WEEGEE'S PEOPLE

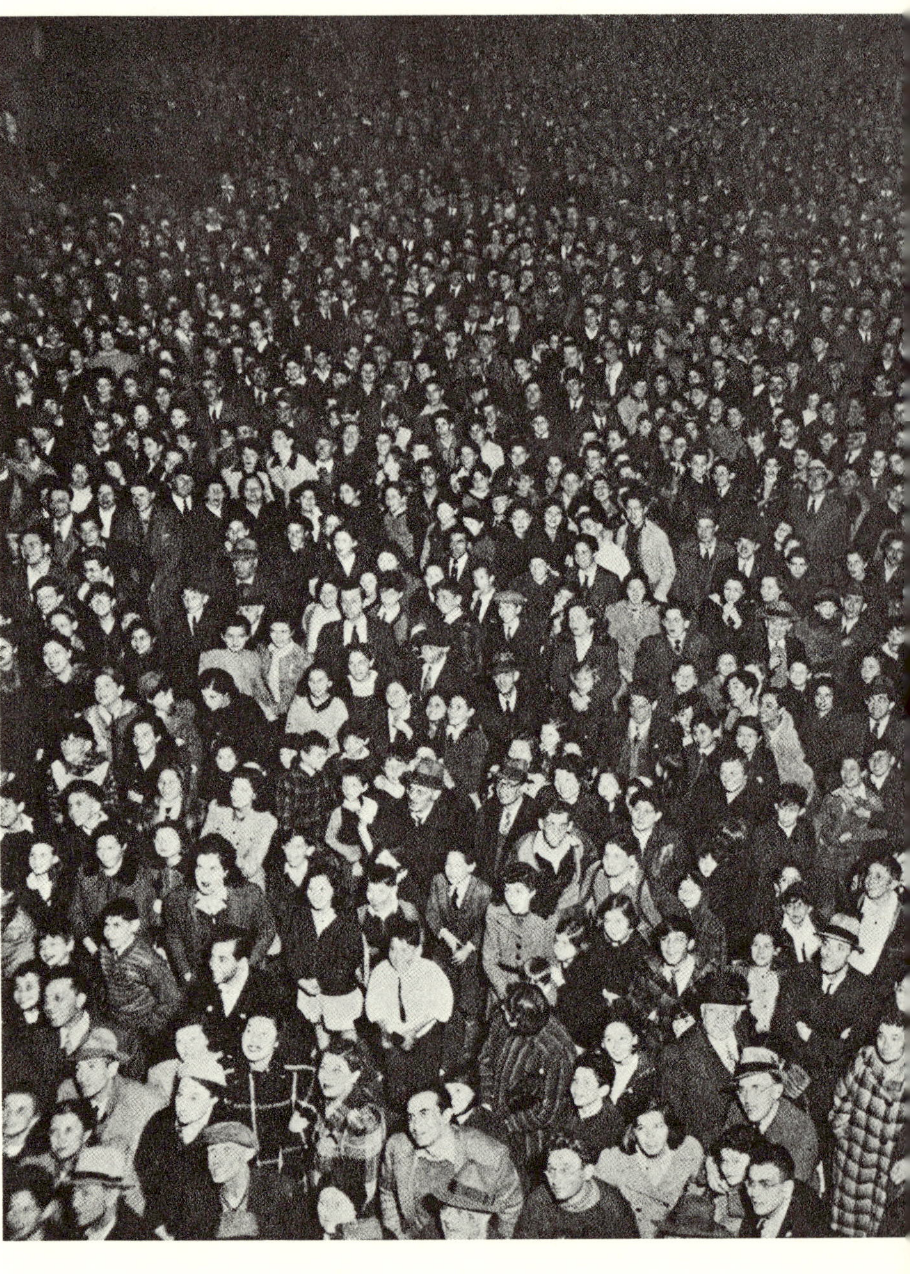

WEEGEE'S PEOPLE

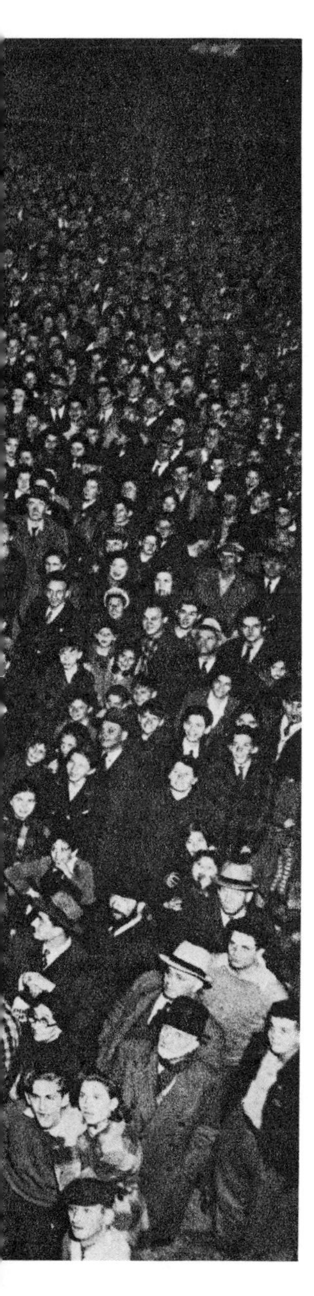

A DA CAPO PAPERBACK

Library of Congress Cataloging in Publication Data

Weegee, 1899–1968.
  Weegee's people.

  1. New York (N.Y.) — Description — Views.
2. New York (N.Y.) — Social life and customs — Pictorial
works. I. Title.
F128.37.W435   1985   779′.997471   84-29219
ISBN 0-306-80242-2 (pbk.)

This Da Capo Press paperback edition of *Weegee's People*
is an unabridged republication of the first edition published
in New York in 1946. It is reprinted by arrangement with
E. P. Dutton, Inc.

Published by Da Capo Press, Inc.
A Subsidiary of Plenum Publishing Corporation
233 Spring Street, New York, N.Y. 10013

Manufactured in the United States of America

TO MY MOTHER

ACKNOWLEDGMENTS

To my Fellow-Craftsmen

JEAN   POLACHECK

CHARLES SEAWOOD

CYRIL   WEINSTEIN

HOWARD JOHNSON

INTRODUCTION

After my first book, *Naked City*, had run into three editions within a few months, I found myself in a confident and happy mood. And the way I feel—well, that's the way I take pictures, so I parked my car and cut the wires of the police radio set in it. I was through with the newspaper game—through with chasing ambulances to scenes of crime and horror—I was saturated with the tears of women and with children sleeping on fire escapes. Now I could really photograph the subjects I liked—I was free.

A magazine sent a telegram asking me to become a fashion and society photographer. I accepted the offer and the portals of society opened before me. All I needed in order to make the change from patrol wagon to Rolls Royce was a tuxedo. The art director warned me on my first assignment to be on my best behavior, and to make sure of it he sent along one of the glamour girls to keep an eye on me. When I received the check for my first night's work, I decided that for that kind of money, I would even wear a tuxedo in the daytime.

In addition to my society high life, I made the rounds until four A.M. when the gay spots close. By that time I would be sufficiently mellow to get a good night's sleep. I slept all day long . . . arose at nine P.M. and then would go to a late breakfast. My first stop would be Julius' in the Village, to see if there were any messages for me . . . then to the Café Royal for blintzes with sour cream, then to Sammy's on the Bowery for a few highballs—and on to Eddie Condon's for some sweet and hot music. Finally, I would end up at the Waldorf Cafeteria on Sixth Avenue in the Village for coffee and some intellectual talk. Wherever I went I always had my camera with me, and averaged about one picture a night for this book.

I found that being an author of a published book opened doors for me everywhere—fan letters—dates, things I've wanted all my life. And besides no matter where I went I wasn't allowed to pay for anything—food and drinks were all on the house.

How does one produce a book like this? After all, a writer can hear and remember things or just imagine and dream them—but pictures are different, the photographer must be on the scene at the split second of occurrence. Here's my formula—dealing as I do with human beings, and I find them wonderful: I leave them alone and let them be themselves—holding hands with love-light in their eyes—sleeping—or merely walking down the street. The trick is to be where the people are. One doesn't need a scenario or shooting script, all one needs to do is to be on the spot, alert and human. One never knows what will happen. The photographs of the Negro cop against the clouds and the youngster asleep in the telephone booth I took one Saturday afternoon, at the time of the great Navy Day celebration. President Truman was there, not to mention a couple of million New Yorkers. That's the kind of backdrop I like . . . while other photographers were getting seasick picturing the battleships in the harbor, I was photographing the people.

Then take skyscrapers, it seems to me that readers must have dizzy spells from looking at too many of them, yet photographers apparently become stupefied after they have pictured the Empire State and Radio City buildings from all the angles including the monotonous ones. They forget about the millions of people who work in them. I chose just one building, the Cities Service 60 Wall Street Tower in the financial district, because to me it is the most beautiful building of all. I went all through the place and finished up with the picture of the lone scrub woman working at night. Incidentally, another cleaning woman took the shot after I instructed her, because I had to be up front with the flash bulb. One night Fannie Hurst saw the picture in my studio and asked me for a copy, because, as she explained, the central character in her famous novel, *Lummox,* was a scrub woman.

I spent all summer in Washington Square Park, resting after the publication of my first book, *Naked City,* hence the pictures in the chapter titled "Park Bench." One afternoon I fell asleep and a girl photographer snapped my picture and mailed the film to me. I like this picture of myself because it's real, and I think it's an improvement over the usual pictures of authors— the kind where the author poses with pipe and book in hand and the usual dog by the fireplace—not a care in the world, not even a worry about royalties or sales of movie rights.

For the shots in the society chapter, I used infra-red film and invisible light because they forgot to give me a ticket to the Opera opening and I had to sneak in with Mrs. Cornelius Vanderbilt's party and had to take pictures in the dark in order not to receive the bum's rush. I wish to apologize to the men in tuxedos who look as though they had forgotten to shave, it's really because of the invisible infra-red rays which bring out hidden color in the face.

The pictures from the chapter, "A Place to Sleep," were taken night after night on the corner of Hudson and Duane Streets, opposite the plant of the newspaper, *PM* (my Alma Mater). Every night throughout the year the poor unfortunate and homeless flock to this corner—I don't know why this particular corner, but that's the way it is in New York.

The pictures that I enjoyed taking most were the ones in the chapter, "Saturday Night." Couples drinking, making love, and having a good time . . . the things for which I yearned myself. My subjects and I were really having a wonderful time. This was the life, far better than being out in the cold, photographing a five-alarm fire.

I am often asked what kind of a Candid Camera I use—there really is no such thing—it's the photographer who must be candid. I took all the photographs in this book with a 4x5 Speed Graphic Camera, using Eastman Super Pancro Press Type B film, midget-sized bulbs, the exposure 1/200 part of a second stopped down to F.16.

I work alone because there are no problems that way. I find in my work that people are as nice as you want them to be. If it wasn't for their cooperation this book would not be possible. I want to thank them for being so kind and helpful to me.

Weegee

WEEGEE'S PEOPLE

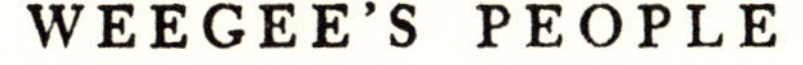

WEEGEE

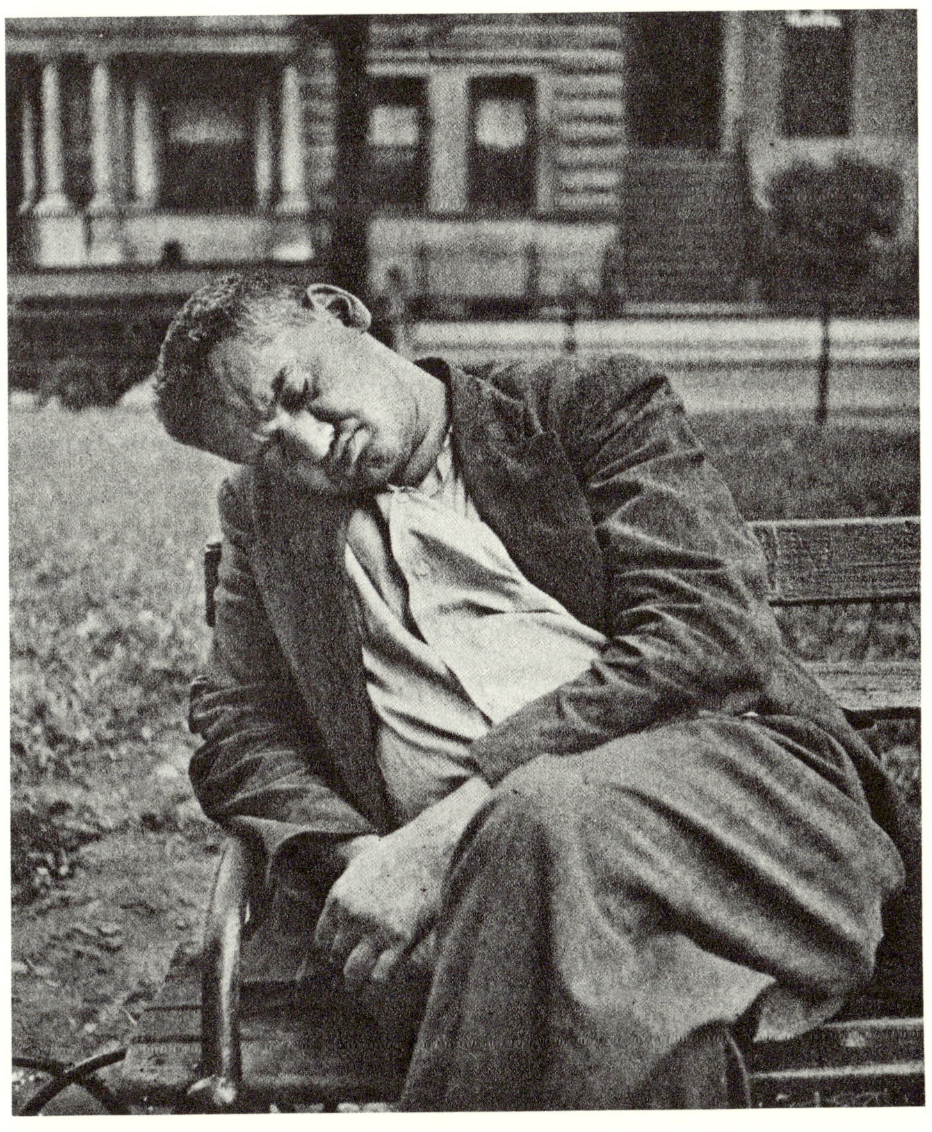

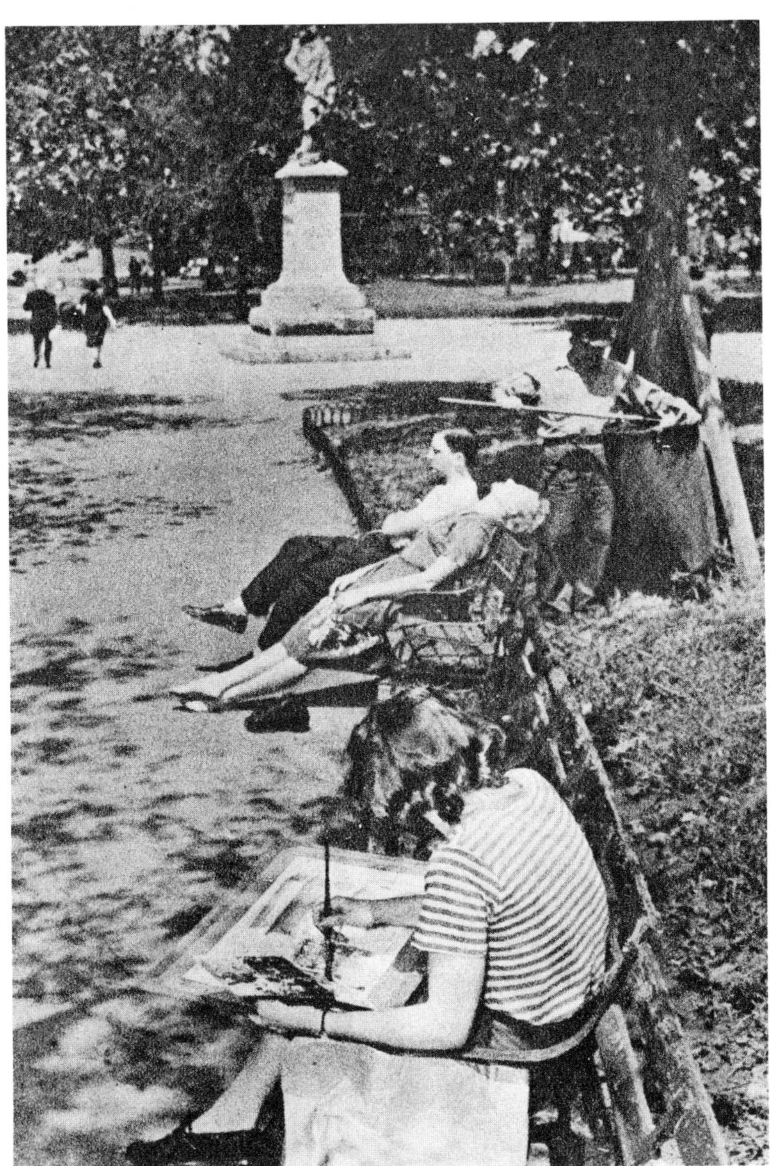

THE PARK BENCH

Washington Square Park in Greenwich Village. This is the friendliest park in the whole city. One rarely sees a cop except at midnight, when everyone but those who have business there, the lovers and the homeless ones, are chased out.

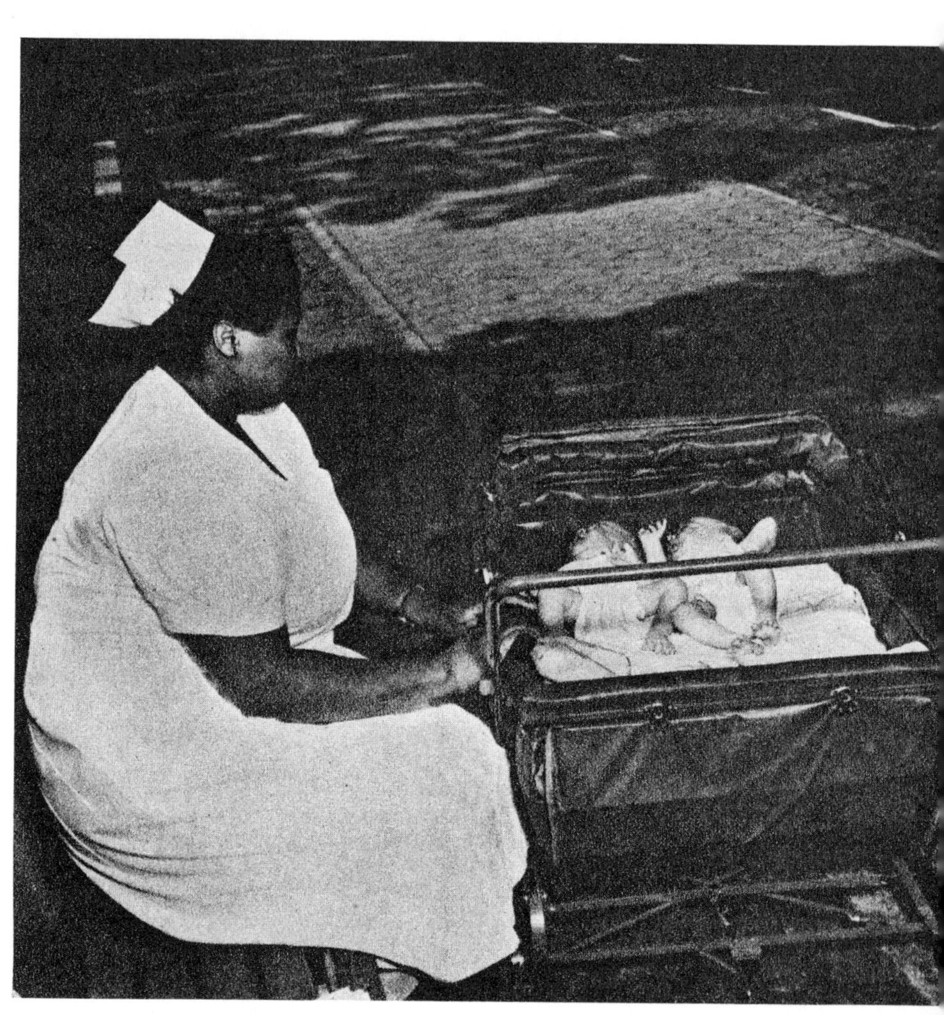

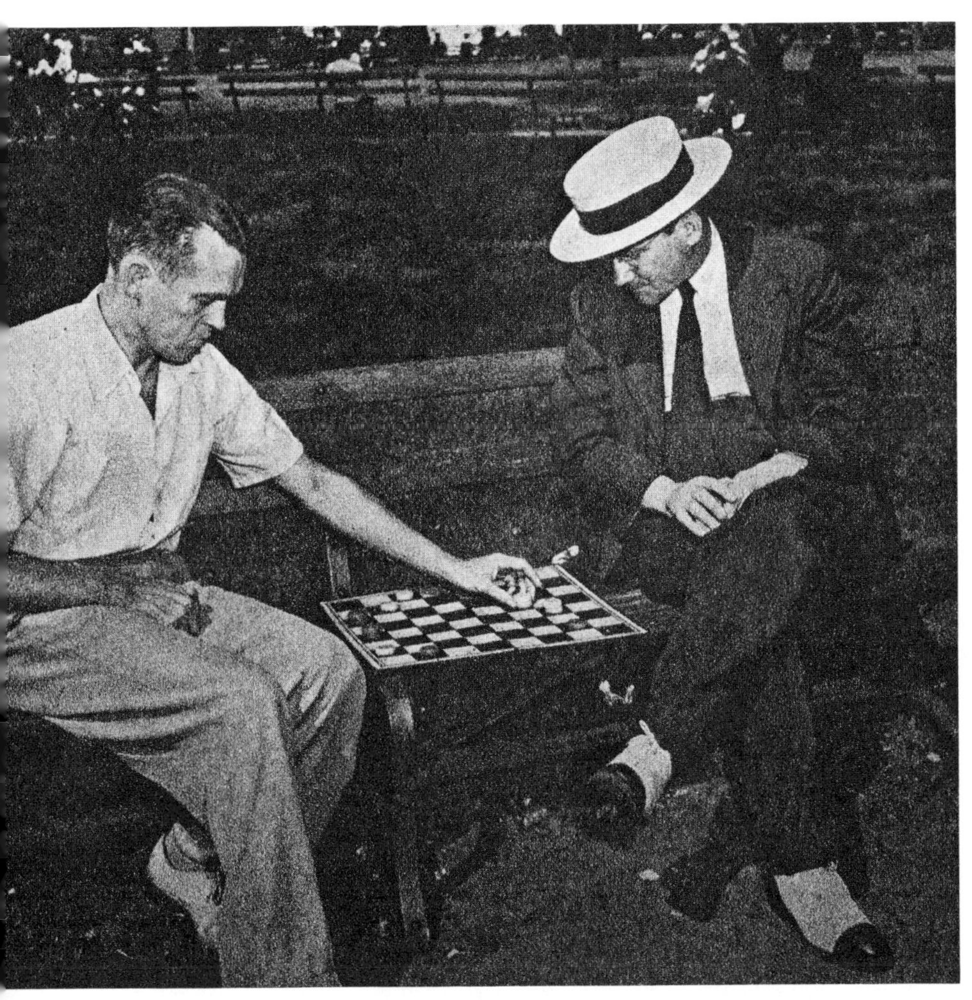

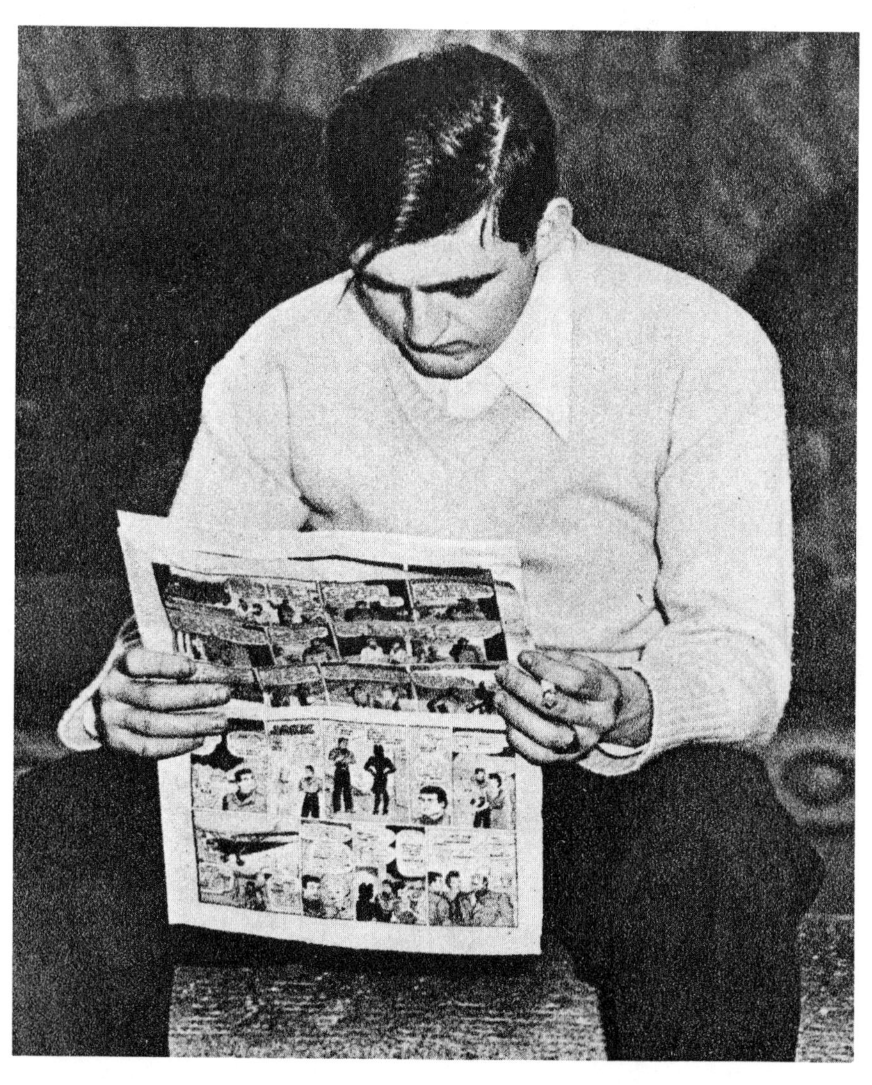

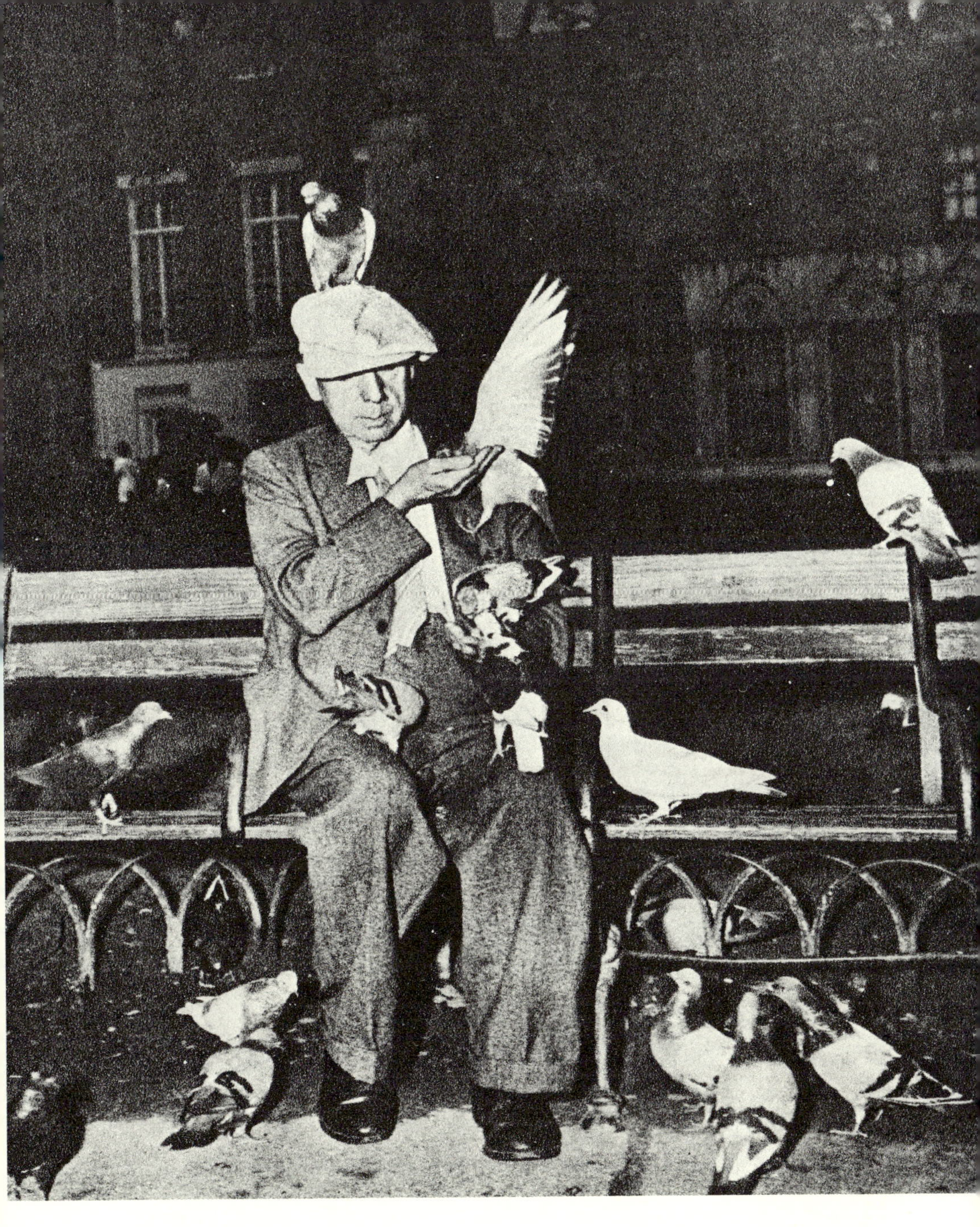

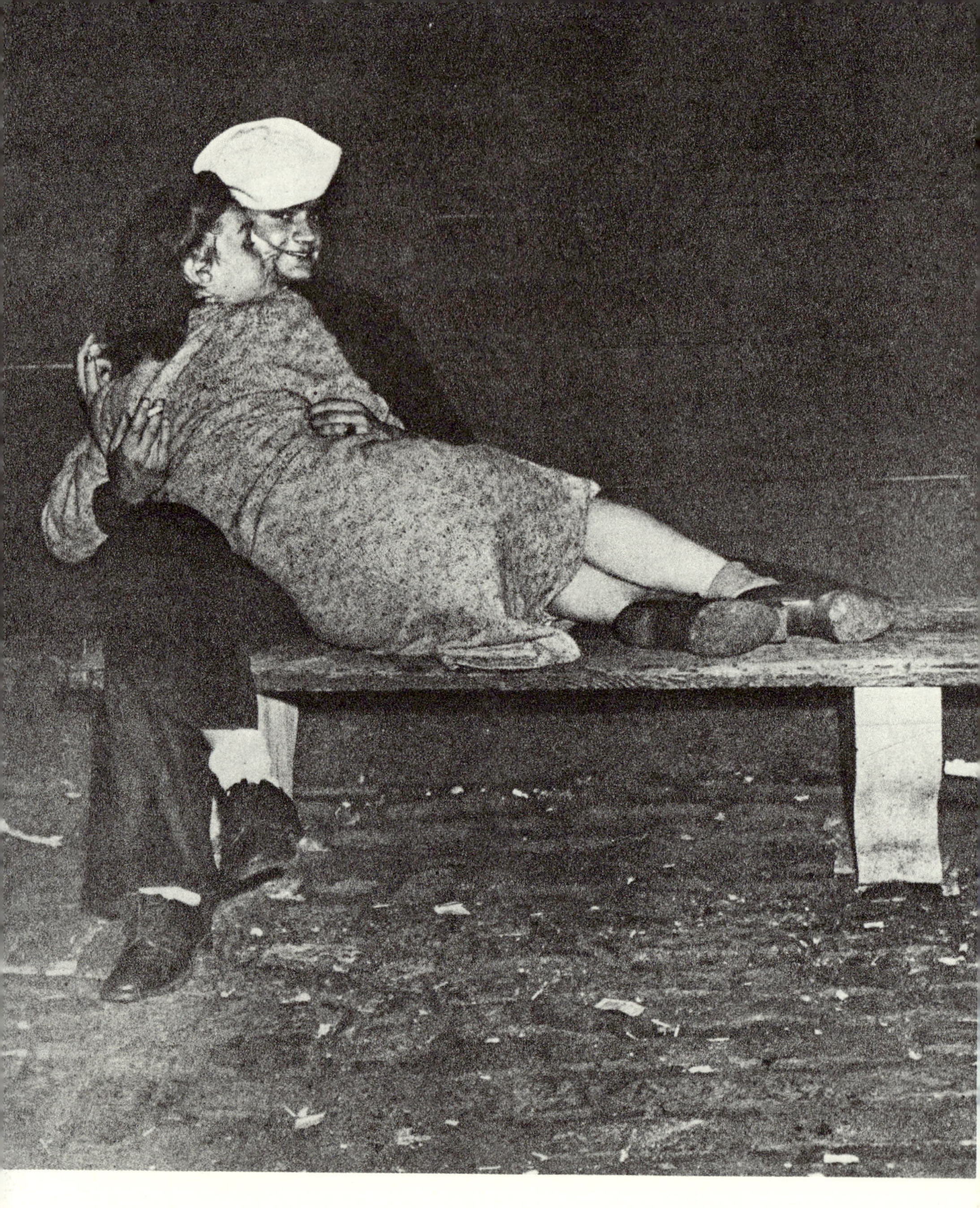

Two o'clock in the morning

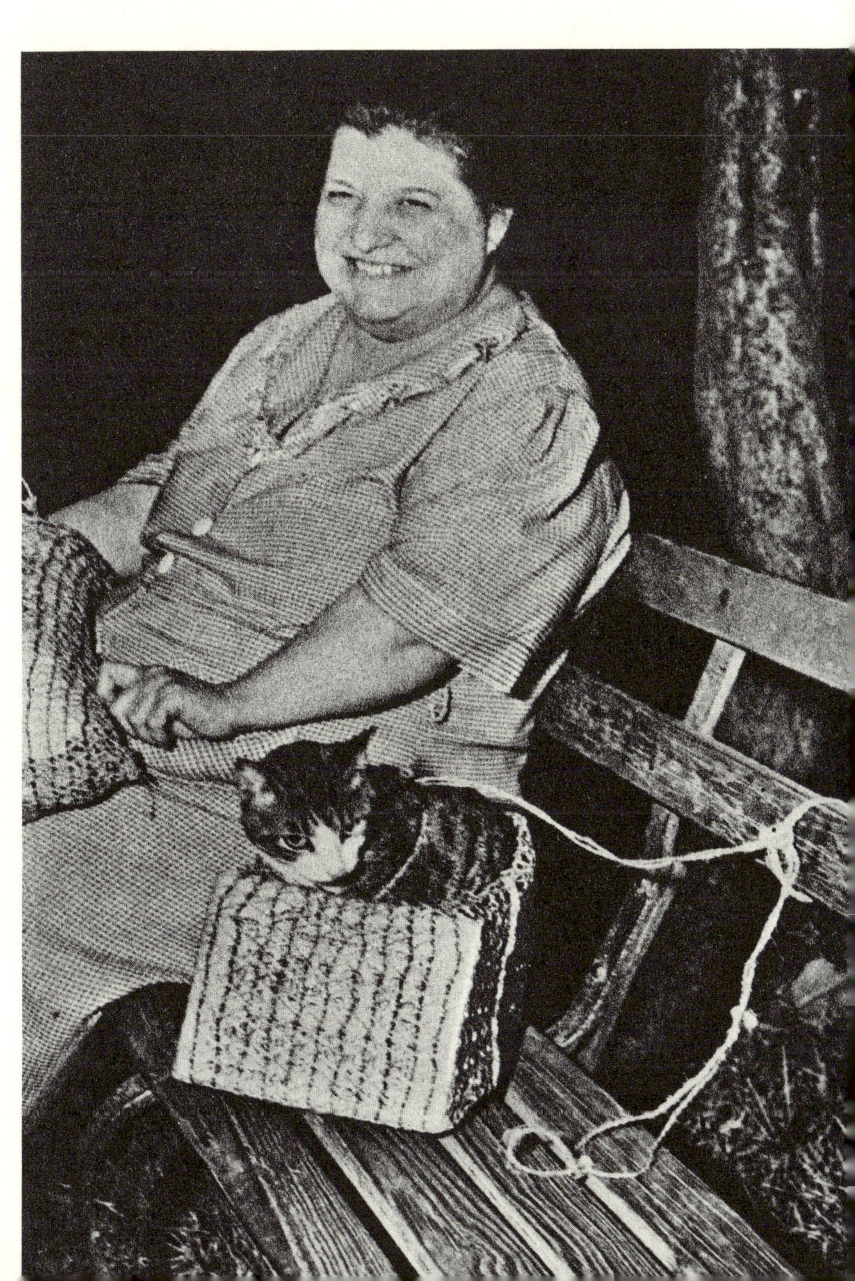

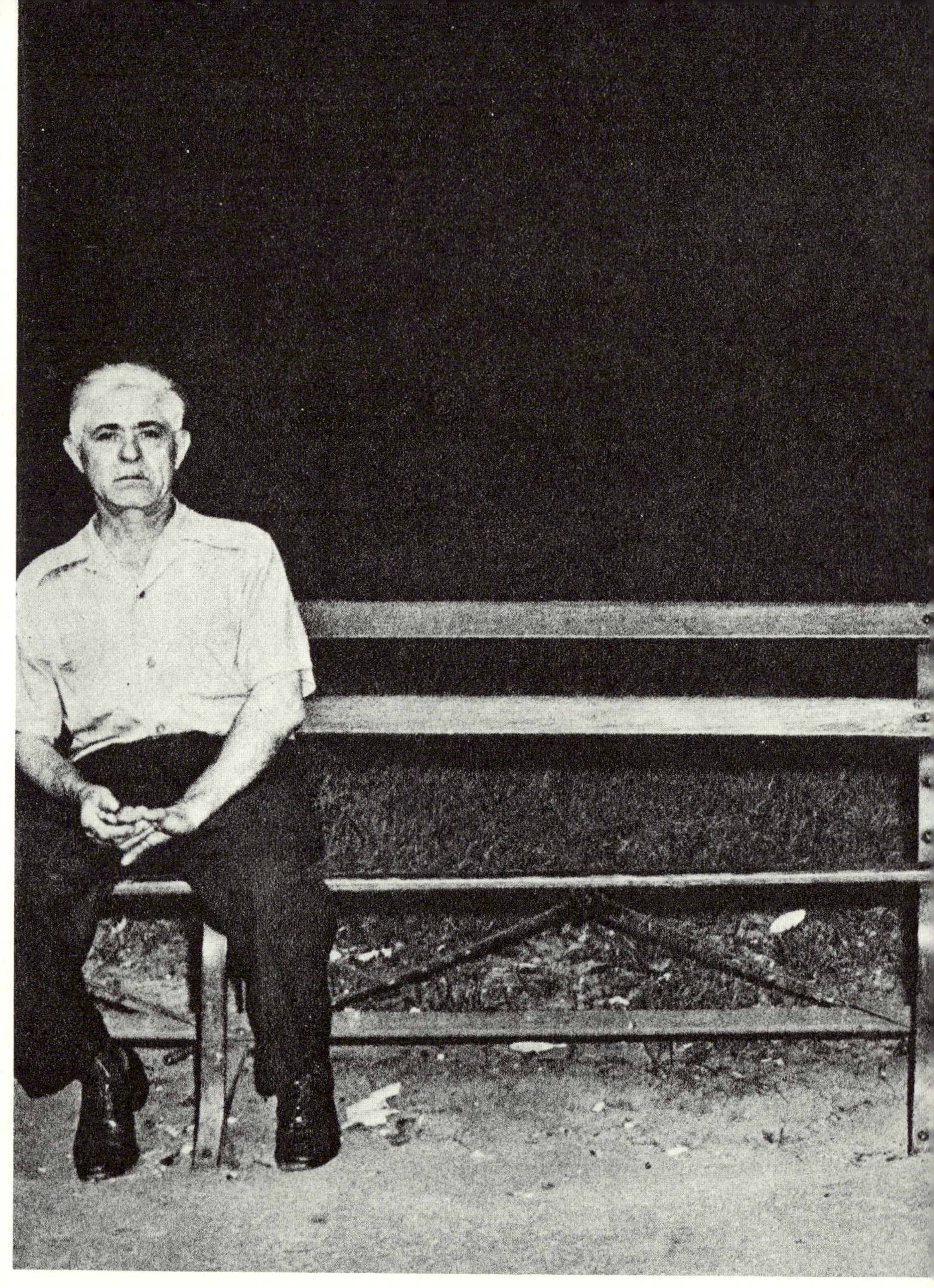

New York City

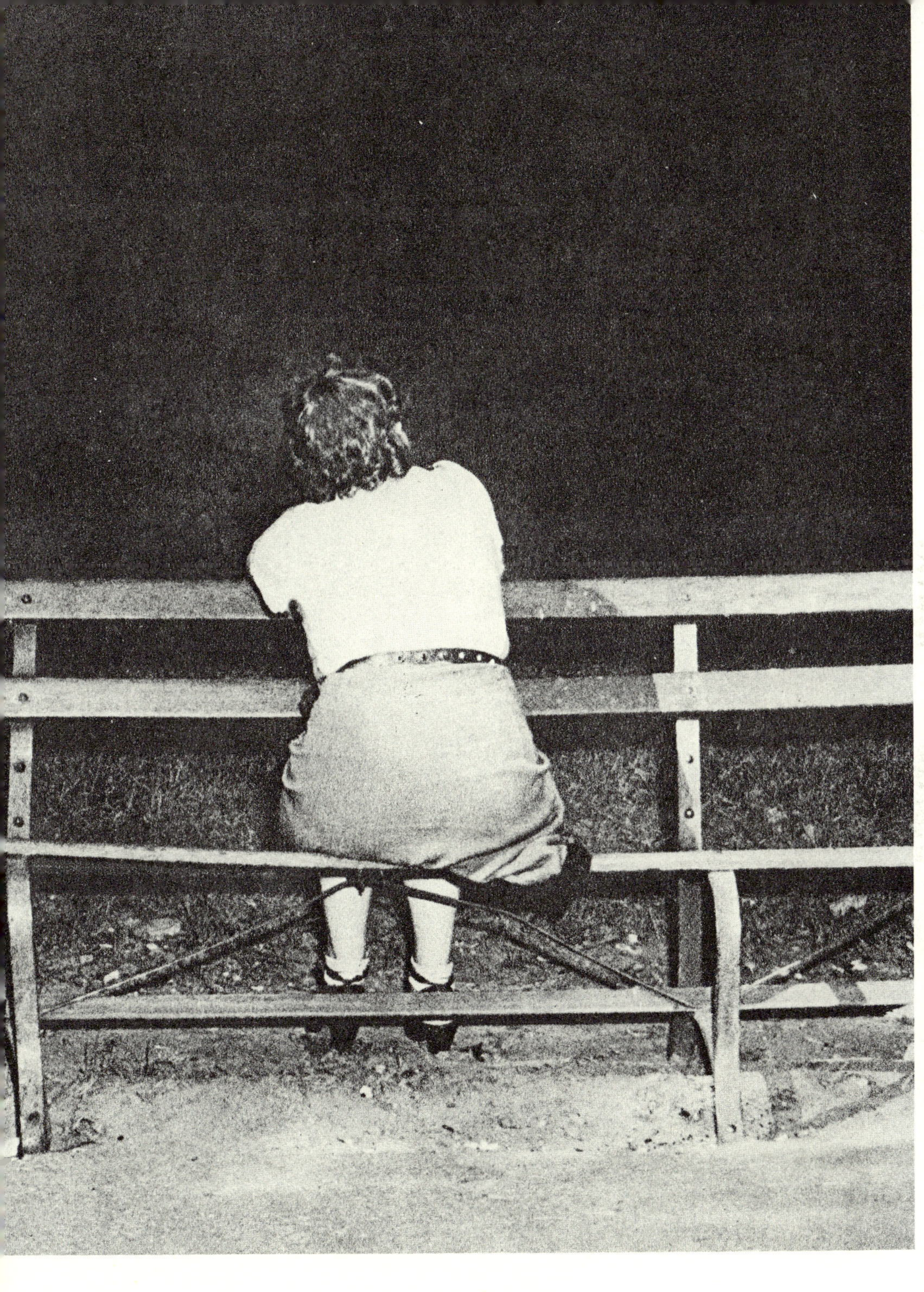

ere seven and a half million people live together in loneliness.

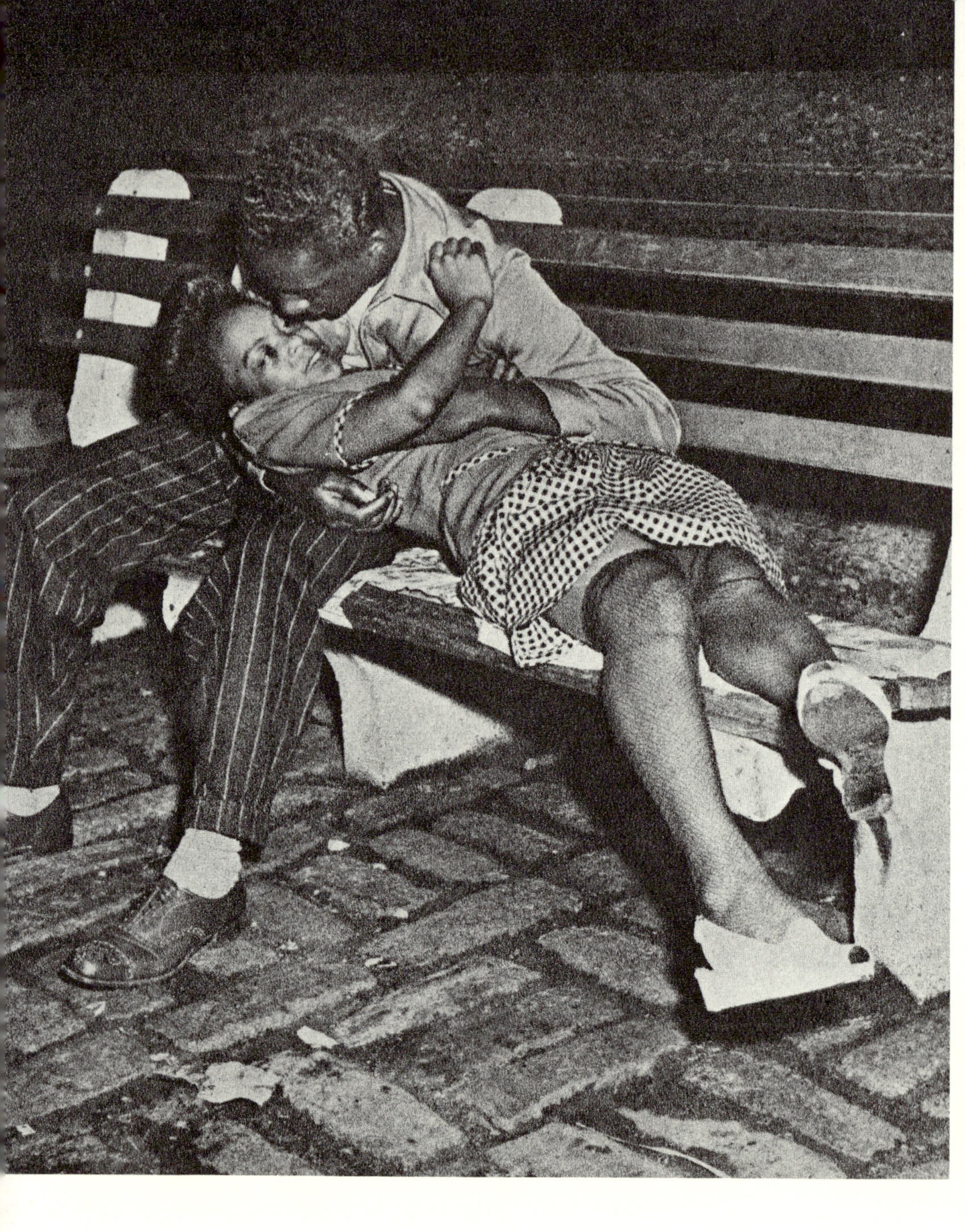

Blowing soap bubbles is fun, too . . .

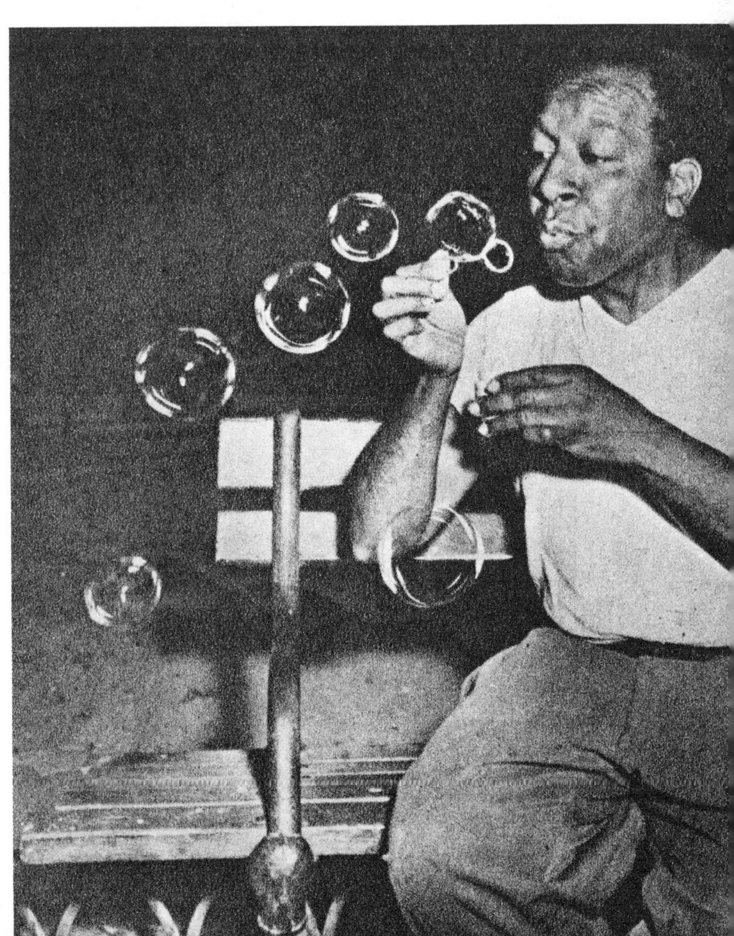

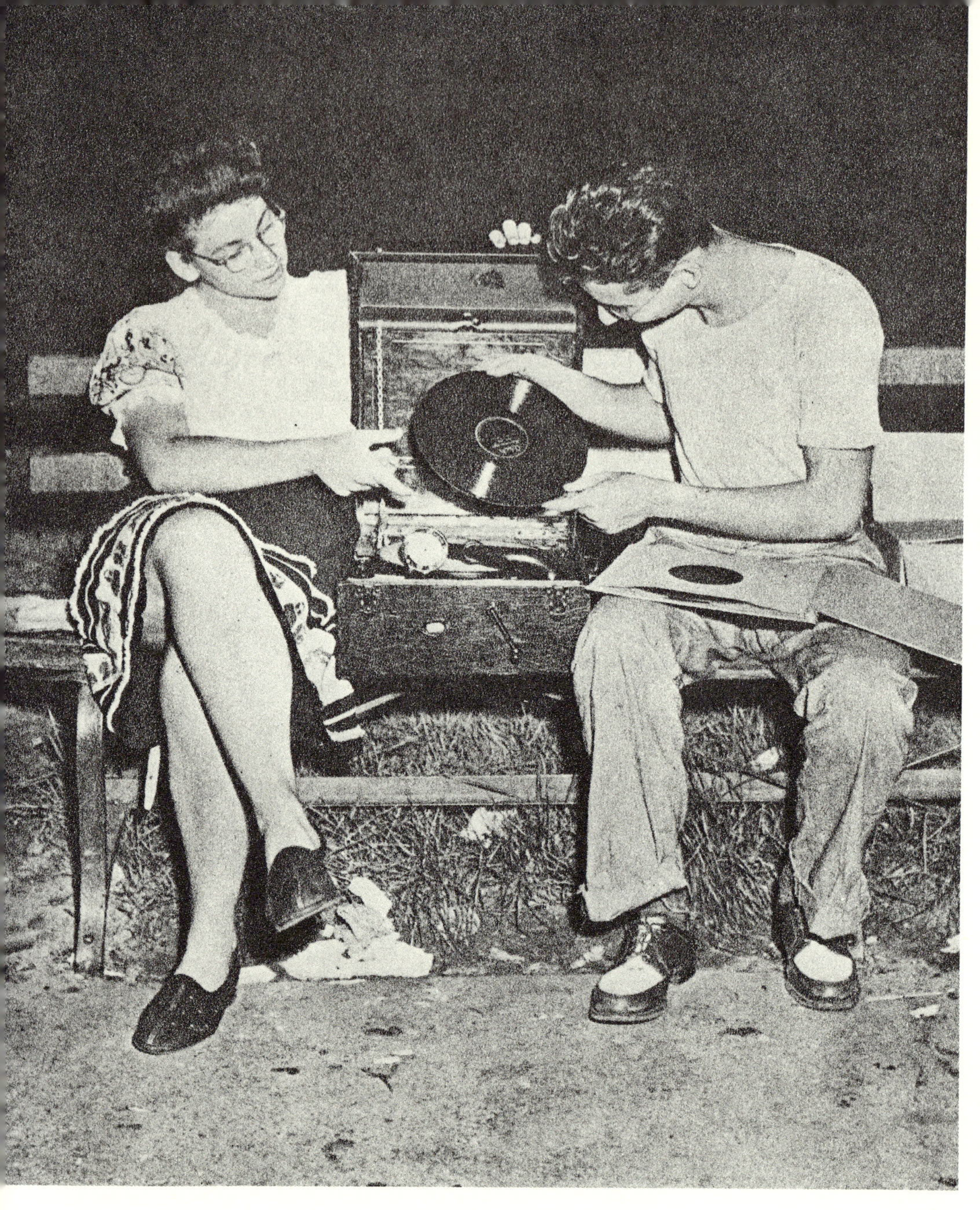

Slumber music

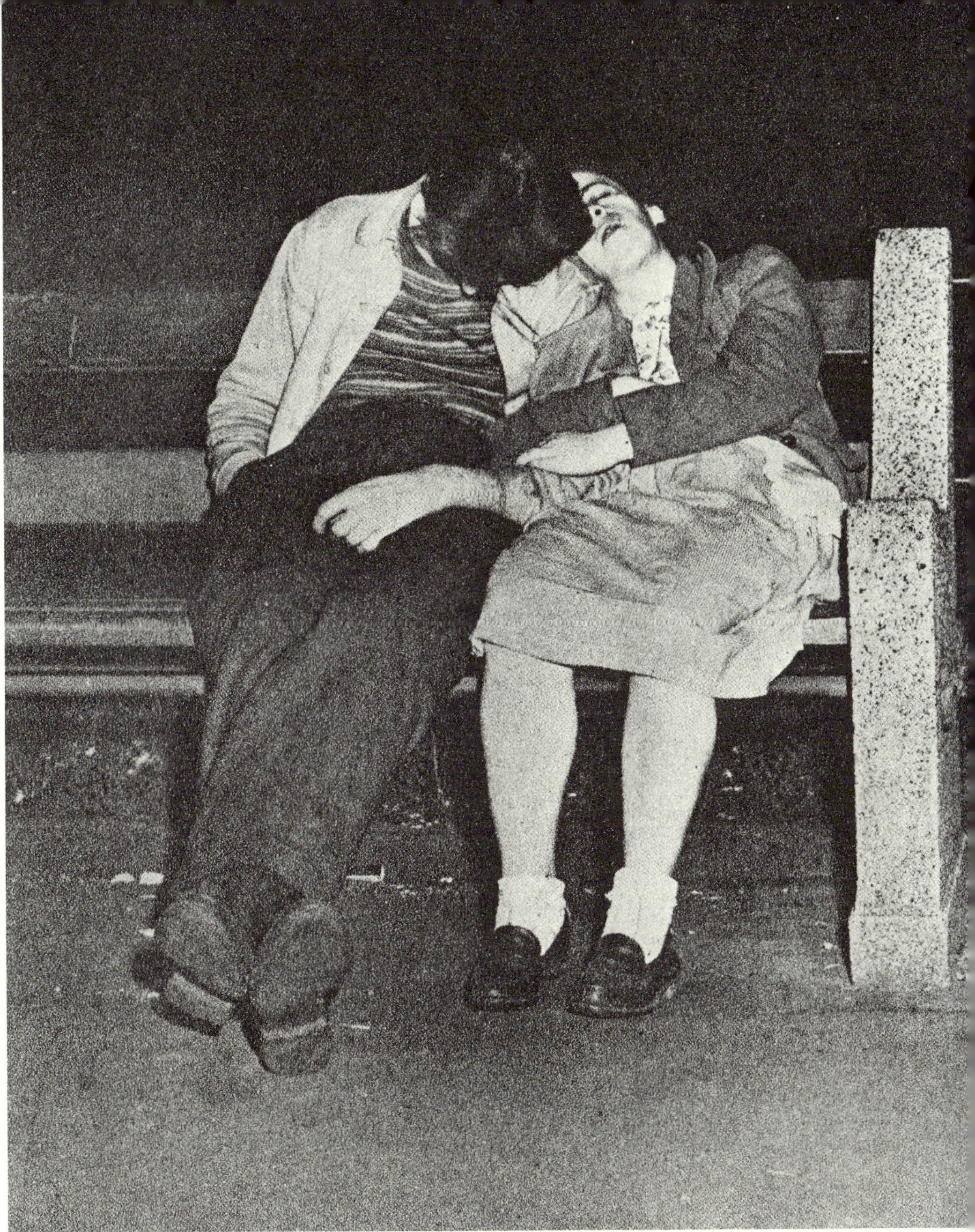

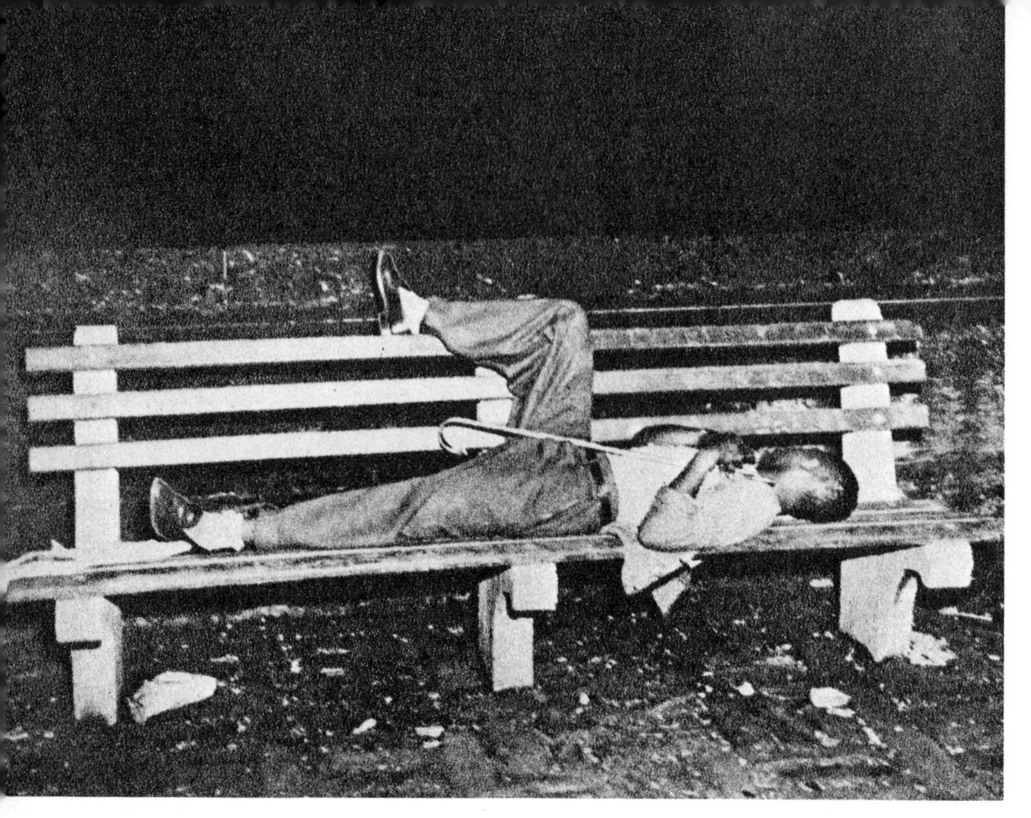

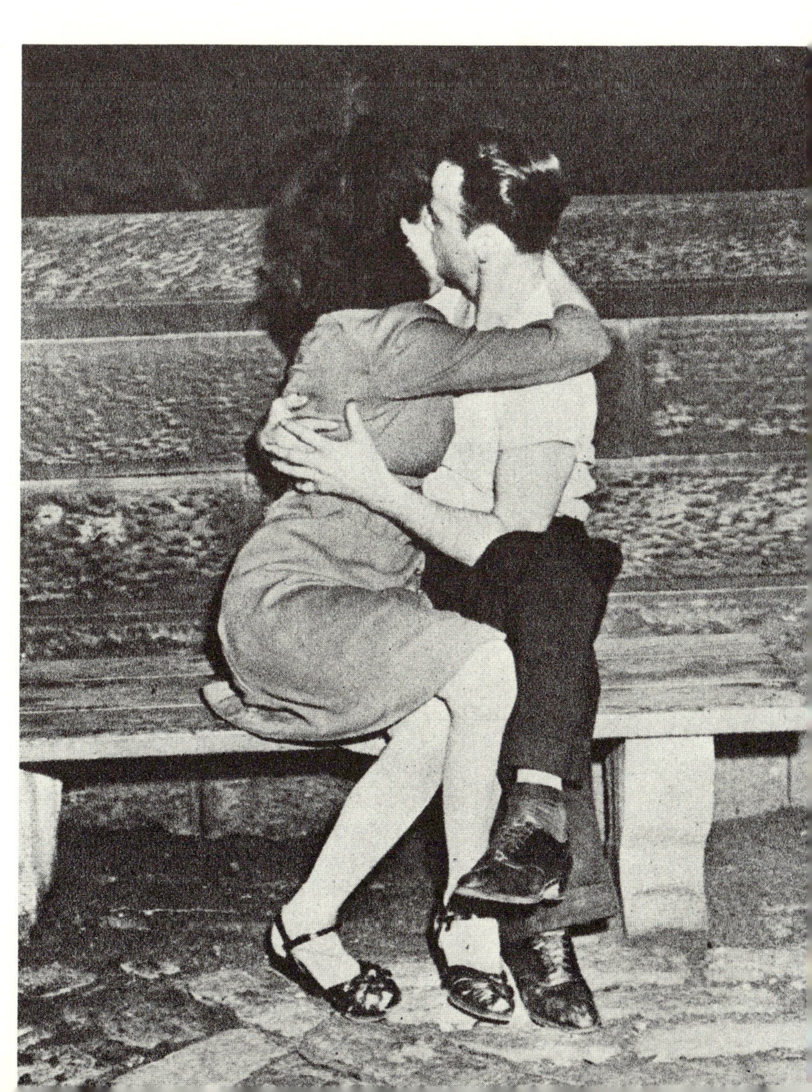

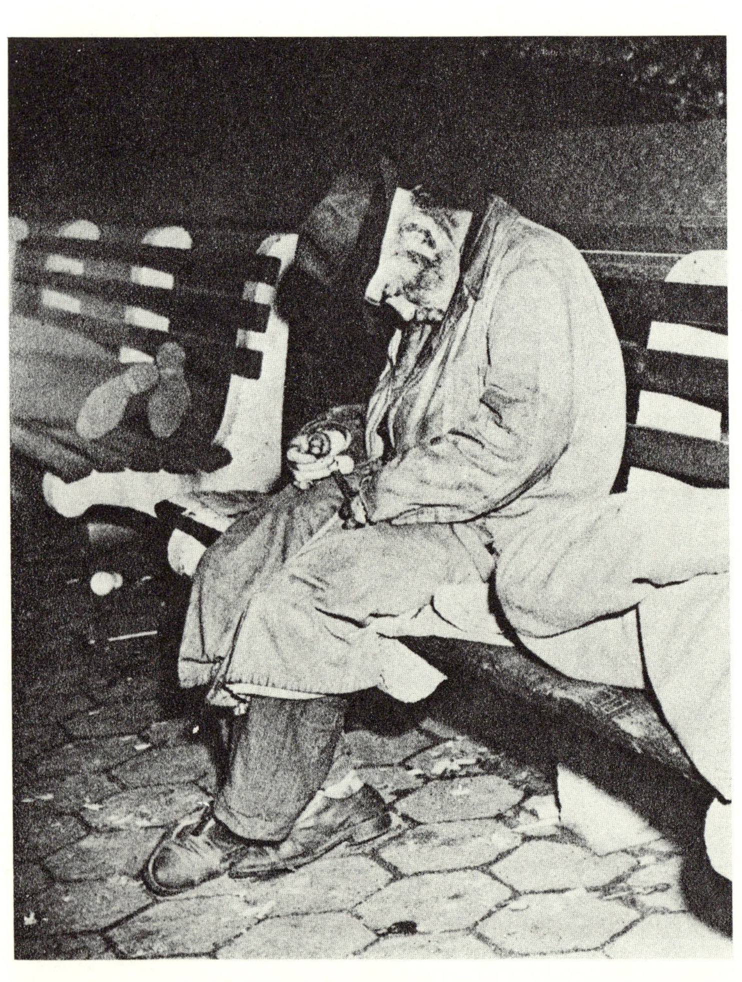

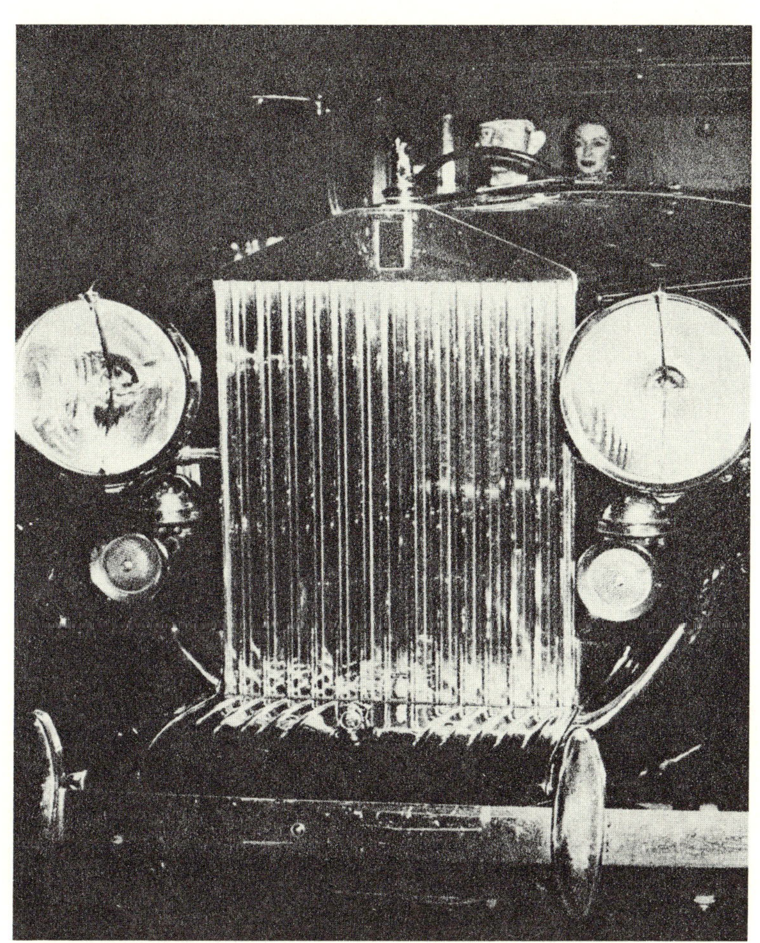

2

Society

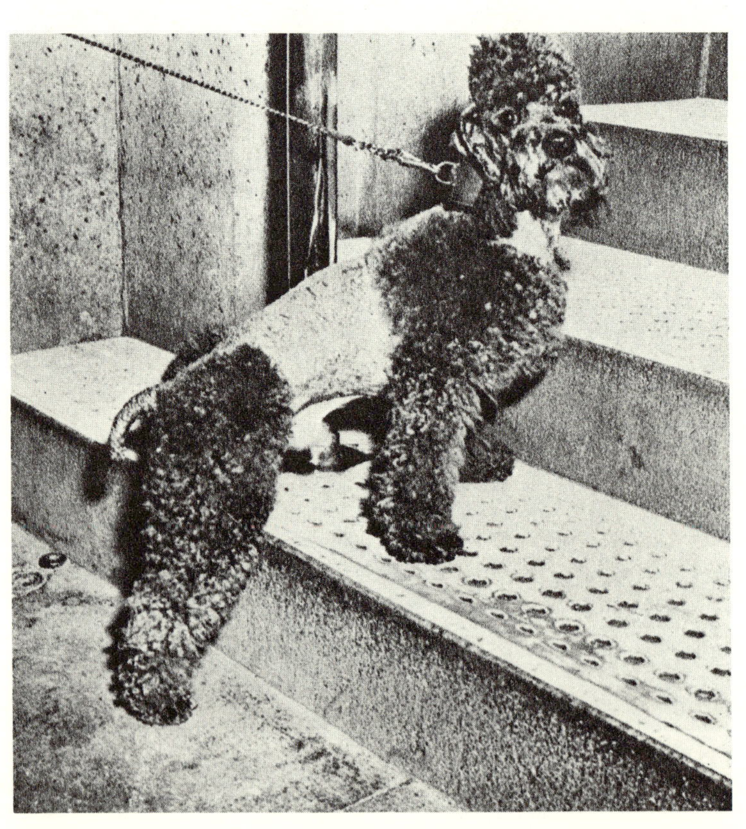

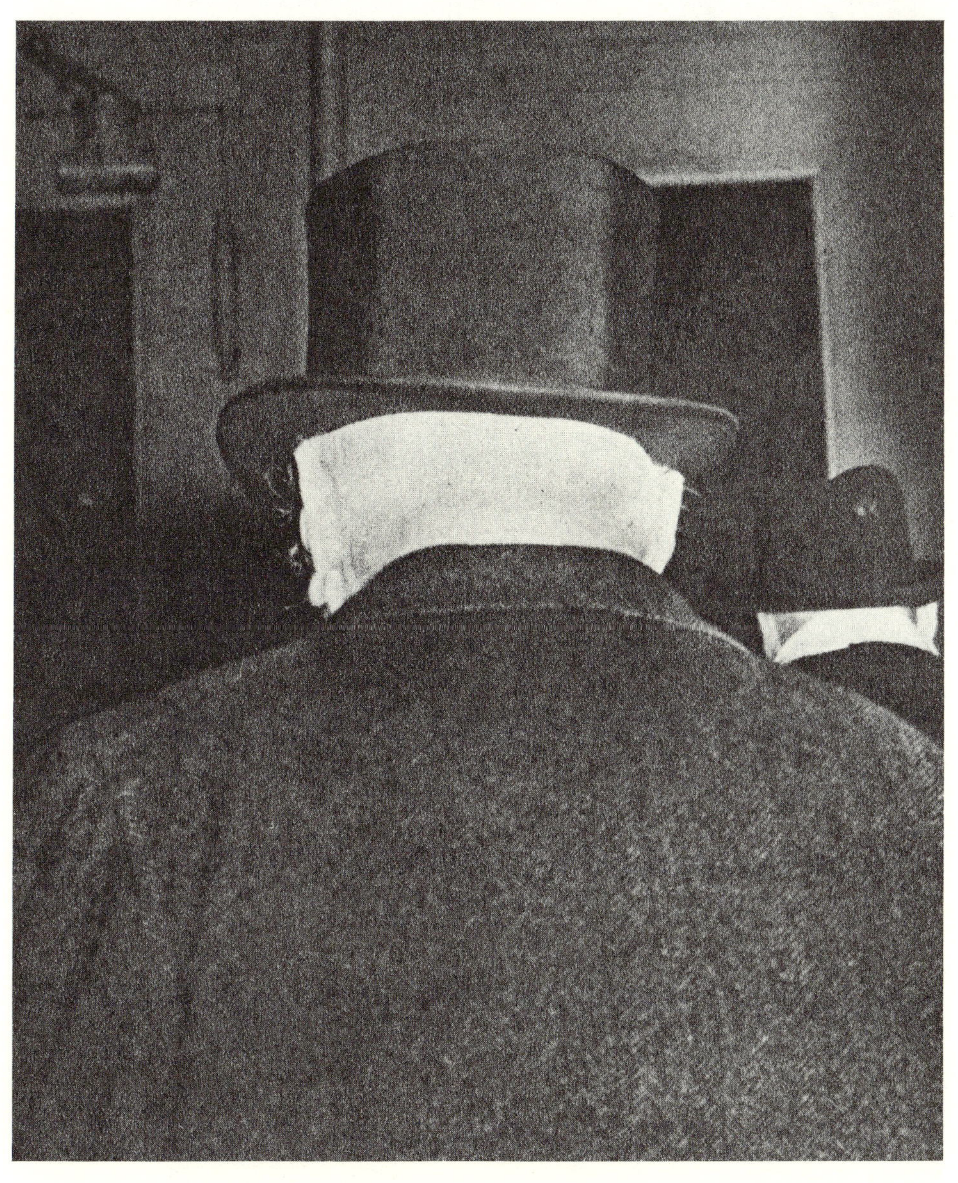

Early arrivals at the Metropolitan Opera House.

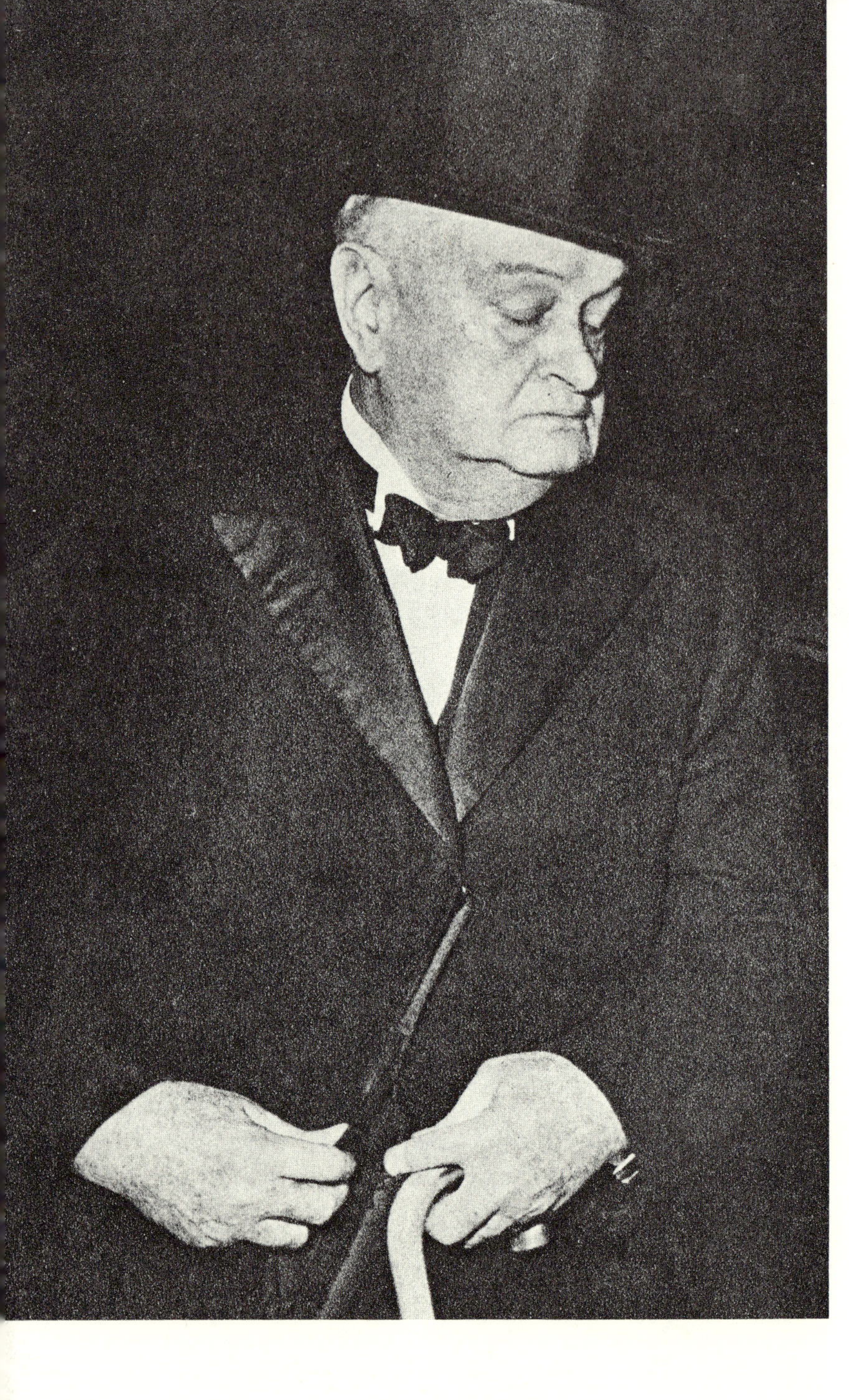

It was a double feature program . . .

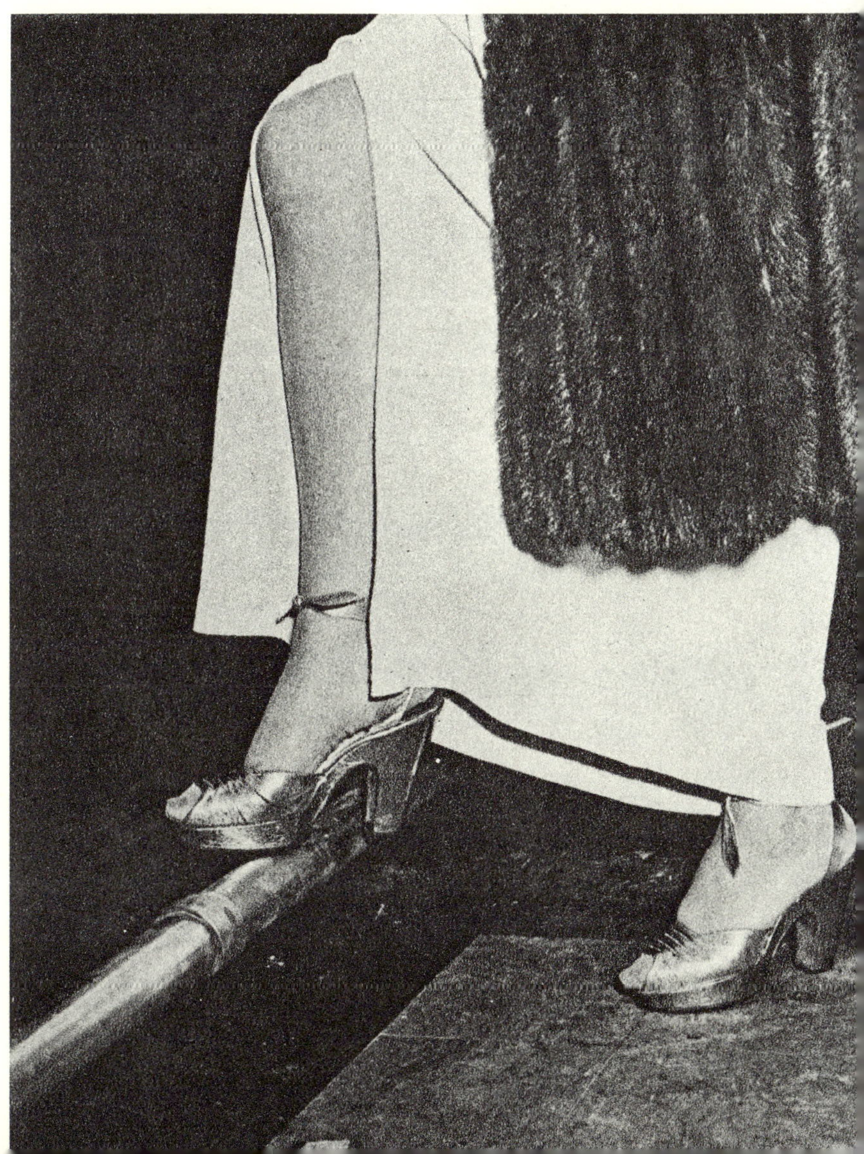

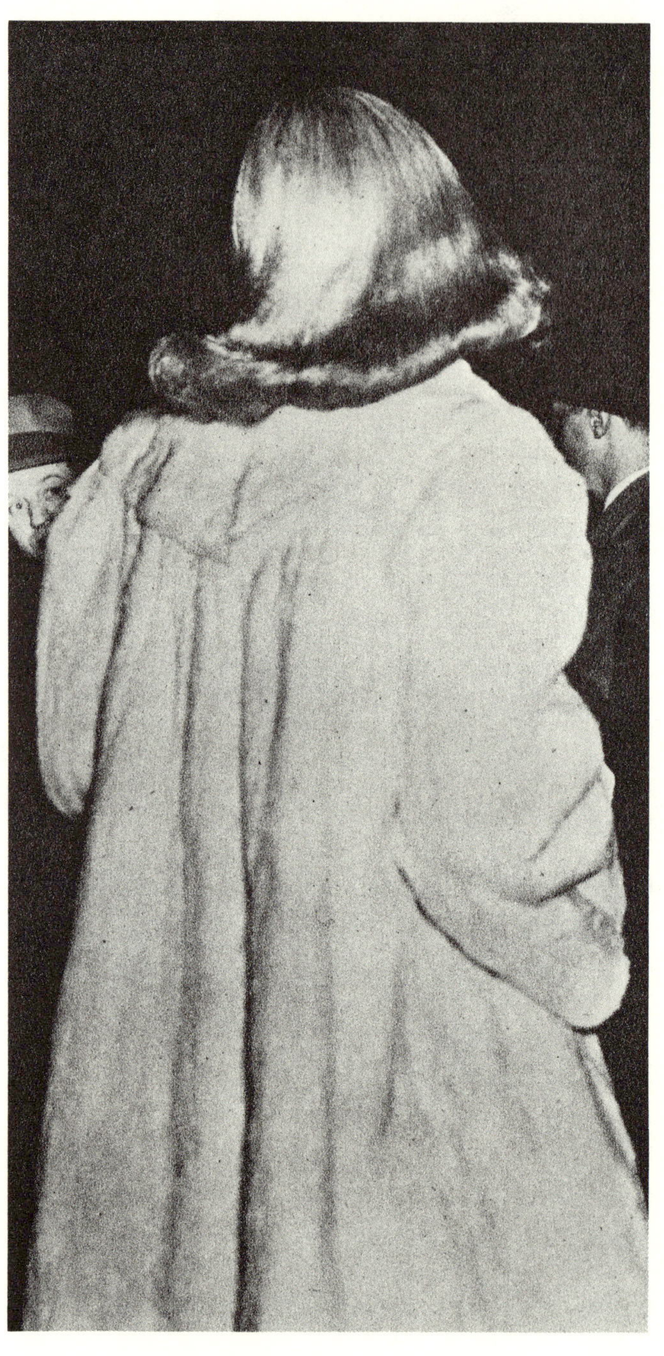

Wagner and champagne

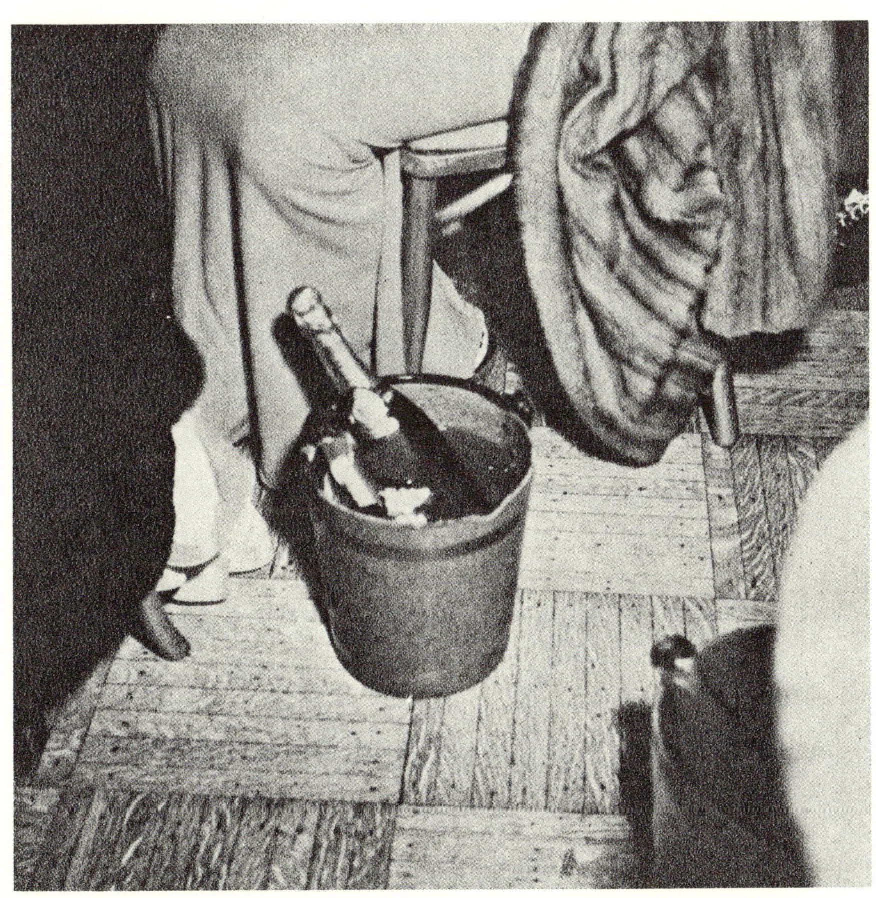

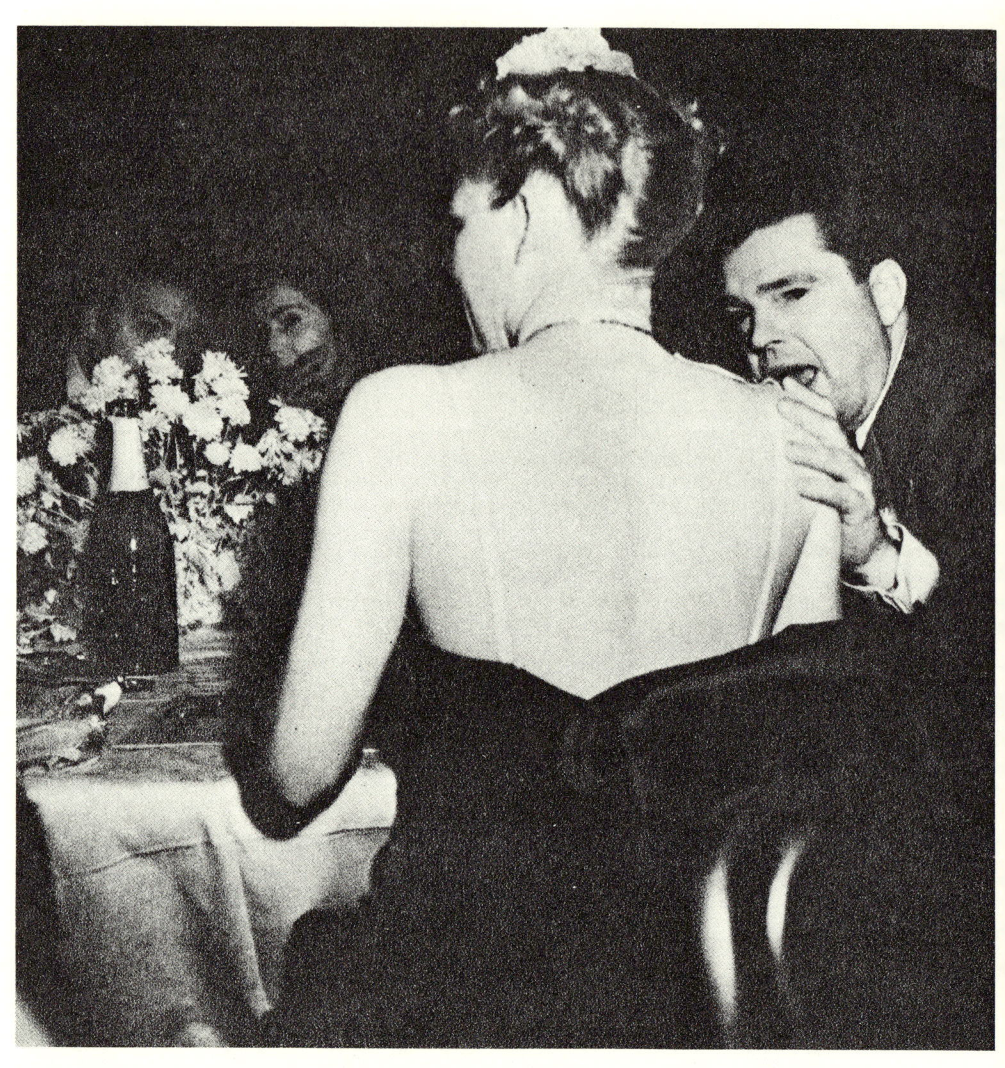

The body beautiful

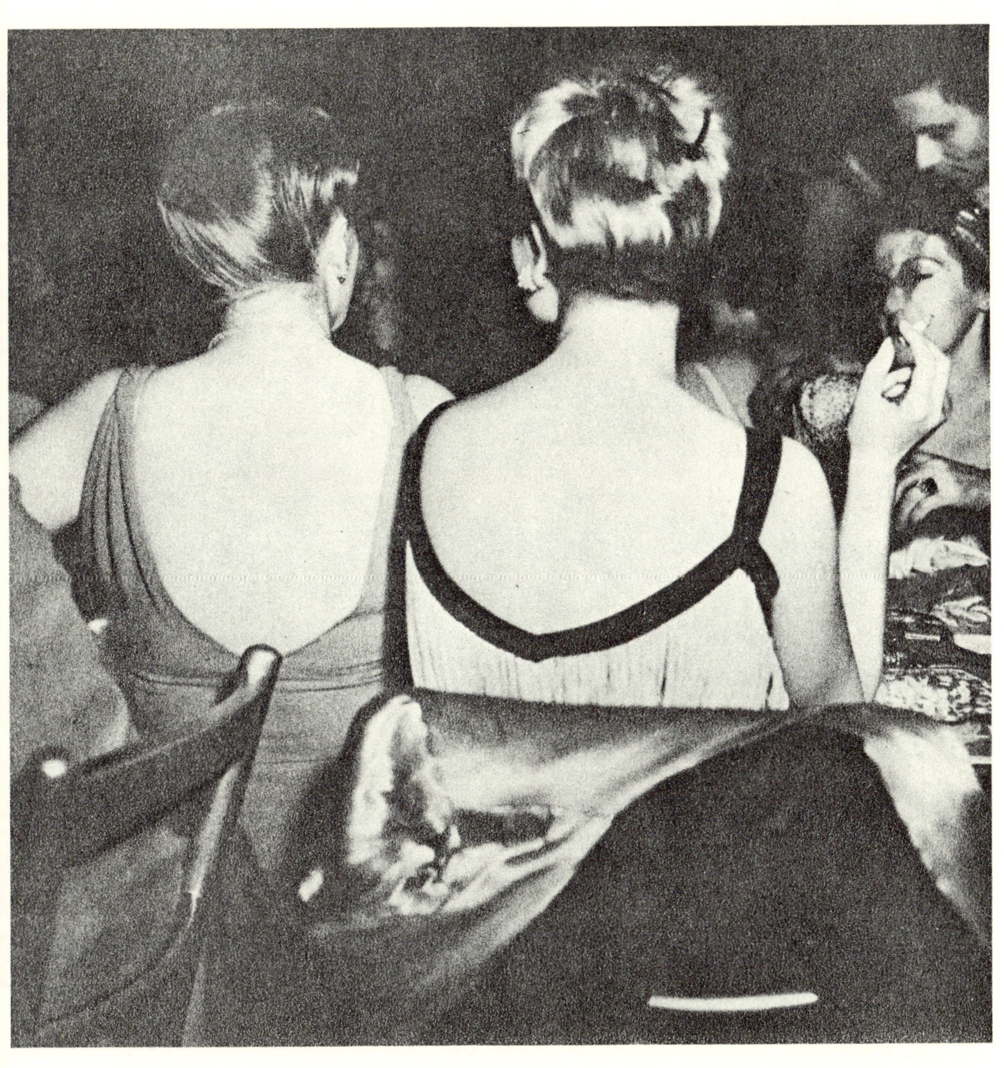

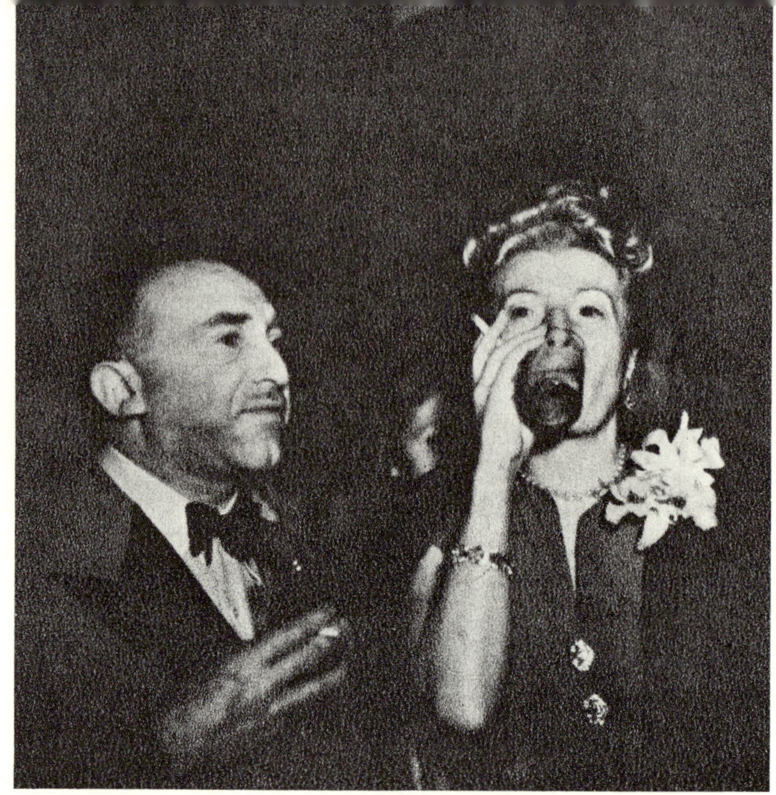

Intermission

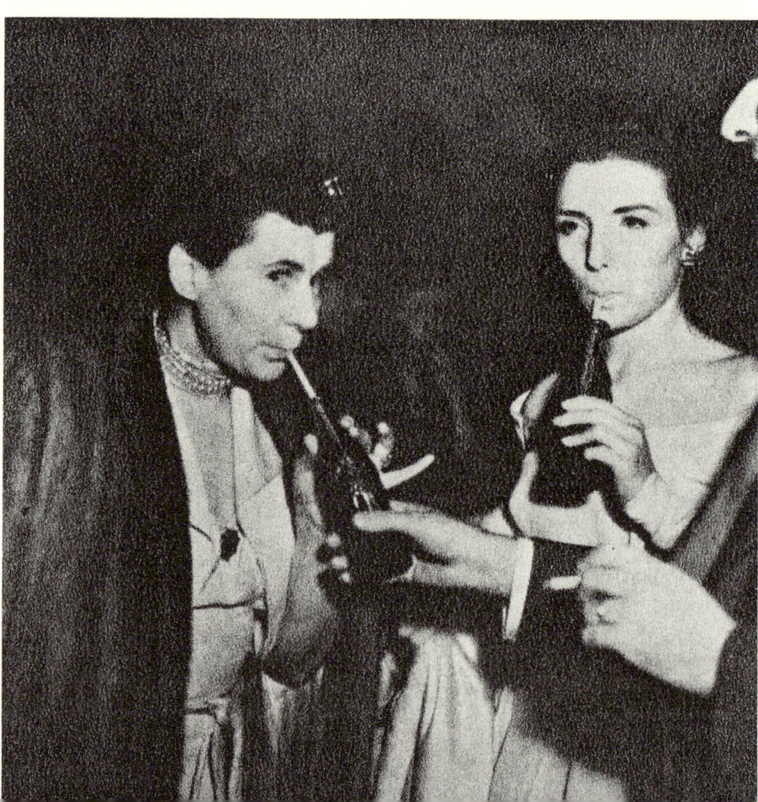

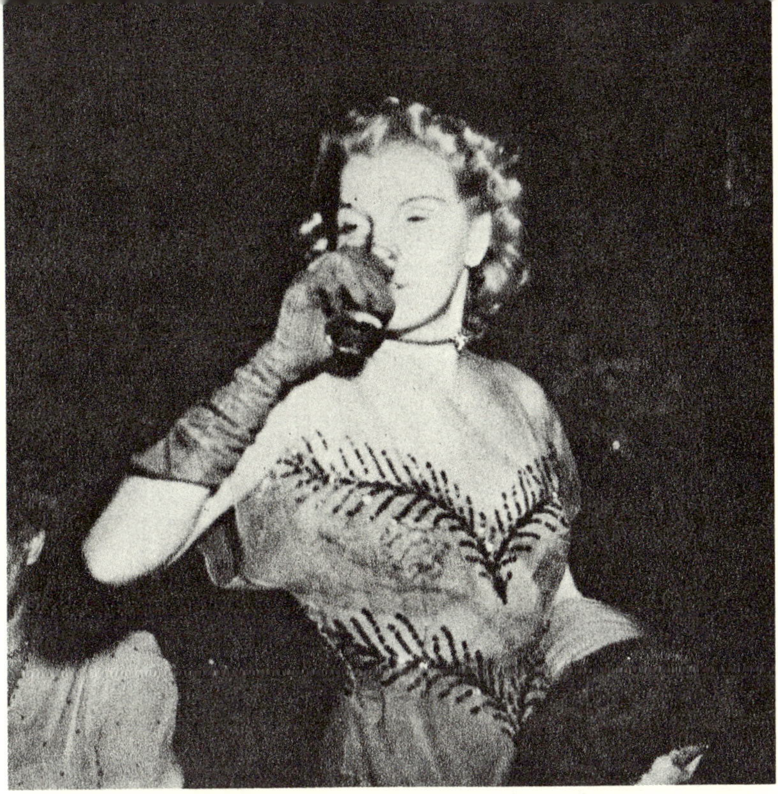

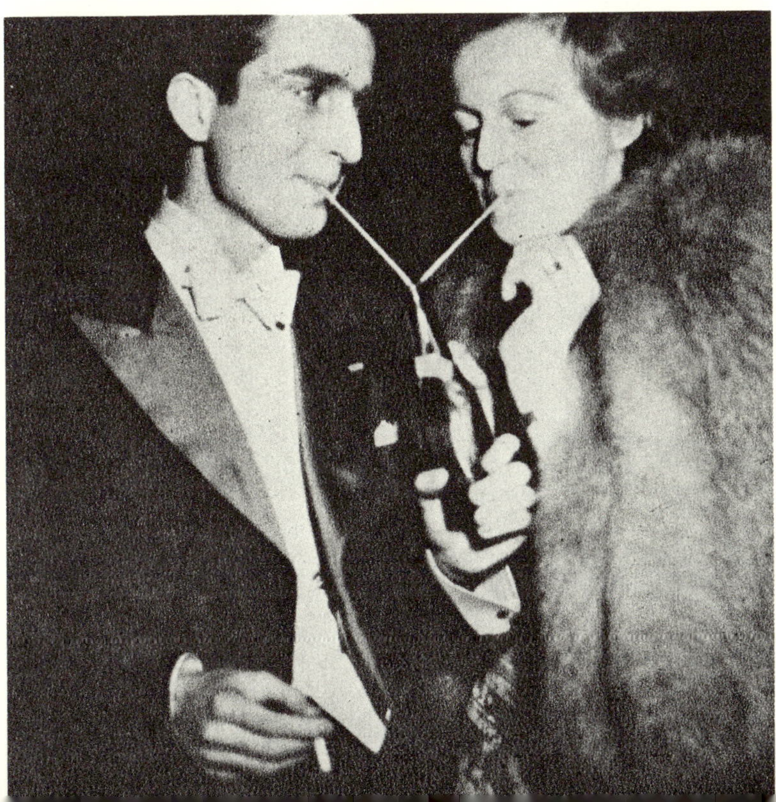

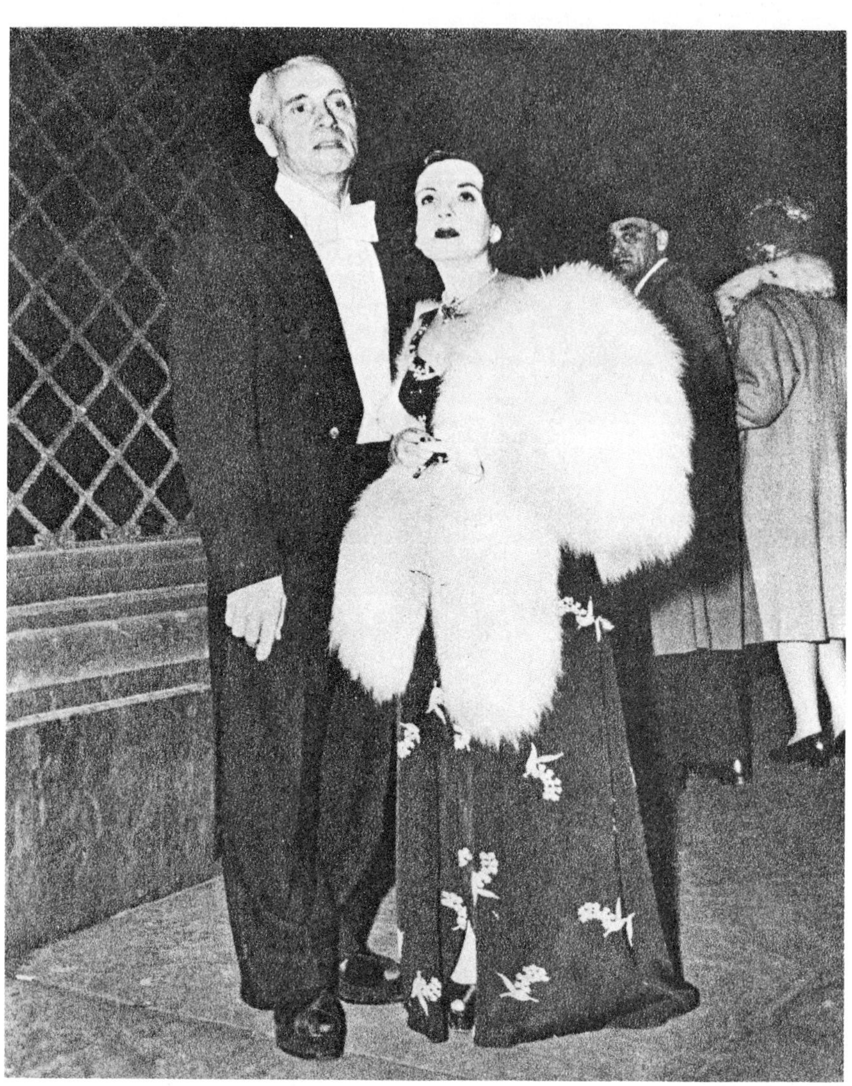

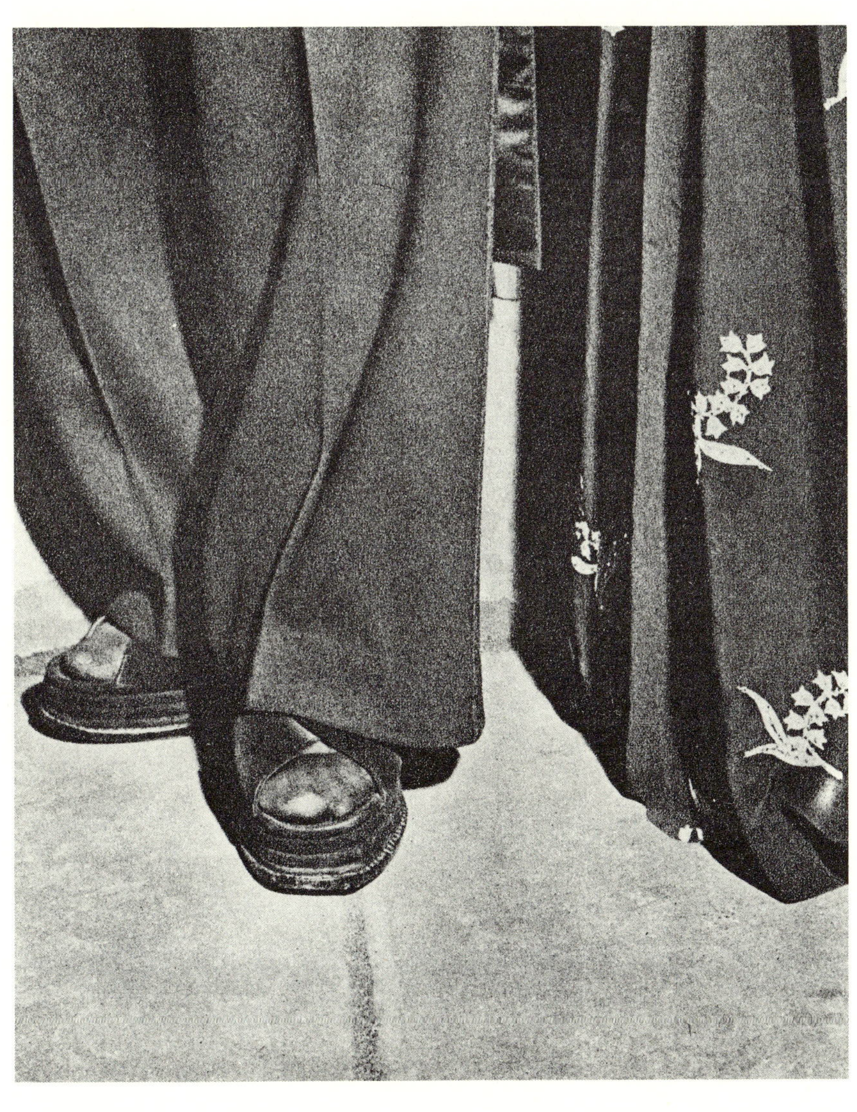

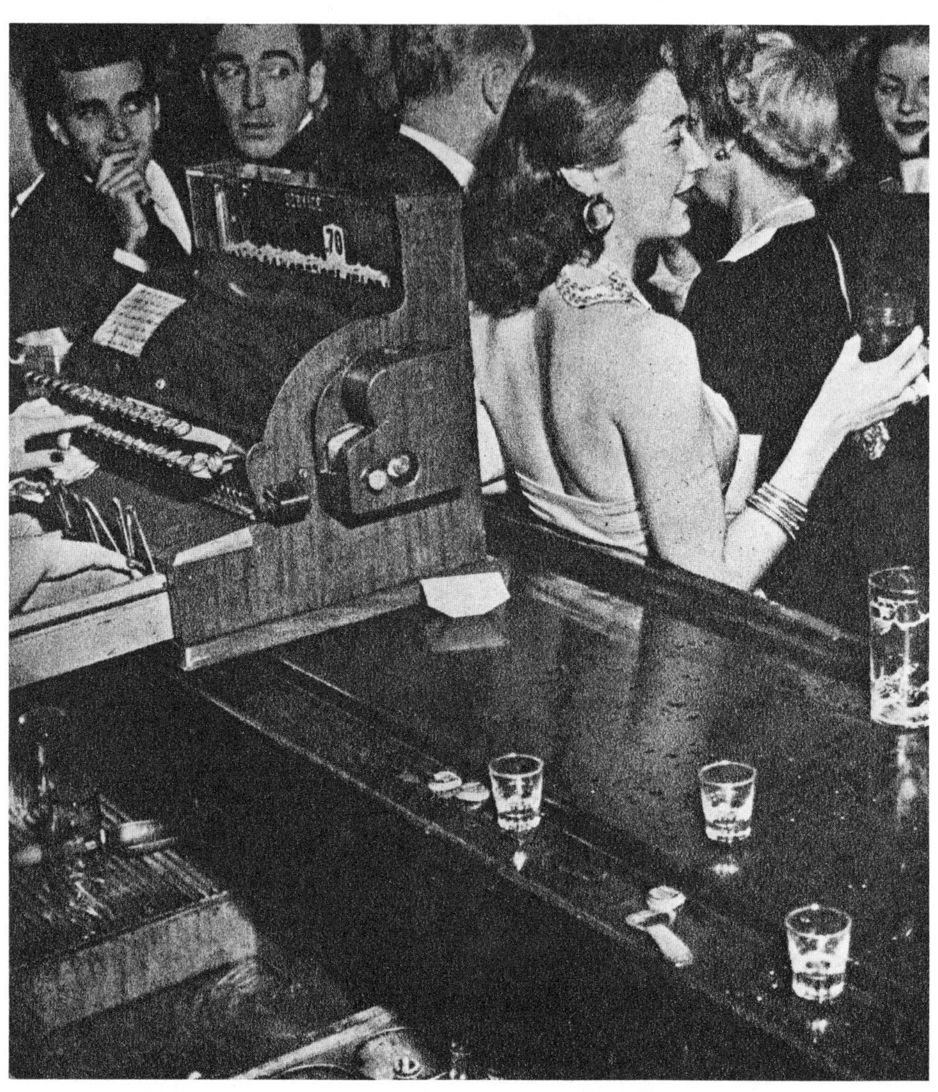

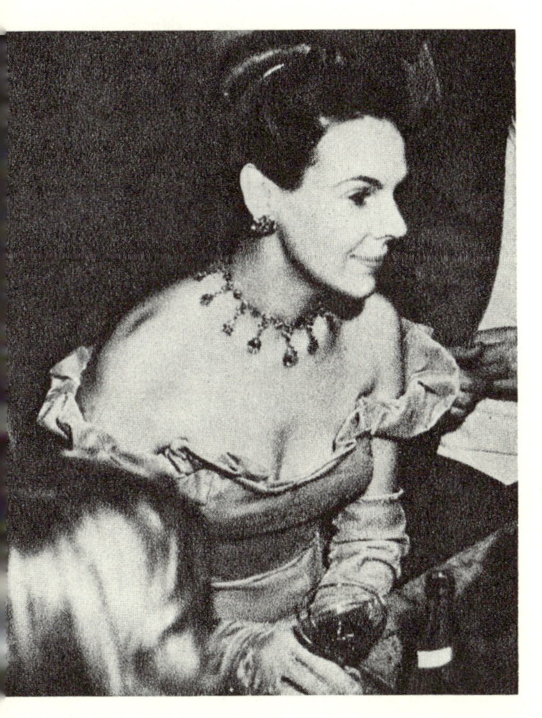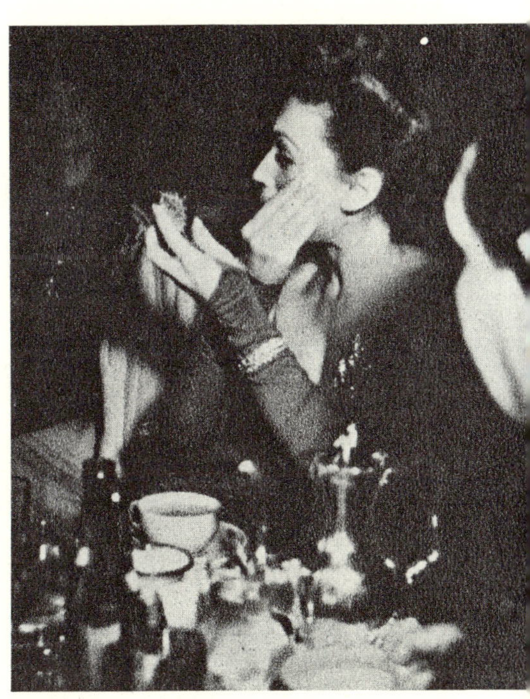

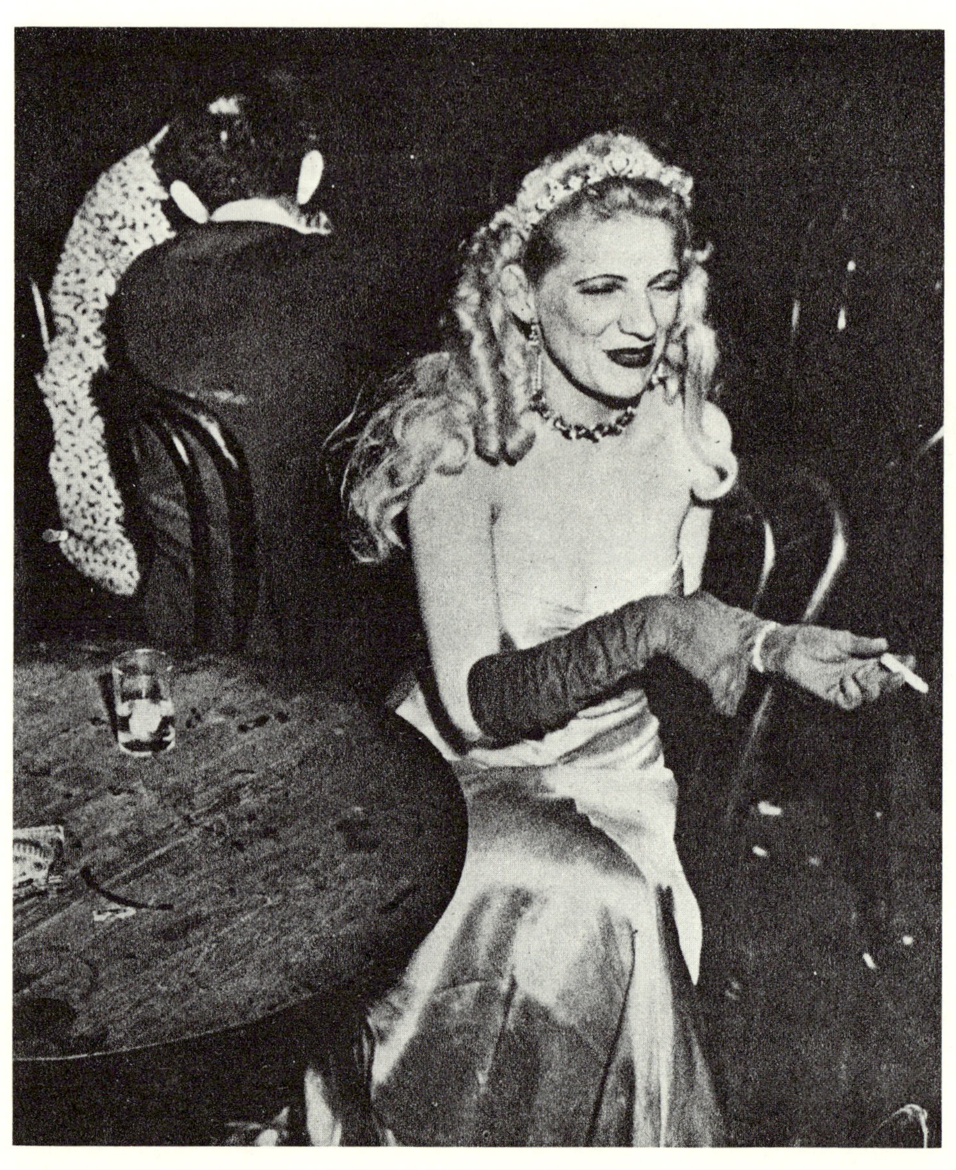

After the Opera . . . at Sammy's Night Club on the Bowery.

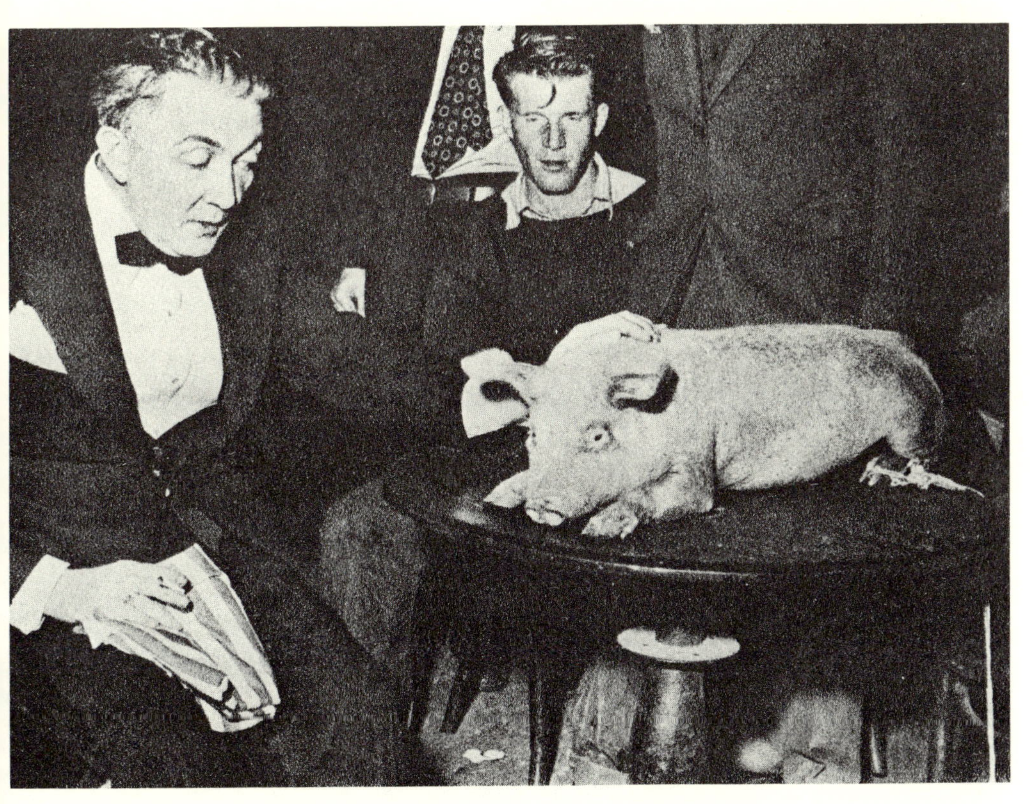

Lost and found department.

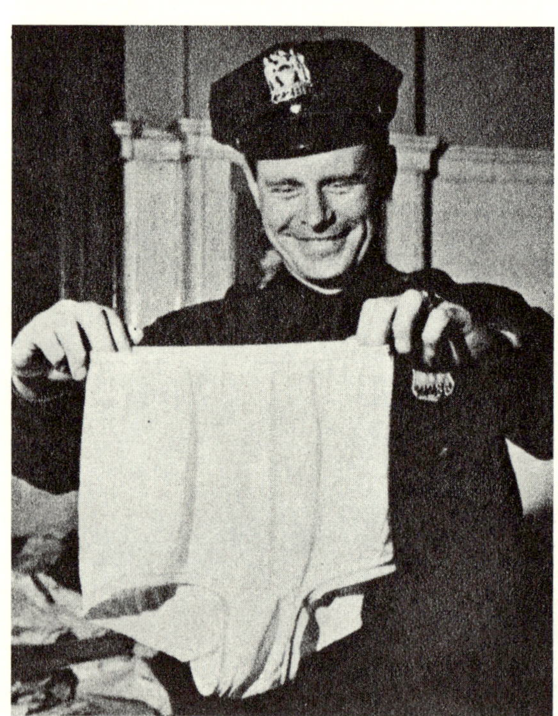

THE SIDEWALK

3

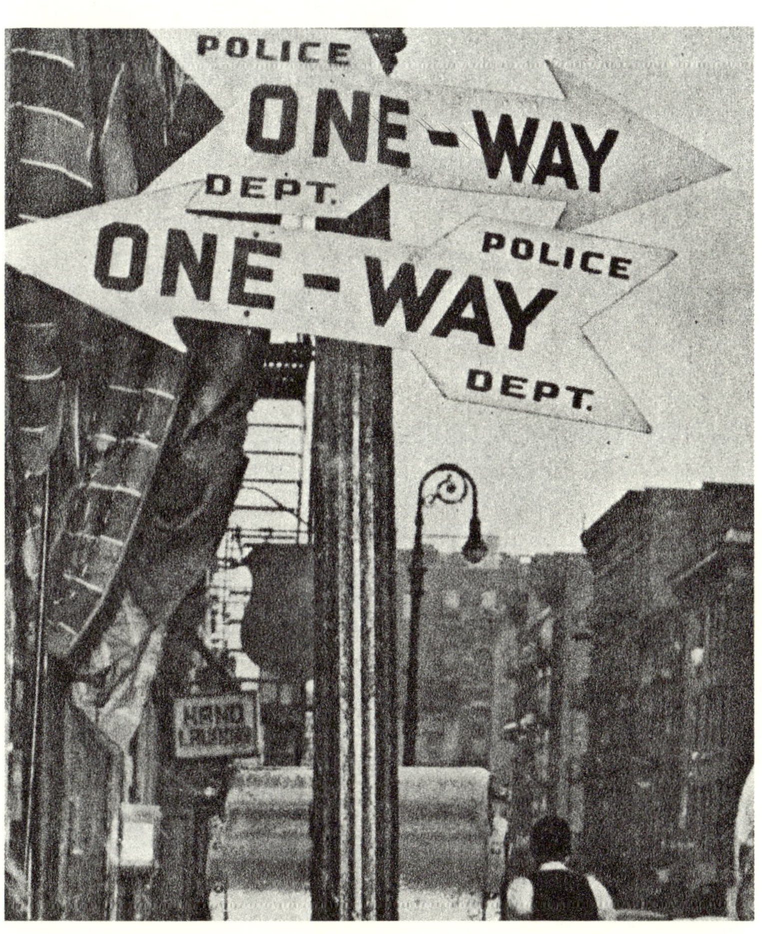

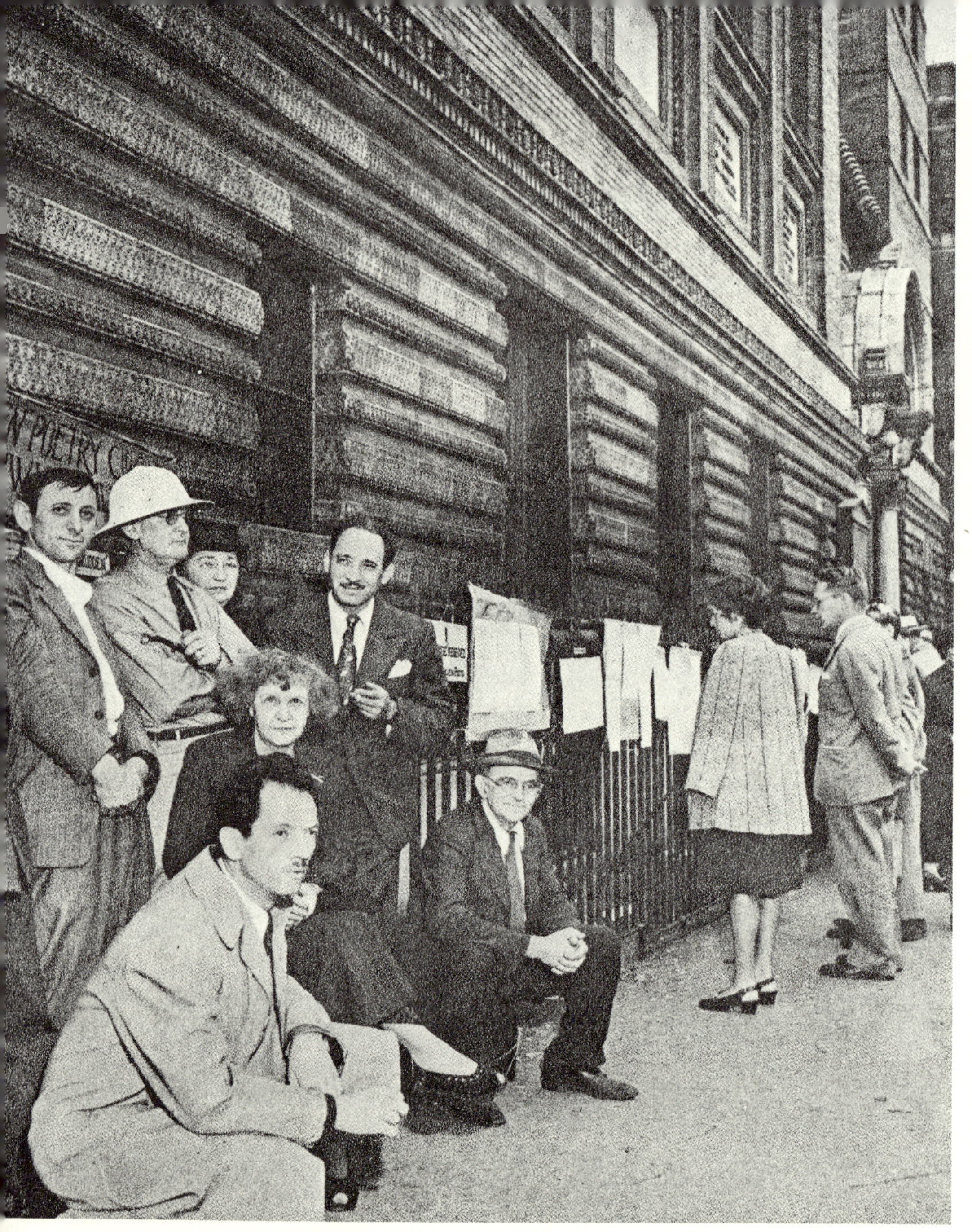

Greenwich Village poets, who like to eat, display their poems for sale at an open air poetry exhibit . . . but there were few buyers.

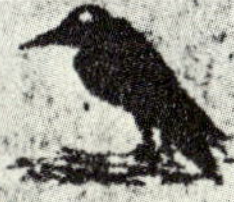

JOE GOULD

TWO POEMS

By

JOE GOULD.

—

SO.

My love for you is uv the cleanus,
Holy and sweet is my emotion.
There should be suthin deep
  between us,
And I suggest the Atlantic Ocean.

———

THE BARRICADES.

(A "Proletarian" Poem.)

This prissy hedge in front of the Brevoort,
Is but a symbol of the coming revolution.
These are the Barricades,the Barricades,
  the Barricades.
  And behind these Barricades,
    Behind these Barricades,
The Comrades die.
  The Comrades die,
    The Comrades die.
And behind these Barricades,the Comrades die---
      of Overeating.

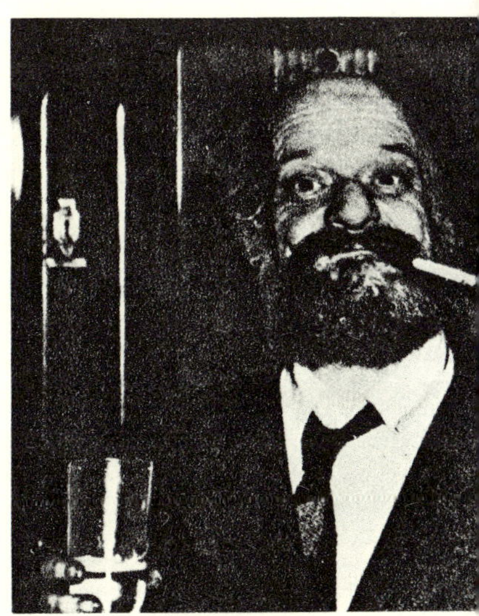

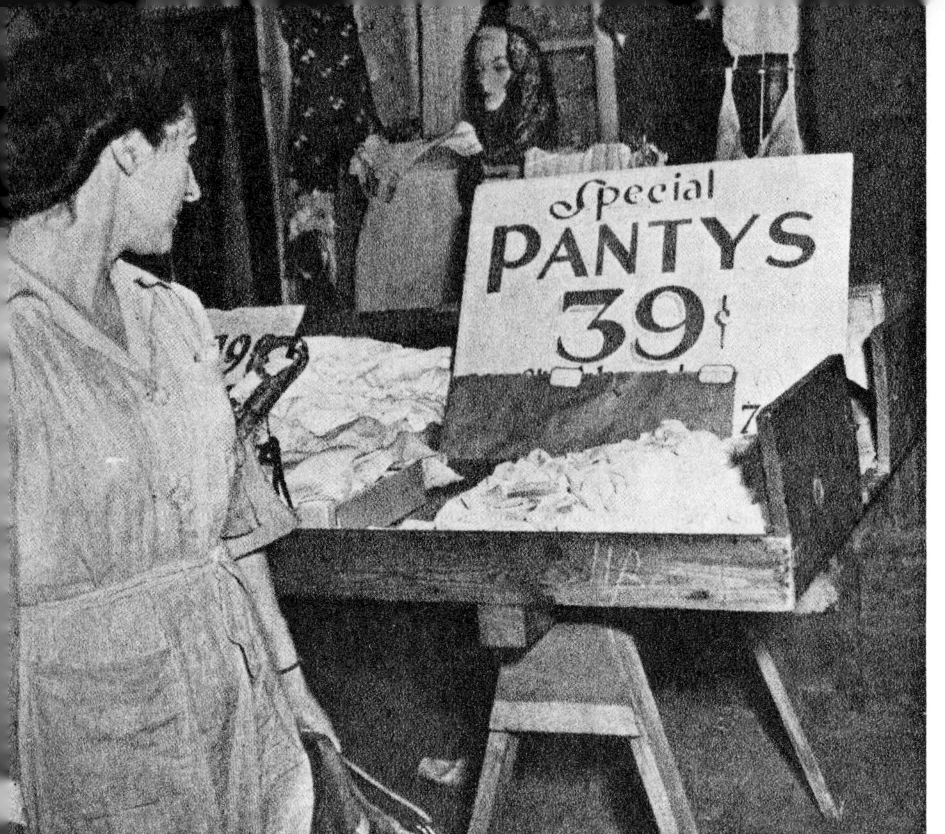
Special
PANTYS
39¢

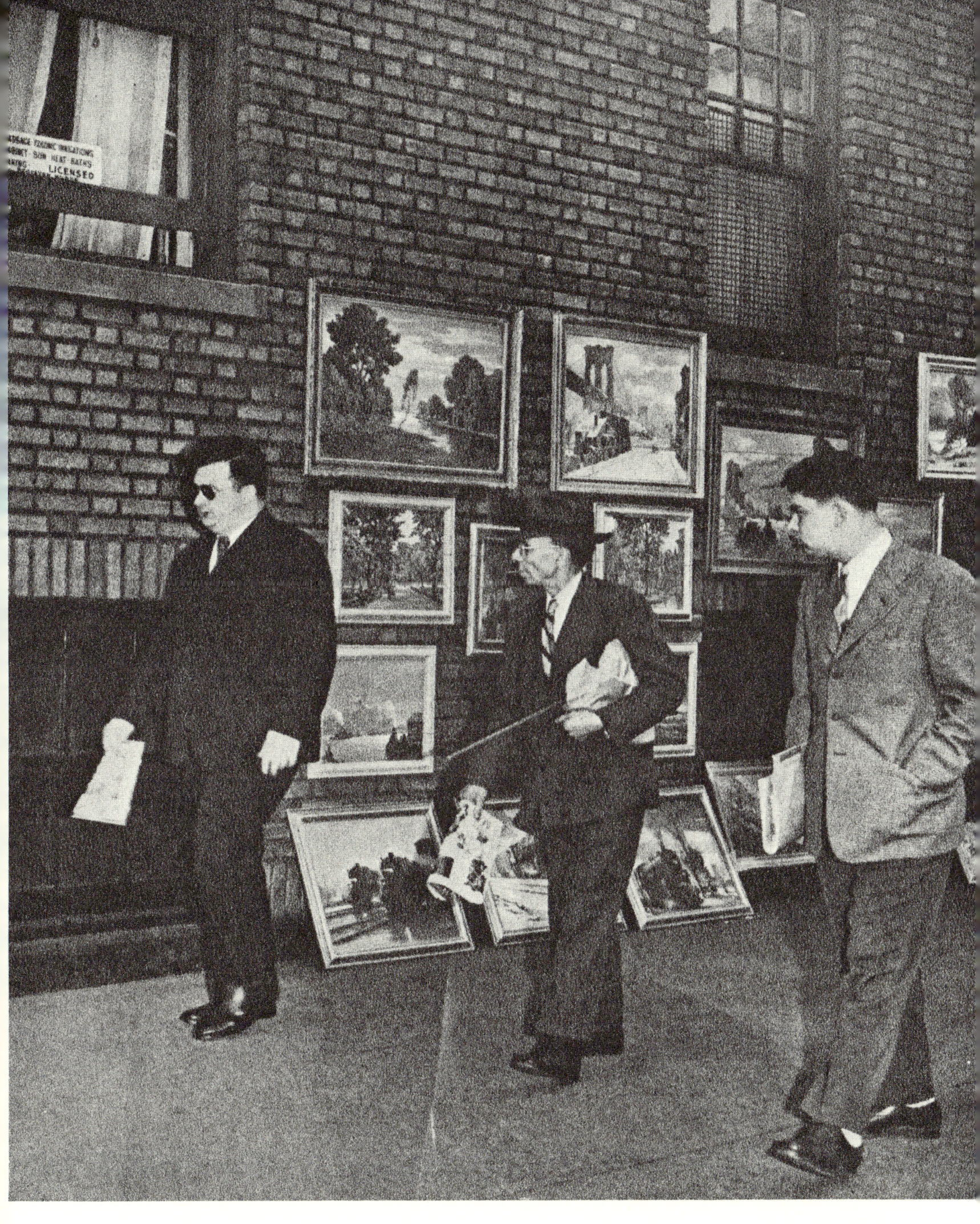
INHALATIONS
HEAT BATHS
LICENSED

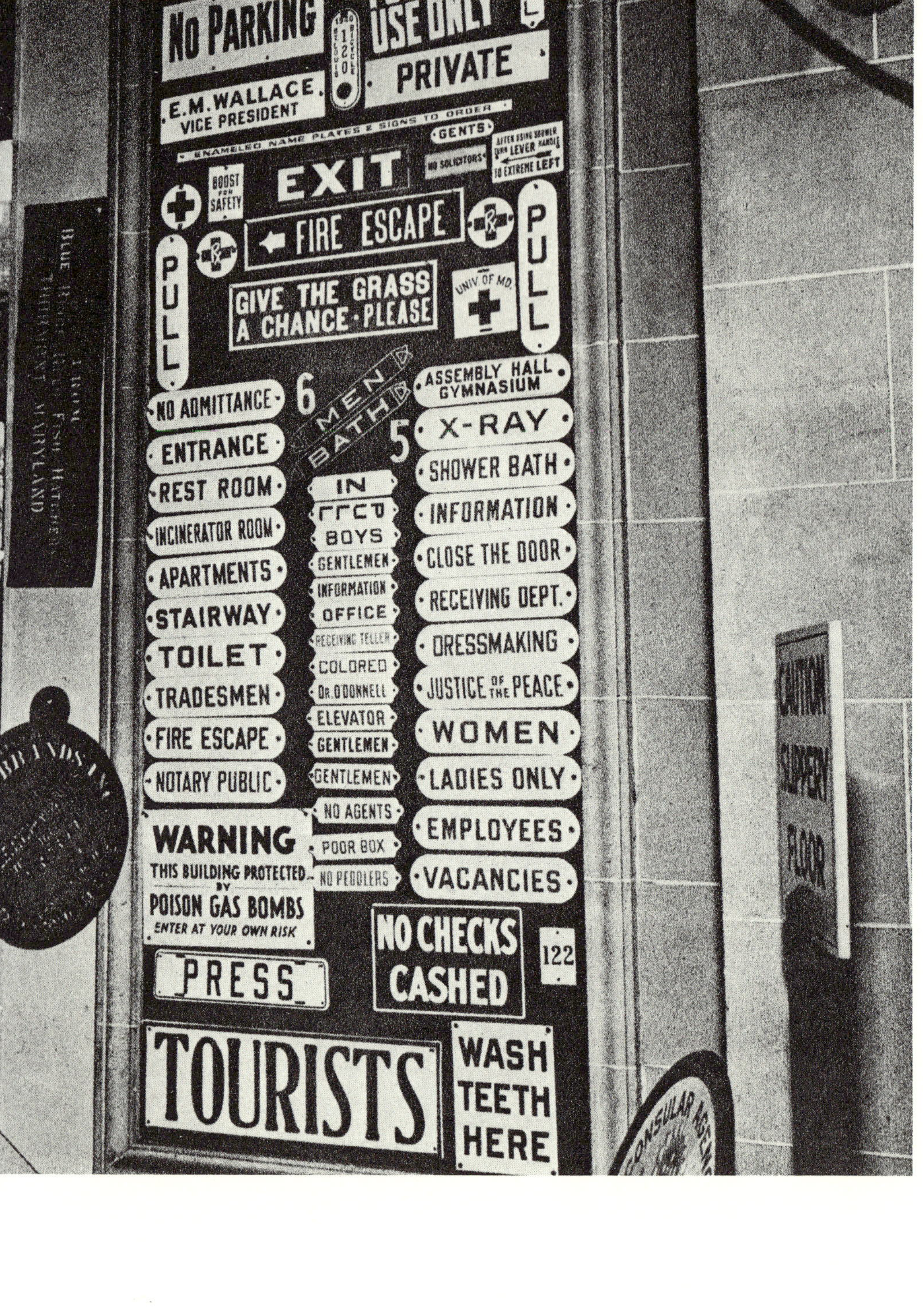
No PARKING
FOR FIRE USE ONLY
PRIVATE
E.M. WALLACE
VICE PRESIDENT
ENAMELED NAME PLATES & SIGNS TO ORDER
GENTS
NO SOLICITORS
AFTER USING SHOWER TURN LEVER HANDLE TO EXTREME LEFT
BOOST FOR SAFETY
EXIT
PULL
FIRE ESCAPE
PULL
GIVE THE GRASS A CHANCE - PLEASE
UNIV. OF MD.
NO ADMITTANCE
6
MEN BATH
ASSEMBLY HALL GYMNASIUM
ENTRANCE
5
X-RAY
REST ROOM
IN
SHOWER BATH
INCINERATOR ROOM
BOYS
INFORMATION
APARTMENTS
GENTLEMEN
CLOSE THE DOOR
STAIRWAY
INFORMATION
RECEIVING DEPT.
TOILET
OFFICE
DRESSMAKING
TRADESMEN
RECEIVING TELLER
JUSTICE OF THE PEACE
COLORED
FIRE ESCAPE
Dr. O'DONNELL
WOMEN
ELEVATOR
NOTARY PUBLIC
GENTLEMEN
LADIES ONLY
GENTLEMEN
WARNING
NO AGENTS
EMPLOYEES
THIS BUILDING PROTECTED BY
POOR BOX
POISON GAS BOMBS
NO PEDDLERS
VACANCIES
ENTER AT YOUR OWN RISK
PRESS
NO CHECKS CASHED
122
TOURISTS
WASH TEETH HERE
CAUTION SLIPPERY FLOOR
BLUE RIDGE RIFLE FISH HATCHERY THURMONT MARYLAND

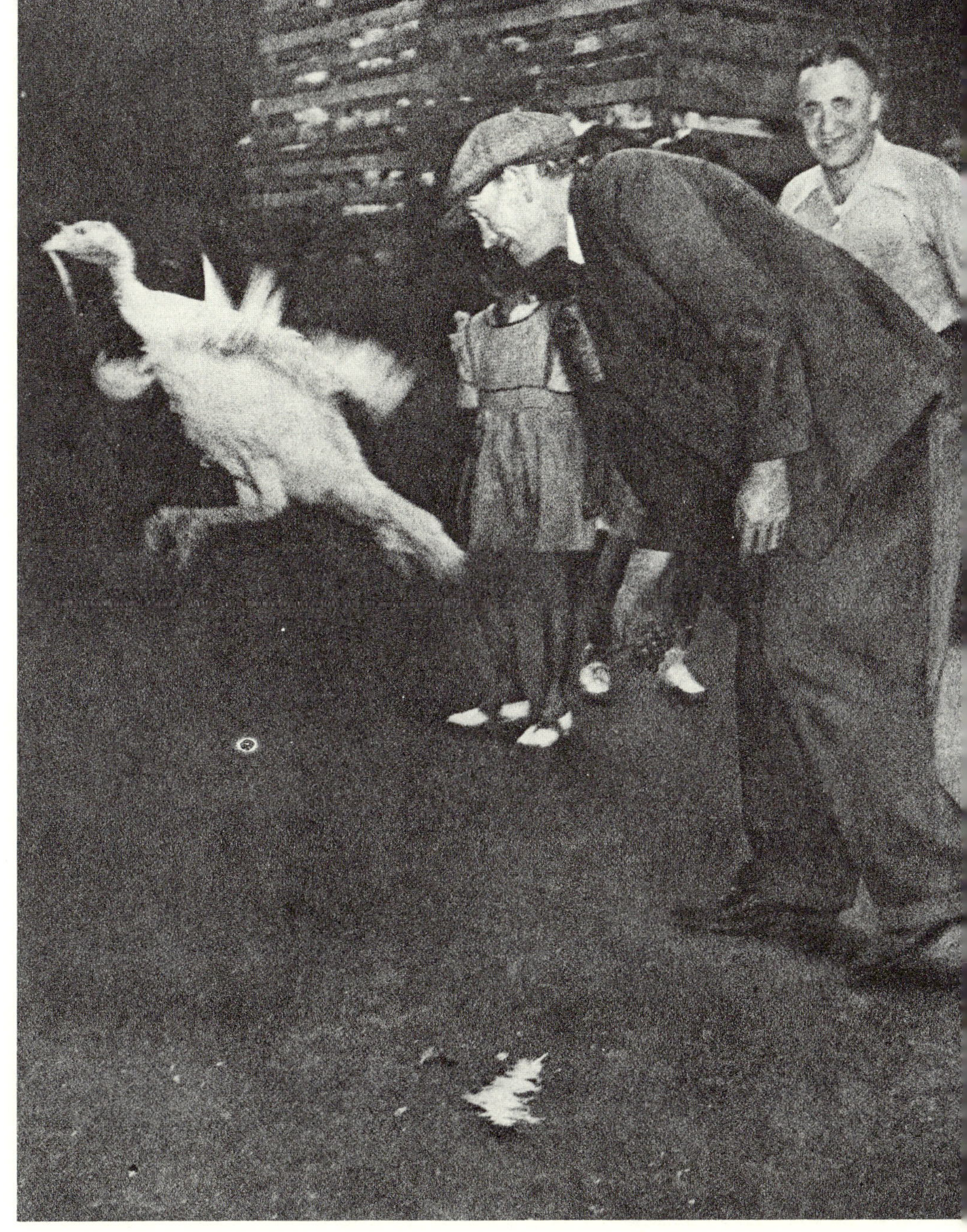

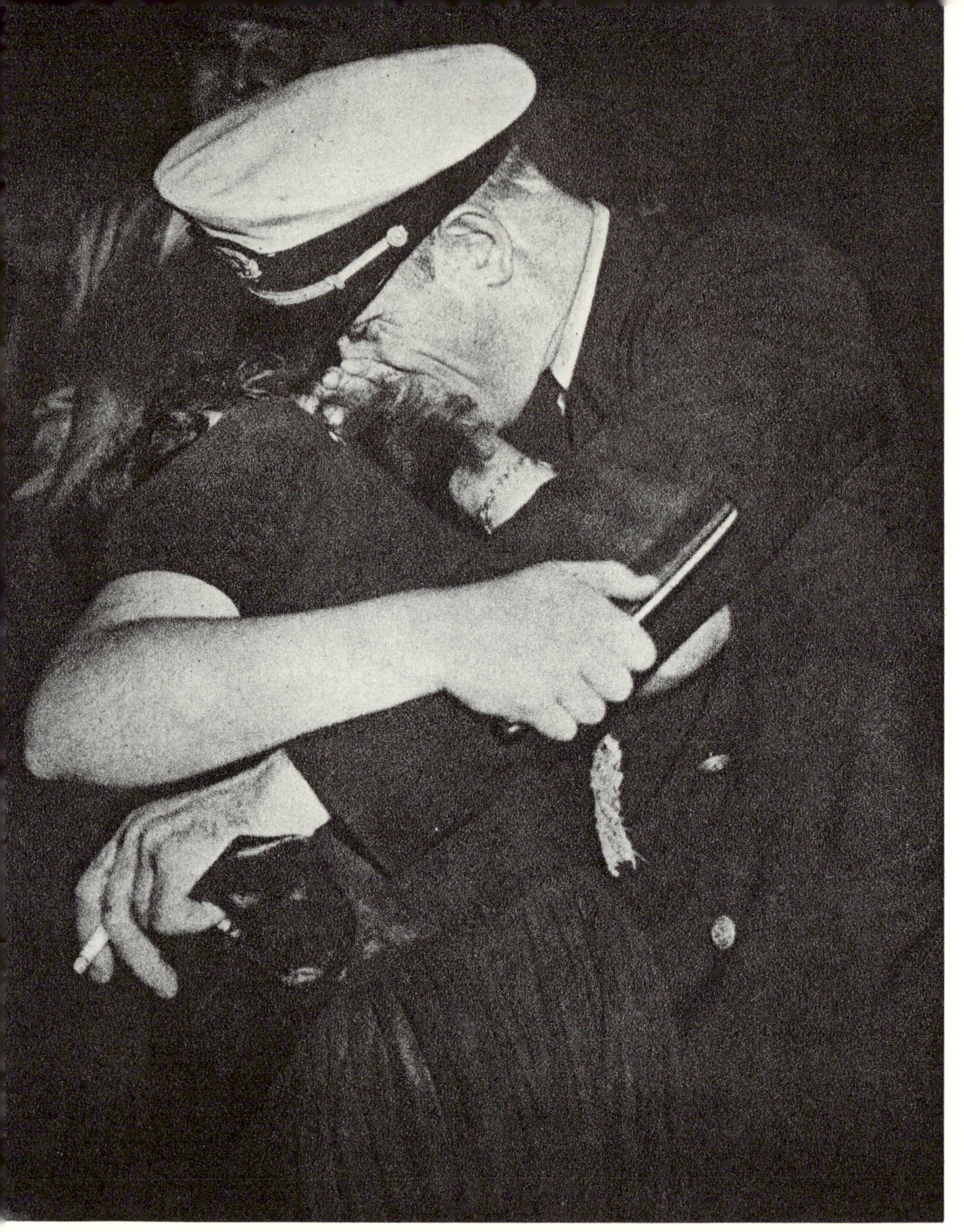

I like this. . . .

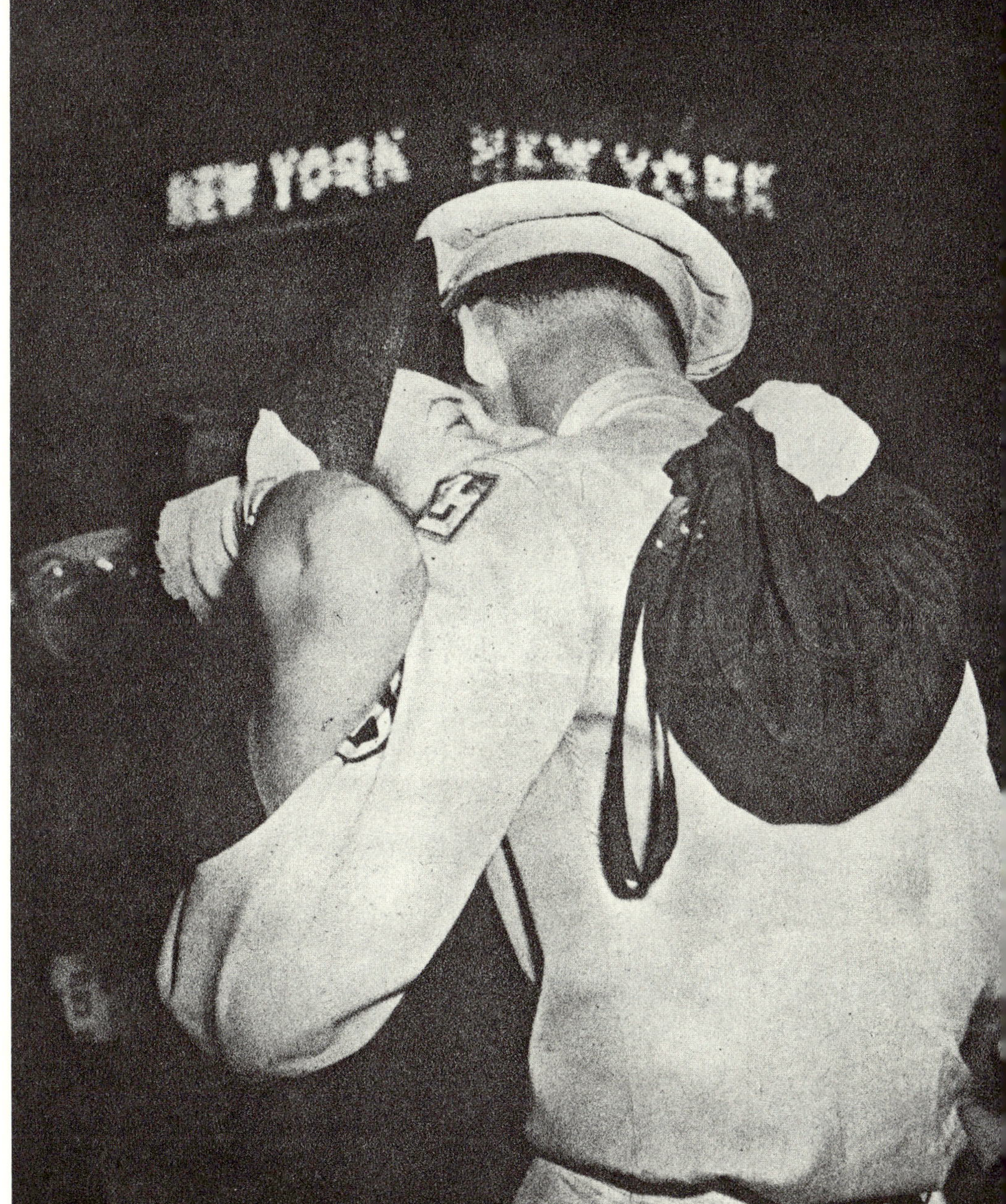
NEW YORK NEW YORK

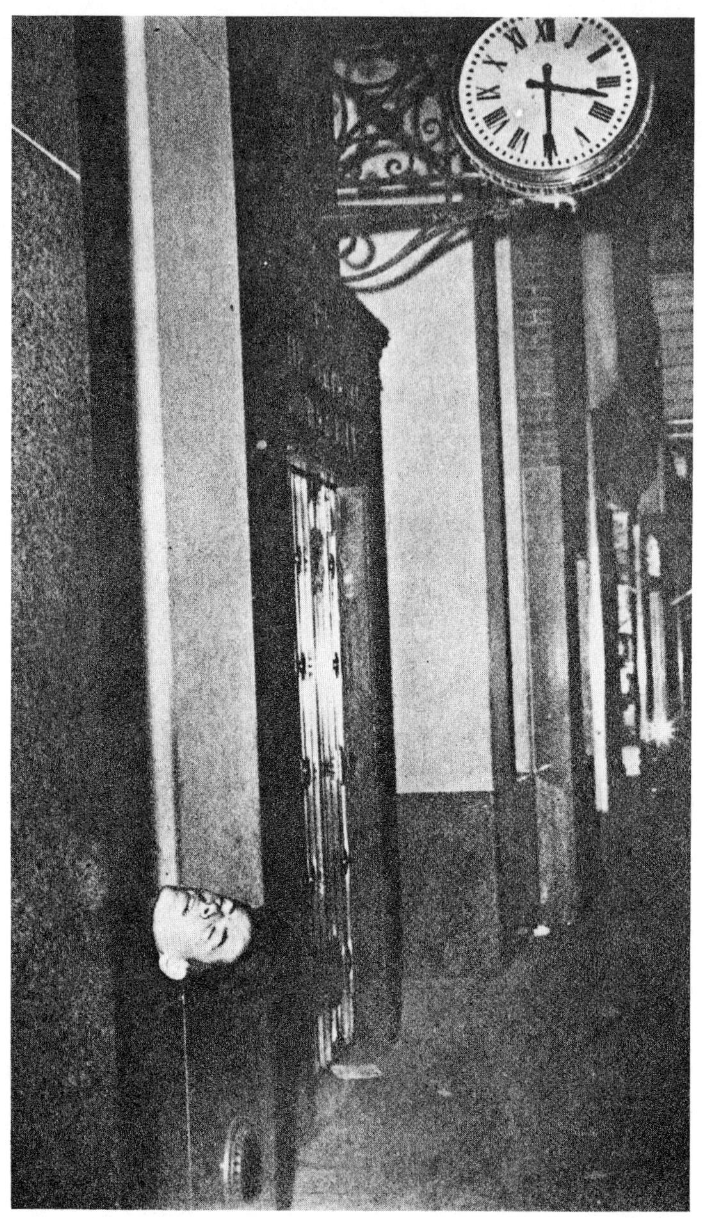

Just a fellow sleeping it off in a Times Square bank window.

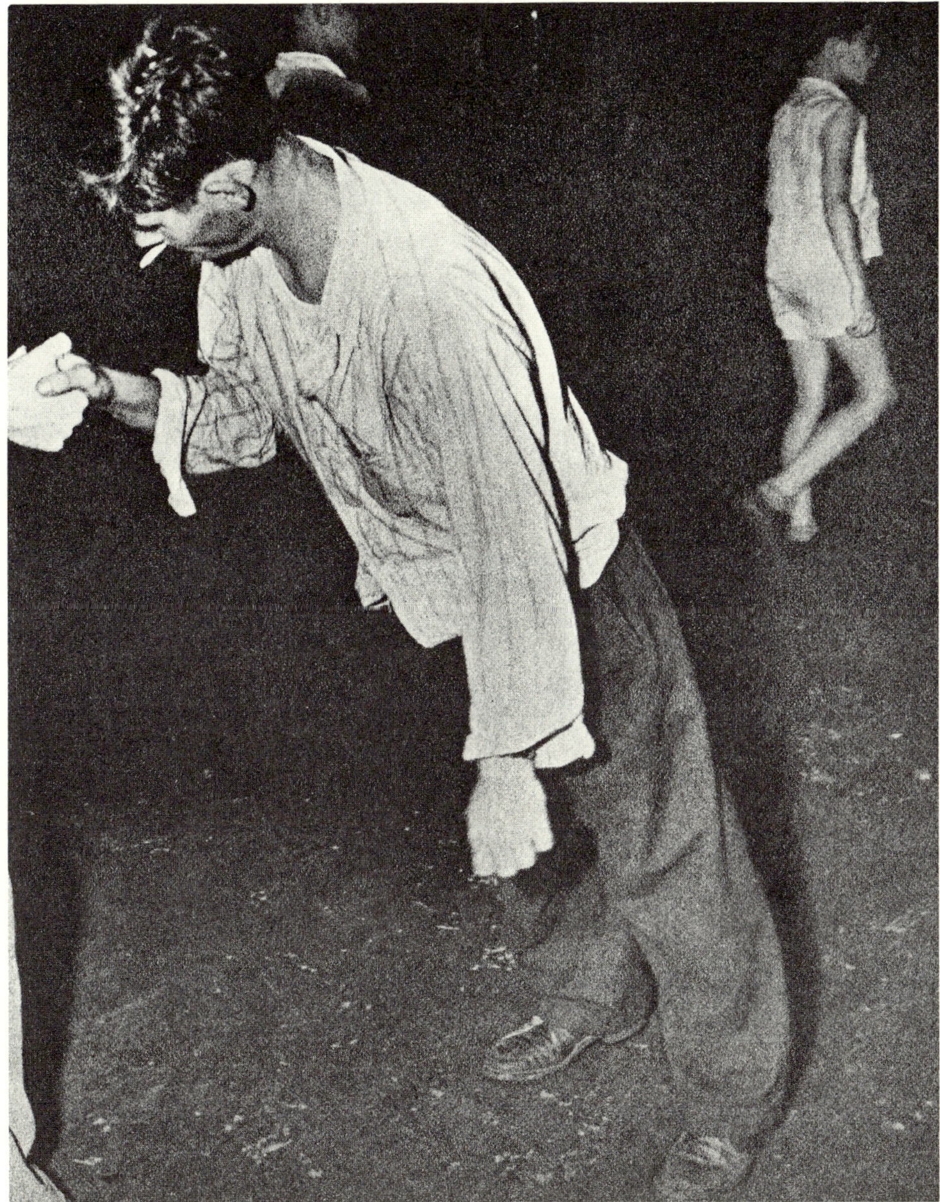

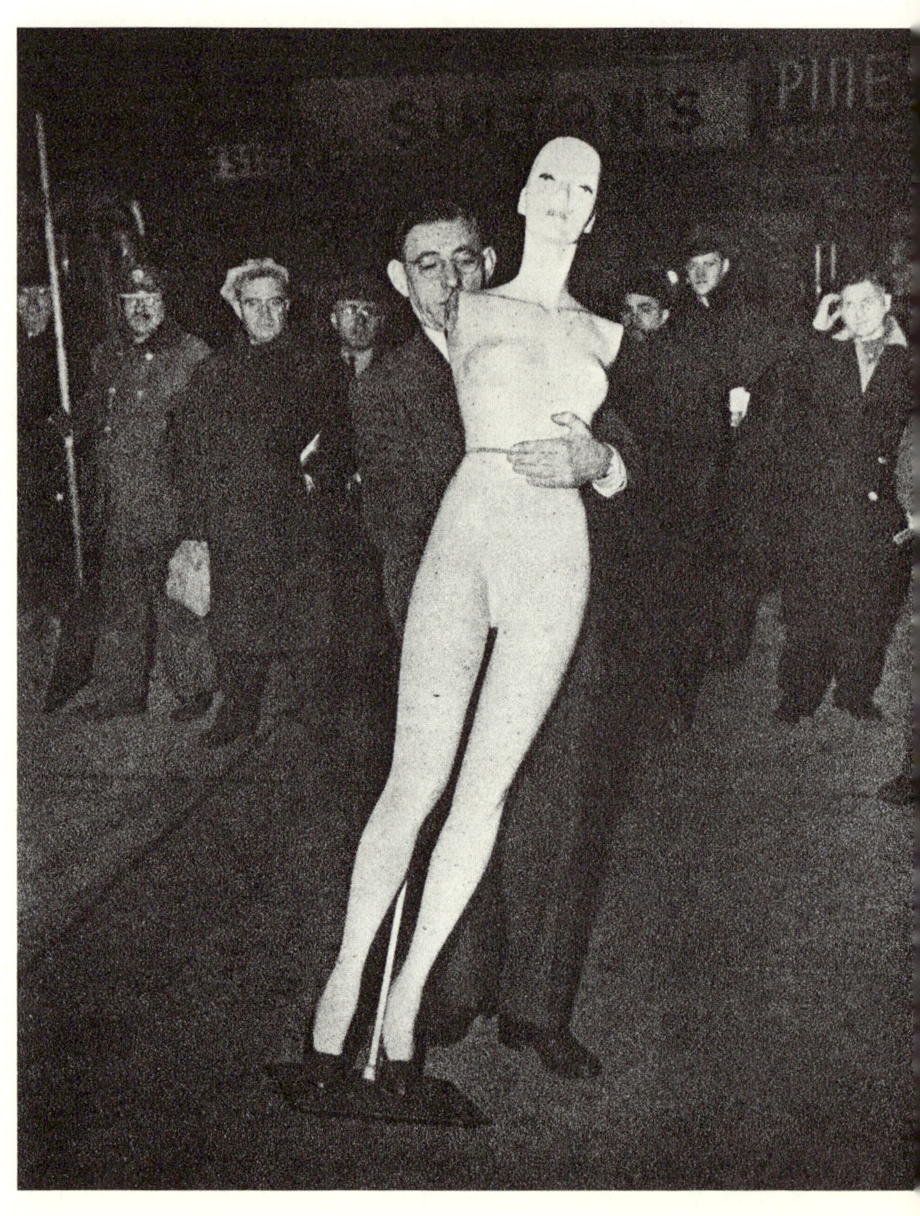

A great metropolis comes to lif

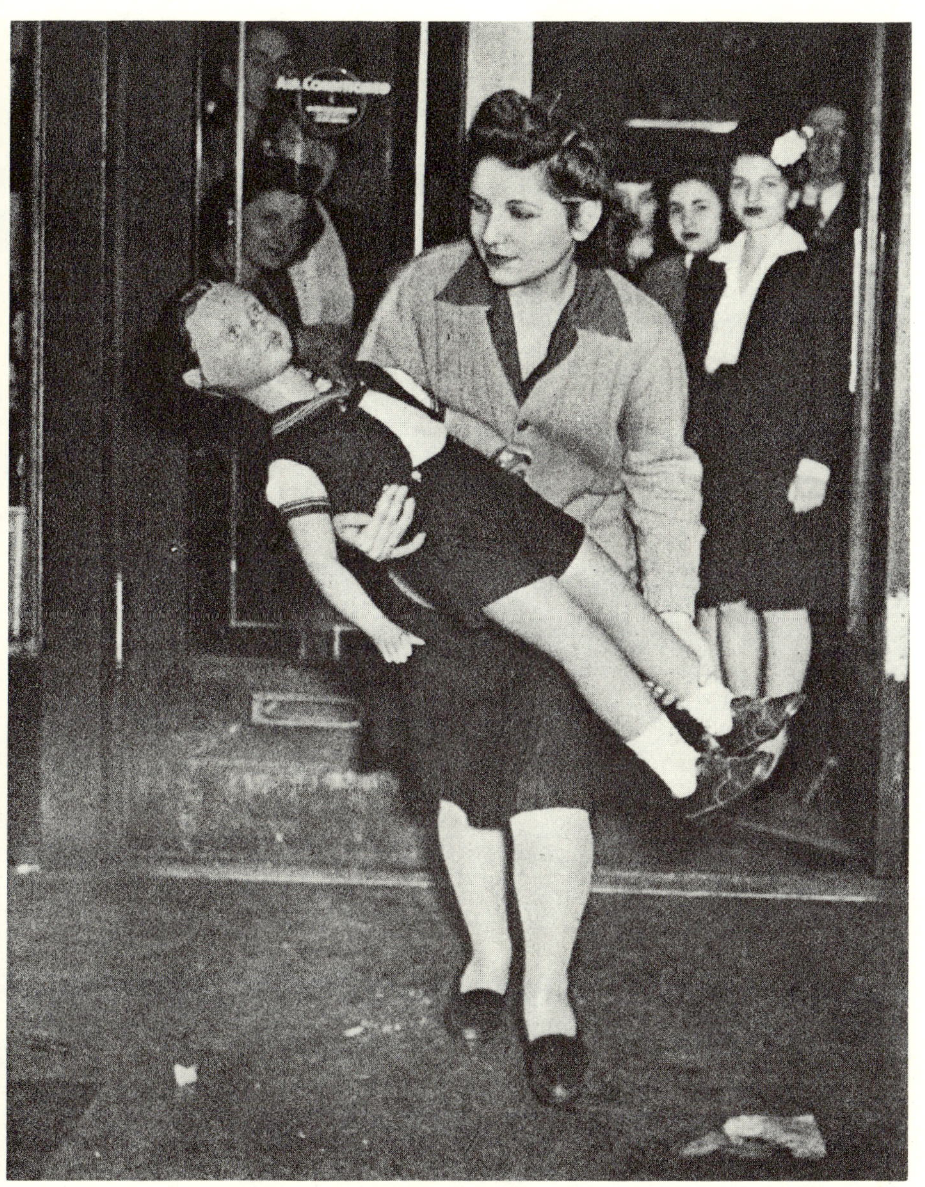

This man stopped every man, woman, and child on the street looking for the most popular beer slogan for an advertising agency.

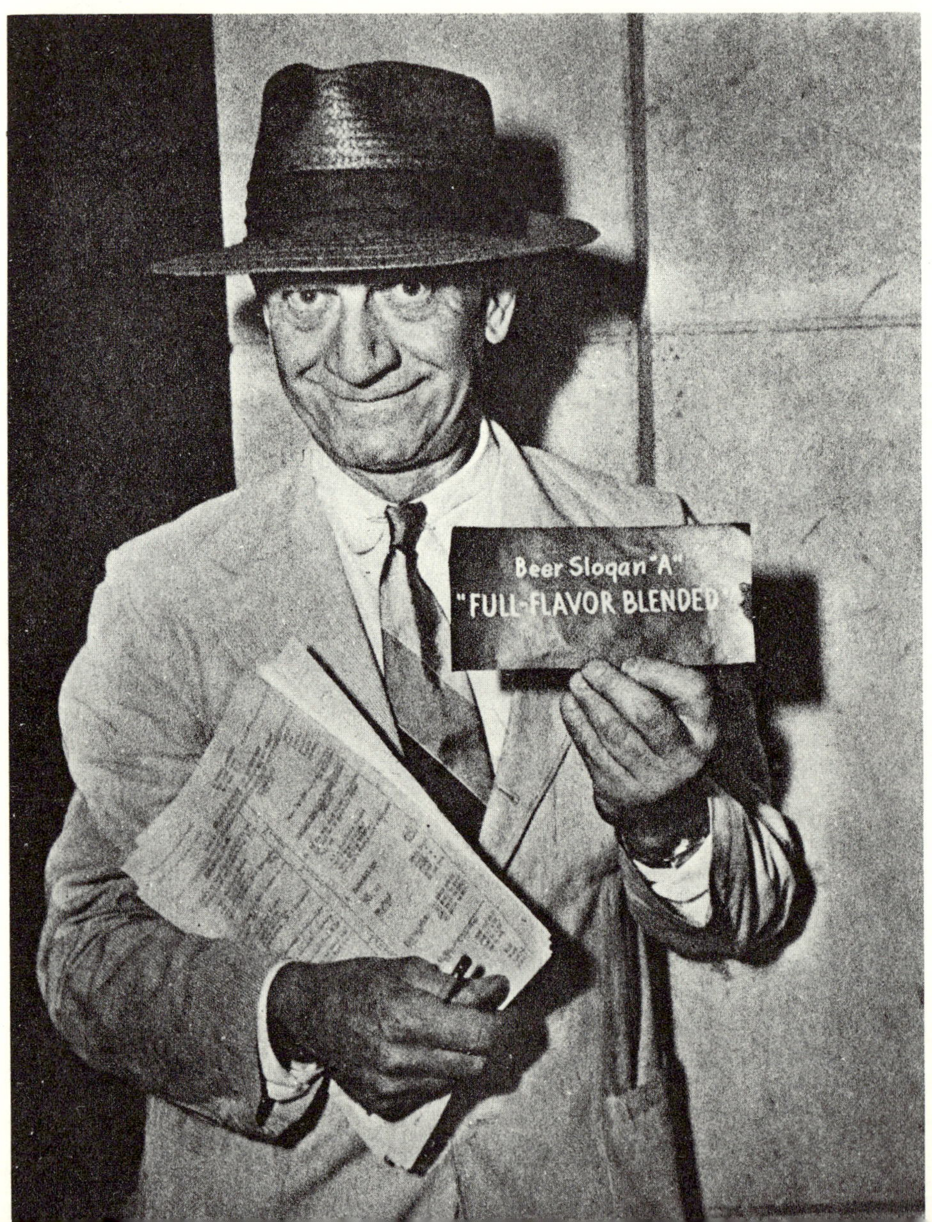

The walking department store

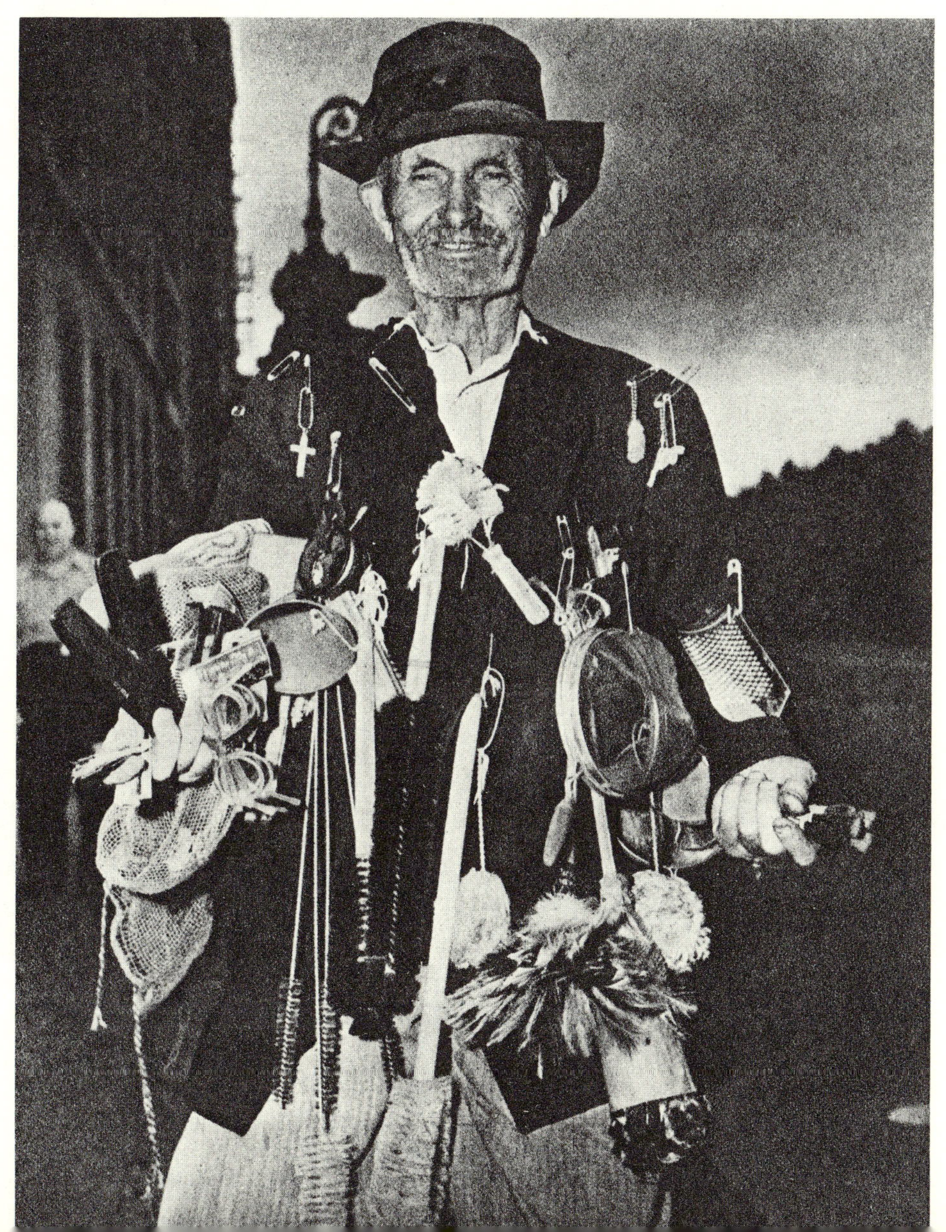

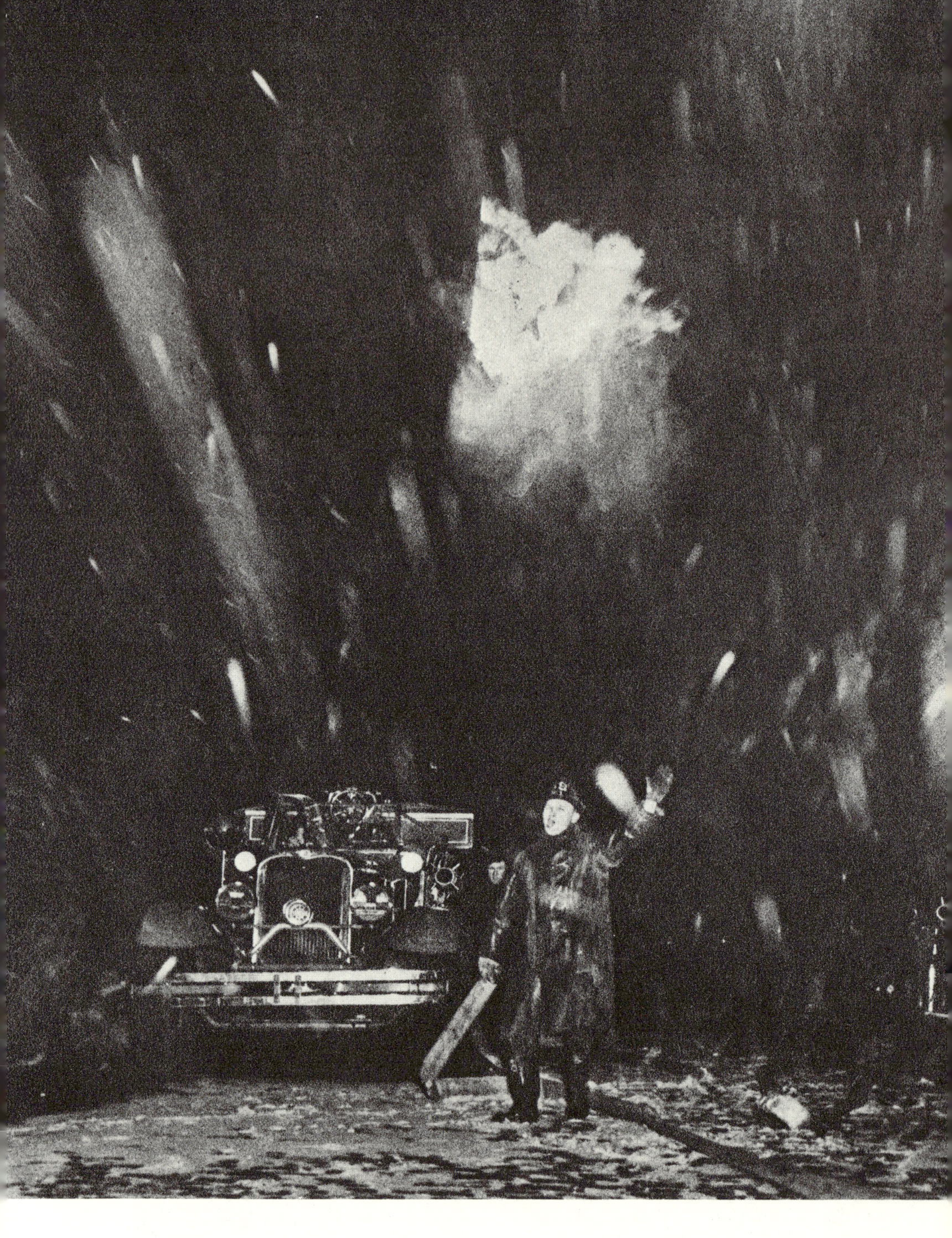

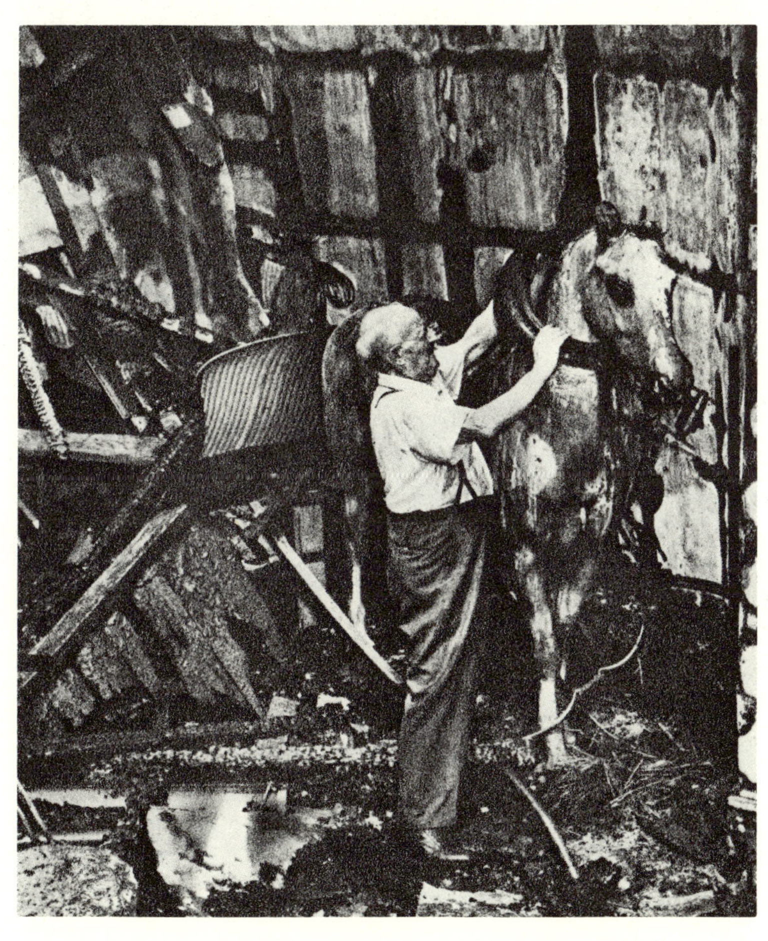

Everyone was saved . . . including the (wooden) horse.

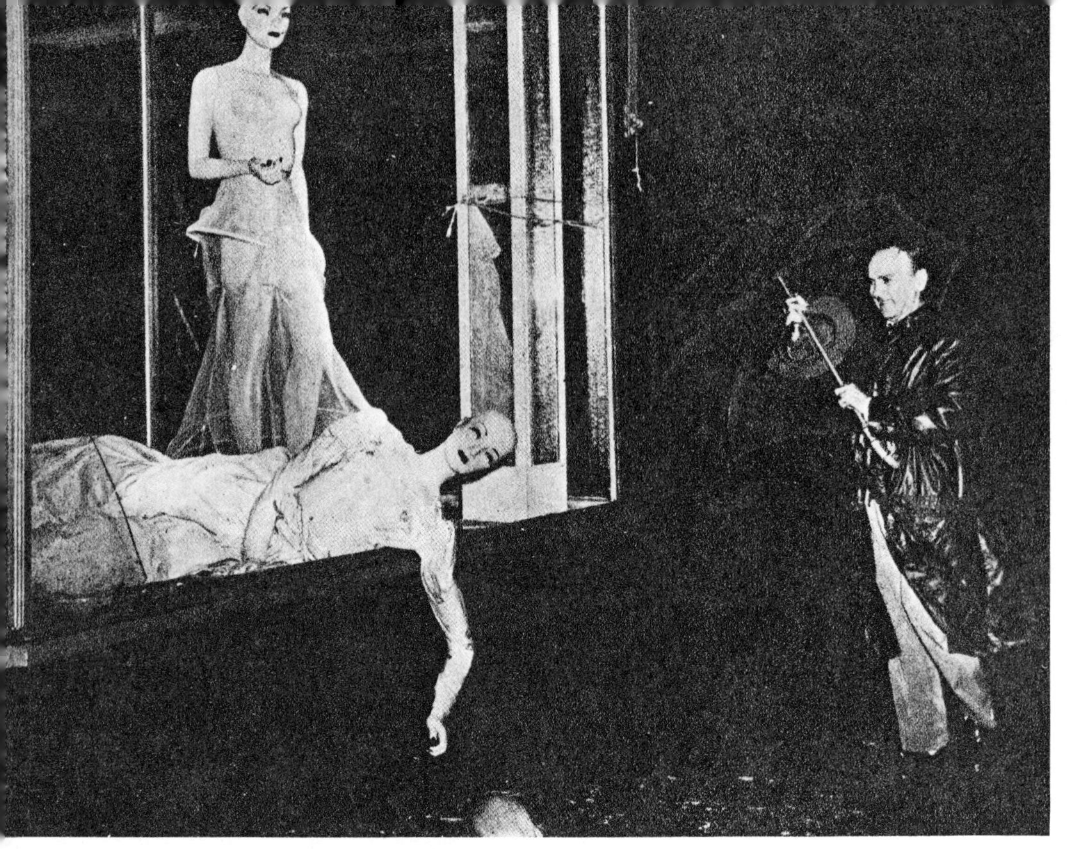

The storm

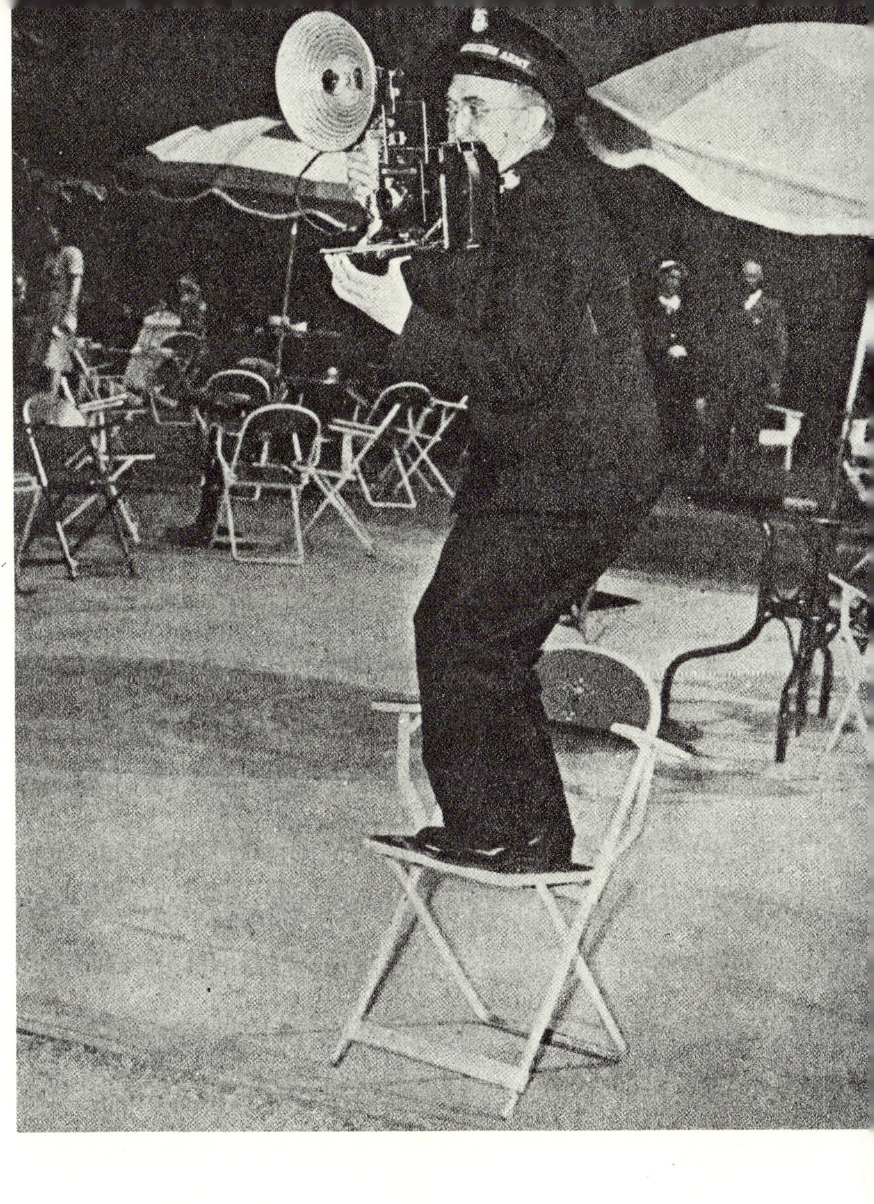

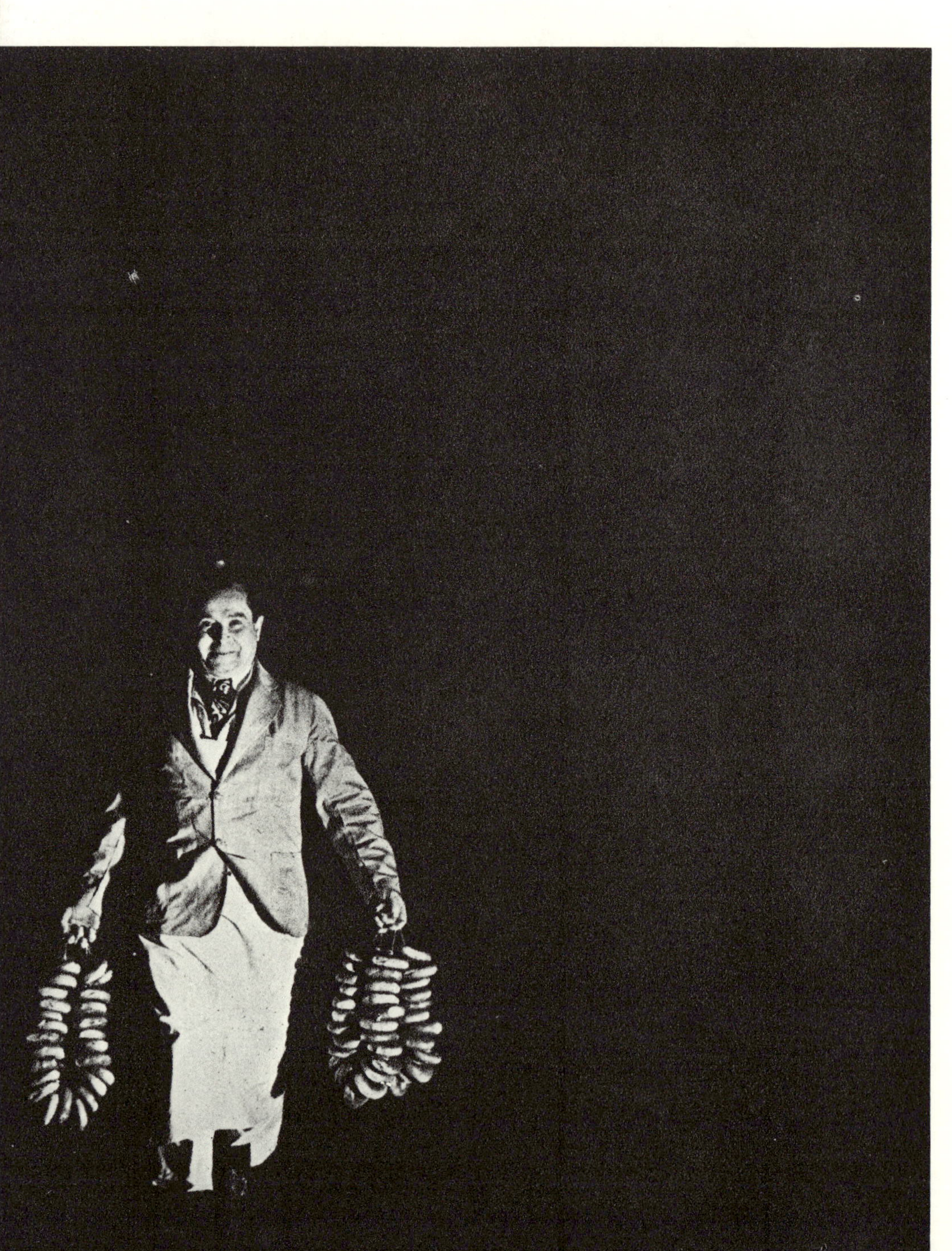

It's six o'clock in the morning on the electric clock on top of the Consolidated Edison Company building on Fourteenth Street. . . . I think they have the clock up there to remind the customers to pay their bills. Max is rushing in the morning's bagles to a restaurant on Second Avenue for the morning trade.

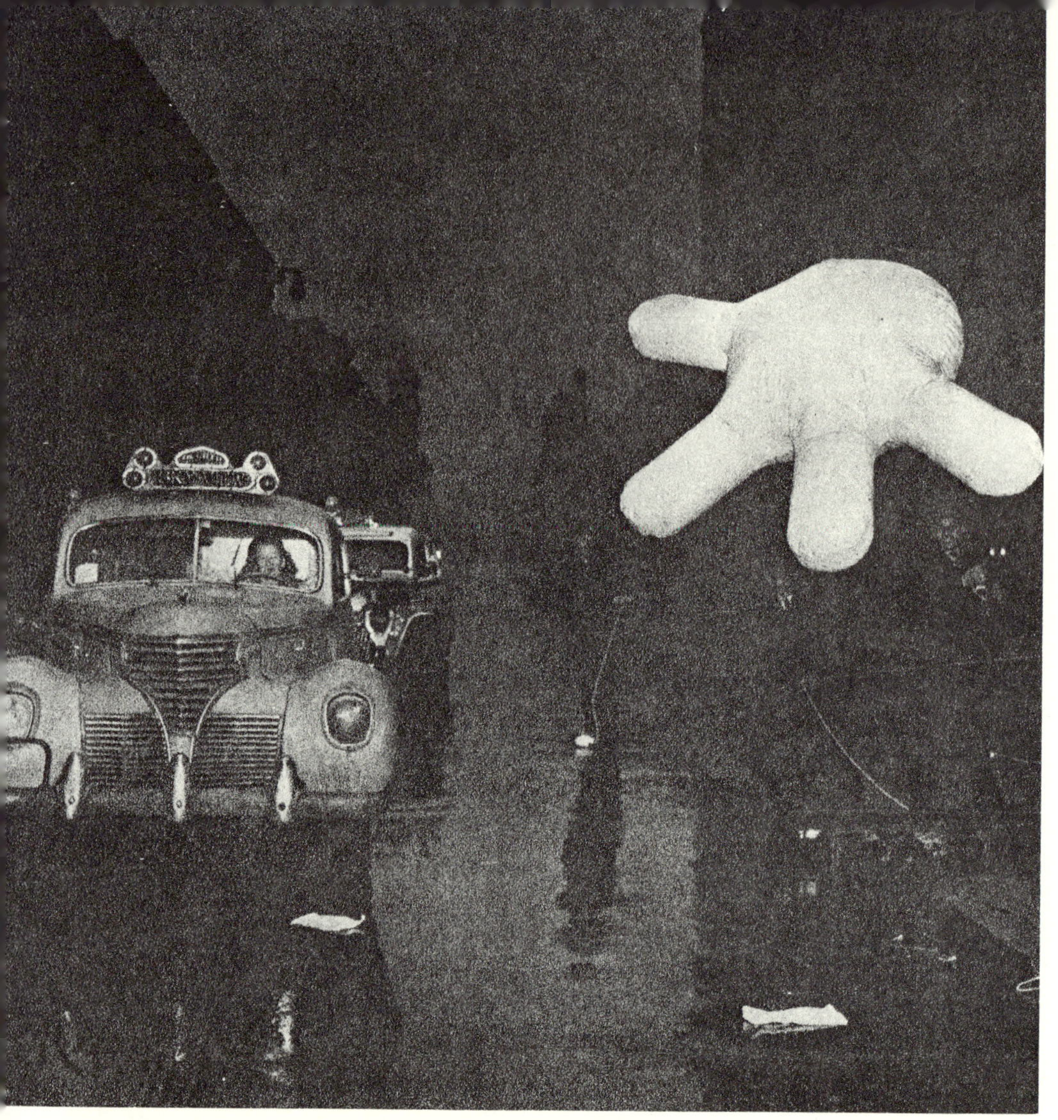

Don't be scared. . . . Lady cab driver cruising in the rain up Columbus Avenue at dawn. . . . It's just the hand of a forty-five-foot clown filled with helium gas for the annual Macy Thanksgiving Day parade.

The Dance

4

Dancing
TO NITE
Monday to Thursday
20 Dances for $1.00
Music By
Lionel Howard
Friday, Sat. & Sunday
15 Dances for $1.00

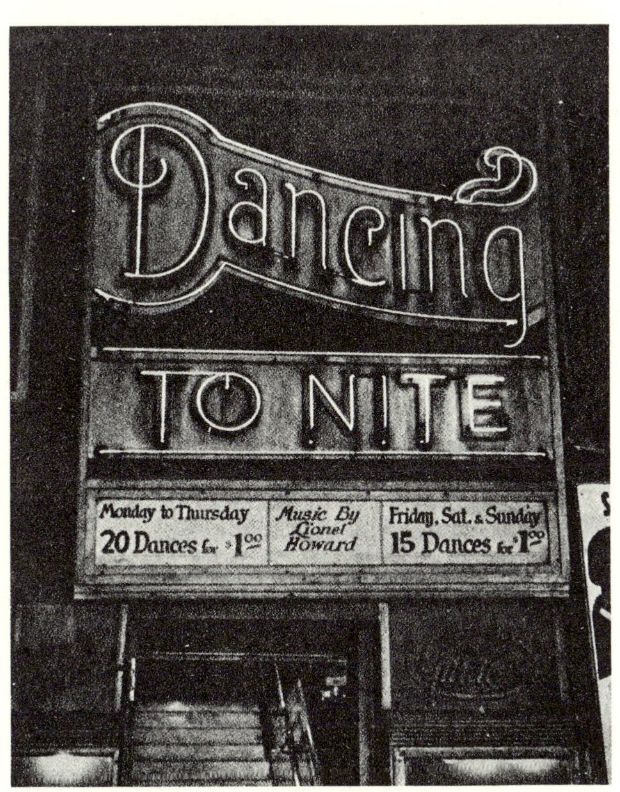

Hostesses waiting for customers in a Broadway ballroom . . . .

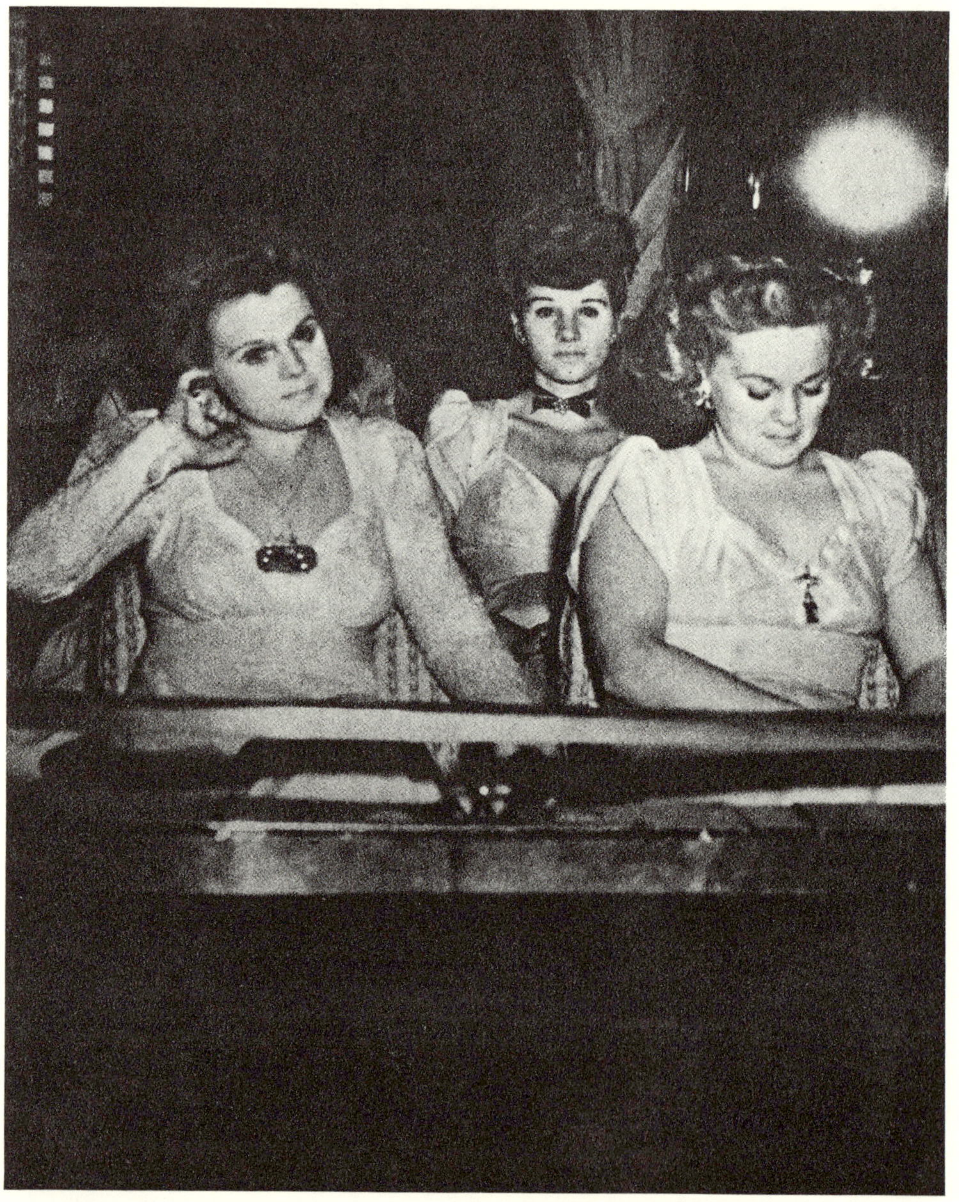

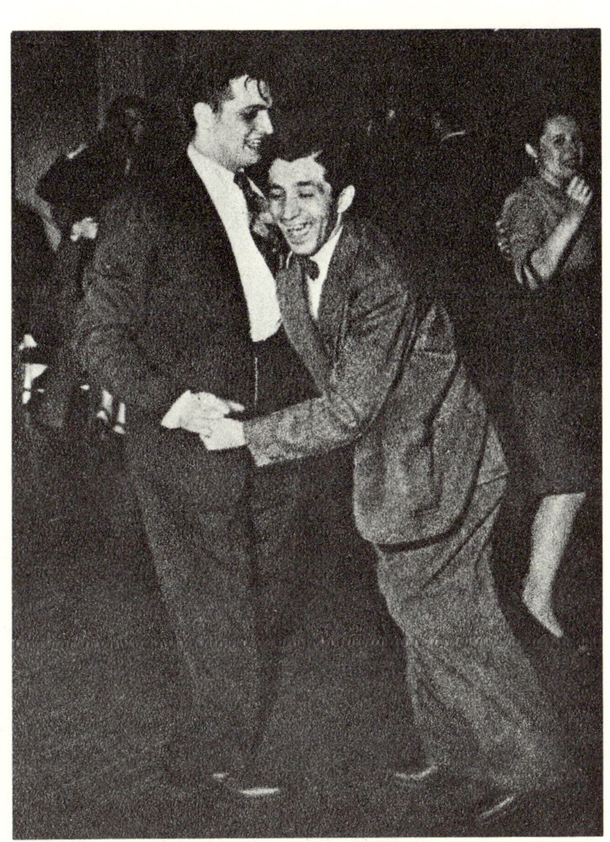

but . . .

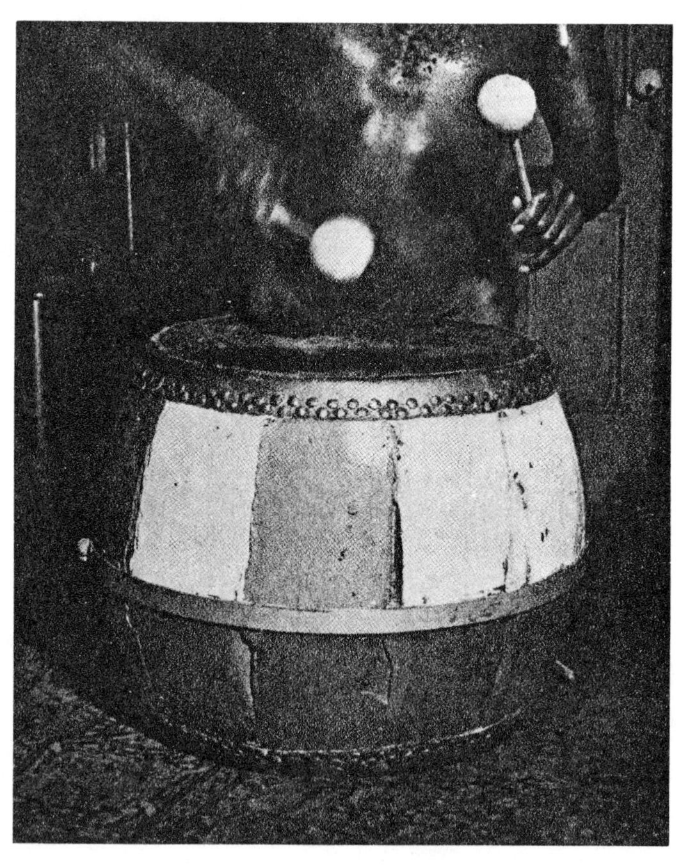

Some prefer the beat of the tom-tom

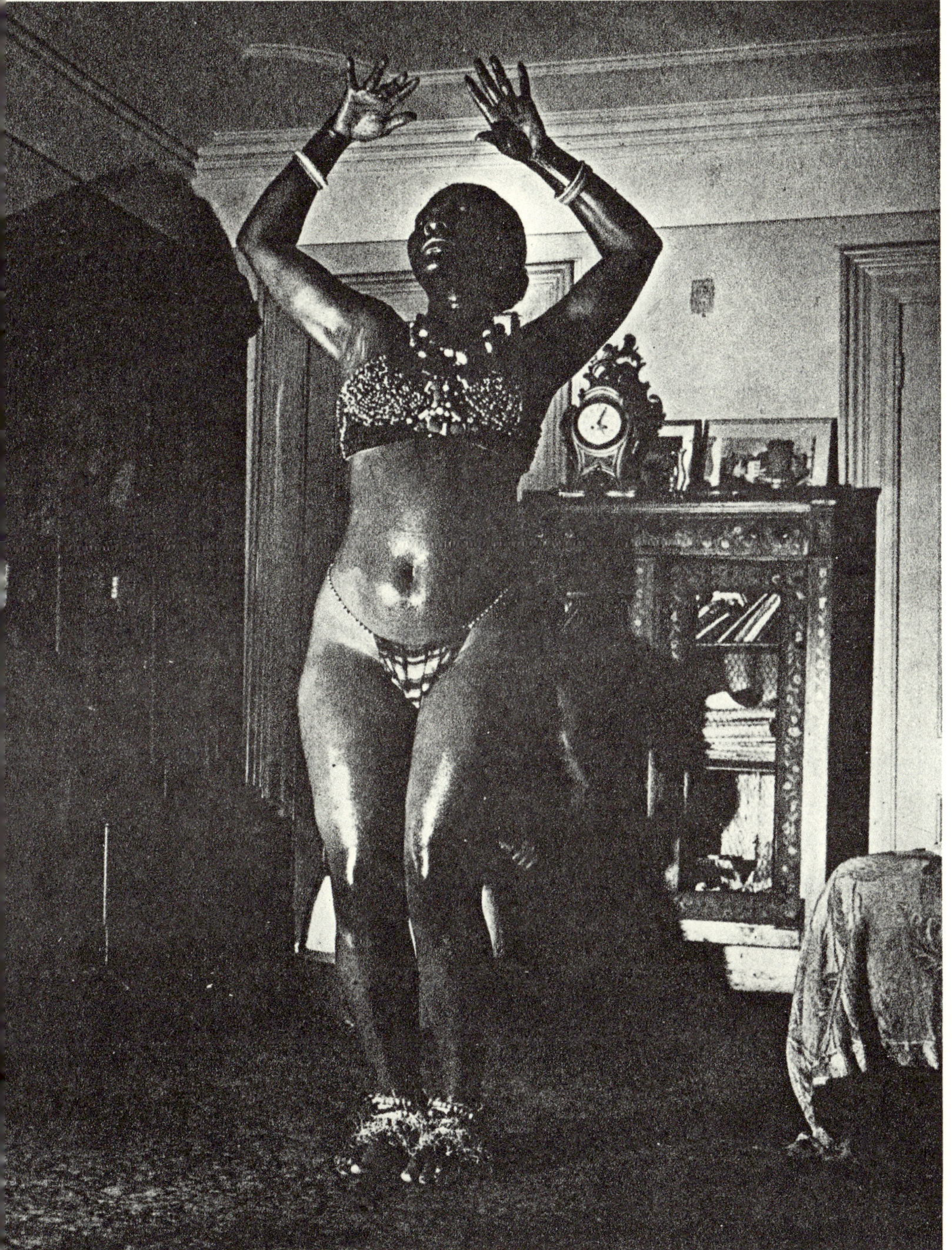

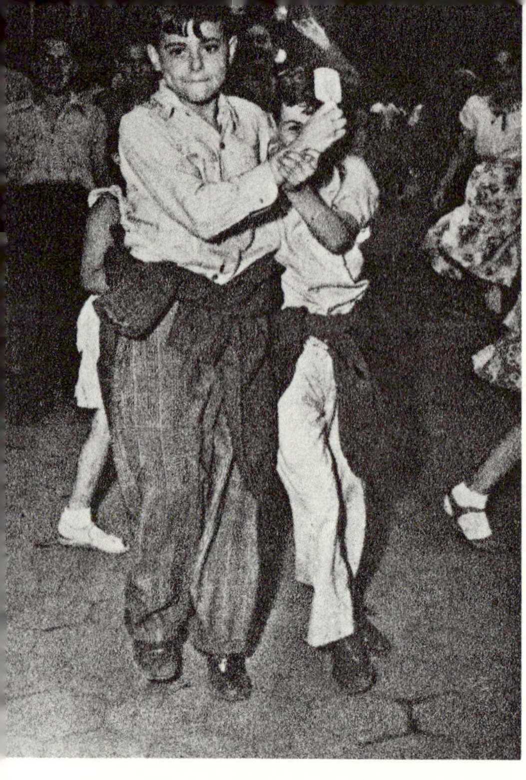

Dancing is free in Central Park

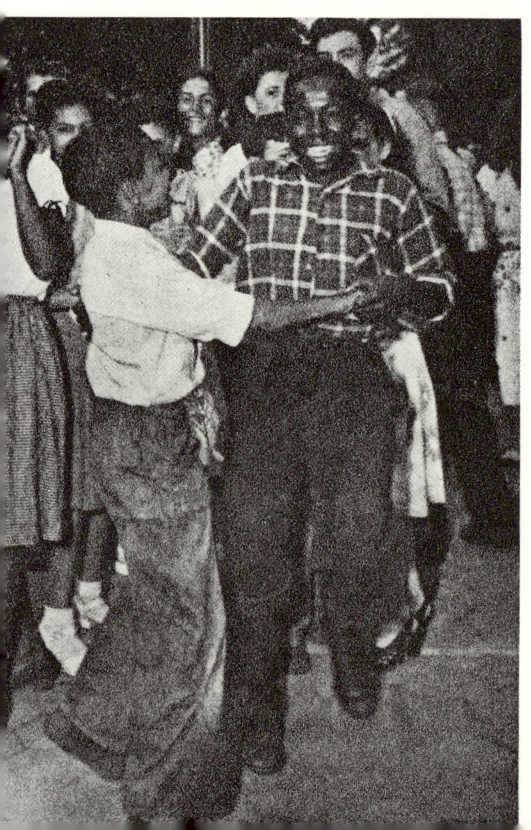

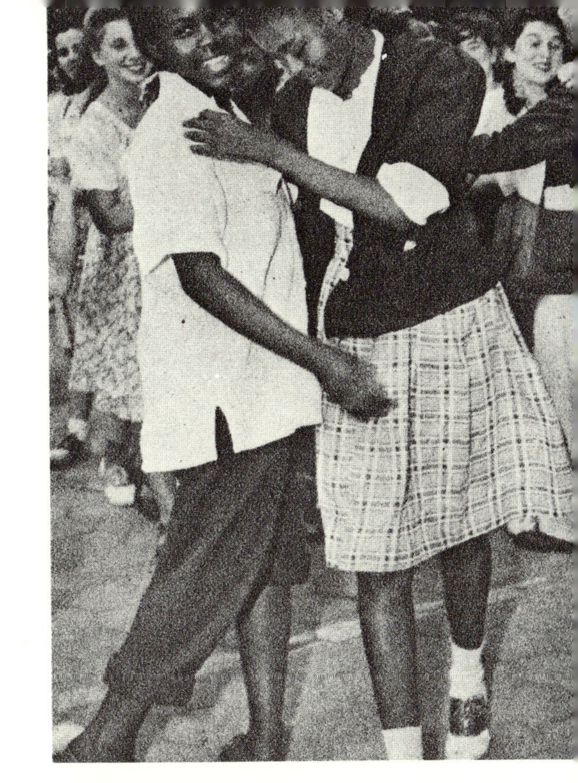

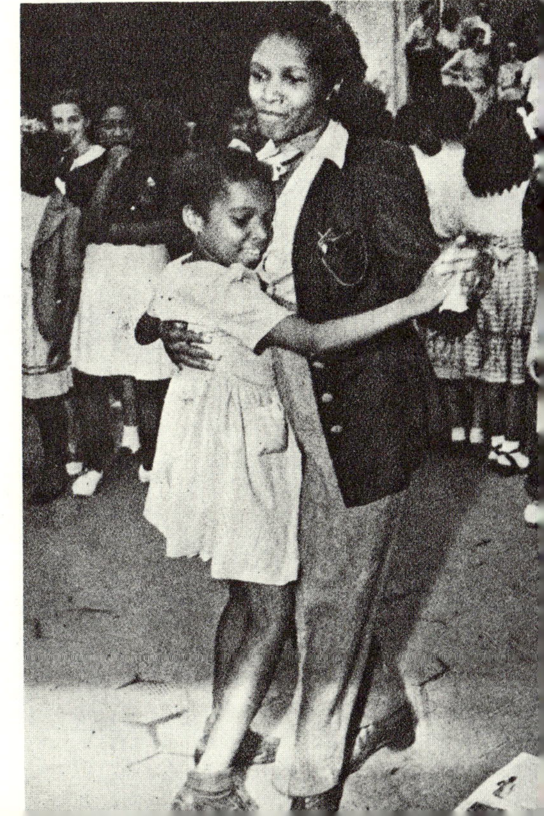

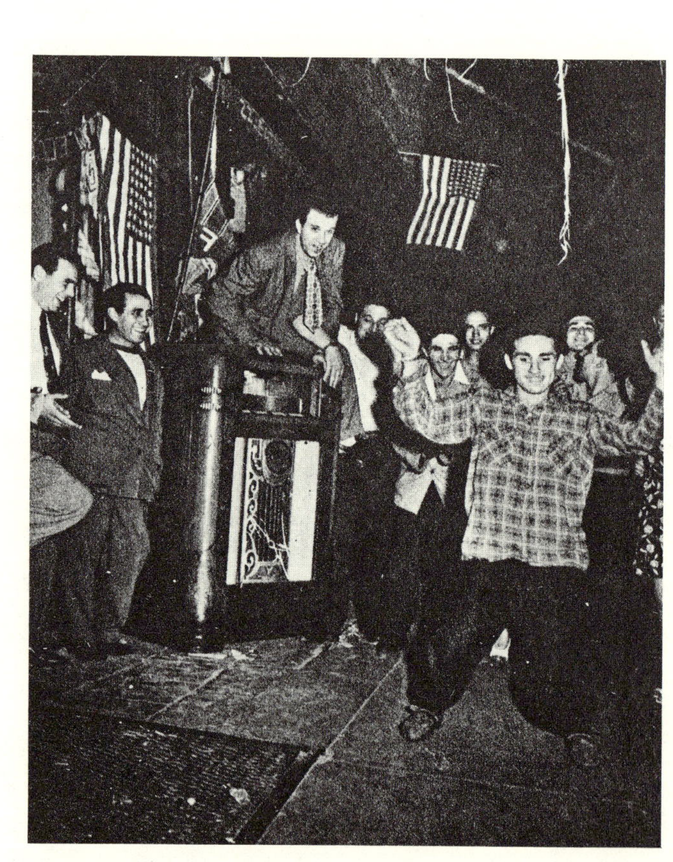

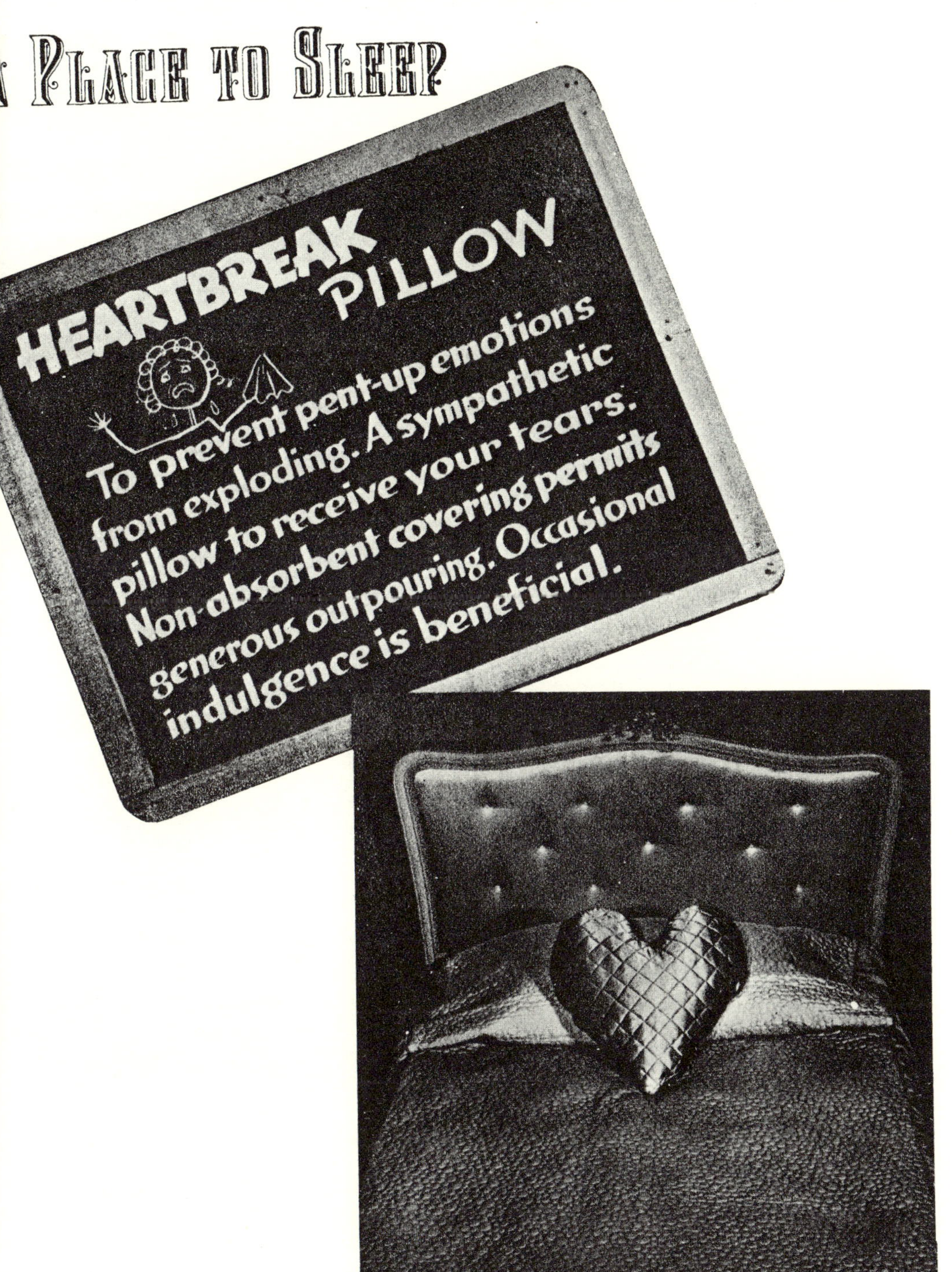

To solve your sleeping problems, go to Lewis and Conger's Sleep Shop at Forty-fifth Street and the Avenue of the Americas. . . . I tried to buy one of these pillows as I, too, am a frustrated soul, but they were all out of stock.

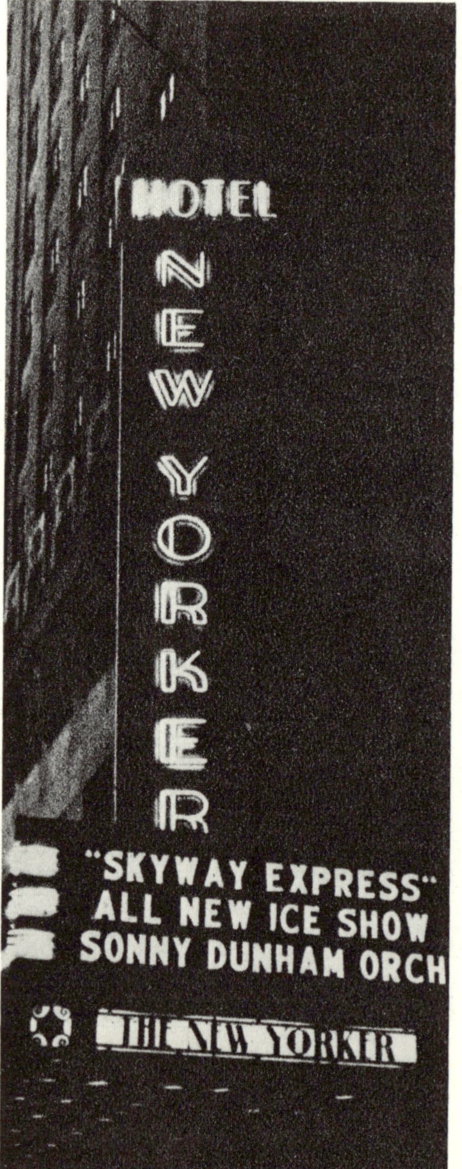

HOTEL
NEW YORKER
"SKYWAY EXPRESS"
ALL NEW ICE SHOW
SONNY DUNHAM ORCH
THE NEW YORKER

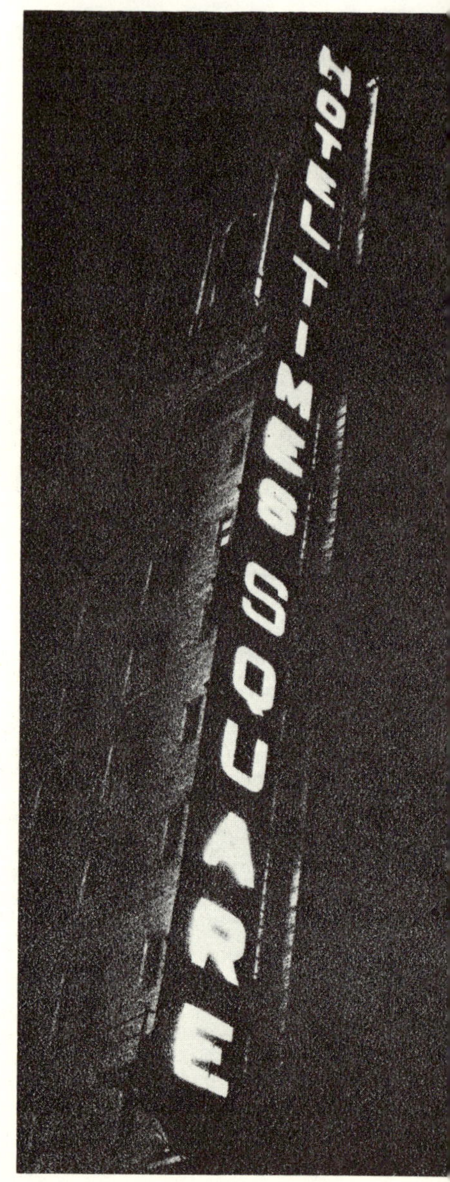

TIMES SQUARE

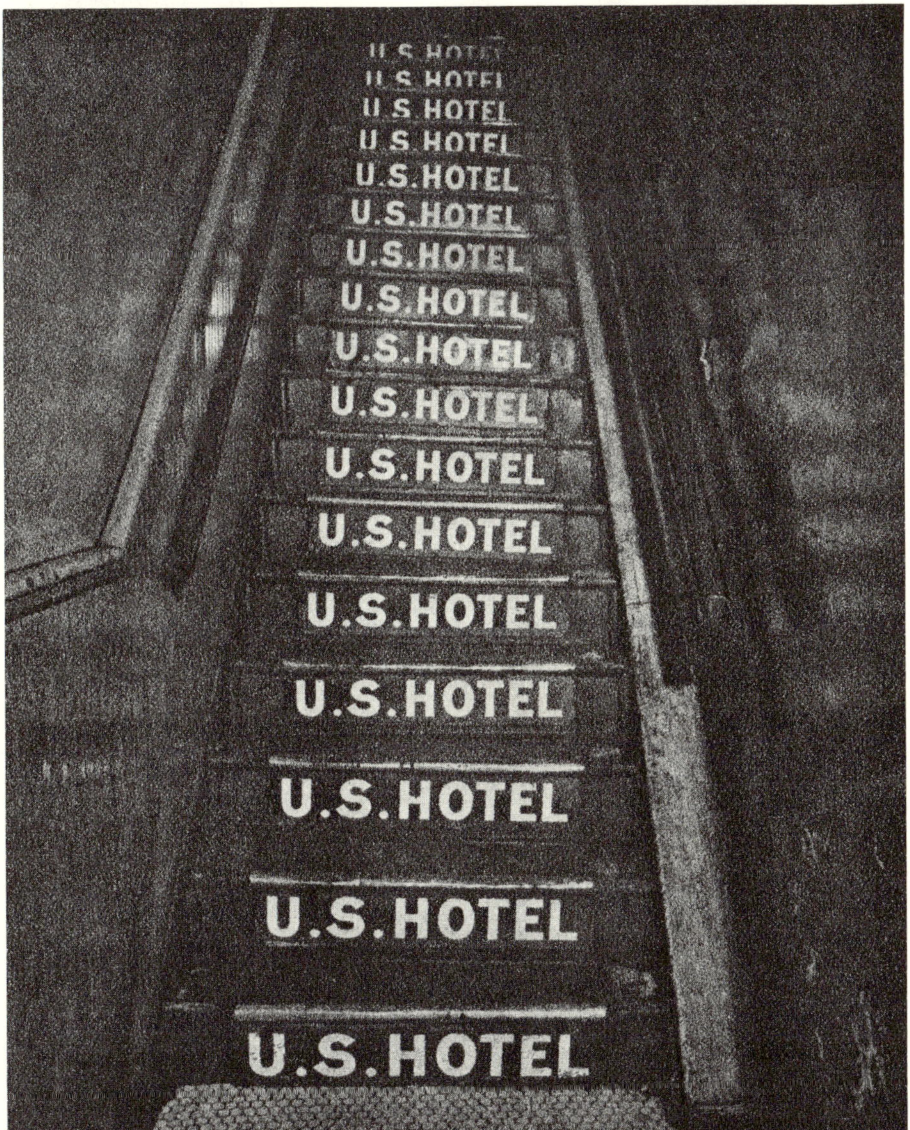

U.S. HOTEL
U.S. HOTEL
U.S. HOTEL
U.S. HOTEL
U.S. HOTEL
U.S. HOTEL
U.S. HOTEL
U.S. HOTEL
U.S. HOTEL
U.S. HOTEL
U.S. HOTEL
U.S. HOTEL
U.S. HOTEL
U.S. HOTEL
U.S. HOTEL
U.S. HOTEL
U.S. HOTEL

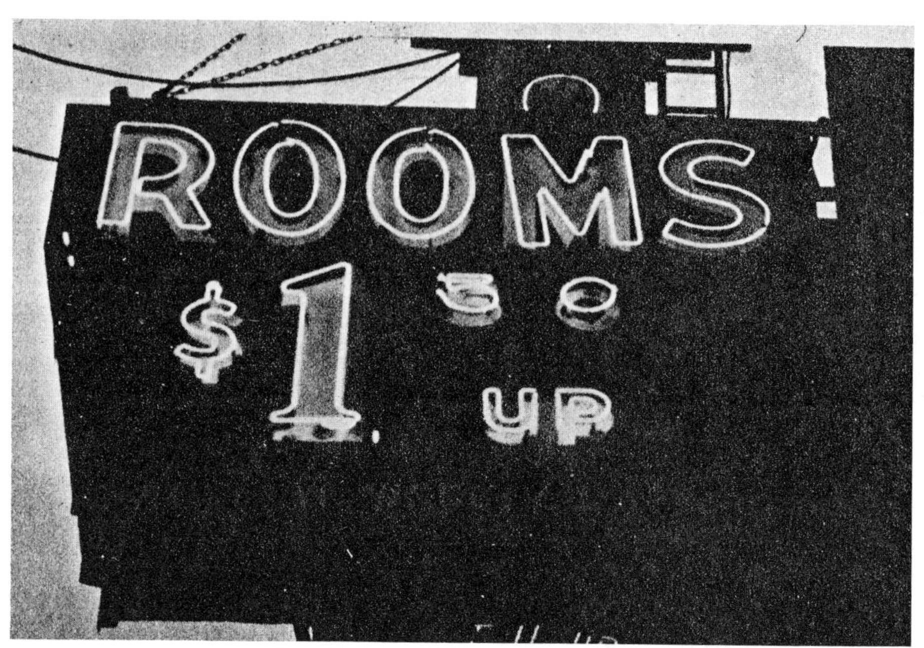

ROOMS!
$1.50
UP

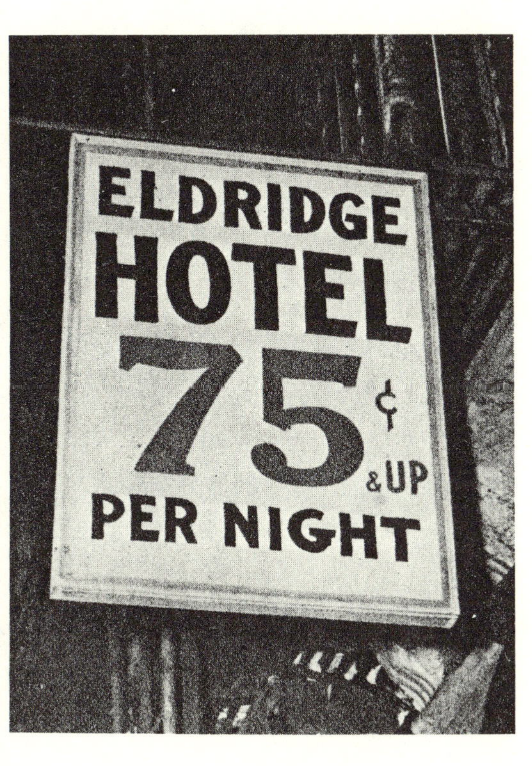
ELDRIDGE
HOTEL
75¢
& UP
PER NIGHT

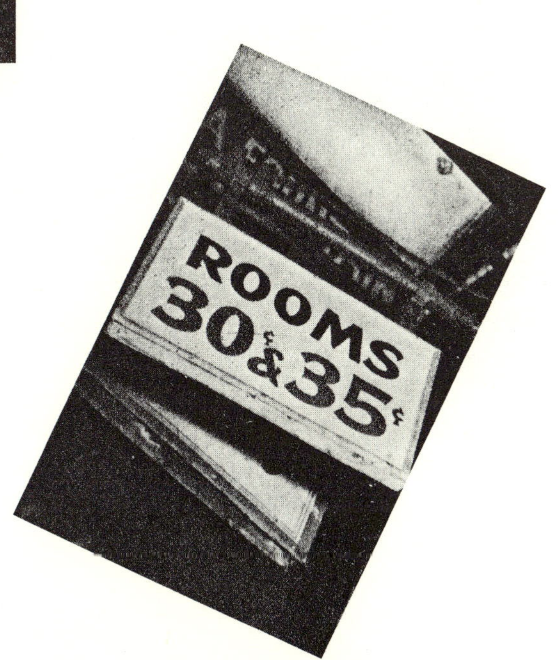
ROOMS
30 & 35¢

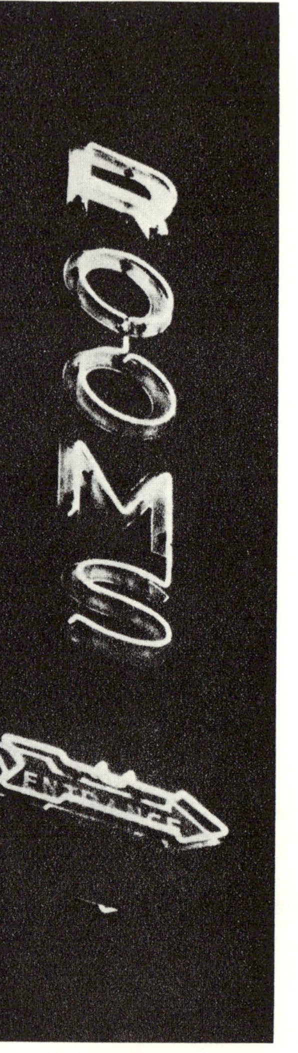

WOODS
ENTRANCE

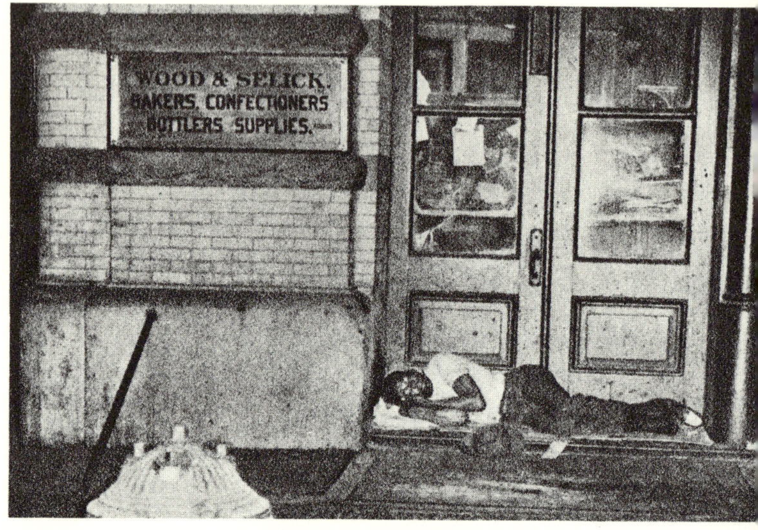

WOOD & SELICK,
BAKERS, CONFECTIONERS
BOTTLERS SUPPLIES.

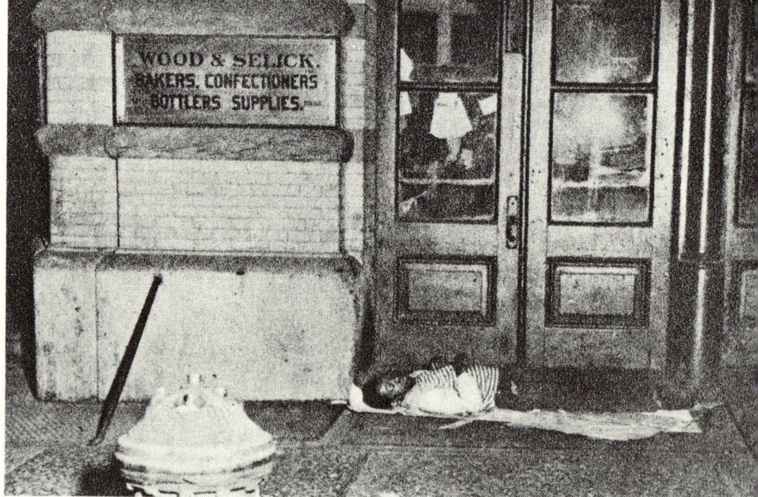

WOOD & SELICK,
BAKERS, CONFECTIONERS
BOTTLERS SUPPLIES.

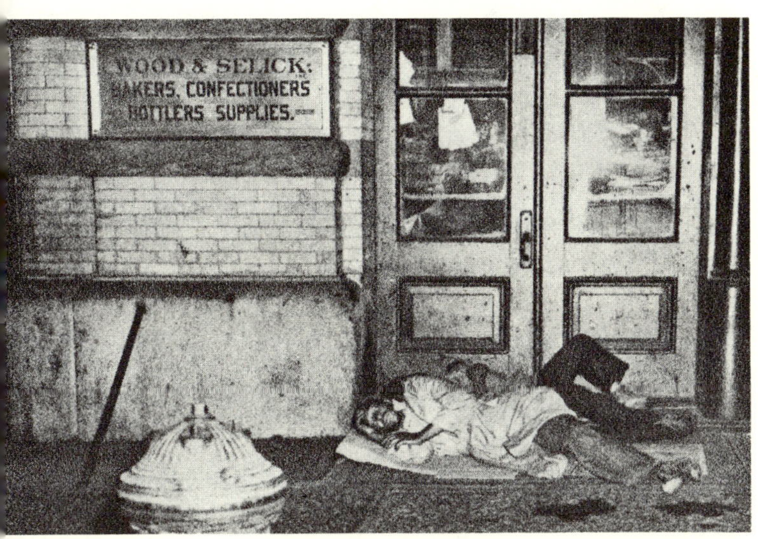

WOOD & SELICK:
BAKERS, CONFECTIONERS
BOTTLERS SUPPLIES.

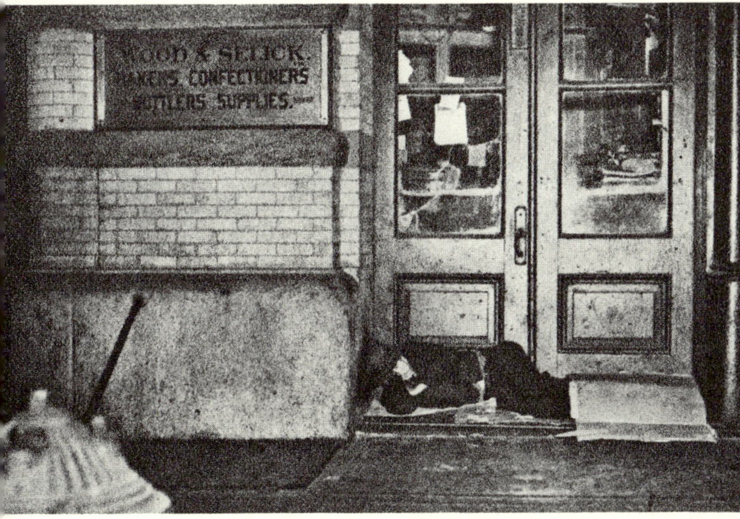

WOOD & SELICK,
BAKERS, CONFECTIONERS
BOTTLERS SUPPLIES.

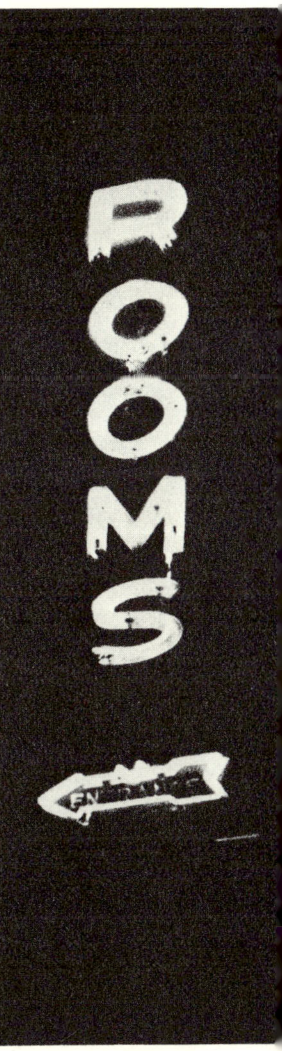

ROOMS
ENTRANCE

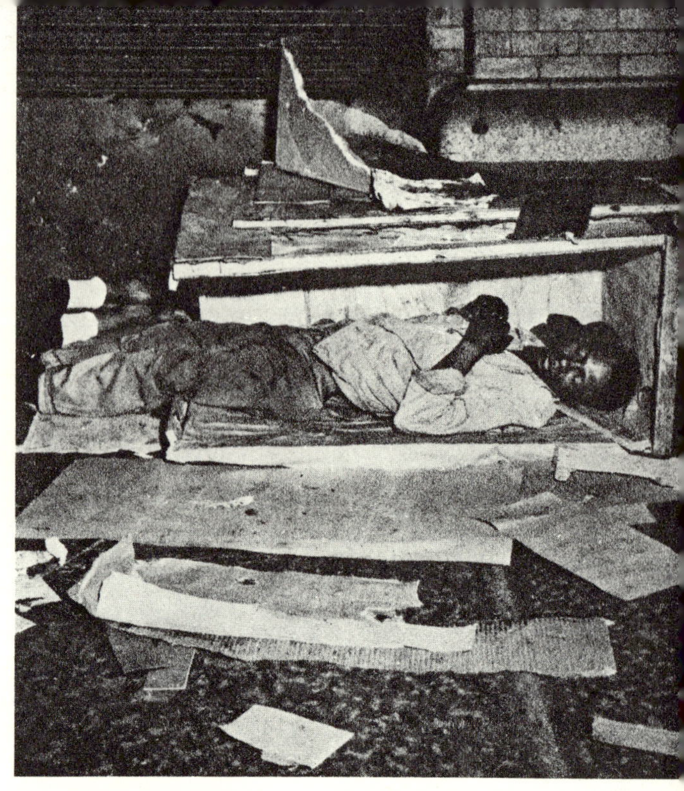

NEW YORK IS A
FRIENDLY TOWN

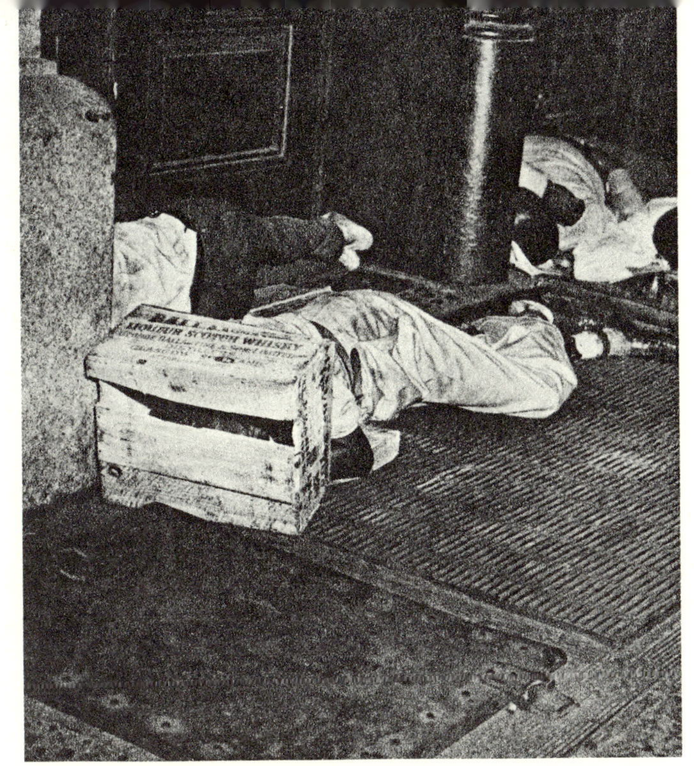

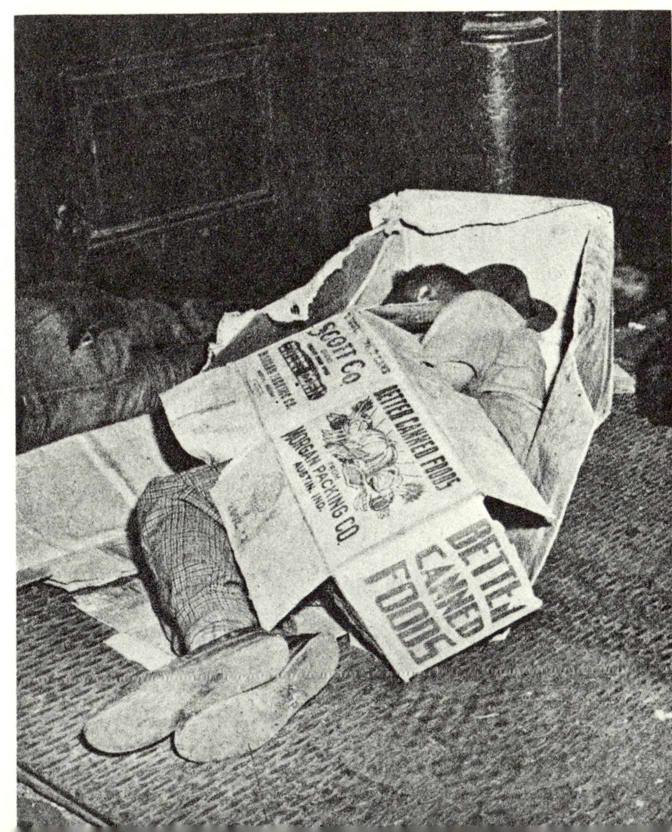

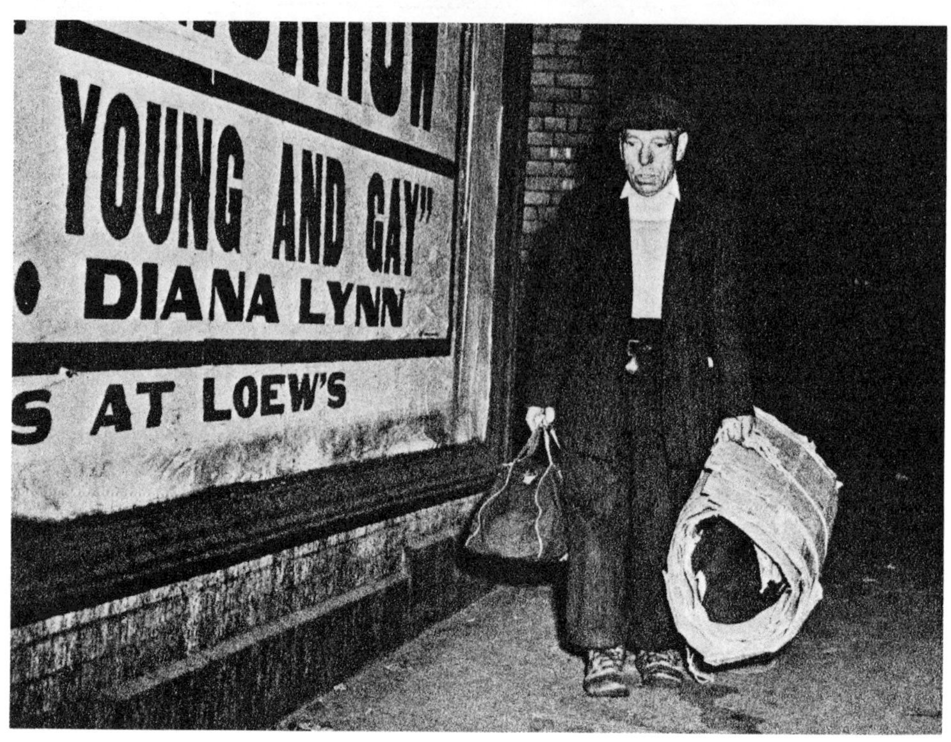

A man walking down Lexington Avenue carries his bed with him. . . . This is a good neighborhood, full of hotels — Commodore, Belmont Plaza, Shelton, Lexington, and Waldorf Astoria. . . . but he doesn't stop at any of them. . . .

Wearily he climbs up the fire escape at Loew's Lexington and goes to sleep. . . . He has been doing this for the past thirteen years, summer and winter, rain or shine. . . . His sleeping problem seems to be solved. . . .

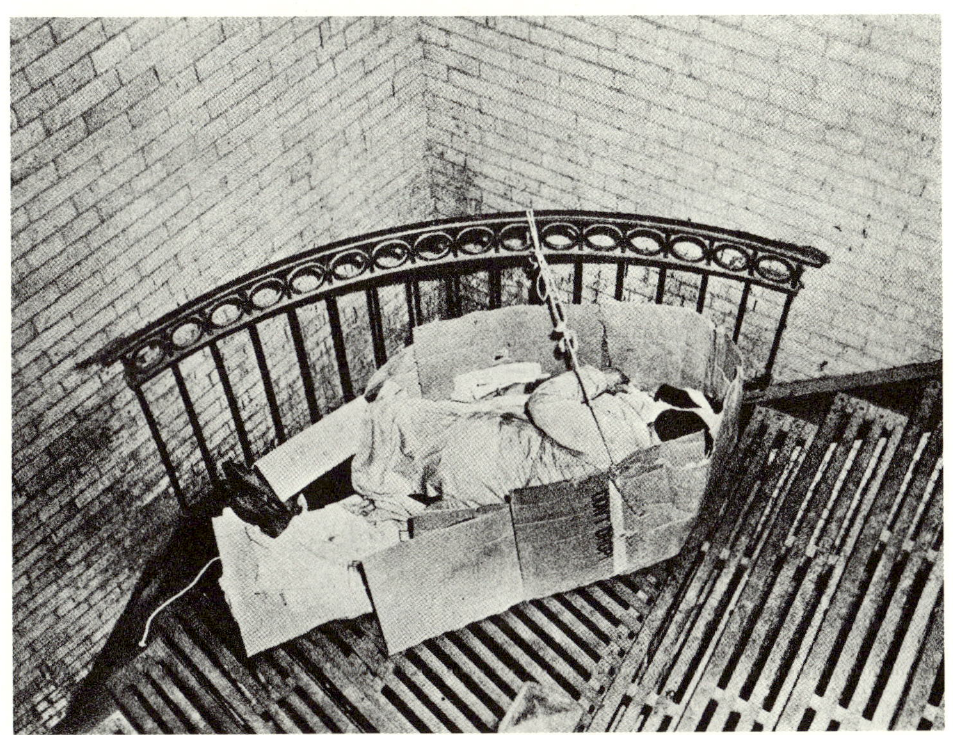

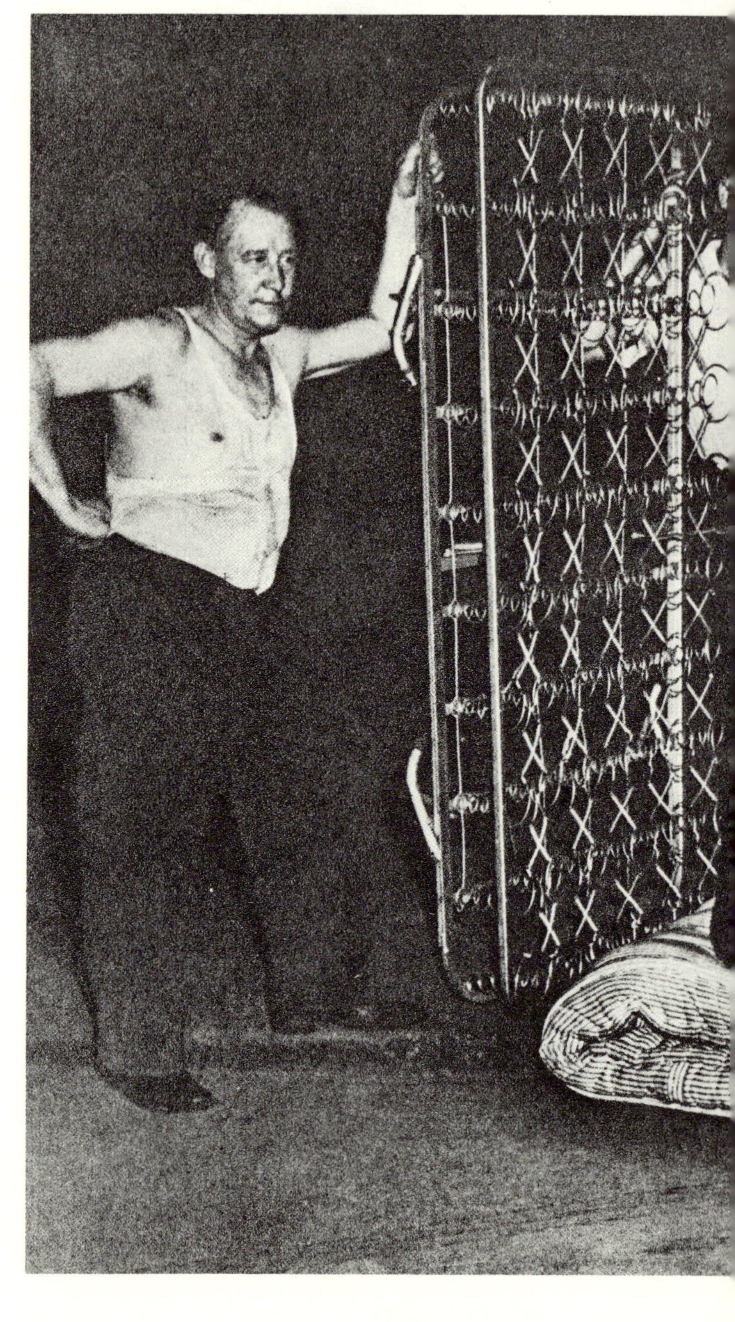

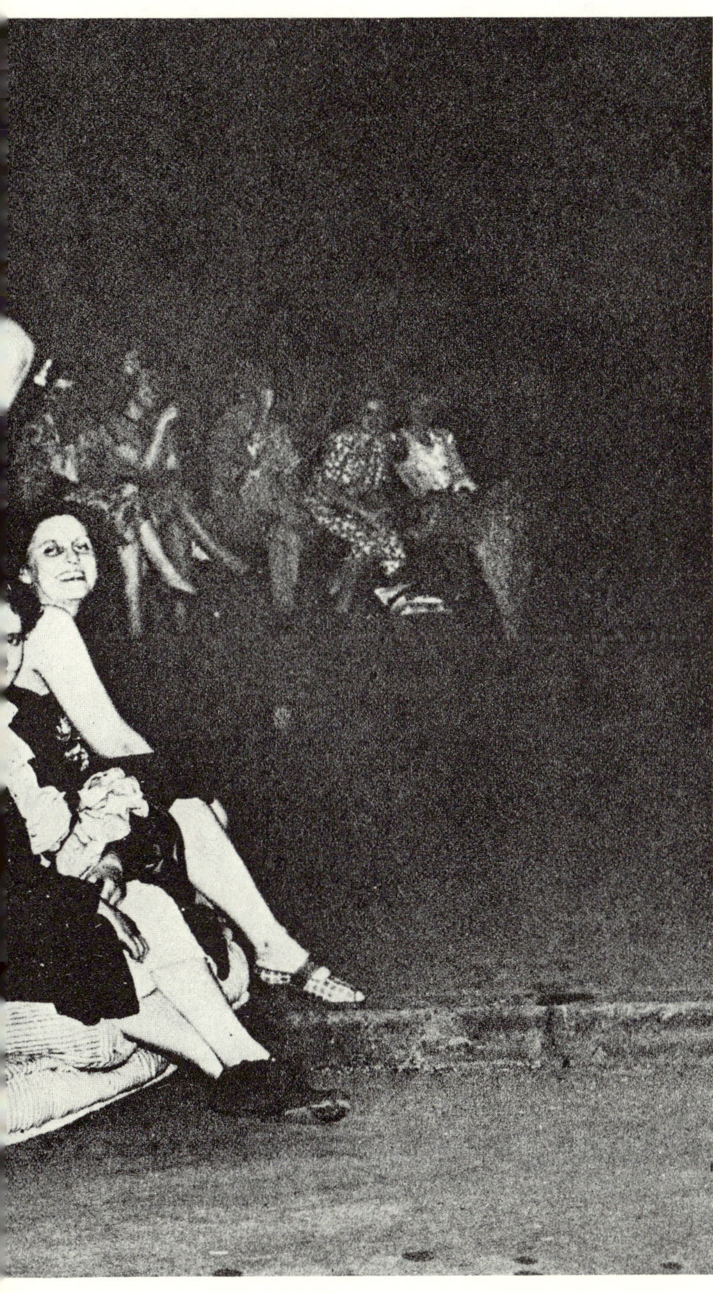

these people still have a problem. . . . I met this quartet, not the least disheartened, one ..rday after midnight in Washington Square Park . . . taking a rest. . . . They told me they .e looking for an apartment. . . . I asked them who wasn't as I wished them good luck.

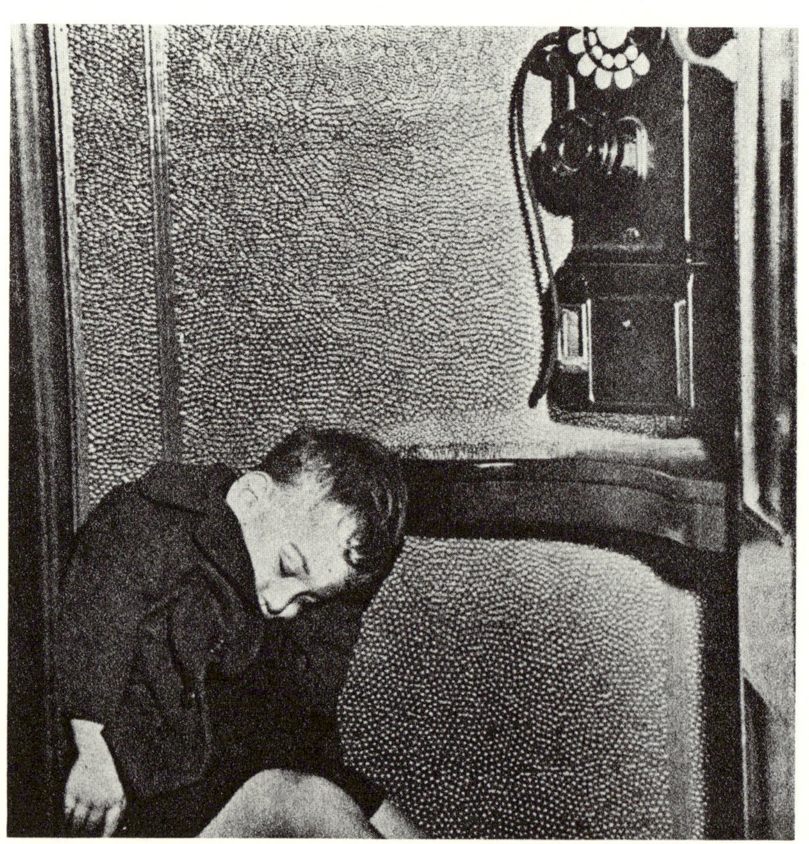

The Children's Hour

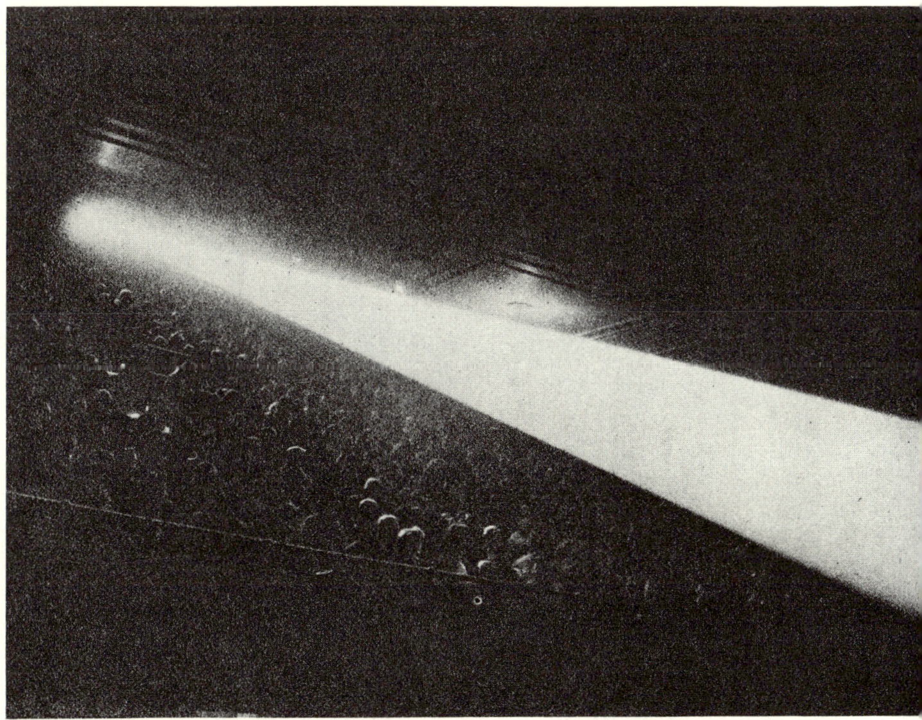

Saturday afternoon show for the youngsters at Loew's
Commodore Theater on Second Avenue. . . . Some of the
kids brought their lunch . . . lolly pops . . . and one fellow
even brought a toy pistol. . . . I took the pictures in the dark
with infra-red rays so that I wouldn't disturb anyone. . . .

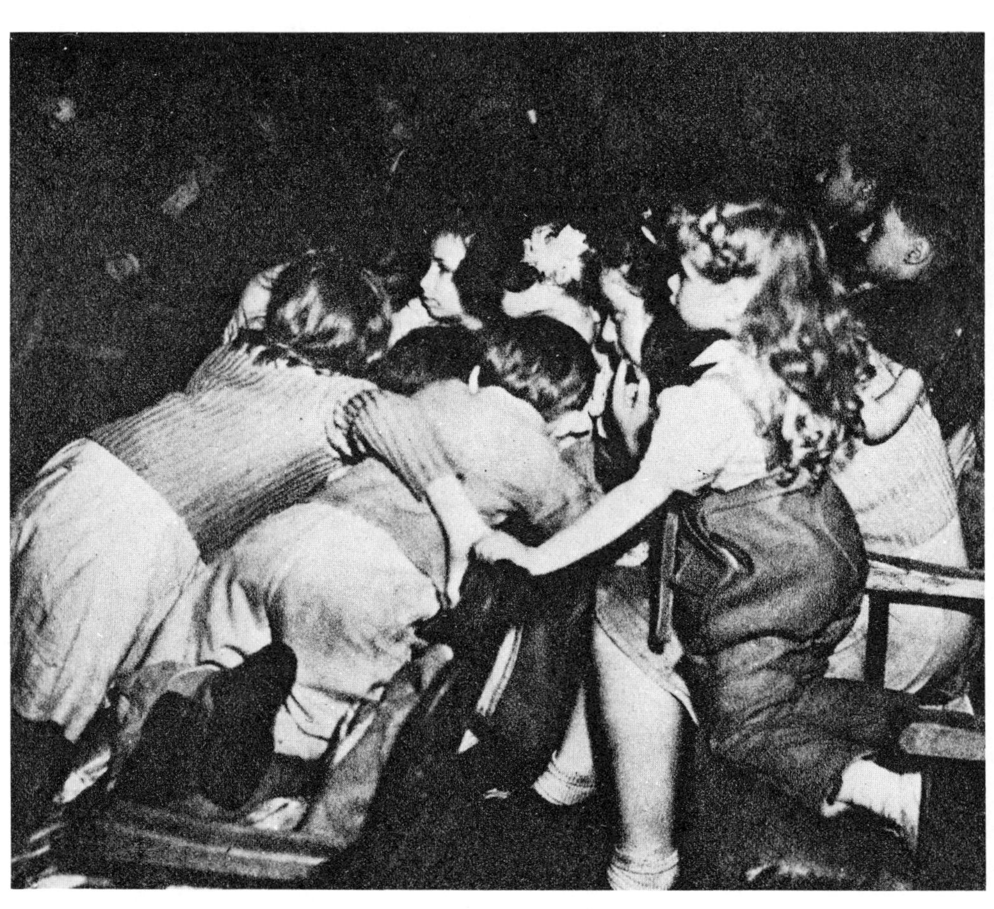

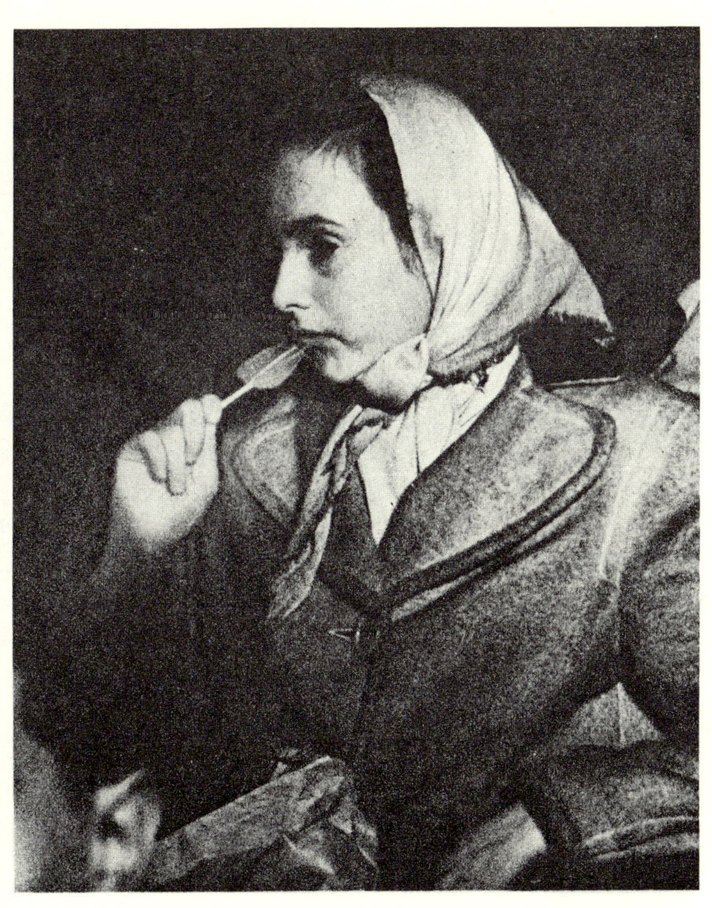

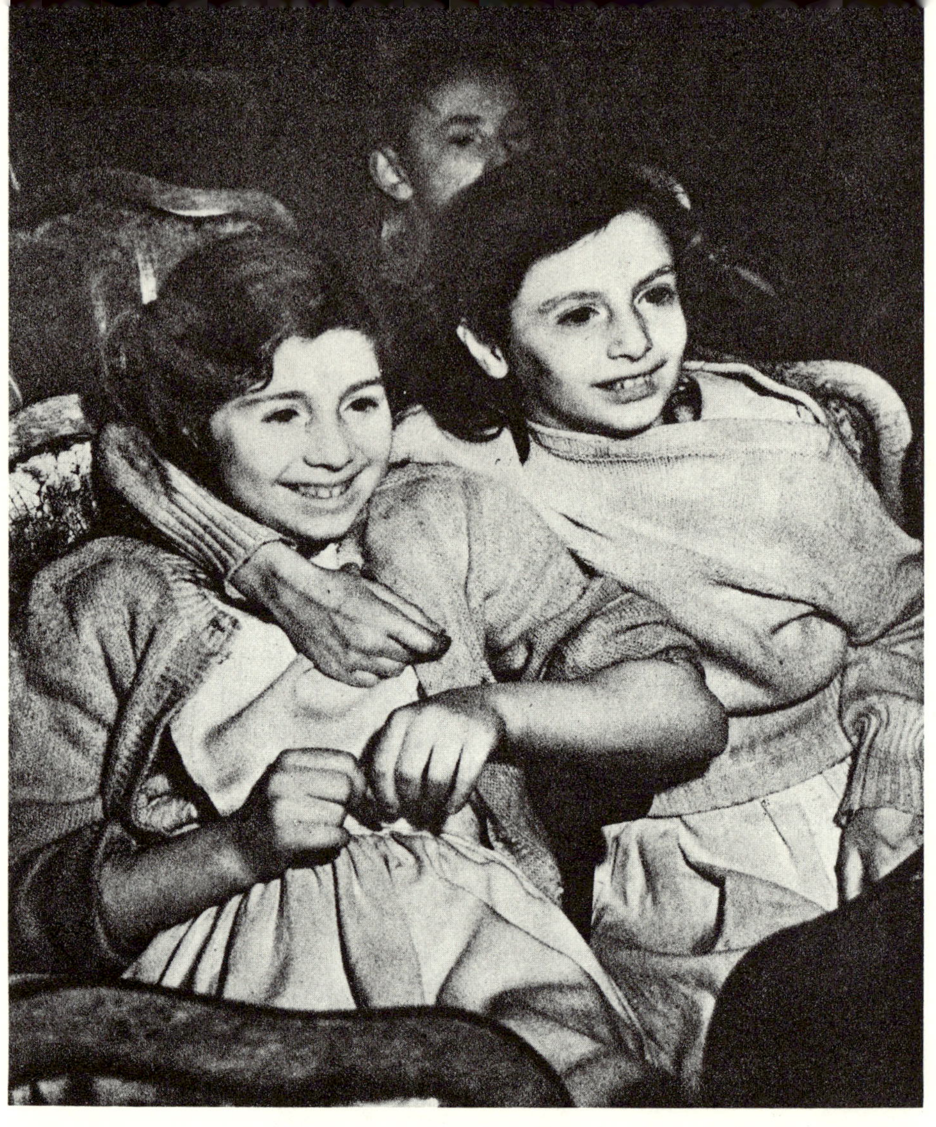

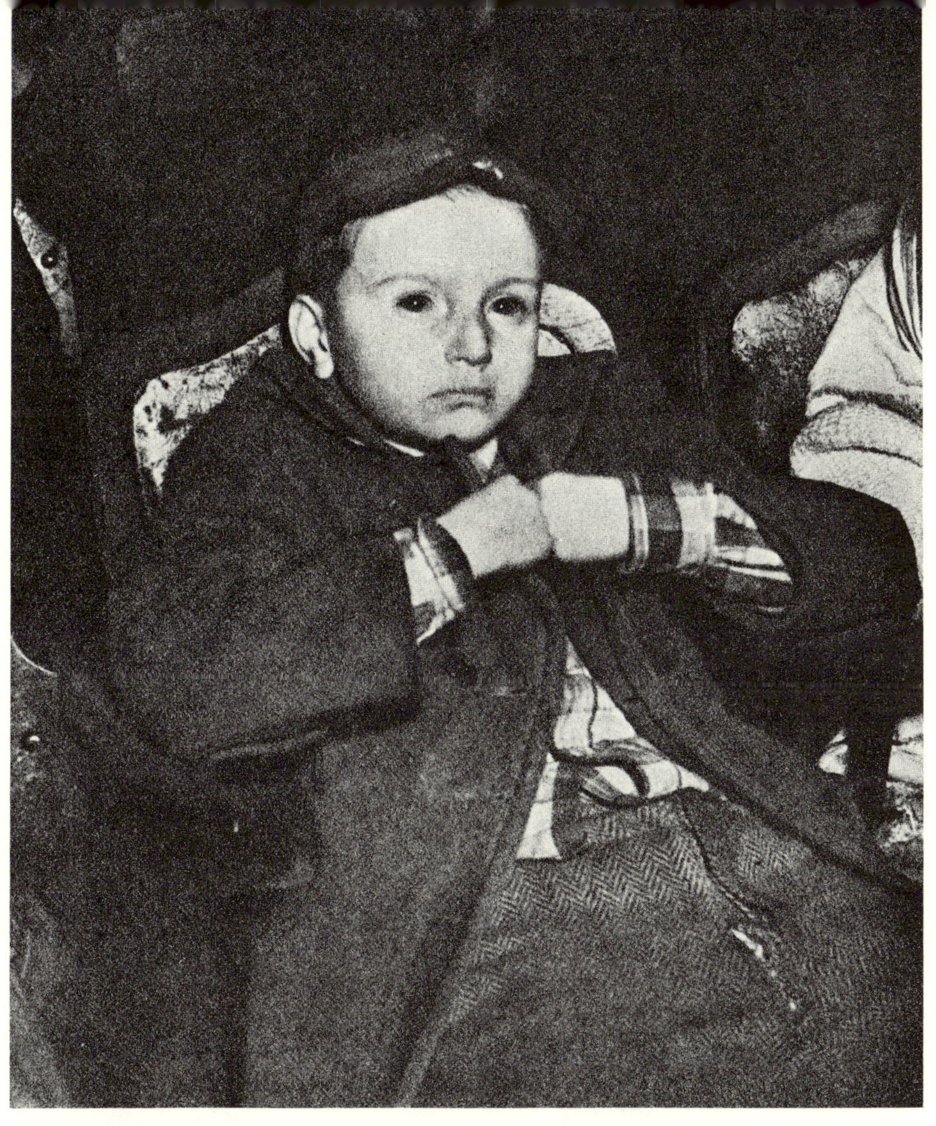

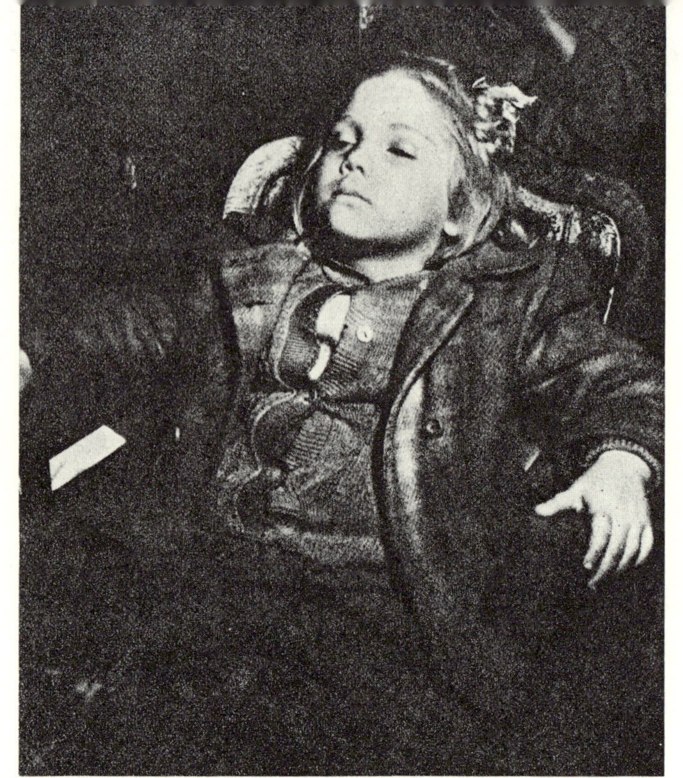

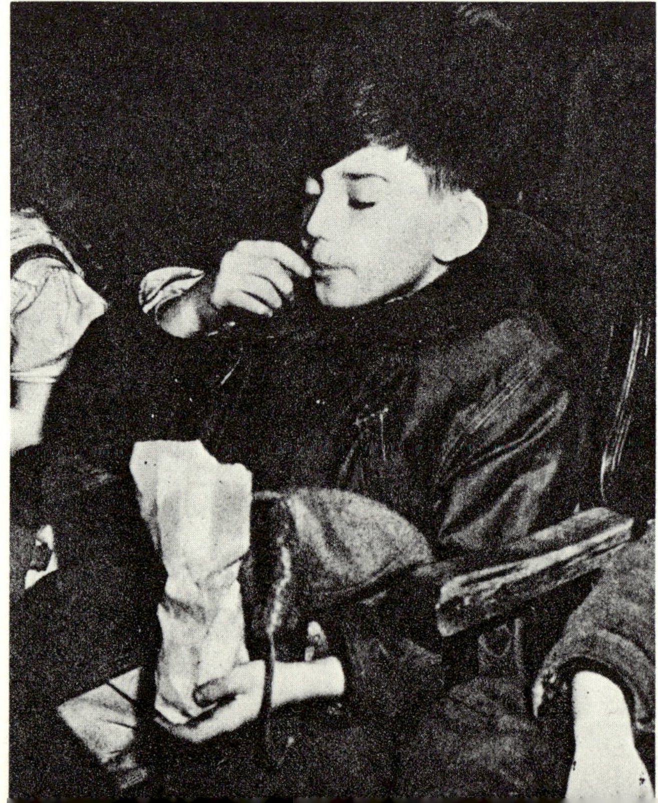

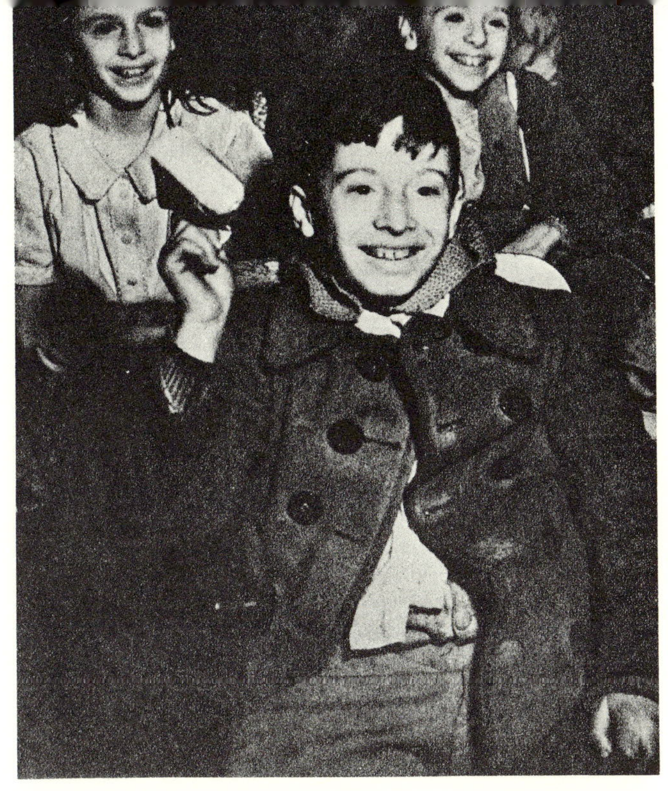

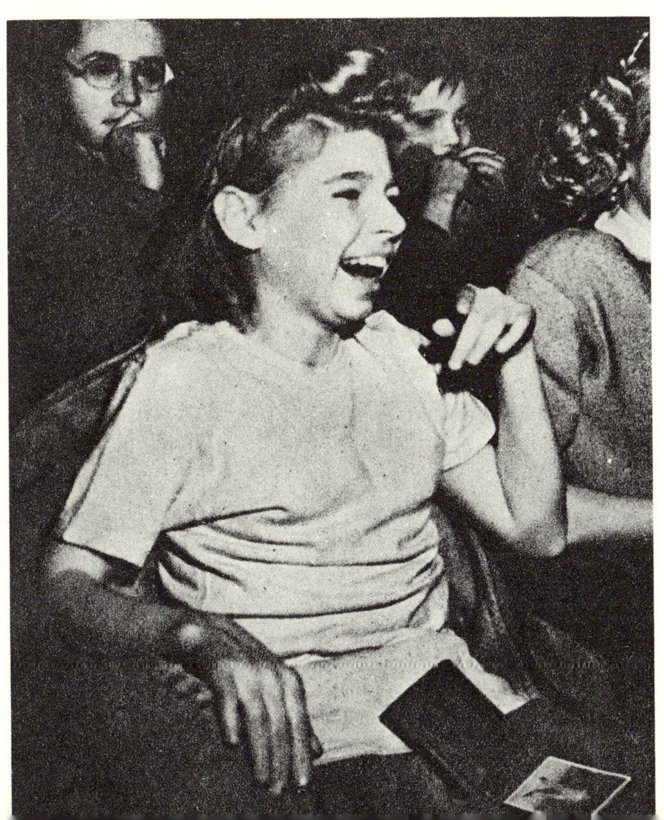

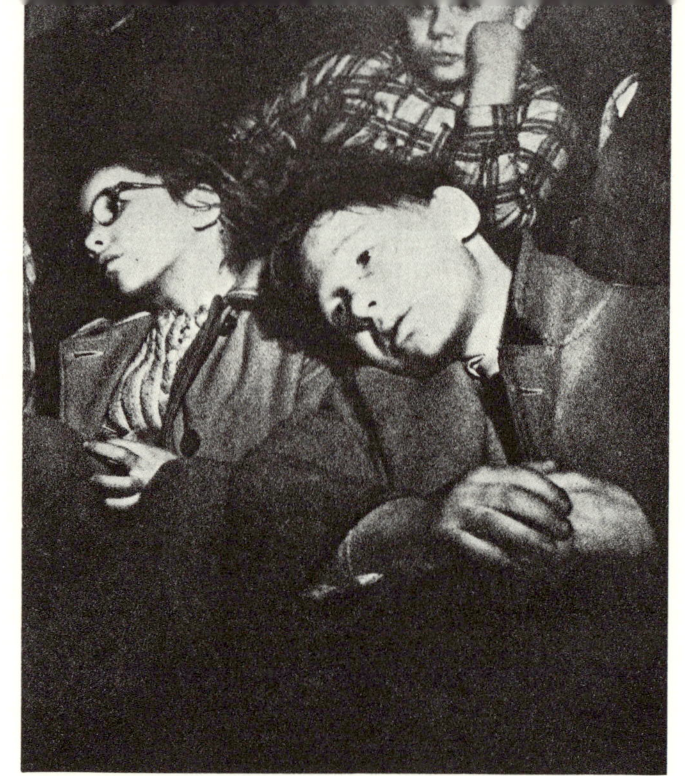

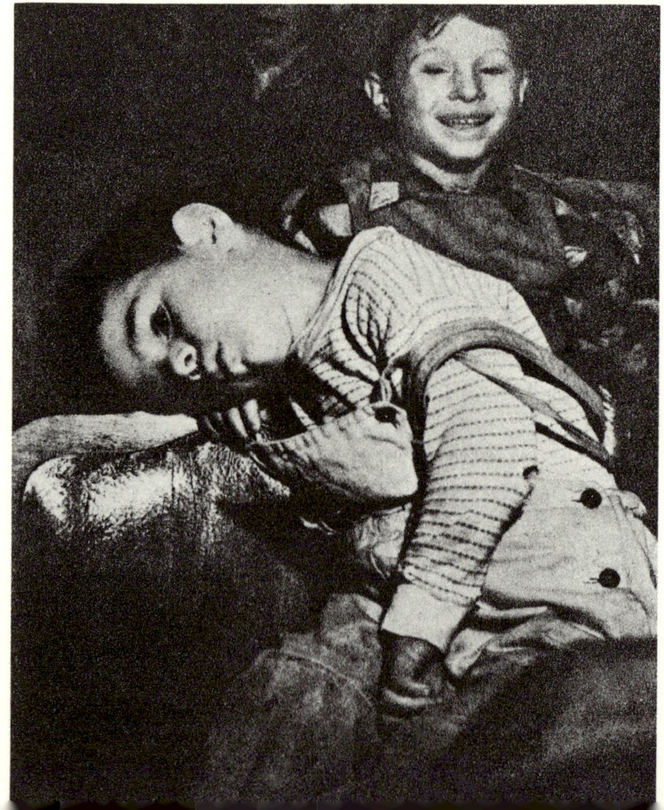

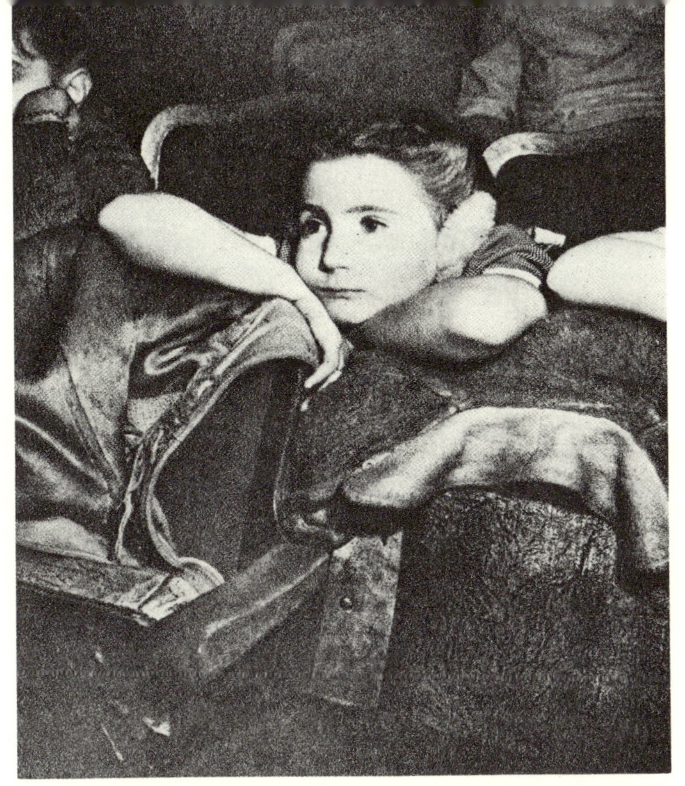

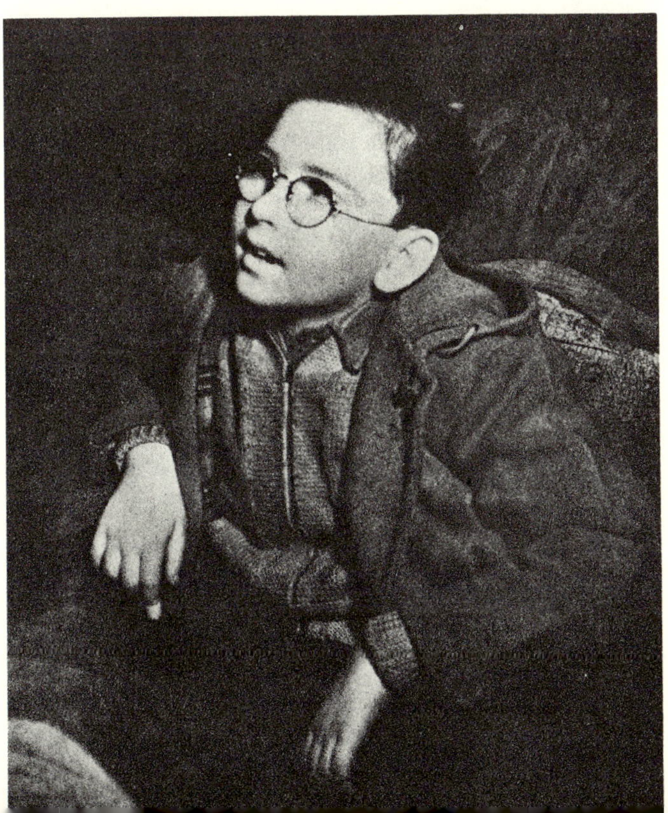

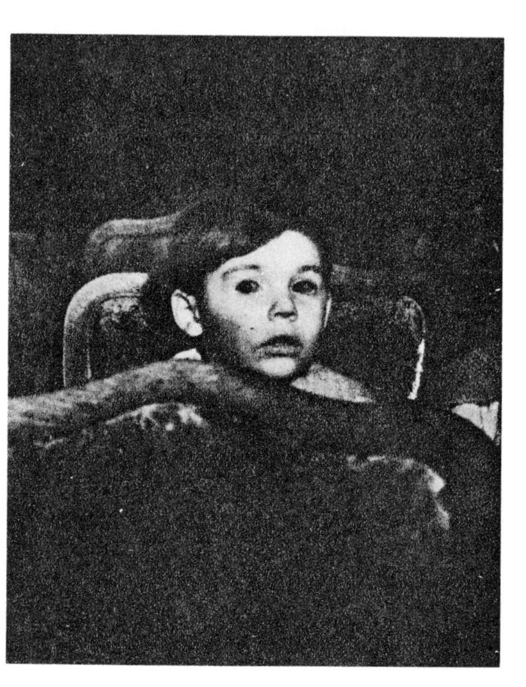

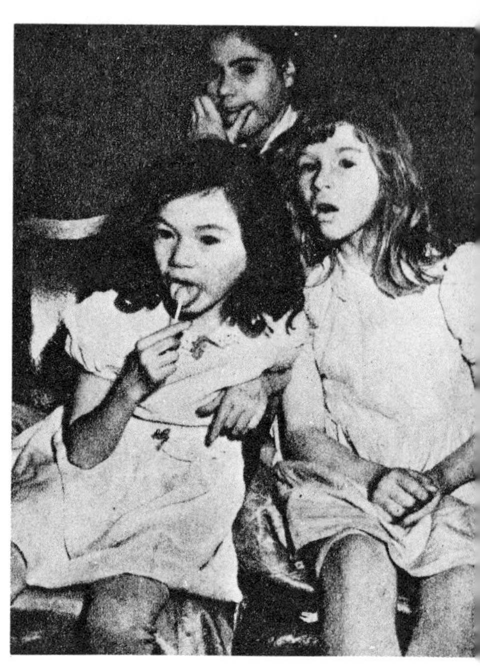

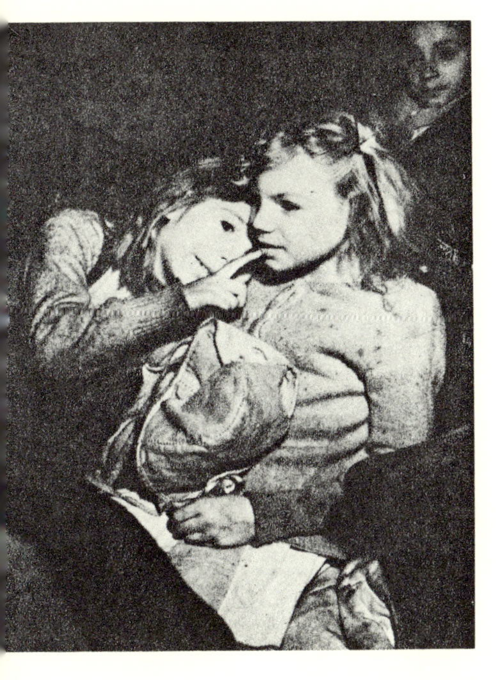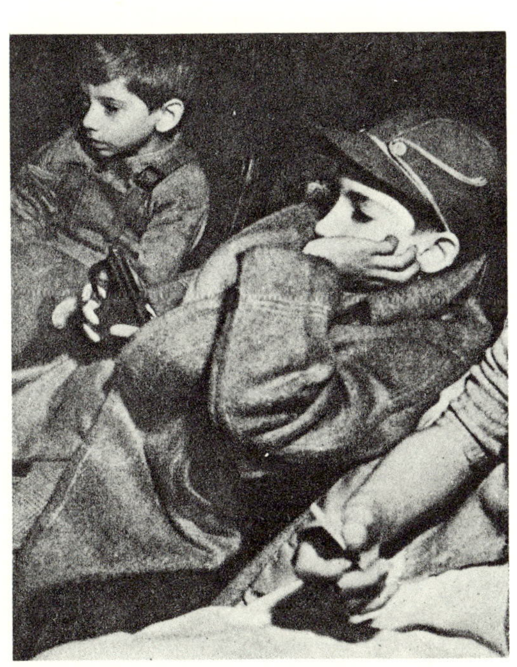

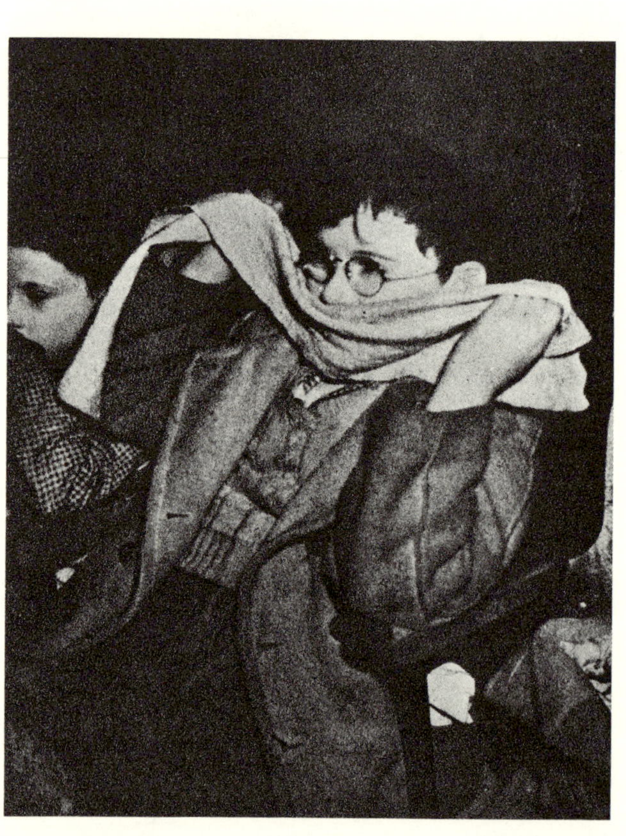

A group of night club musicians, finished with their night's work spread the word that a friendly superintendent would let them hold a "jam" session in the sub-basement of his building. . . . There wasn't a "square in the stach," meaning no outsiders allowed . . . only "kicks," close friends, who brought along a case of beer for the concert. . . . The girl friends broiled hamburgers in the hot furnace . . . an ideal place. . . . The party broke up in the morning when the tenants arrived for work. . . .

SUB-CELLAR BALL

7

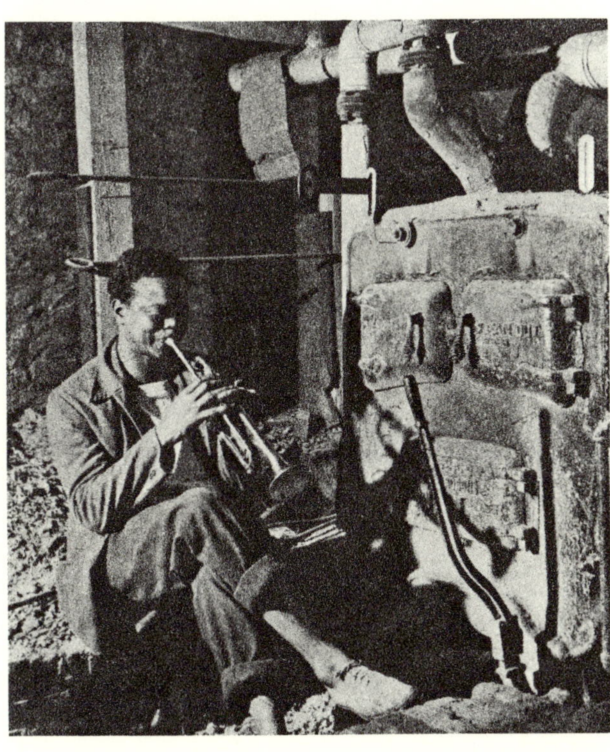

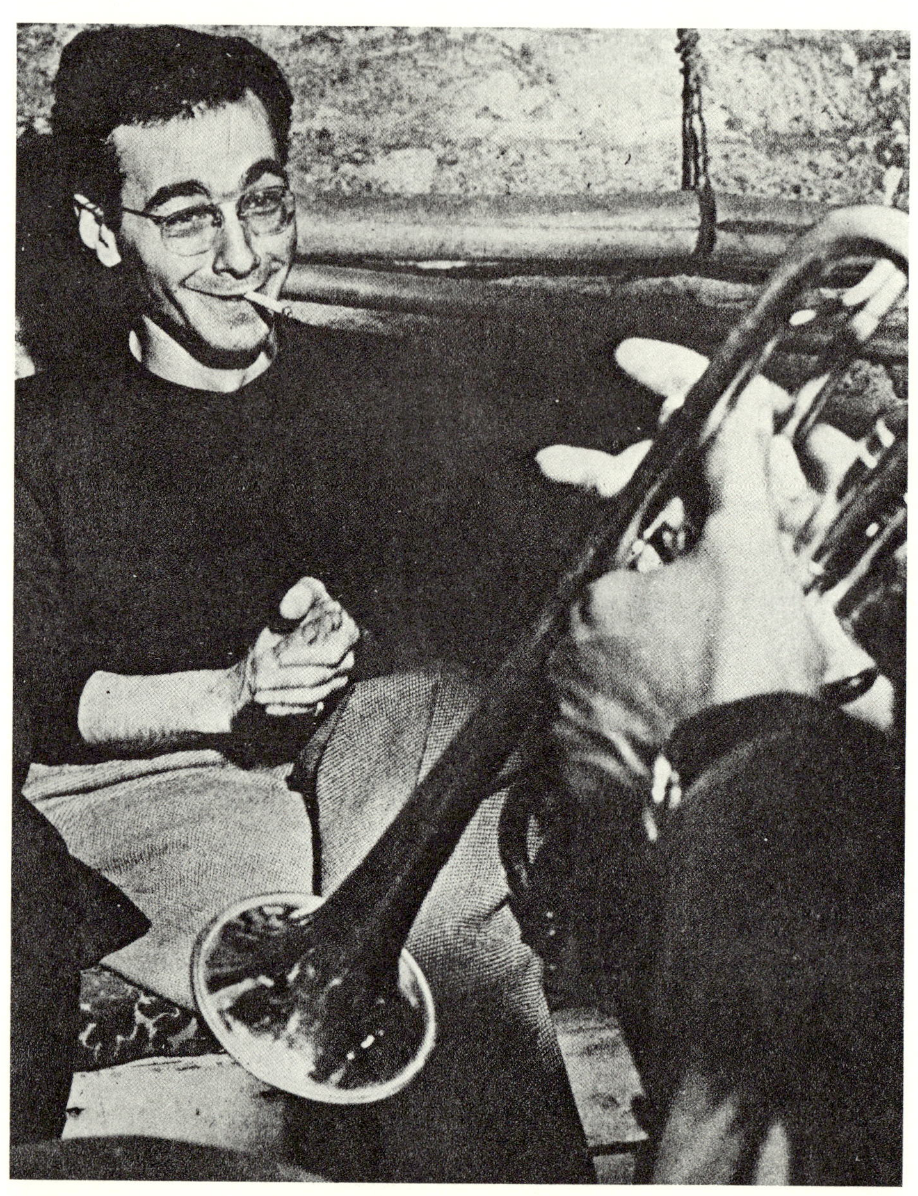

Mad "kick"

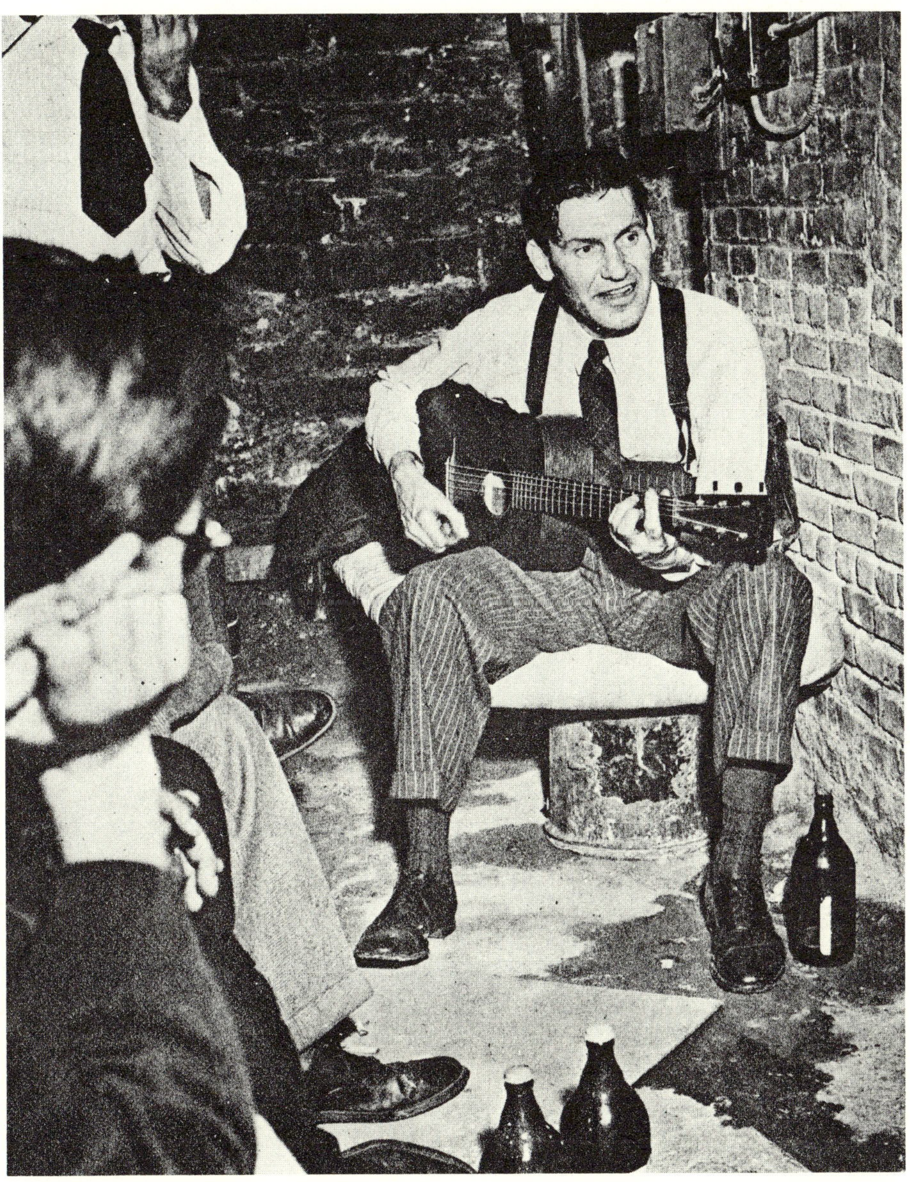

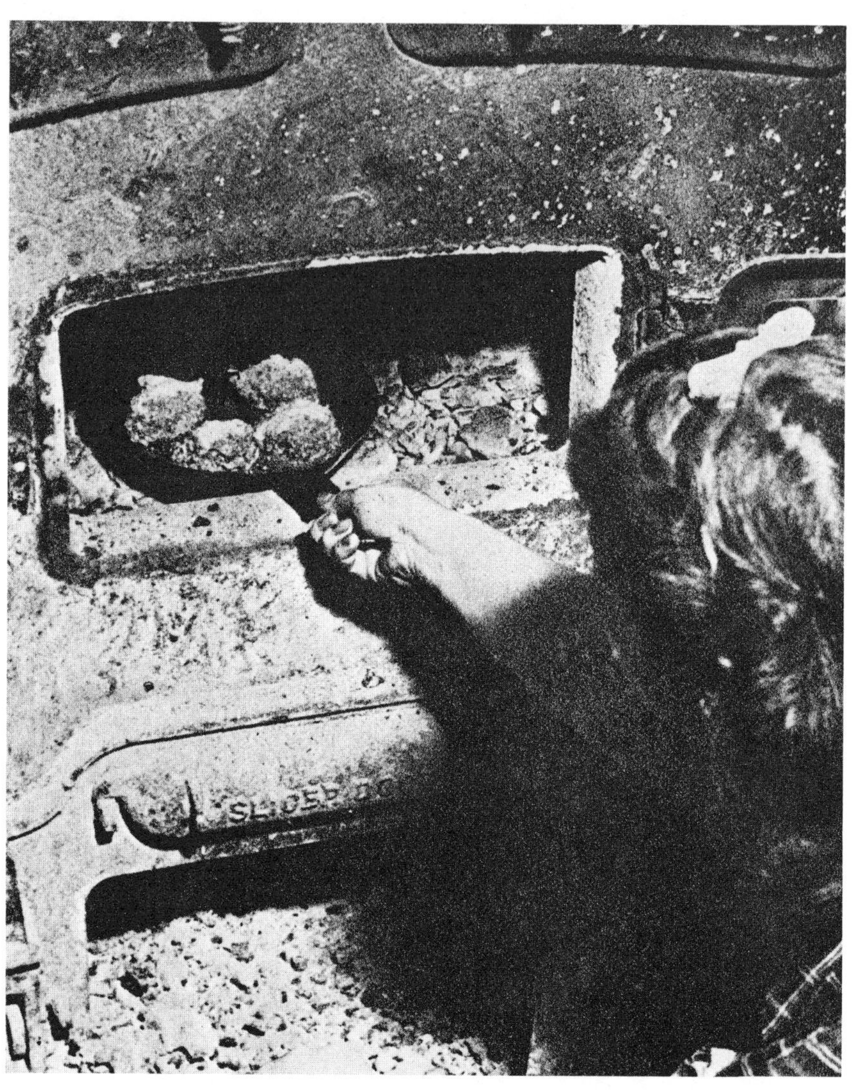

Touching off the groceries

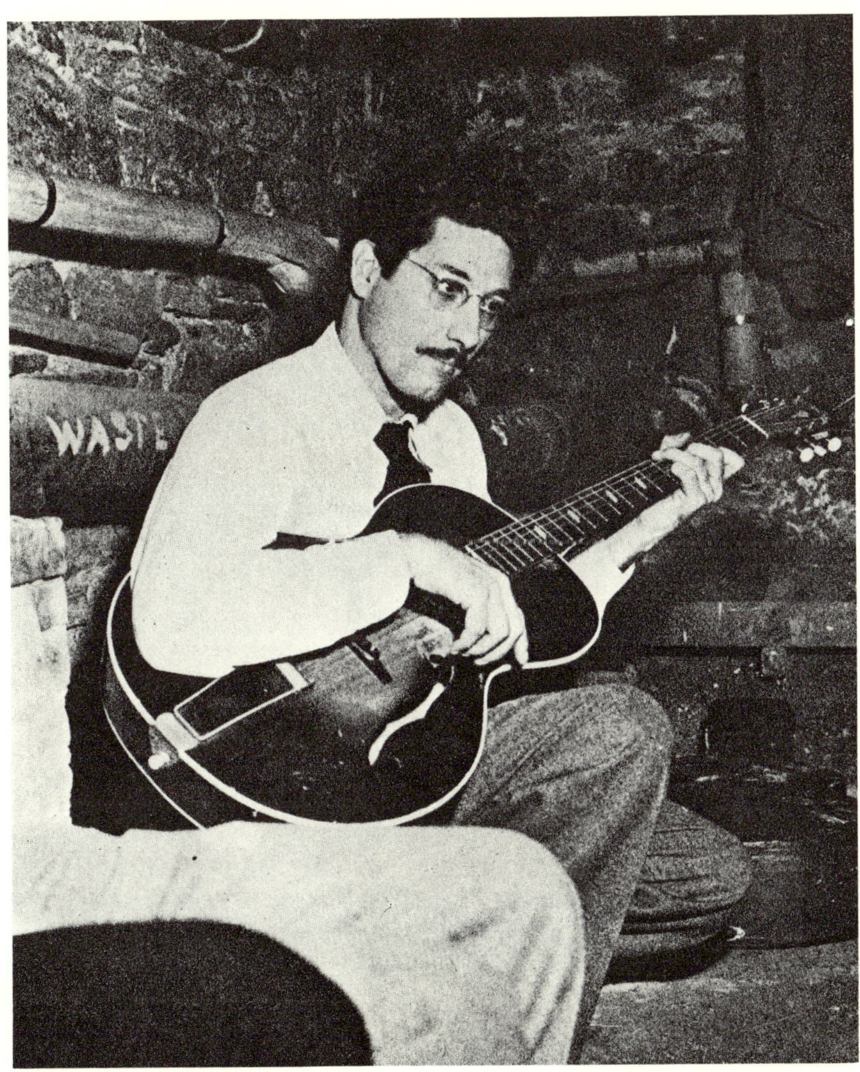

Dreaming up the theme

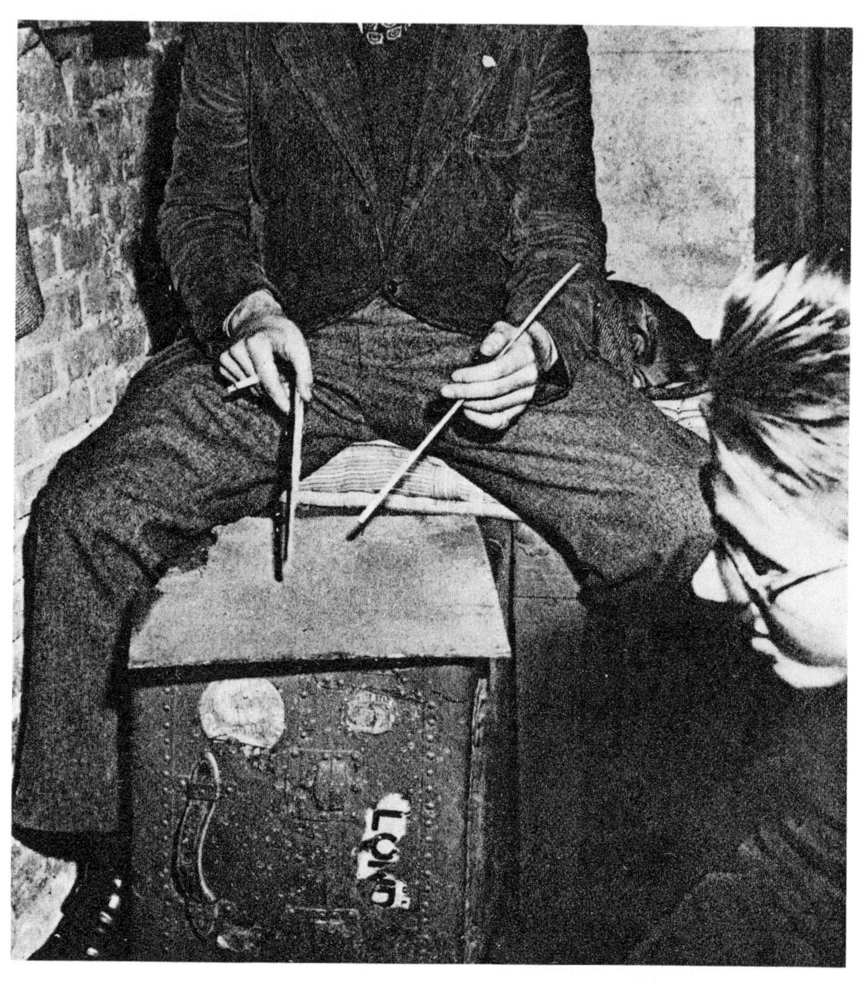

No "skins," so board was used

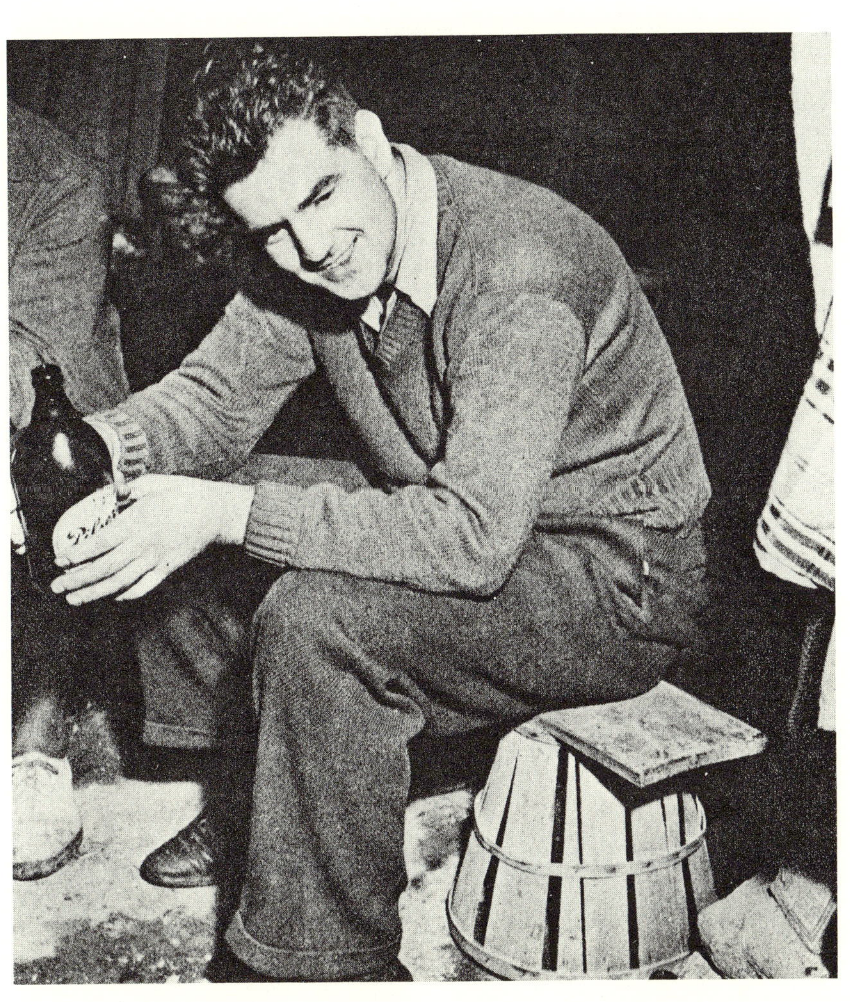

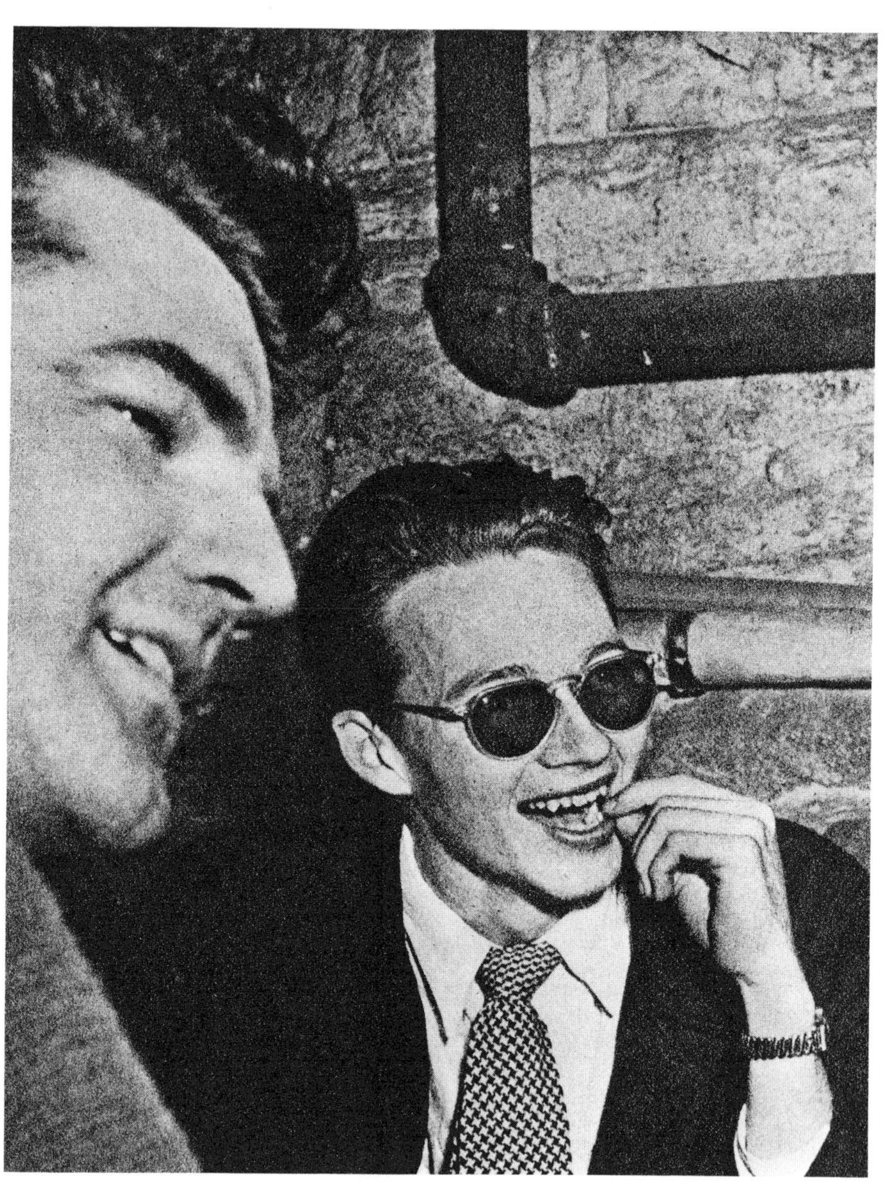

Feeling no pain

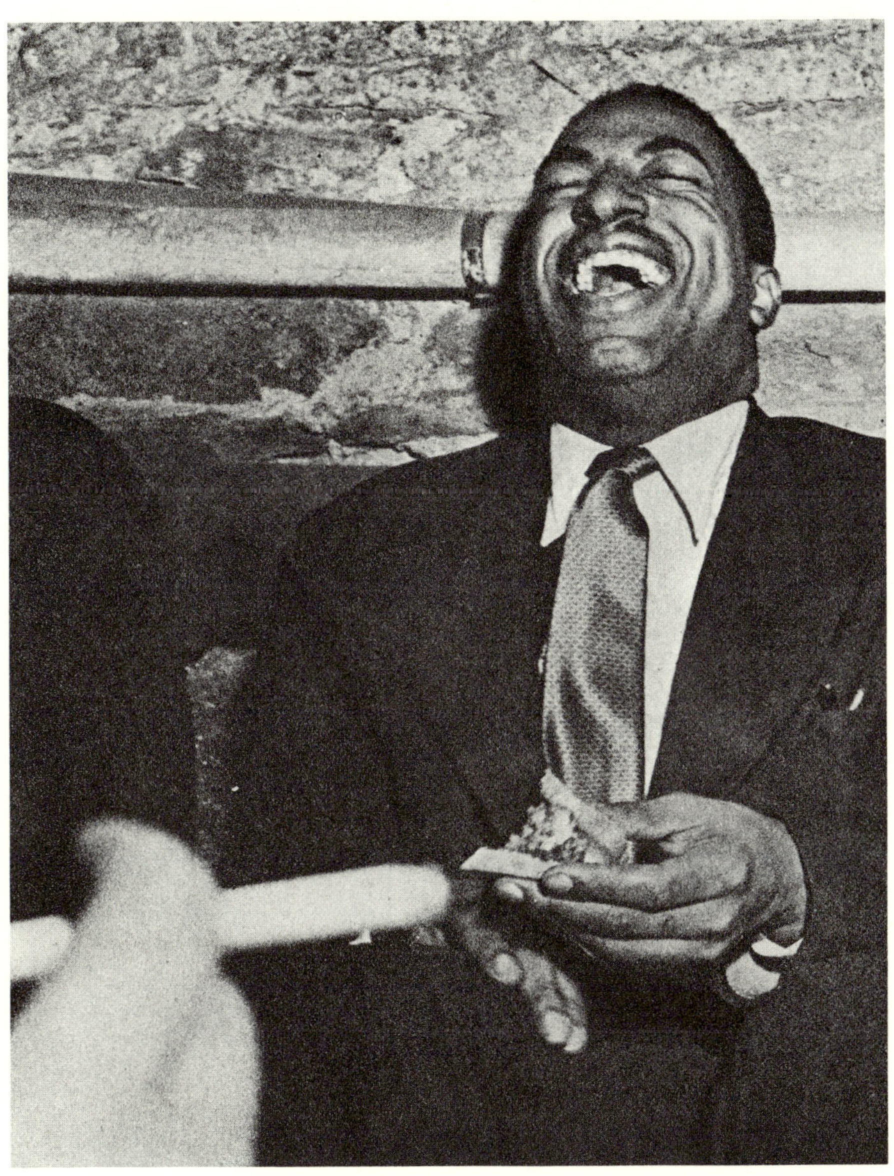

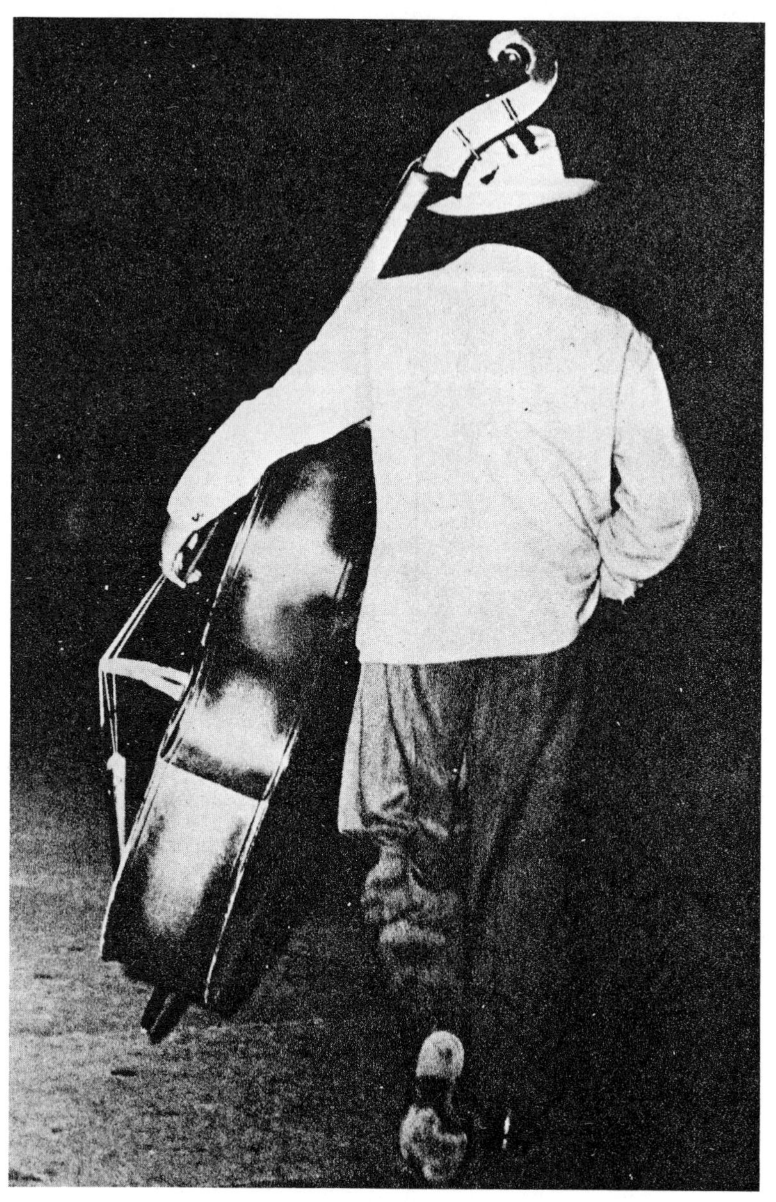

End of concert

BACK STAGE

8

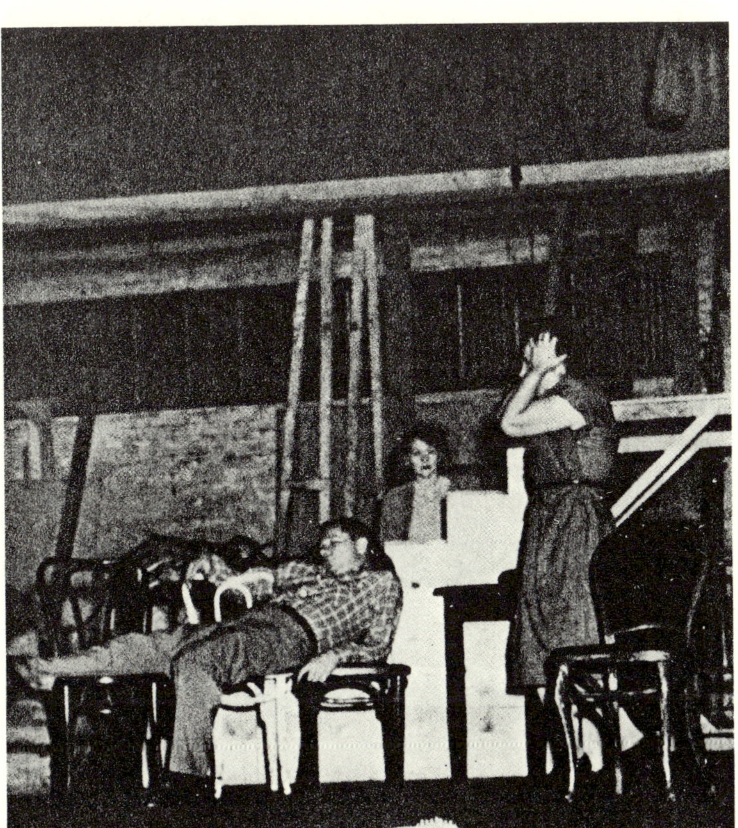

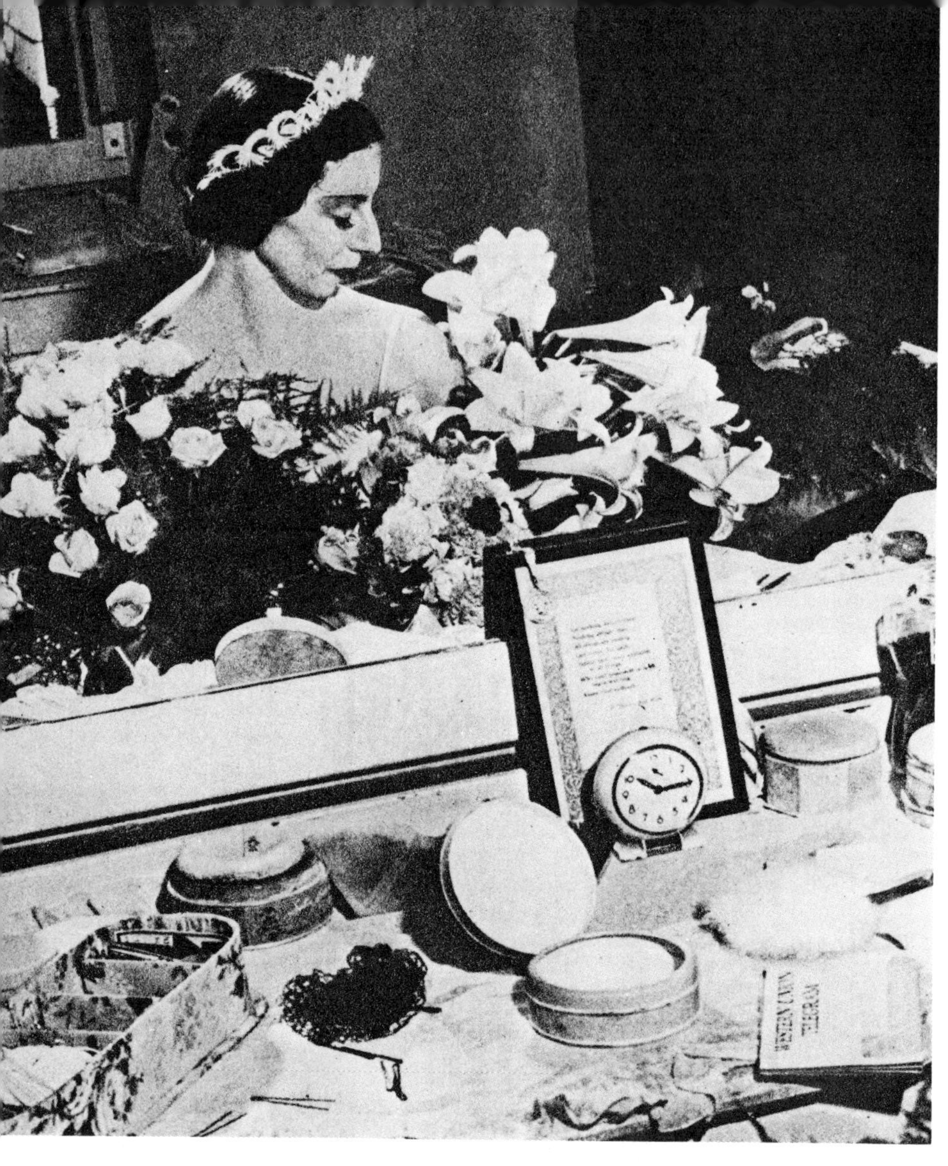

Alicia Markova

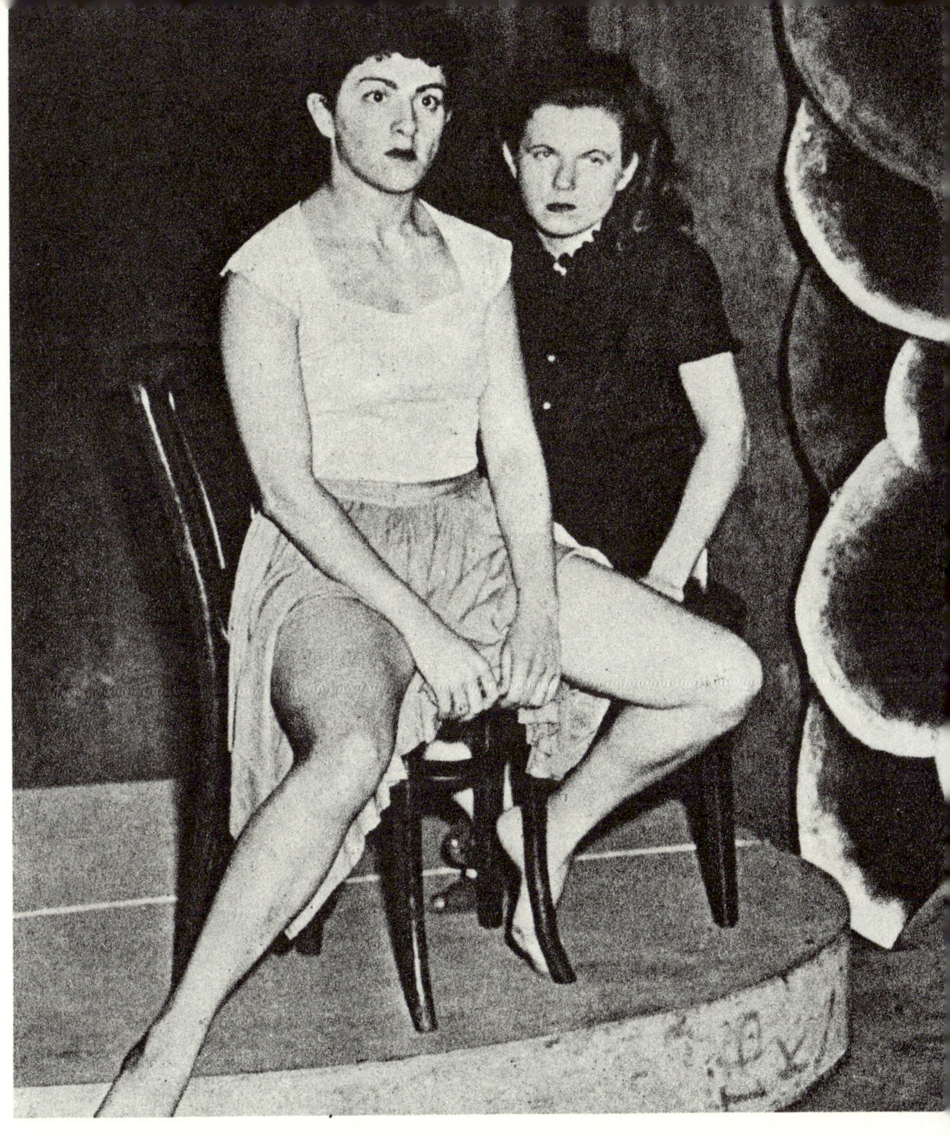

Dreams back stage . . . someday they, too, will be stars . . . have their own dressing room at the Metropolitan Opera House . . . and receive flowers and congratulatory messages on opening night. . . .

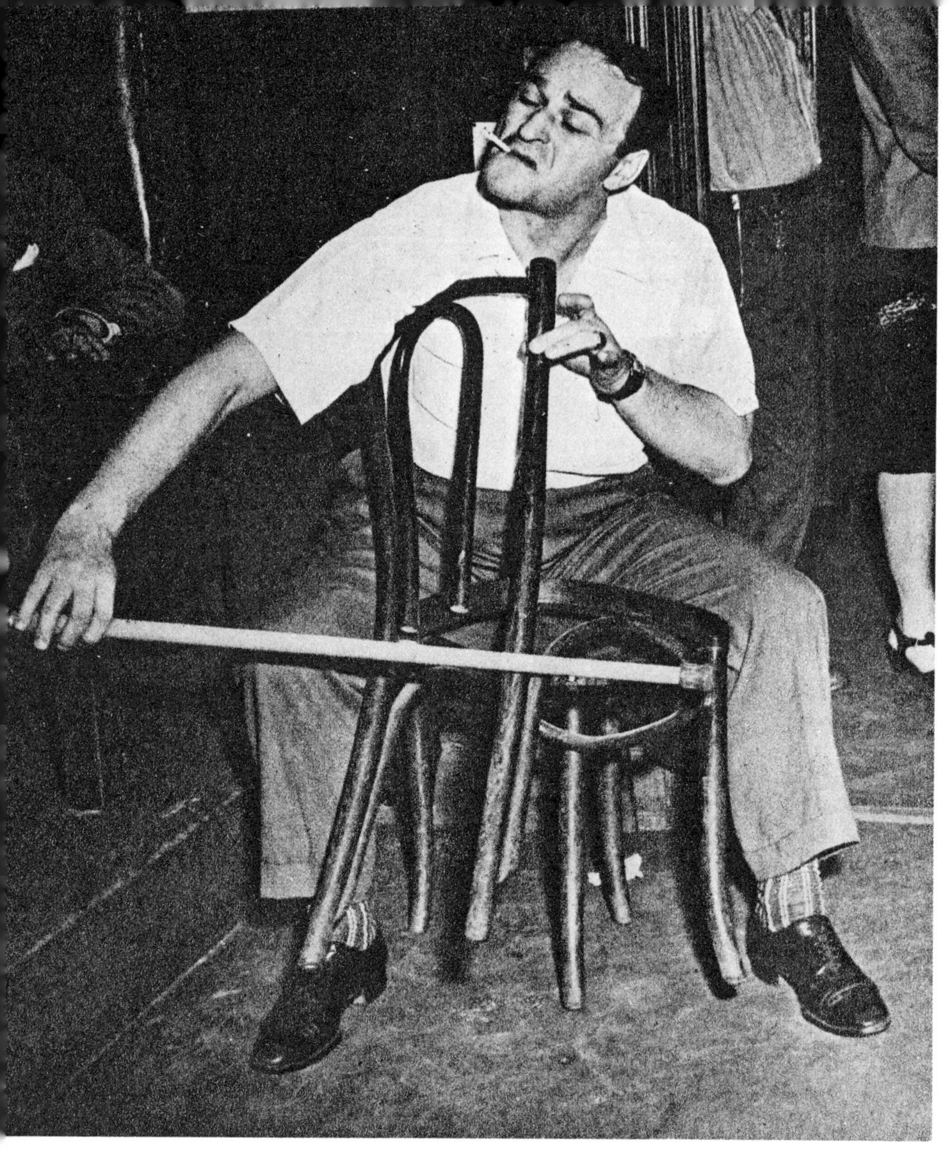

Cello player rehearsing

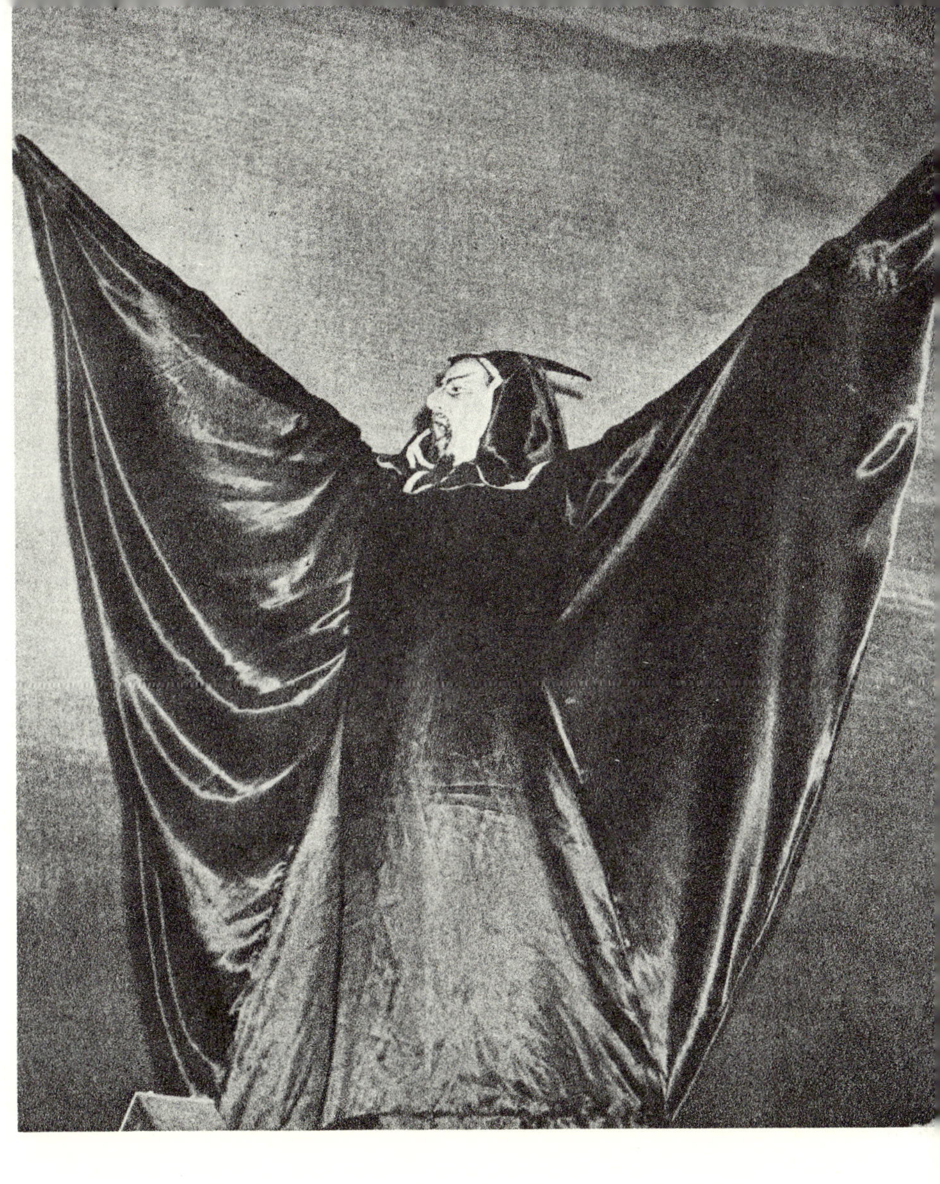

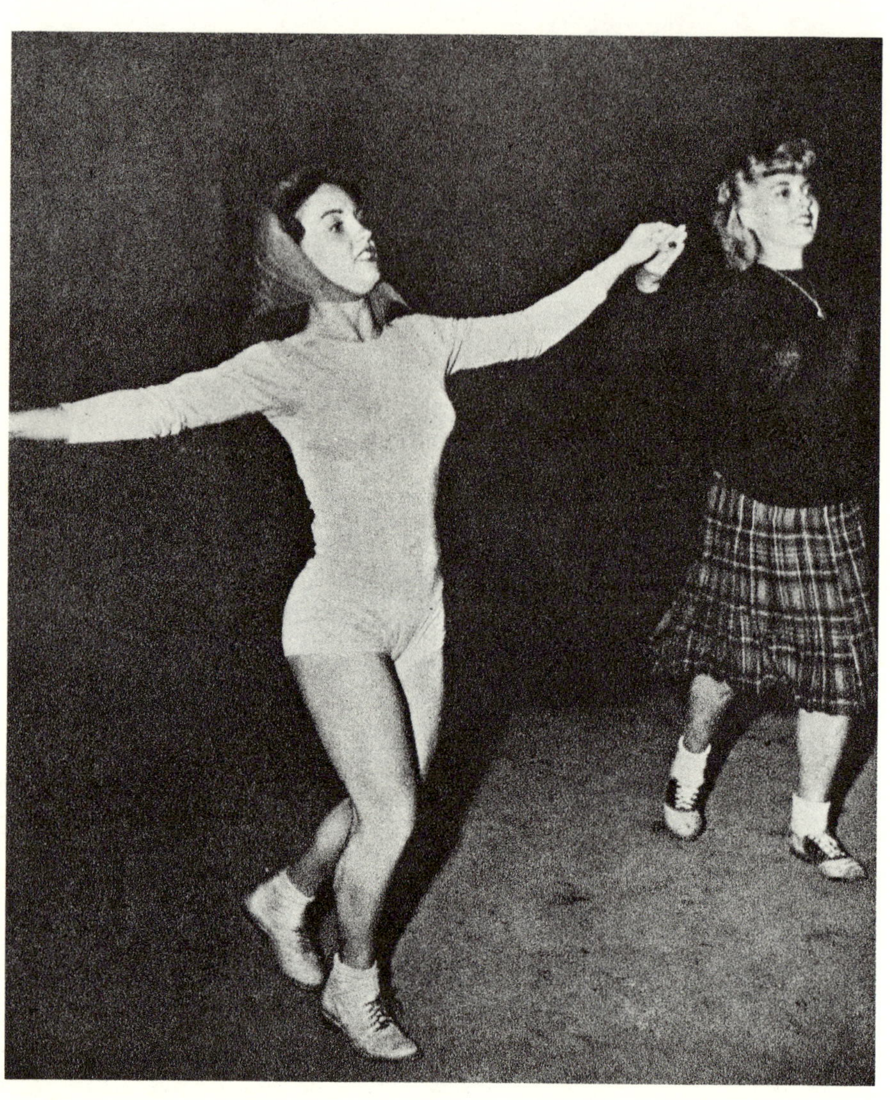

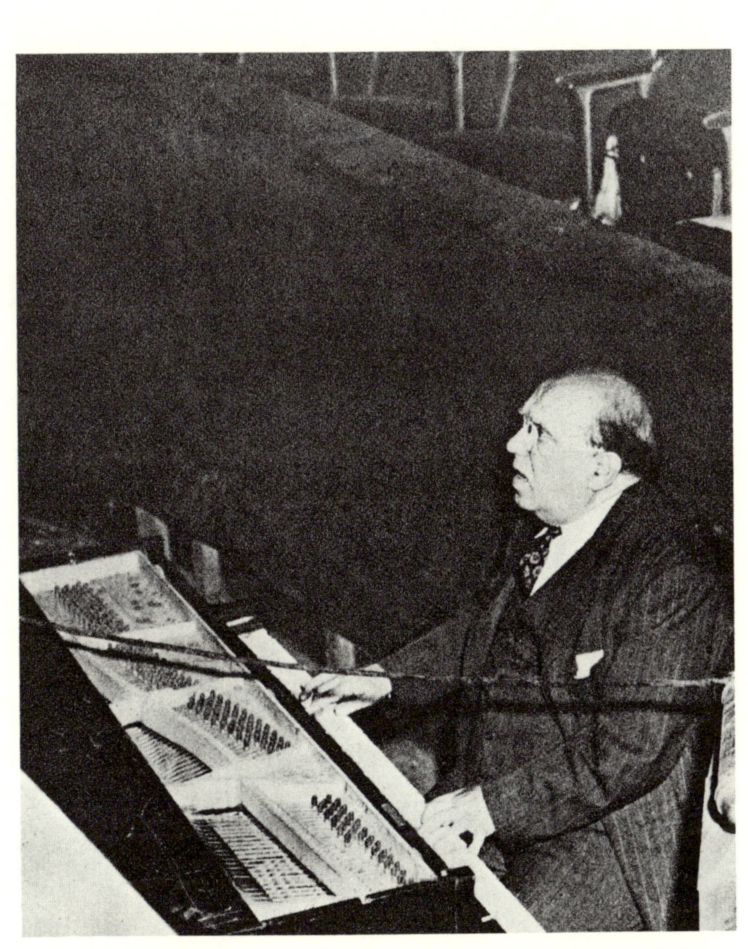

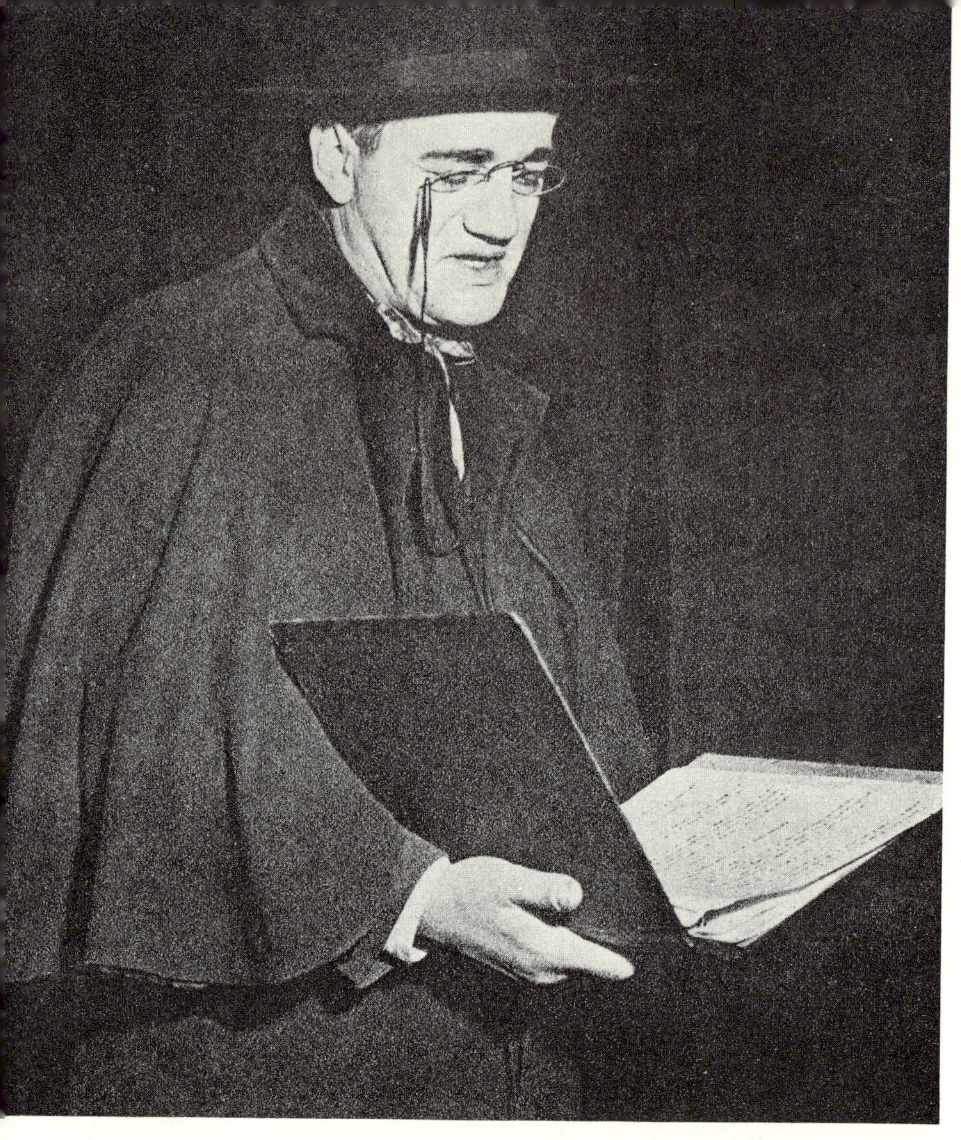

Wolf Mercur, understudy

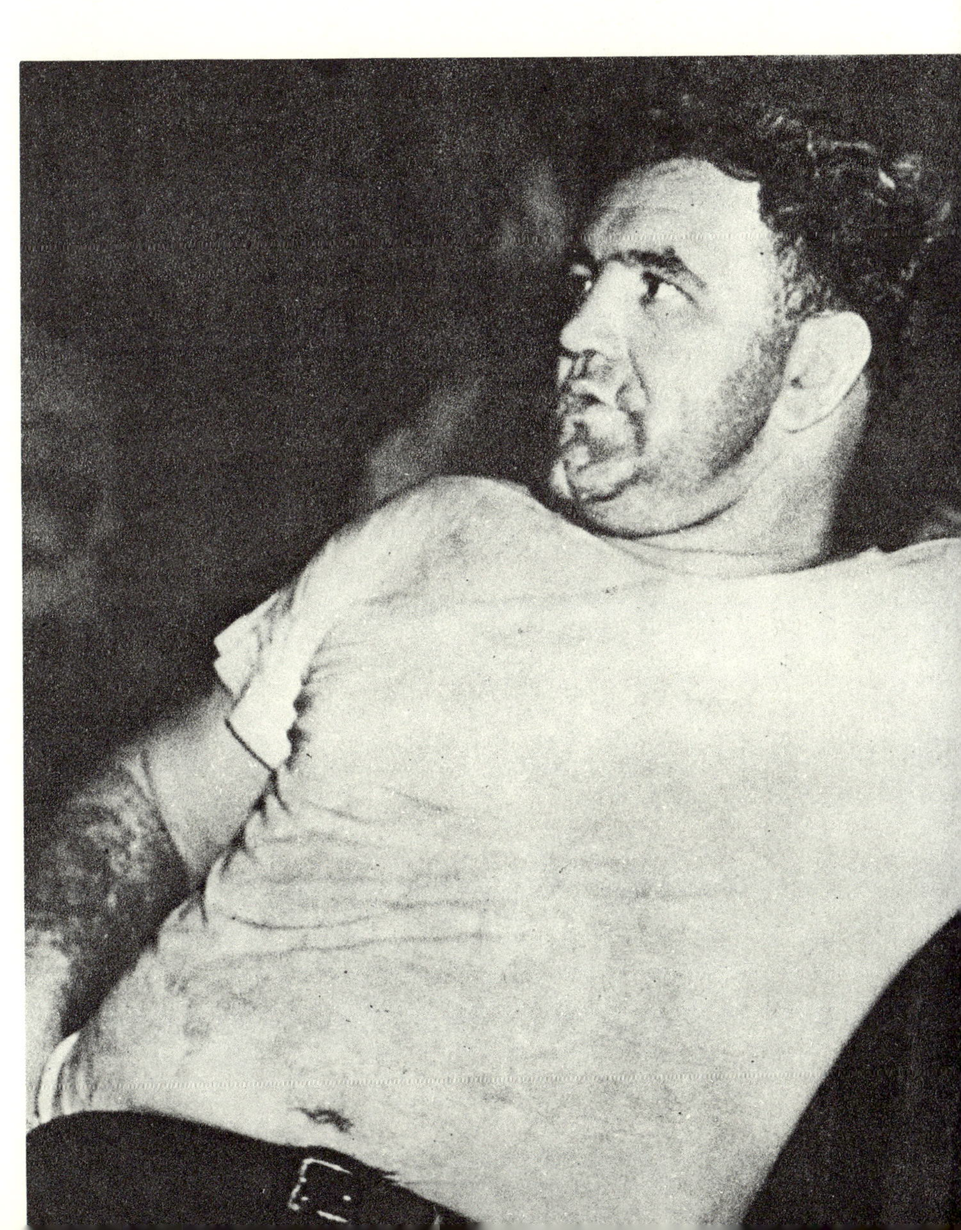

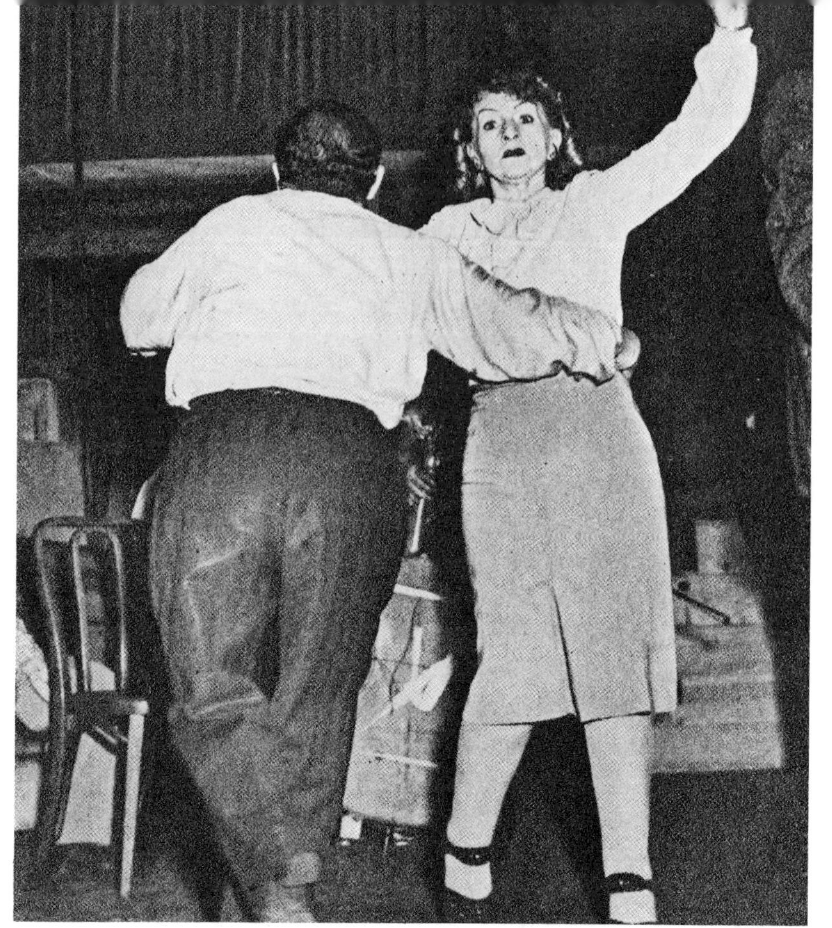

Invitation to the dance

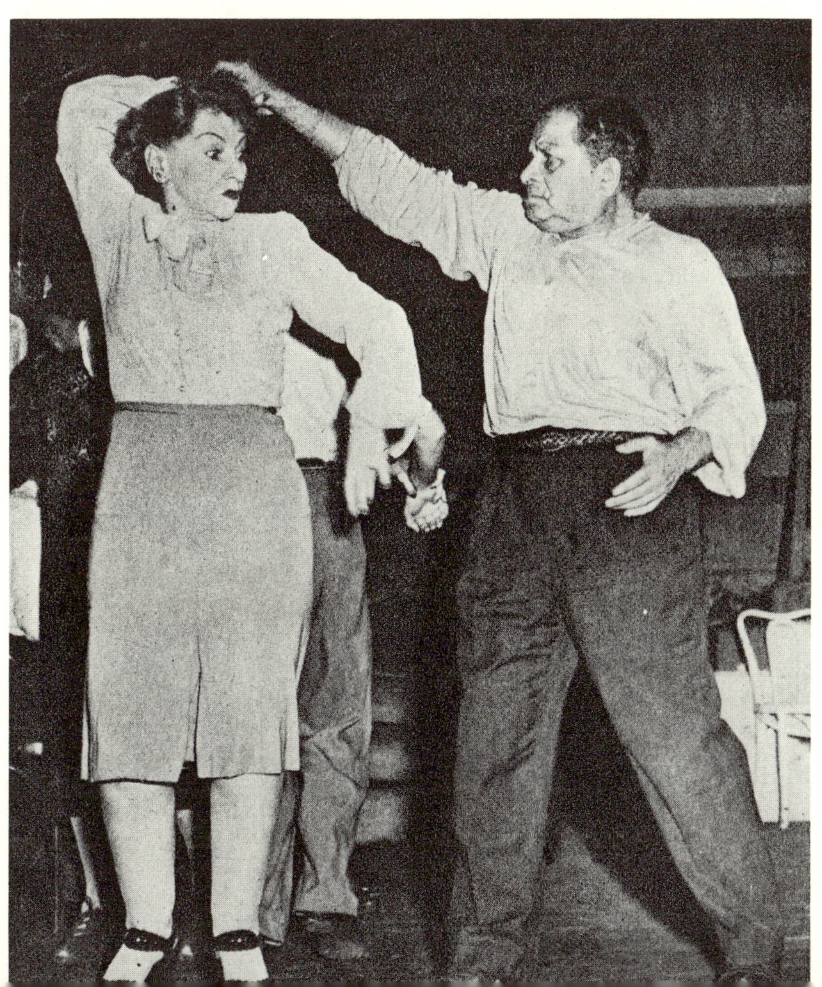

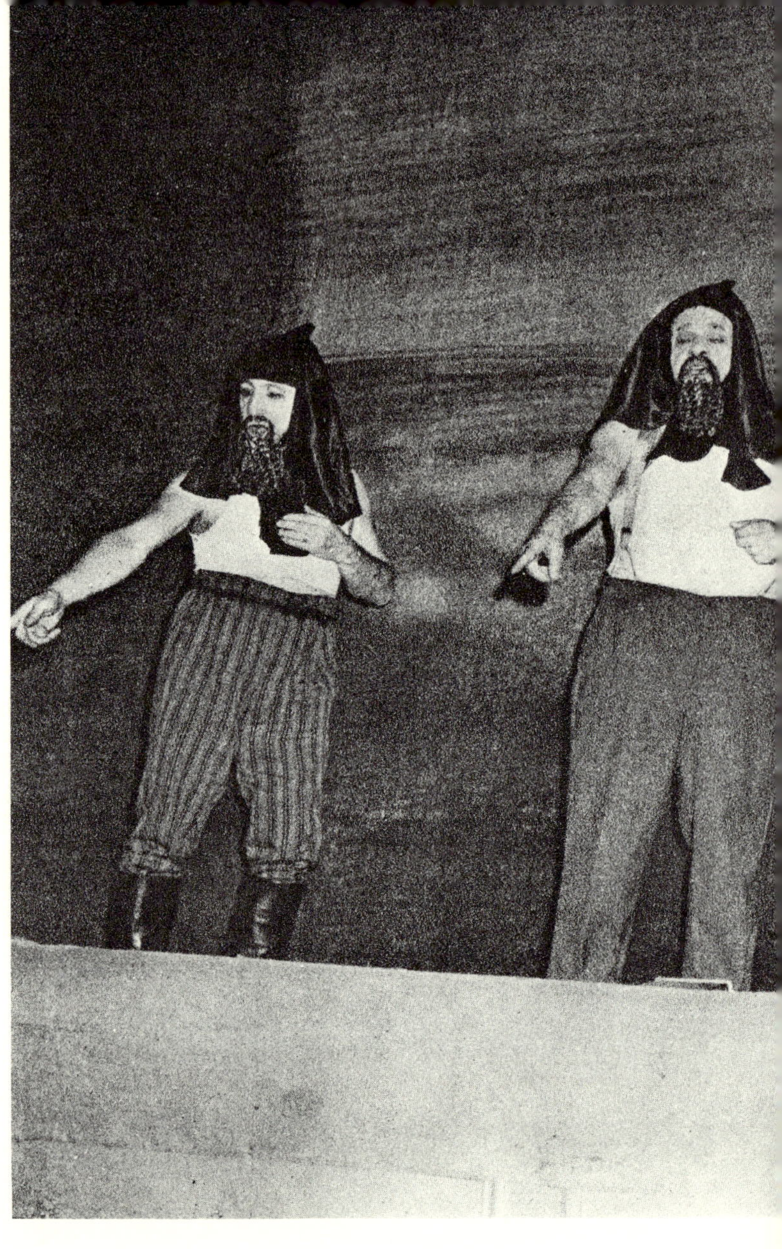

The devils rehearsed in their beards and undershirts. . . .

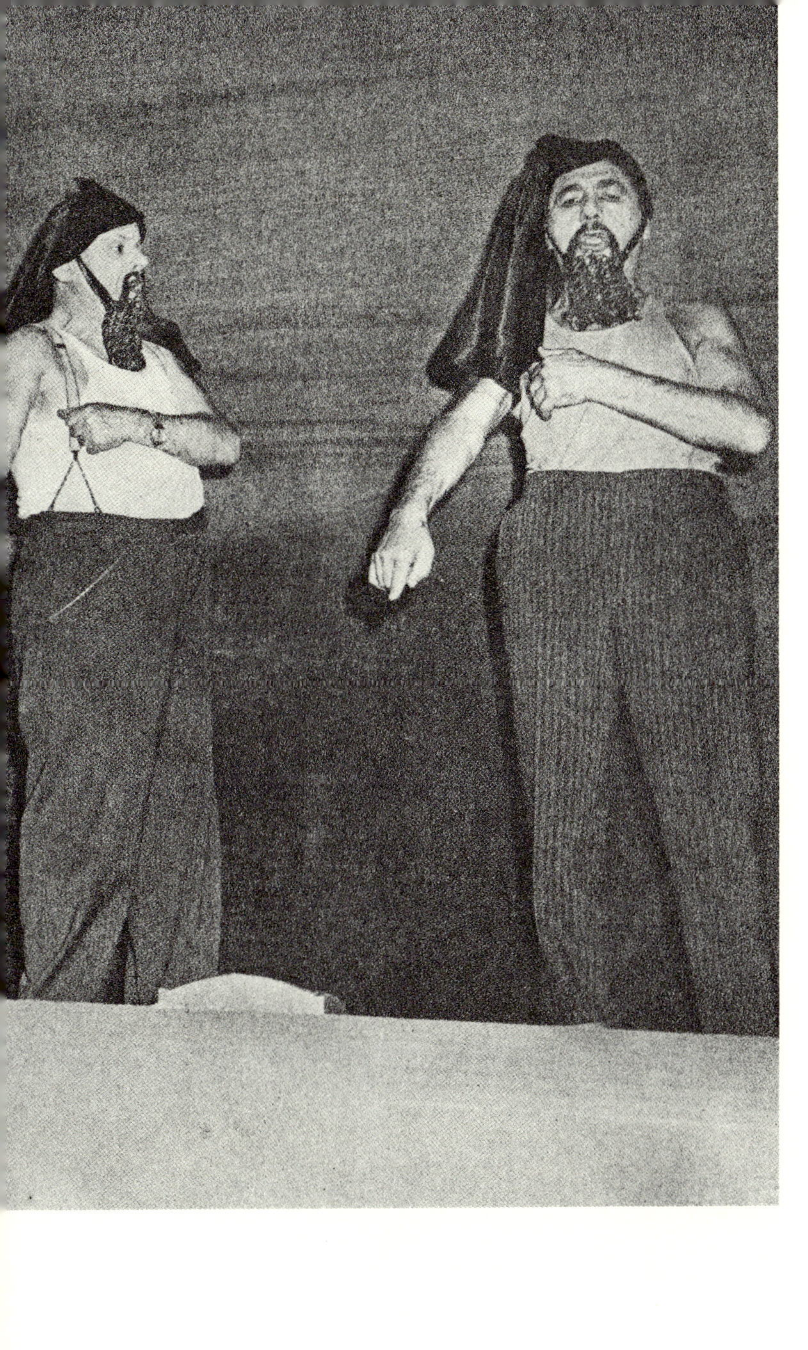

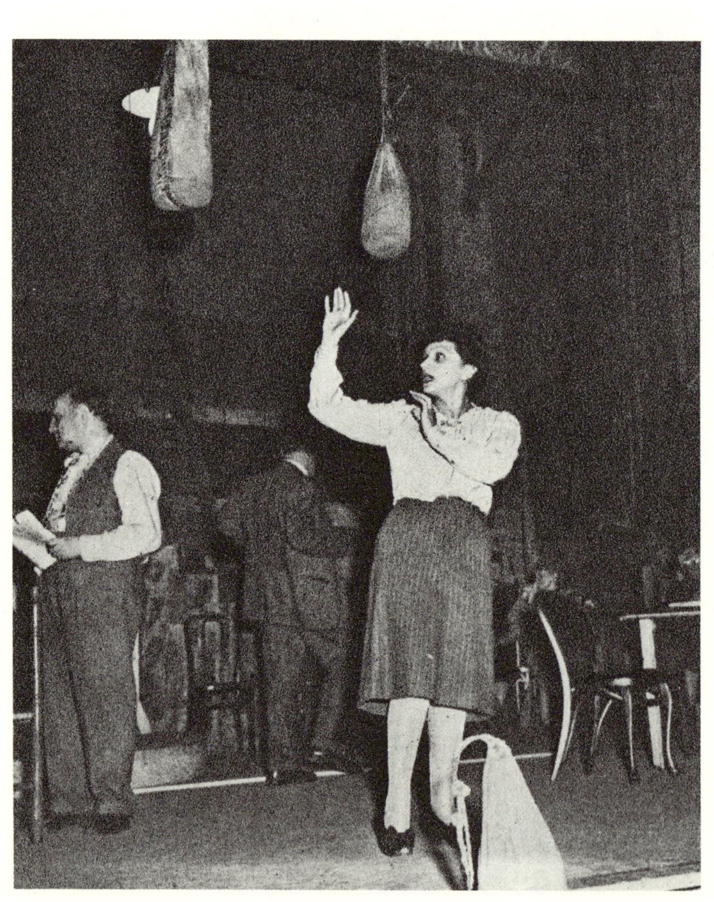

Saturday Night

Saturday night, the big night for the dance halls, night clubs, and saloons . . . Bunk Johnson and his Dixieland Jazz Band at the Stuyvesant Casino . . . with some hot rhythm. . . .

9

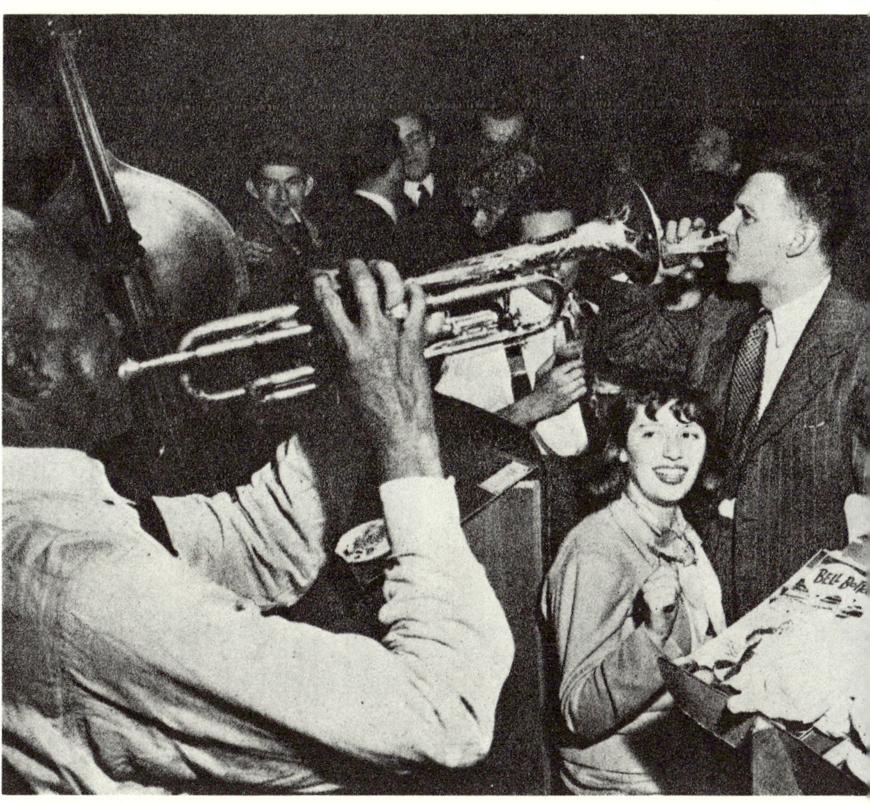

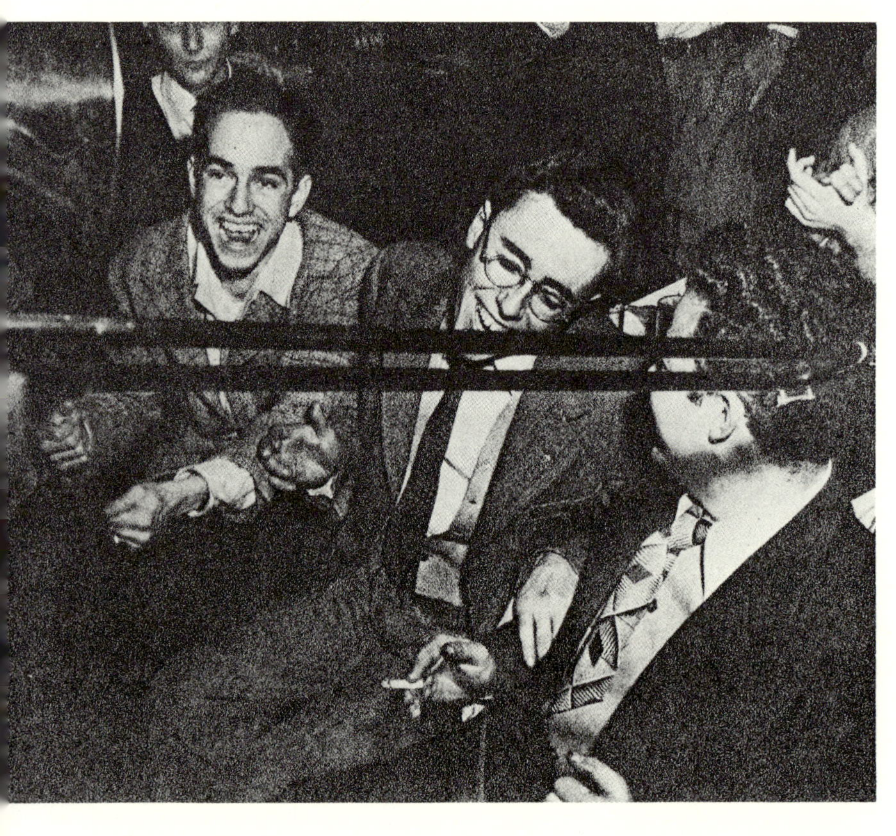

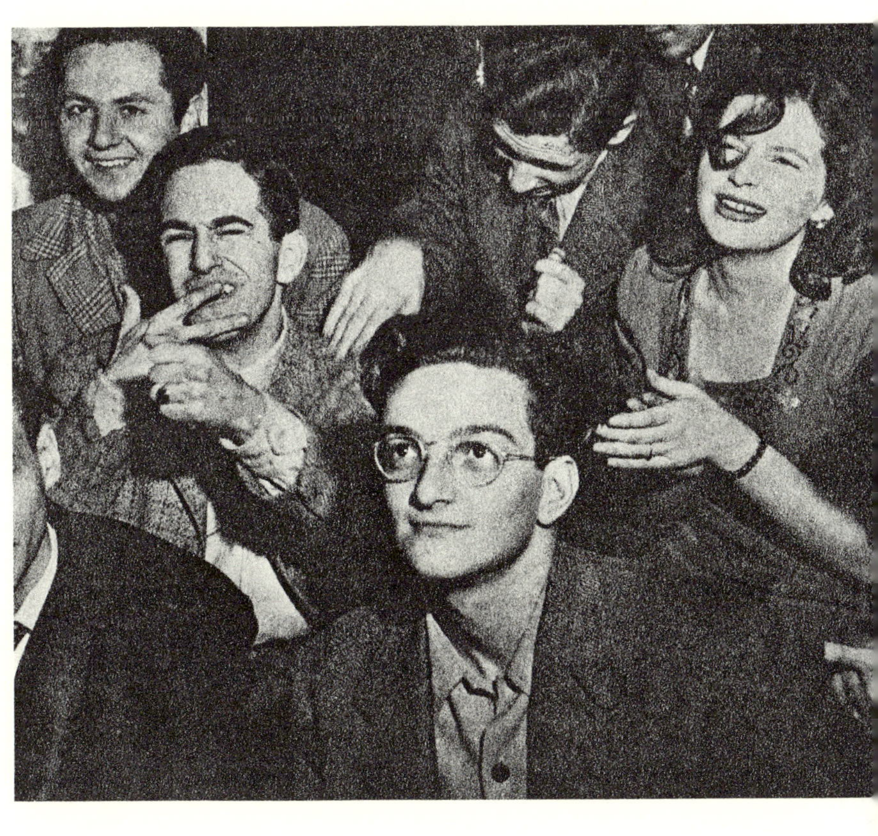

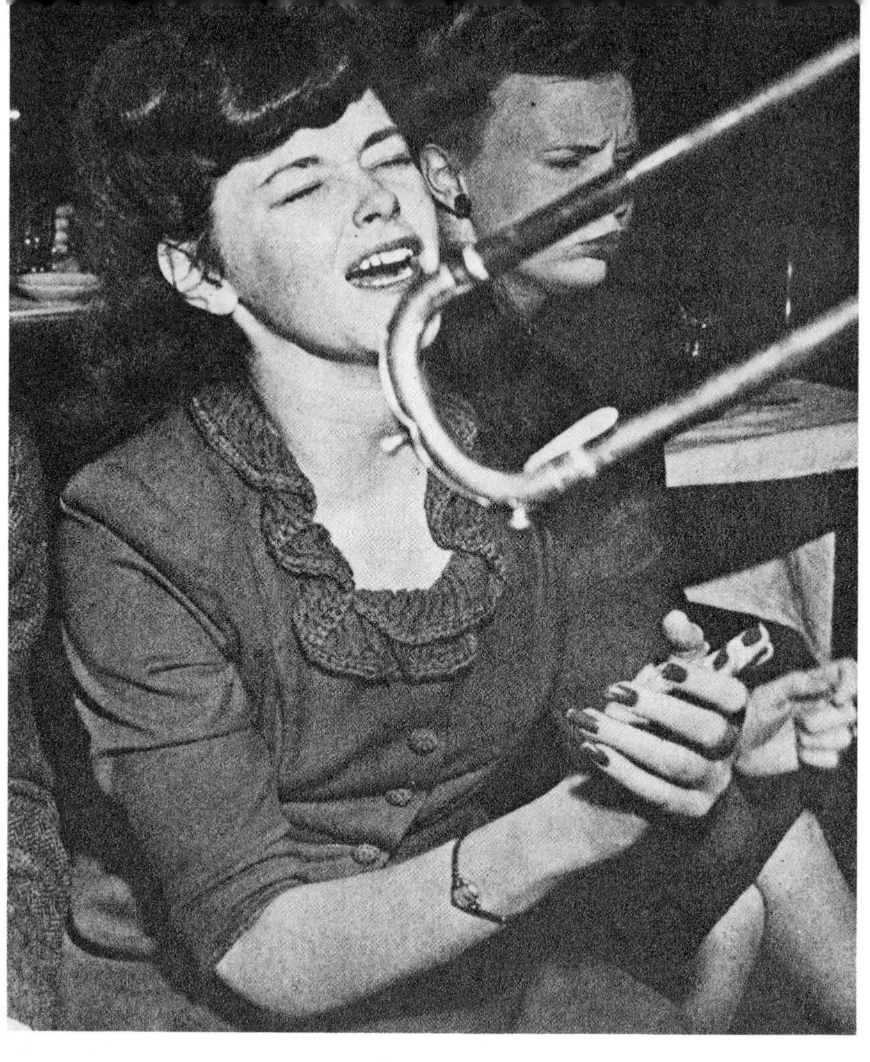

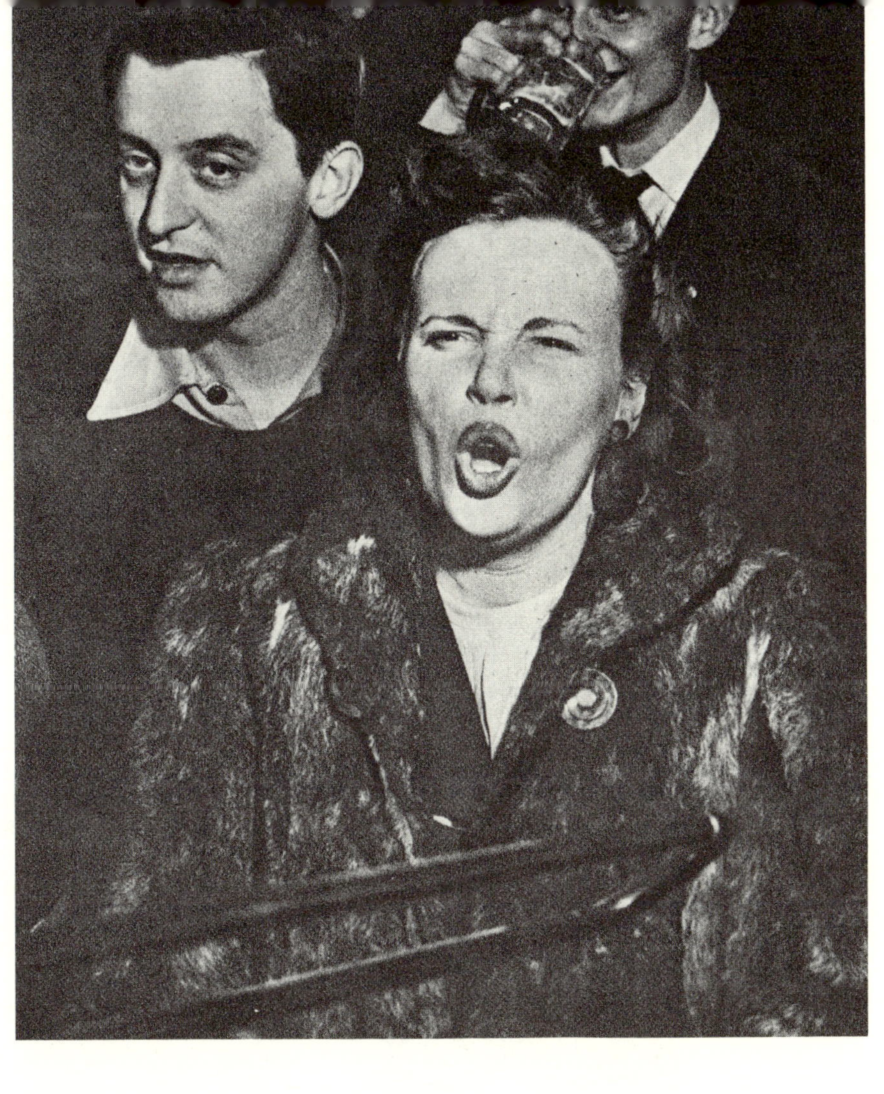

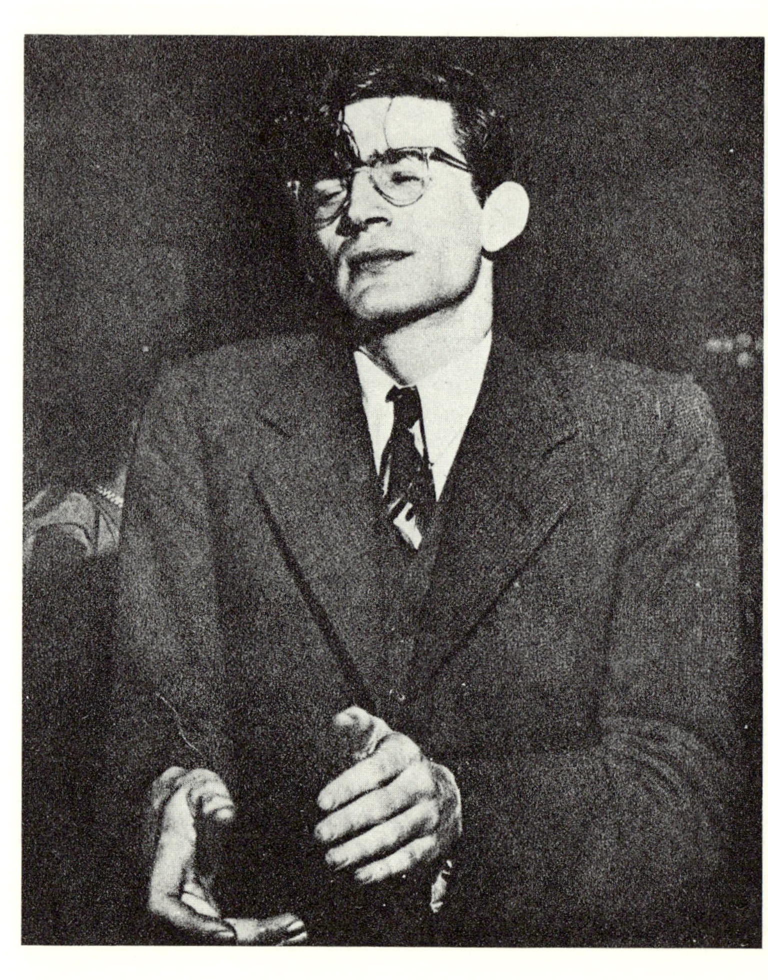

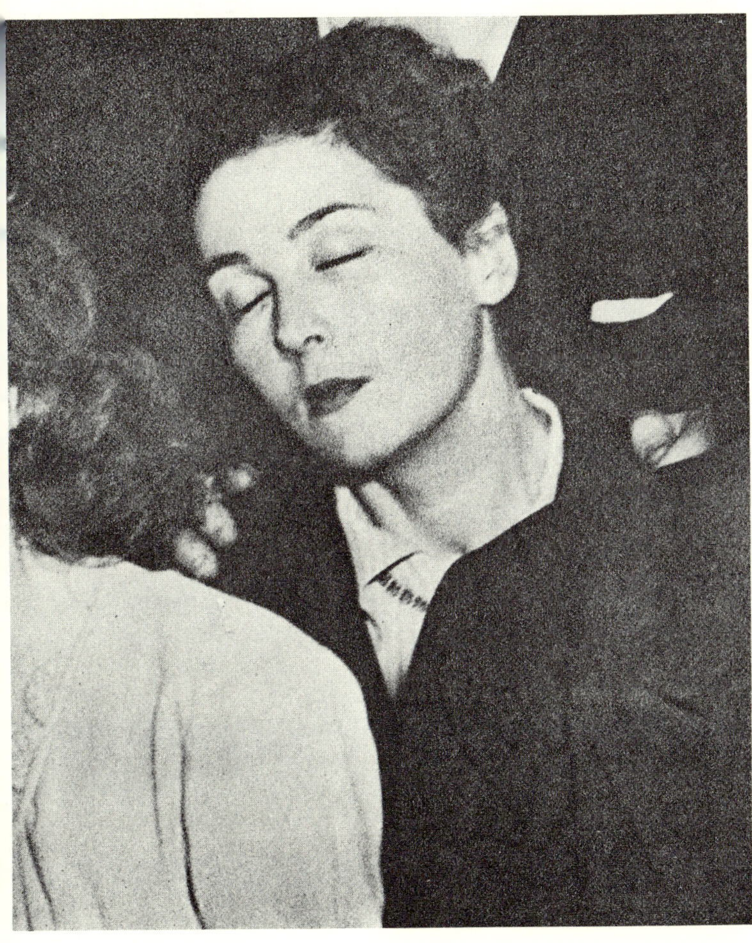

Trance music

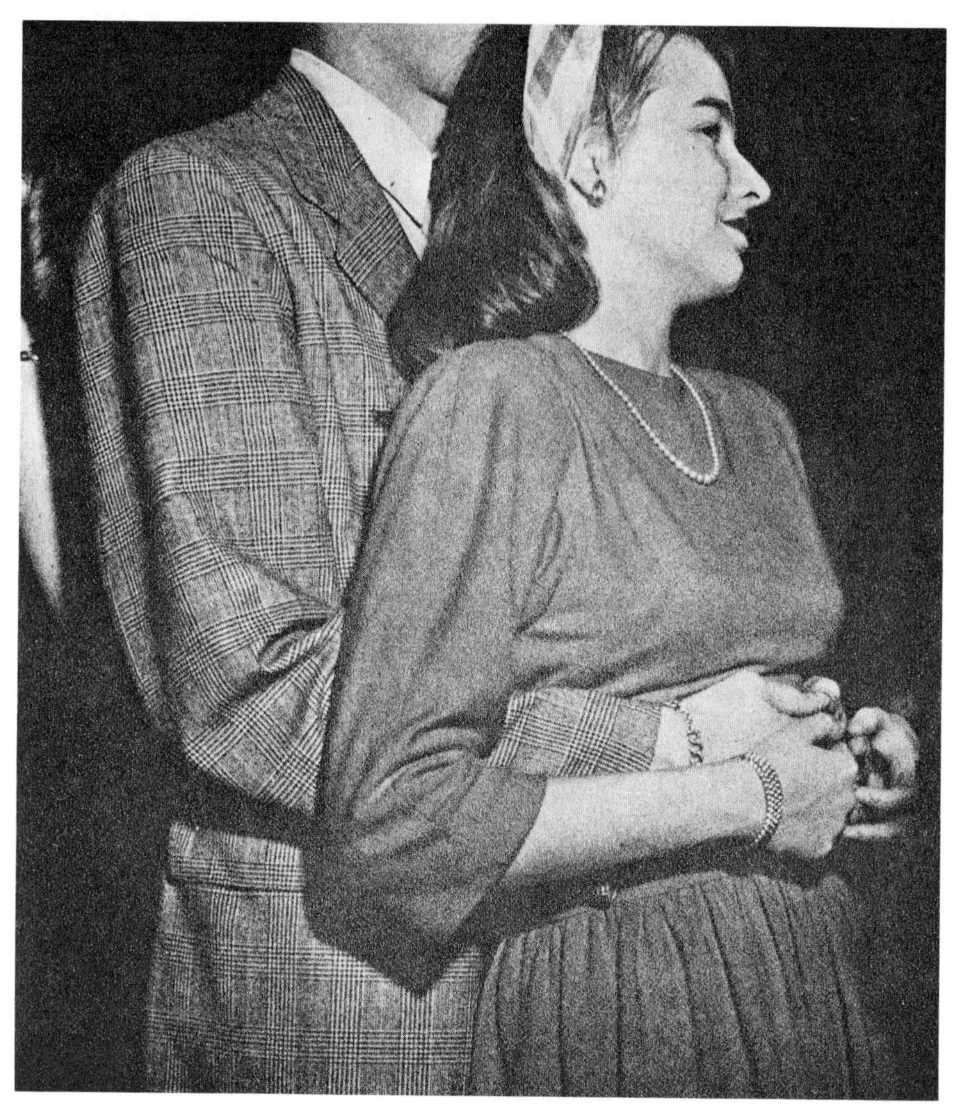

Manhattan lovelight

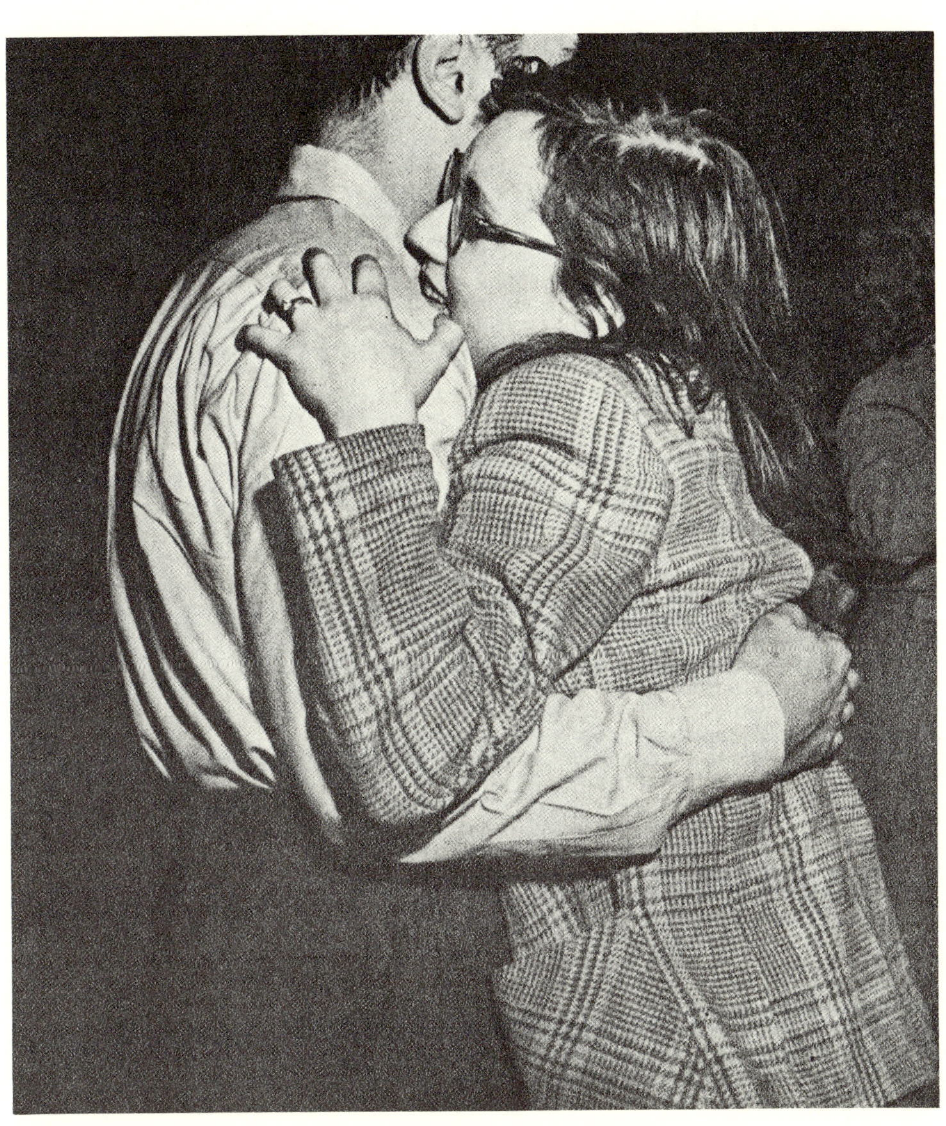

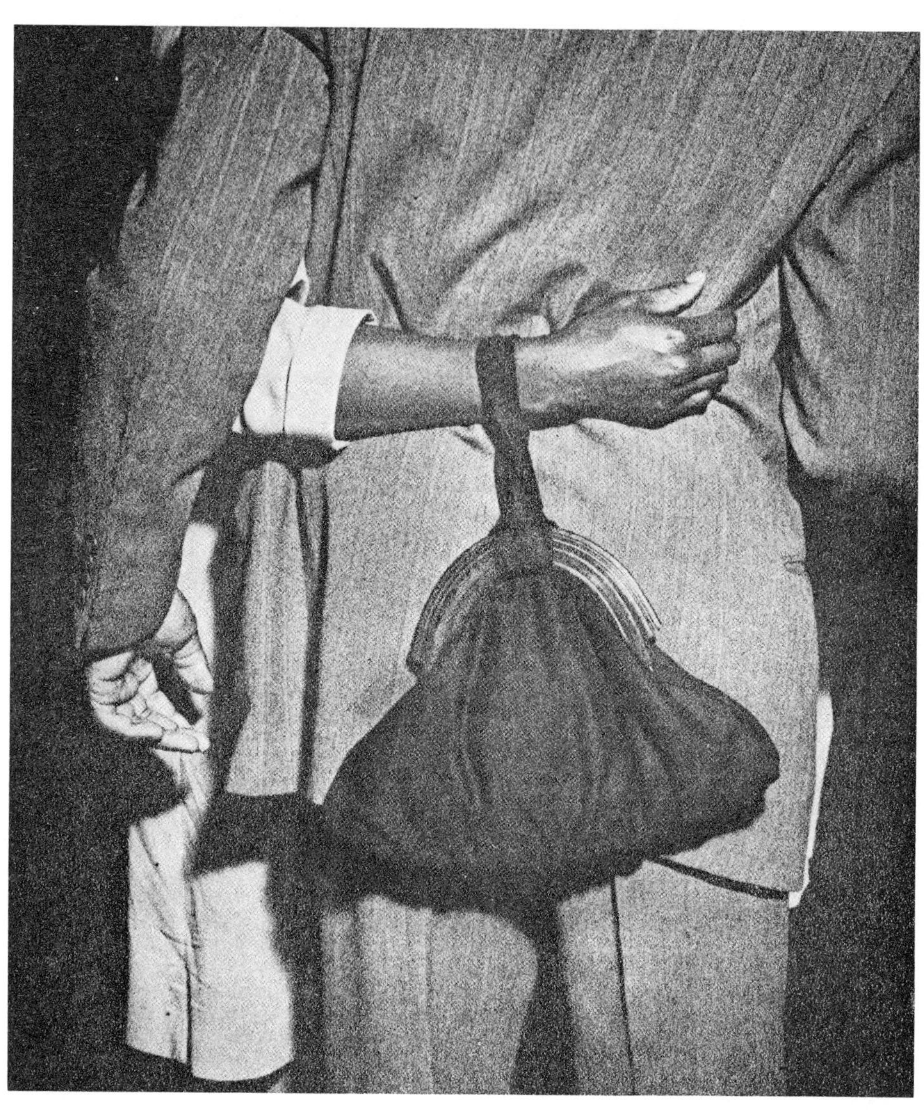

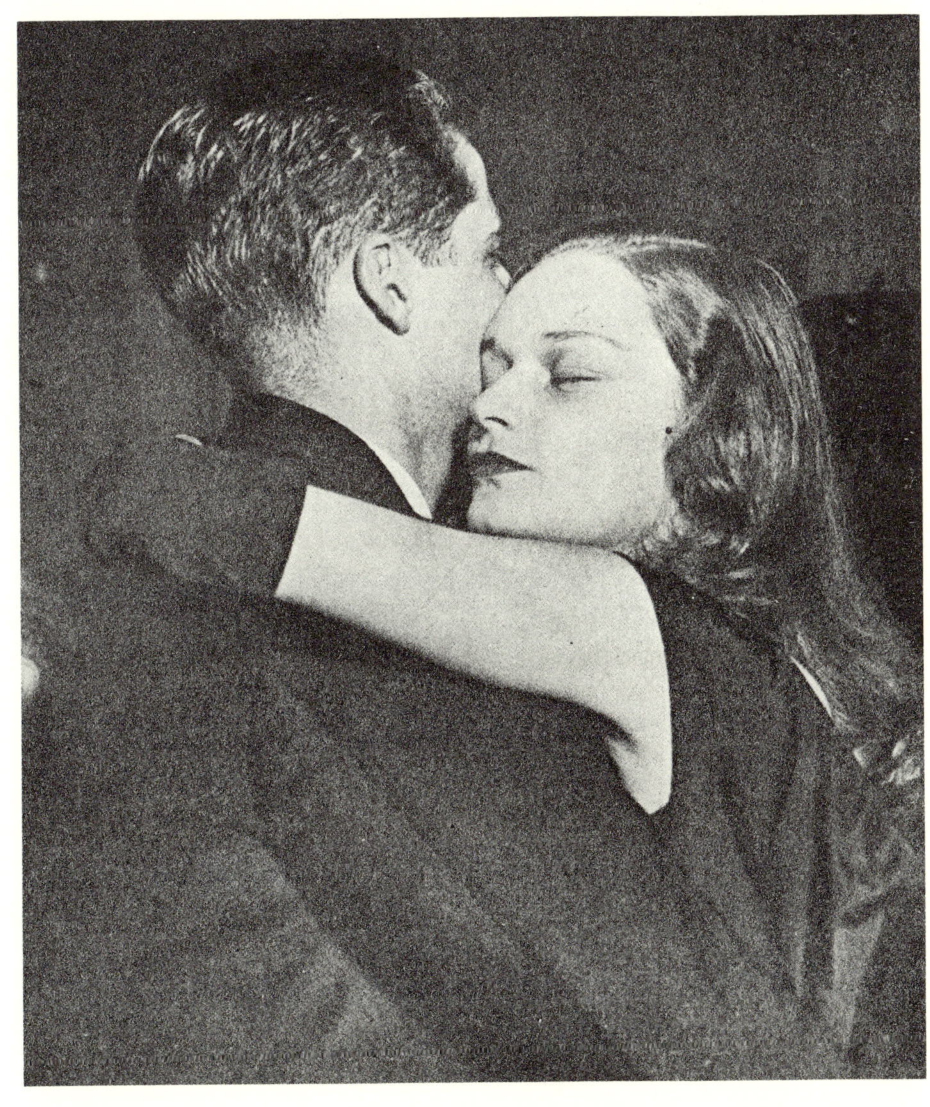

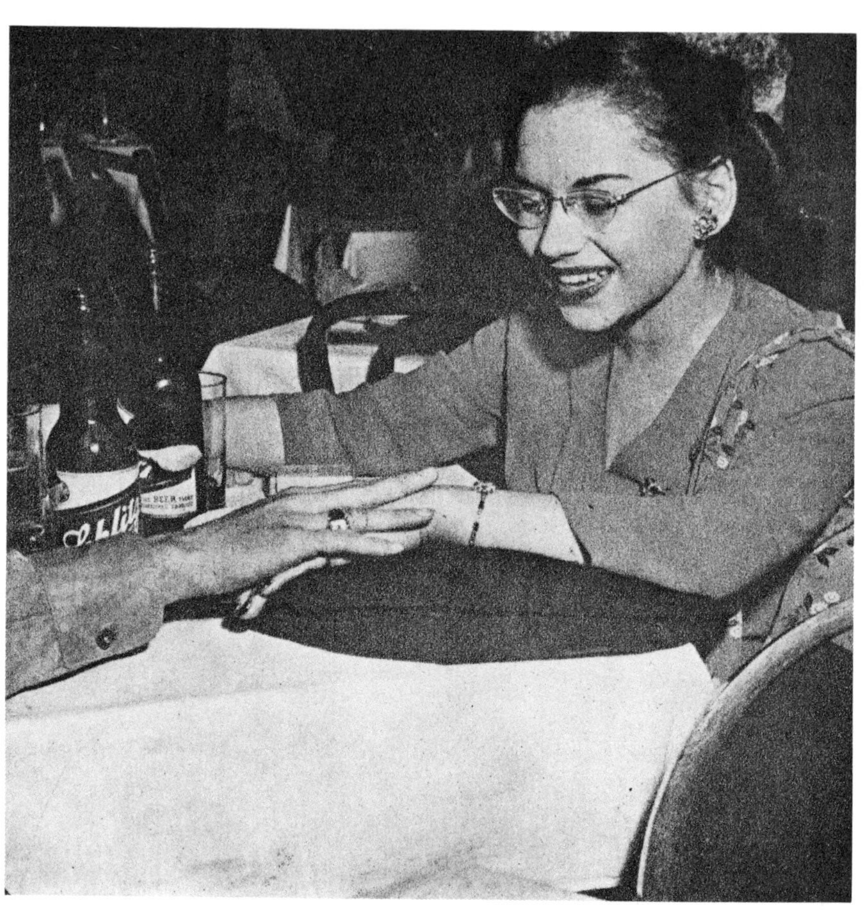

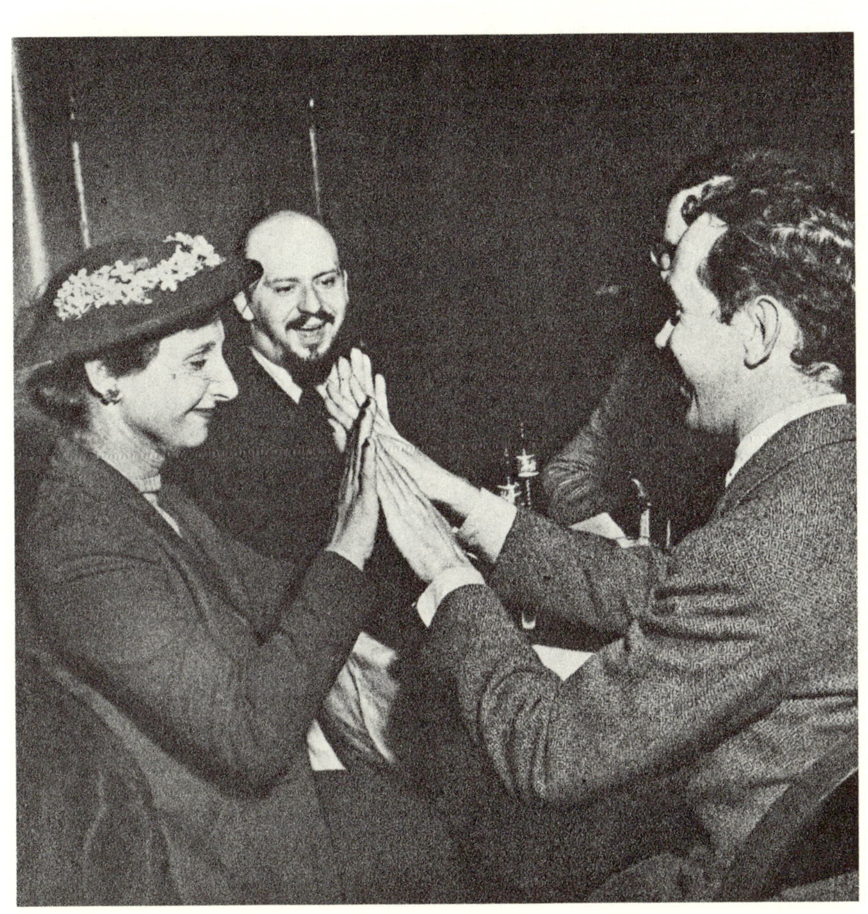

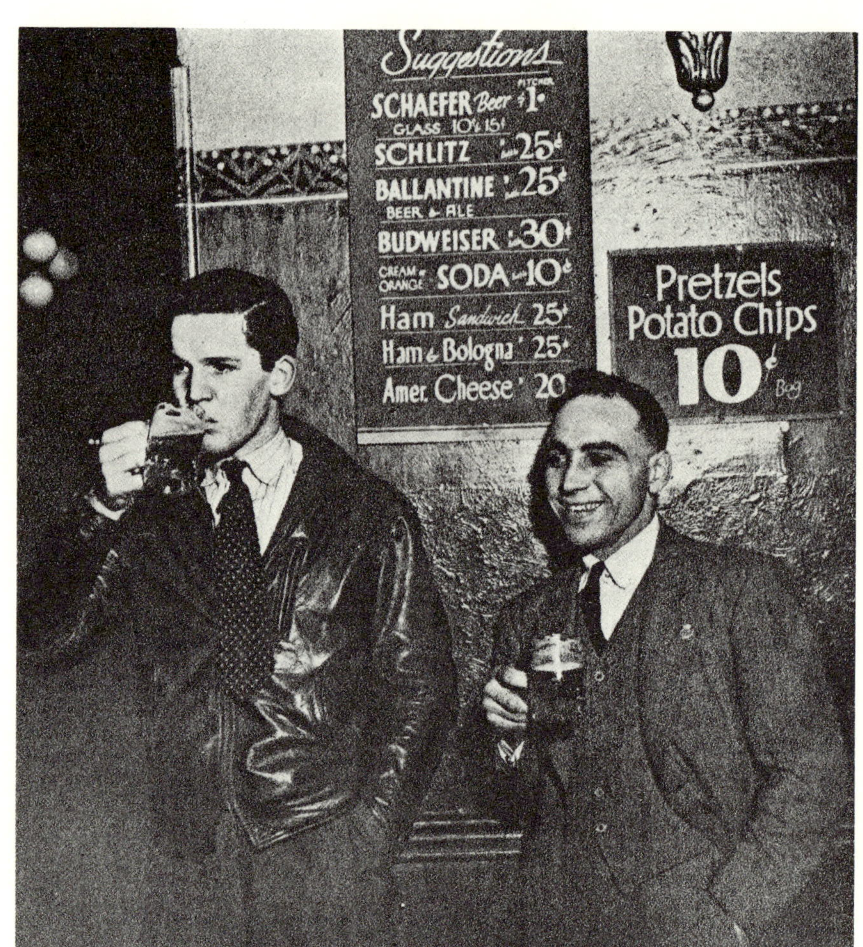
Suggestions
SCHAEFER Beer $1.
GLASS 10¢ & 15¢
SCHLITZ 25¢
BALLANTINE 25¢
BEER & ALE
BUDWEISER 30¢
CREAM & ORANGE SODA 10¢
Ham Sandwich 25¢
Ham & Bologna 25¢
Amer. Cheese 20
Pretzels
Potato Chips
10¢ Bag

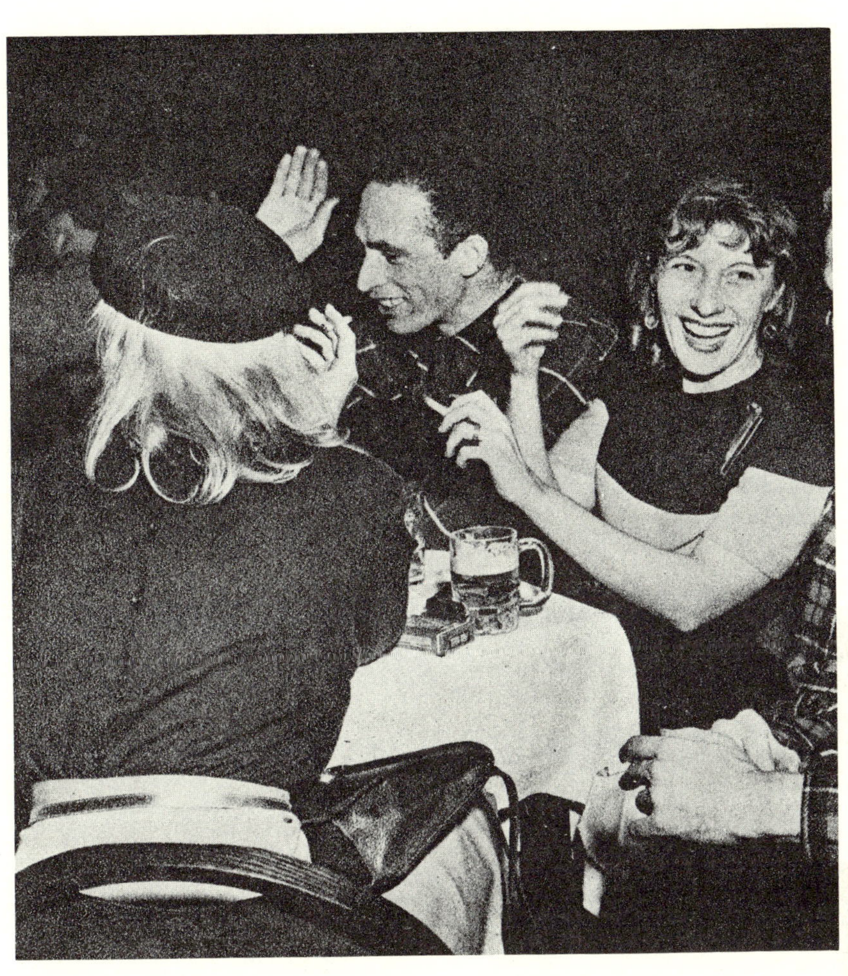

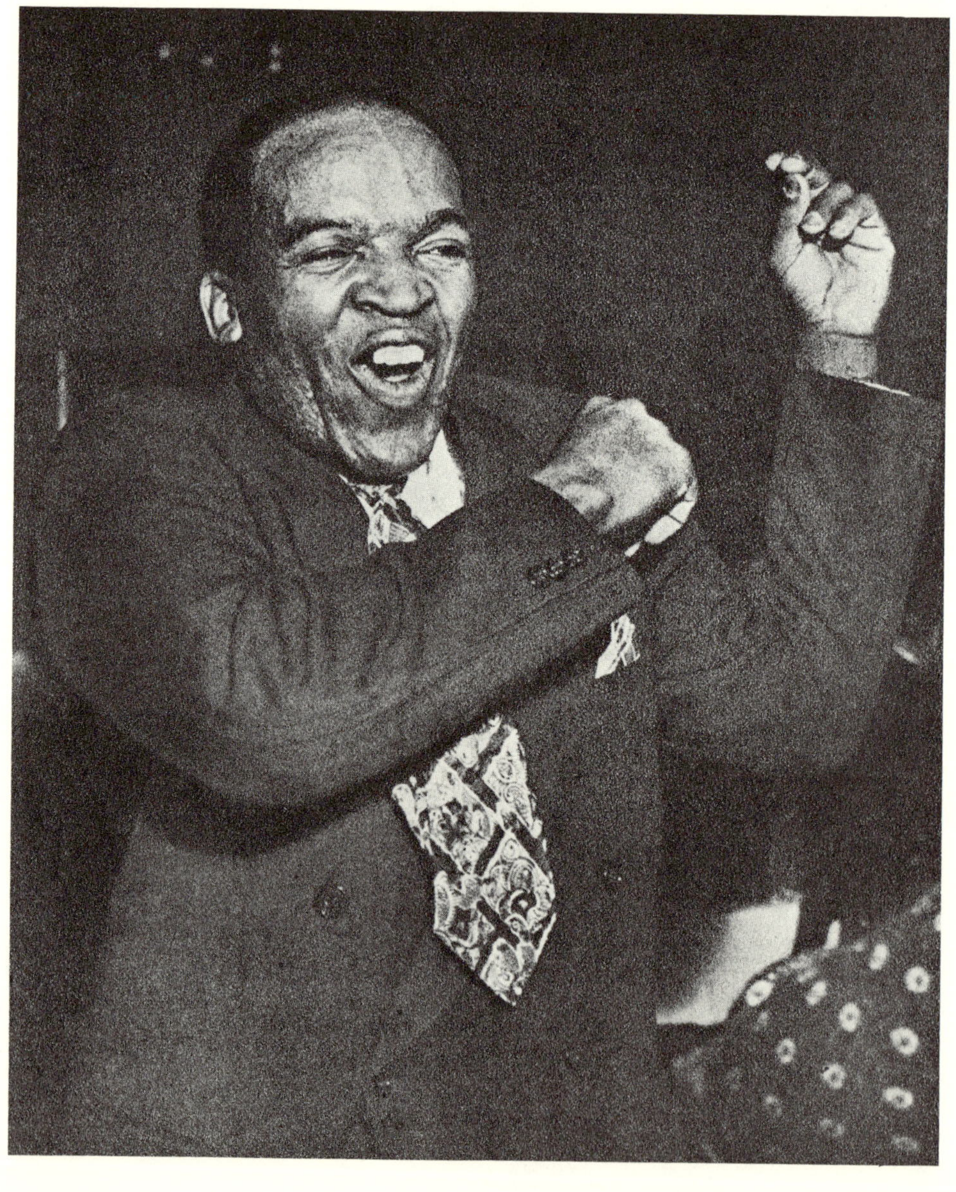

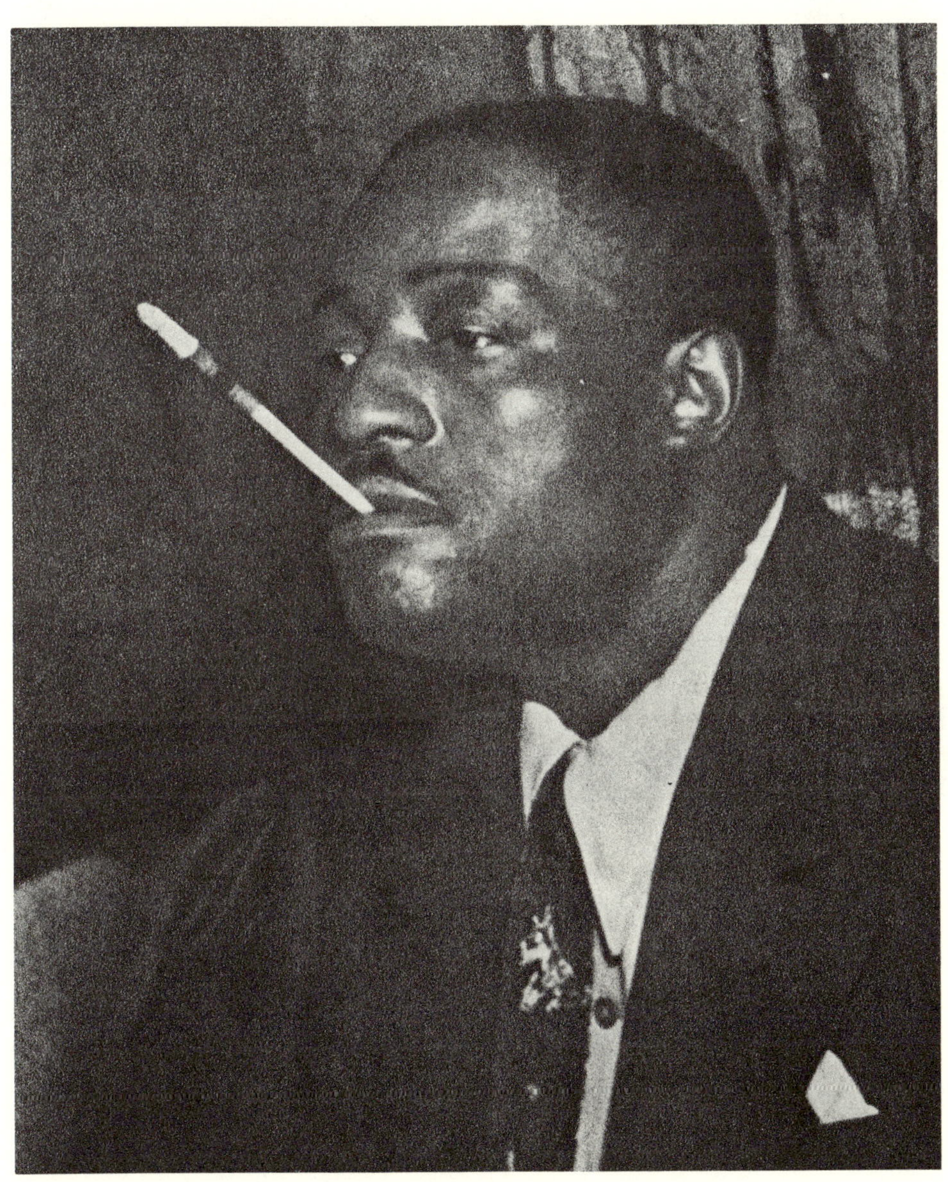

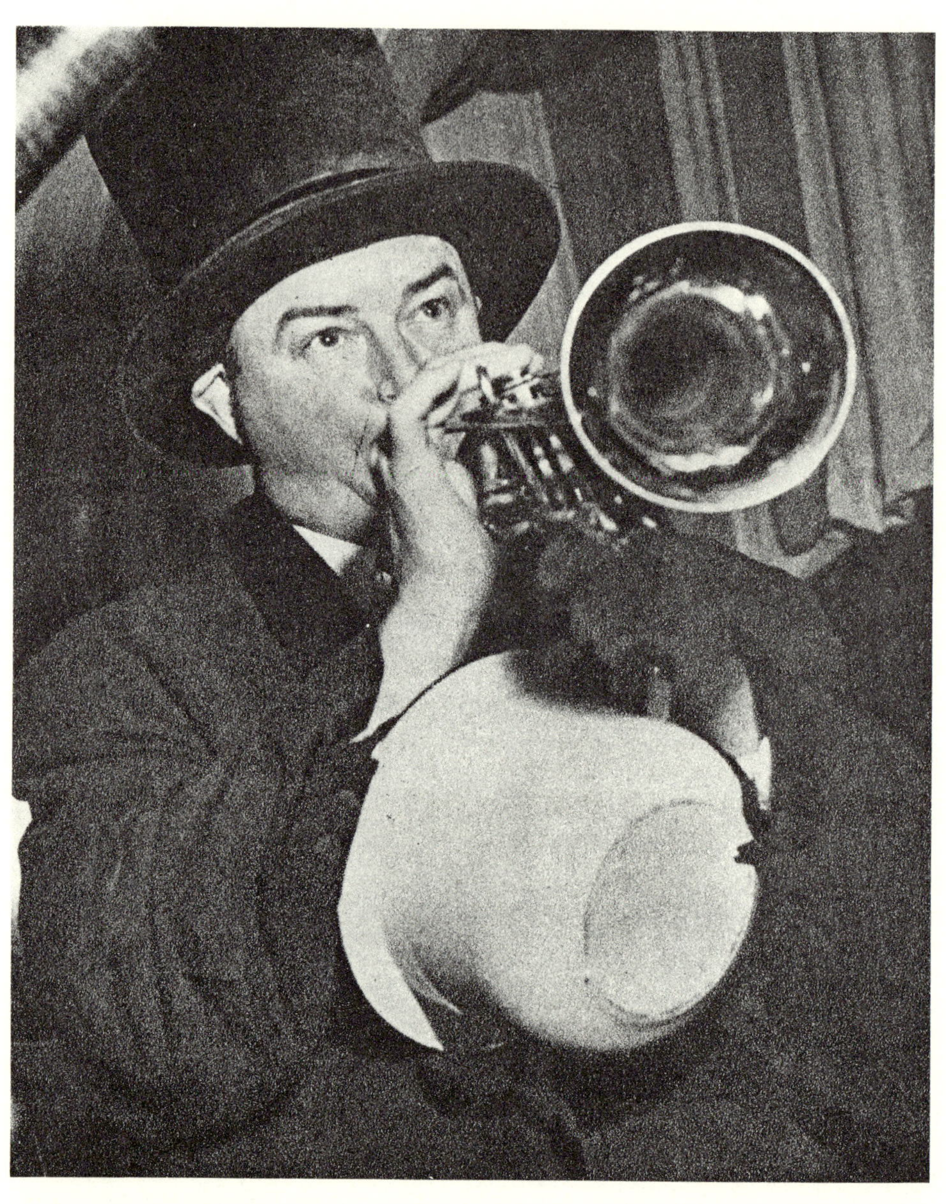

The heckler

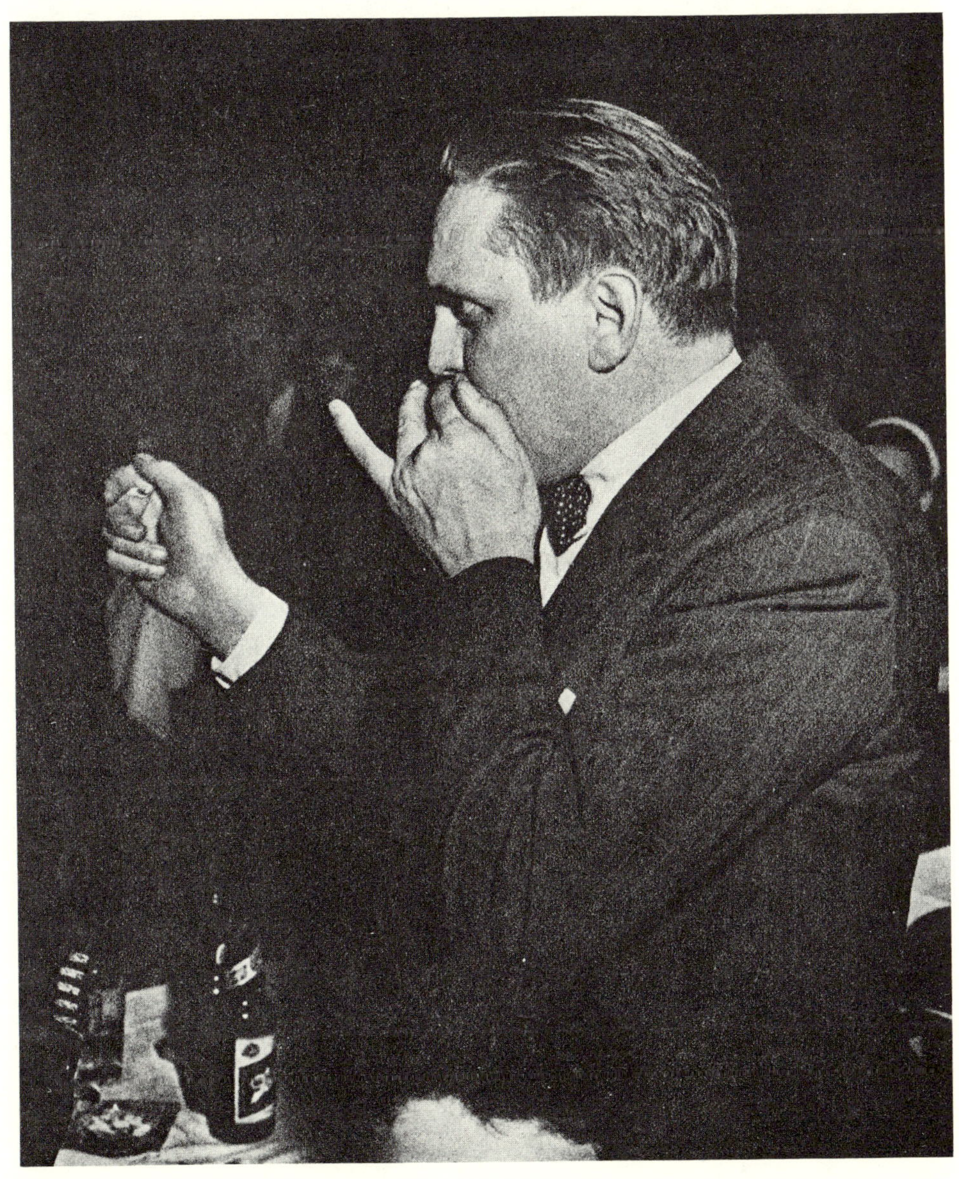

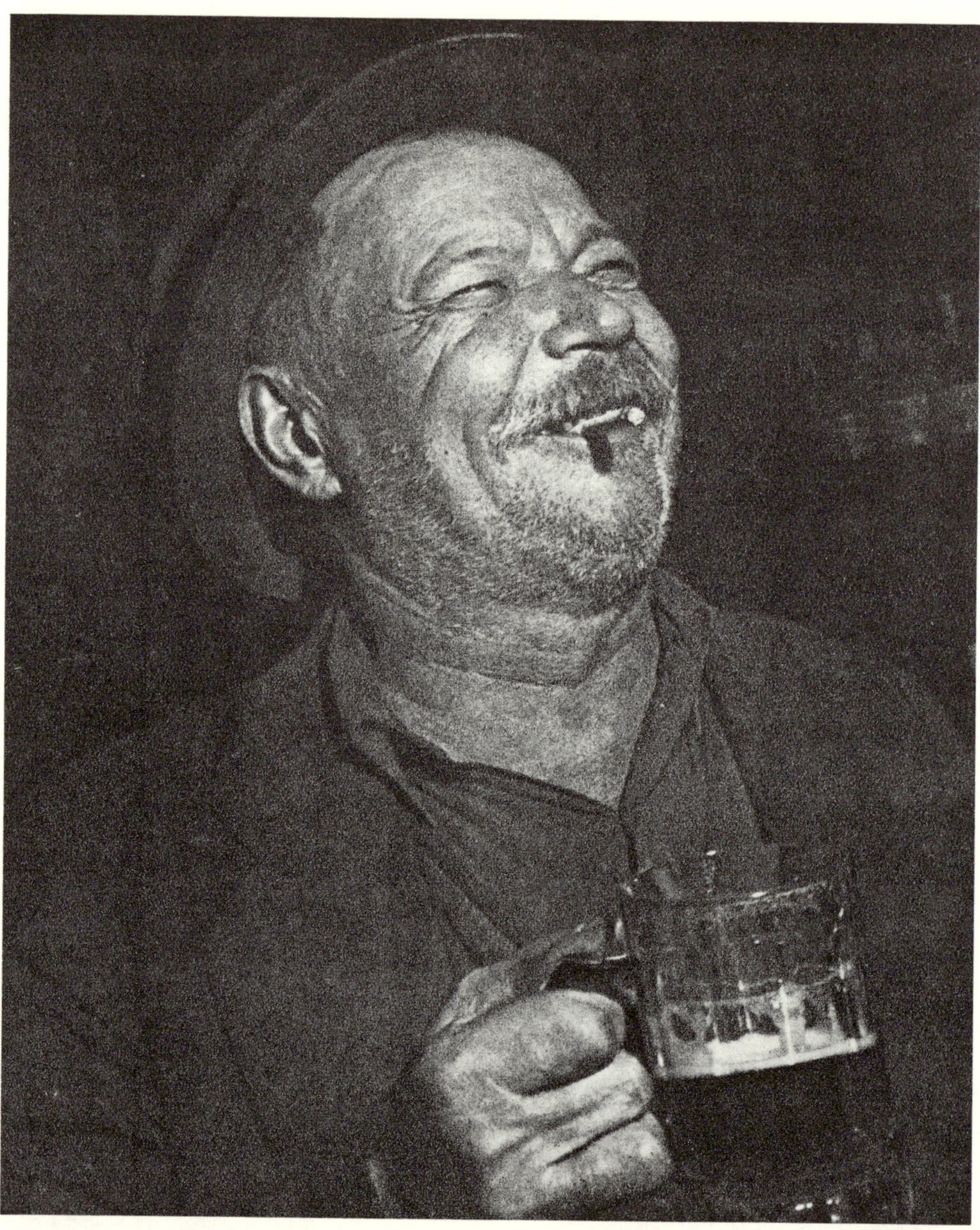

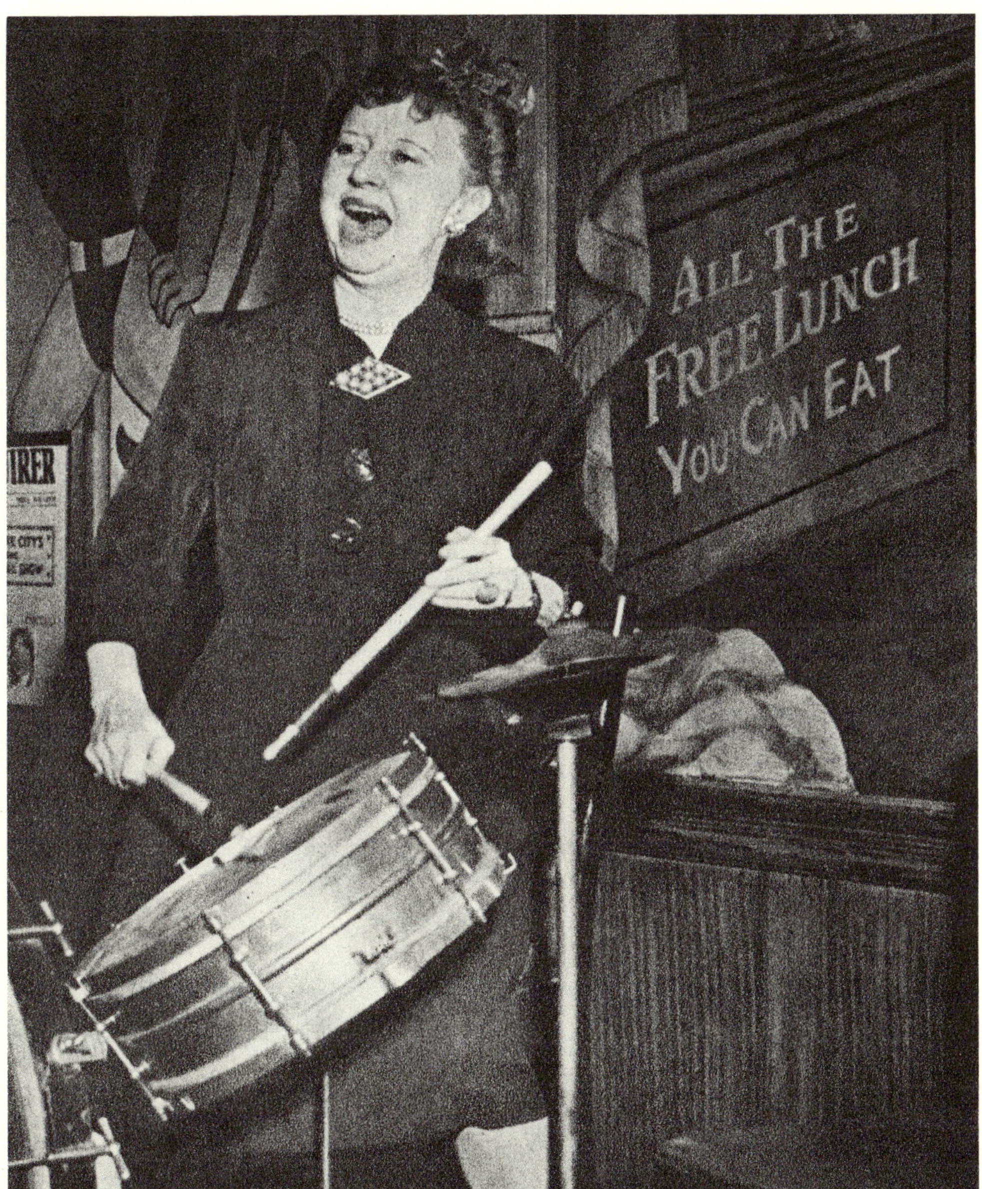

ALL THE
FREE LUNCH
YOU CAN EAT

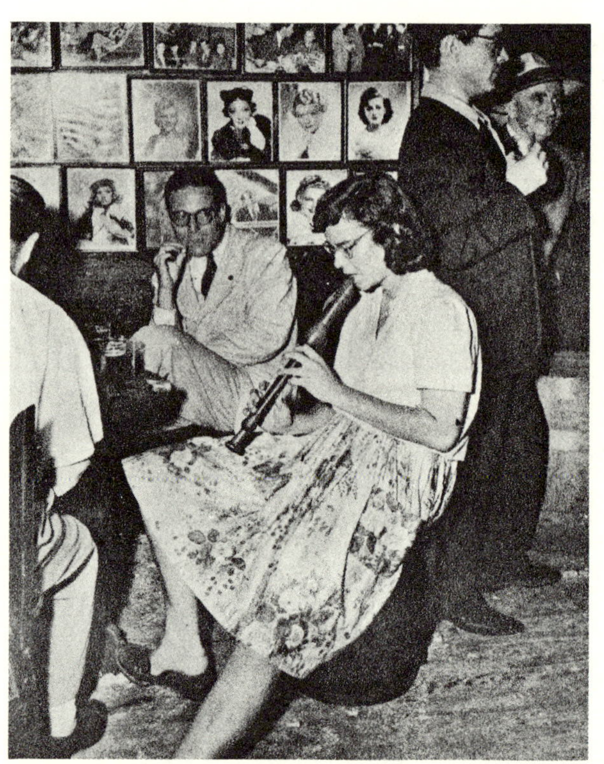

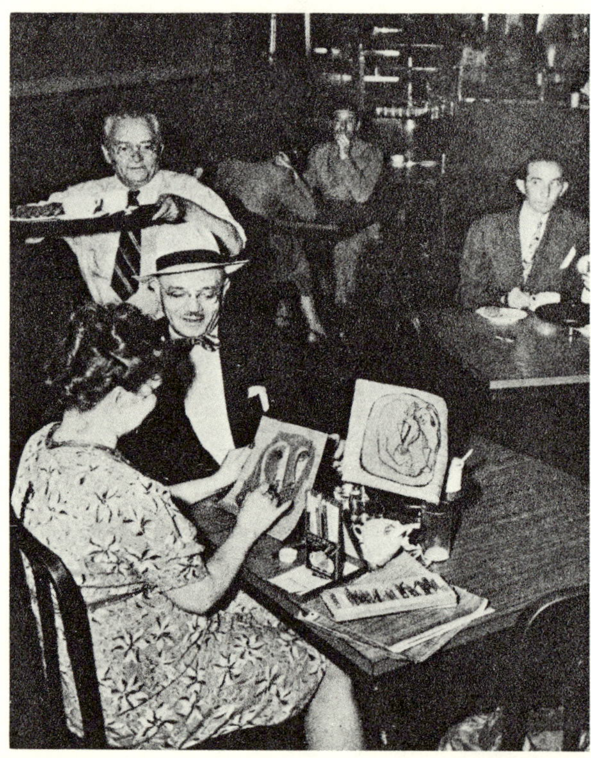

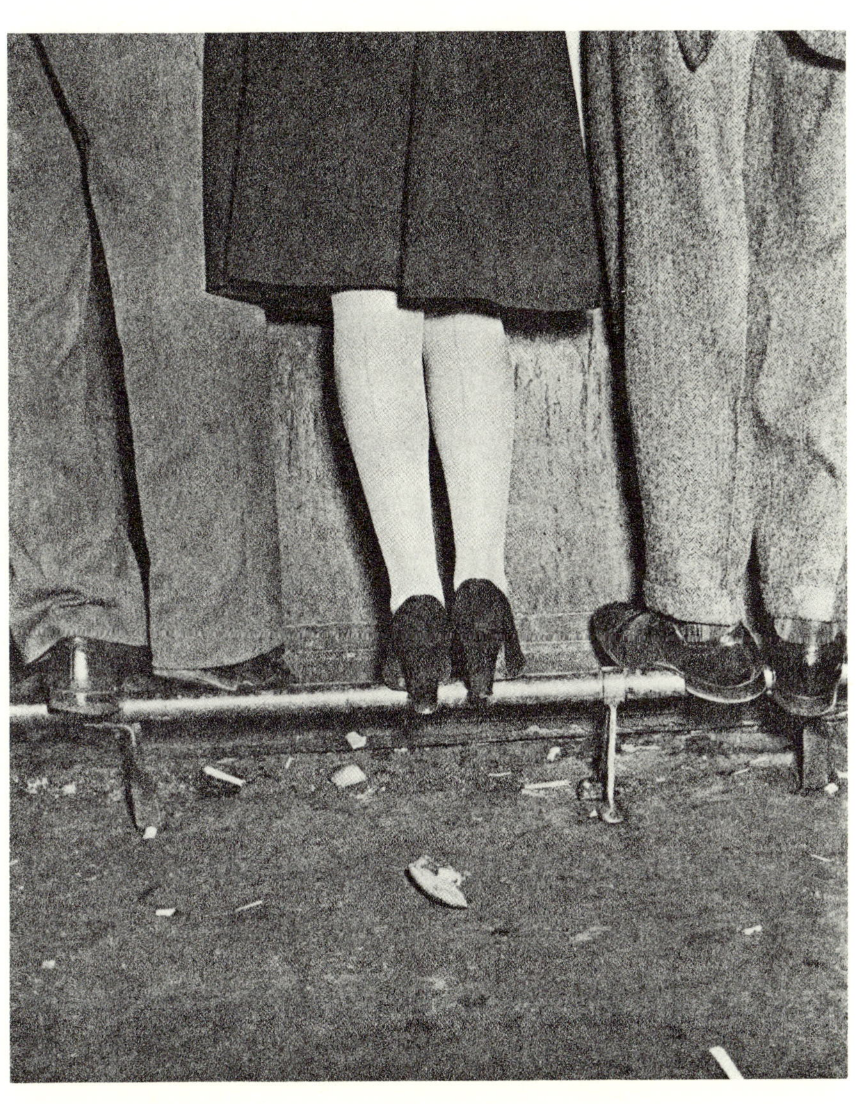

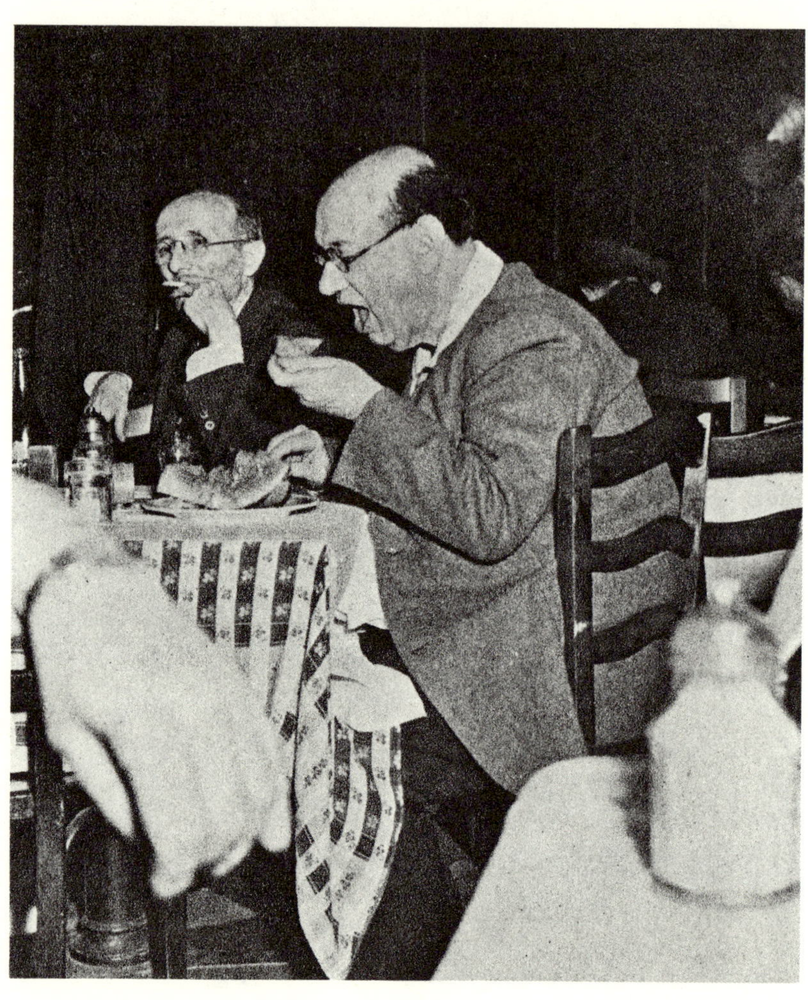

Cafe Royal, meeting place for Yiddish actors on Second Avenue.

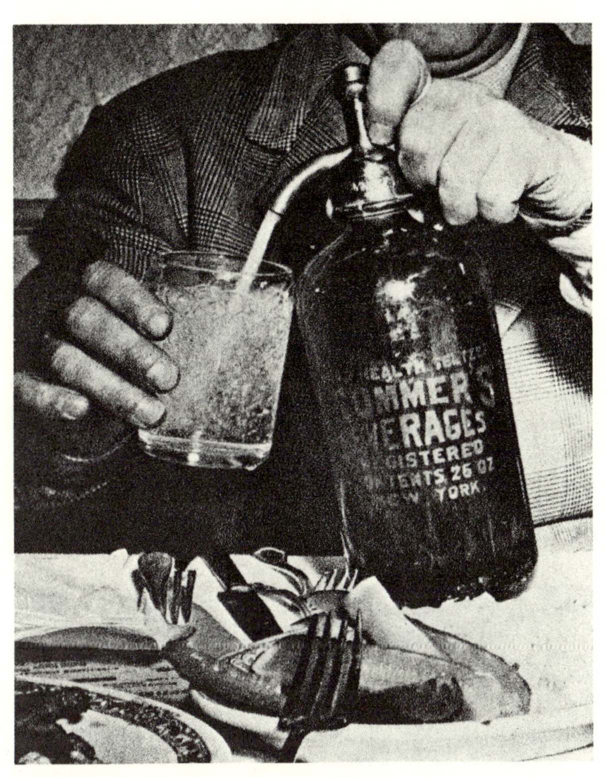
EALTH SELTZ
UMMER'S
VERAGES
GISTERED
NTENTS 26 OZ
EW YORK

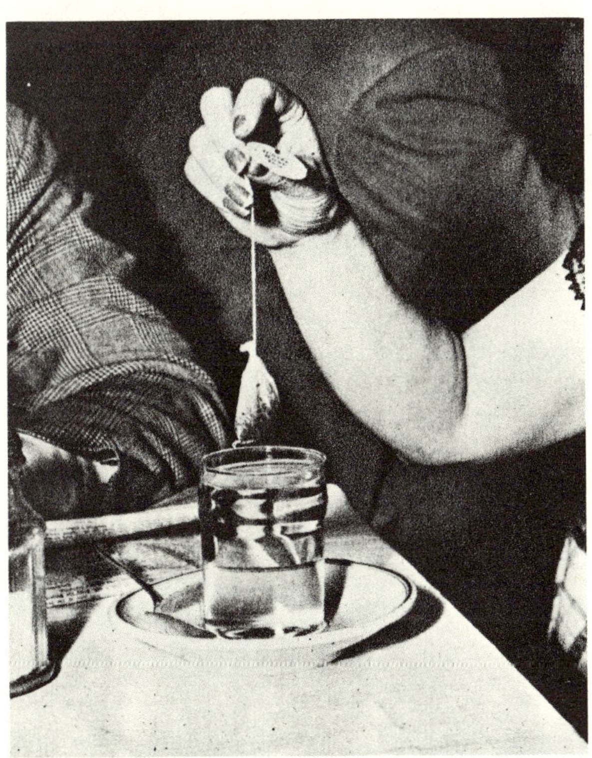

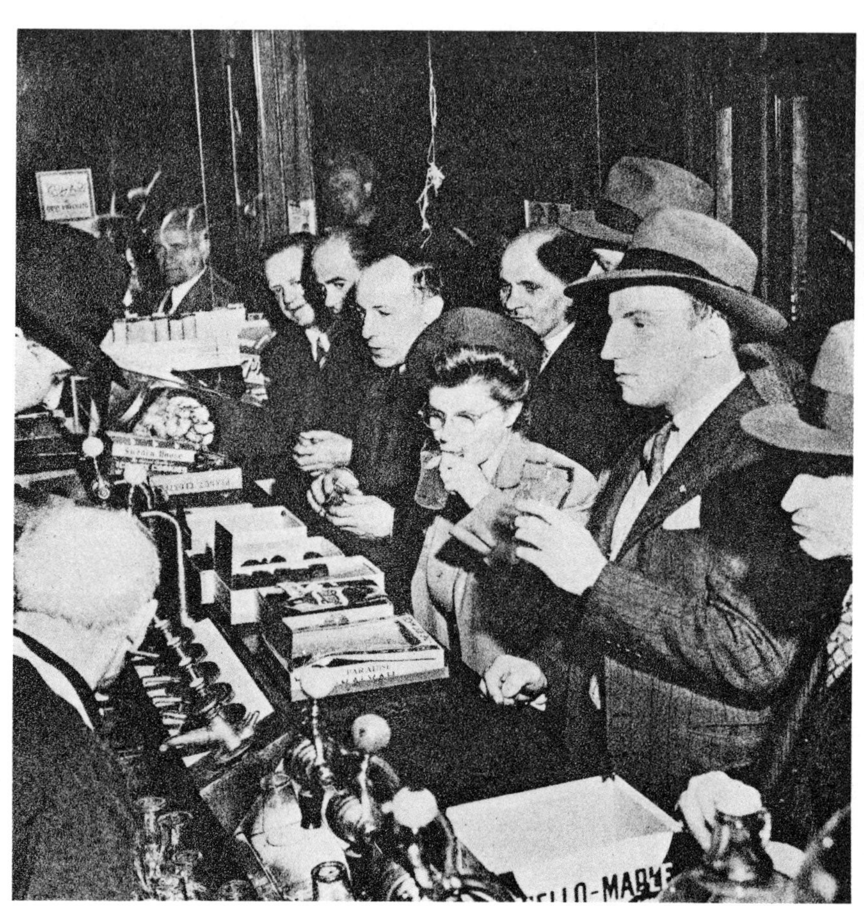

Neighborhood candy store

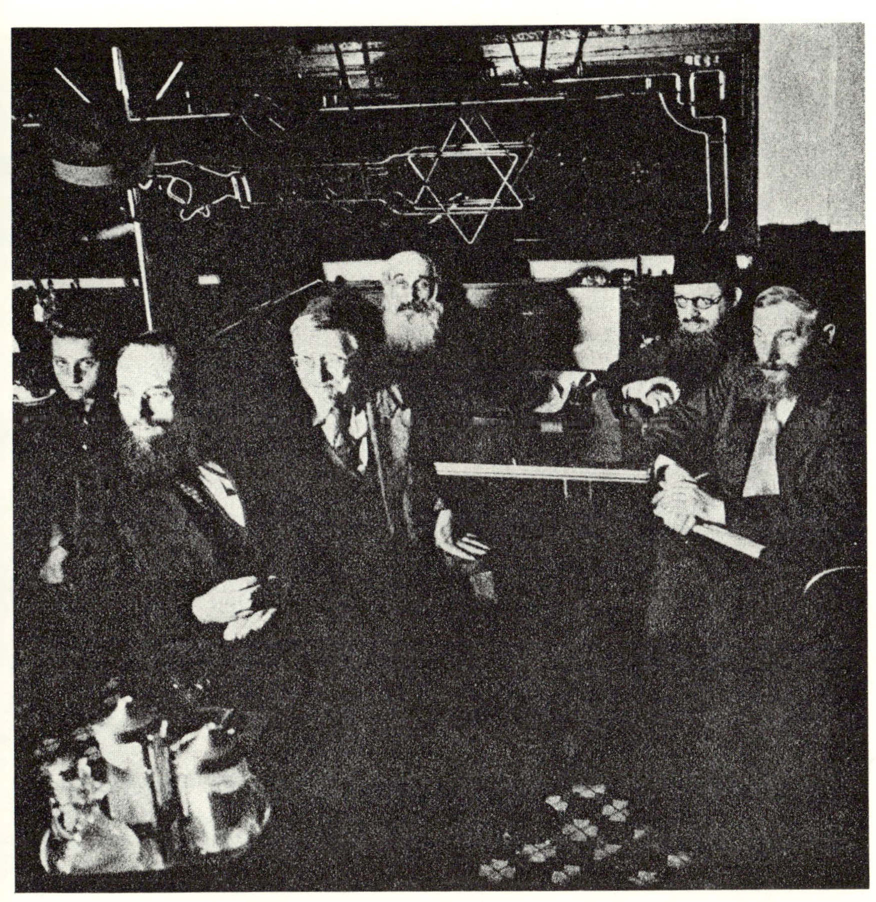

Cafeteria on East Broadway

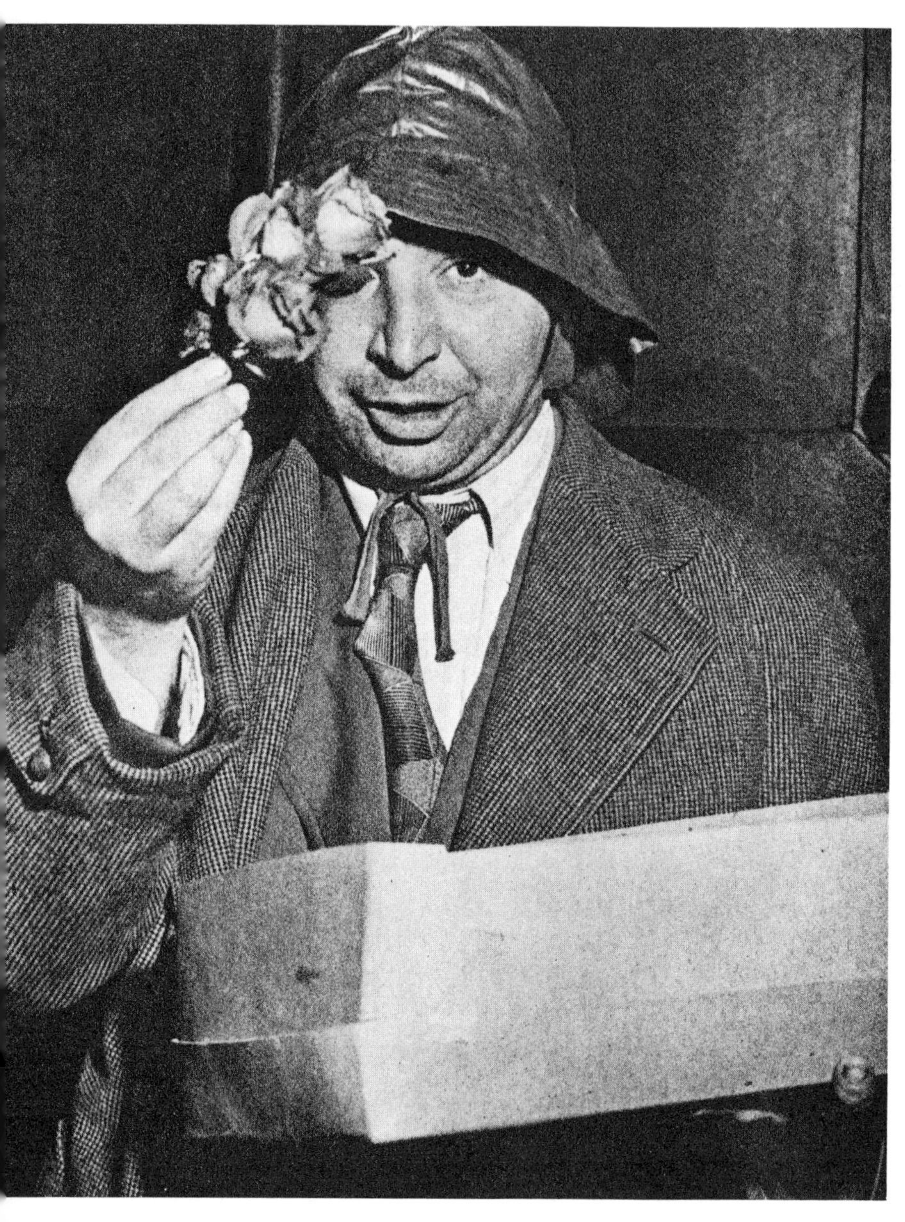

Buy a rose for your honey . . .

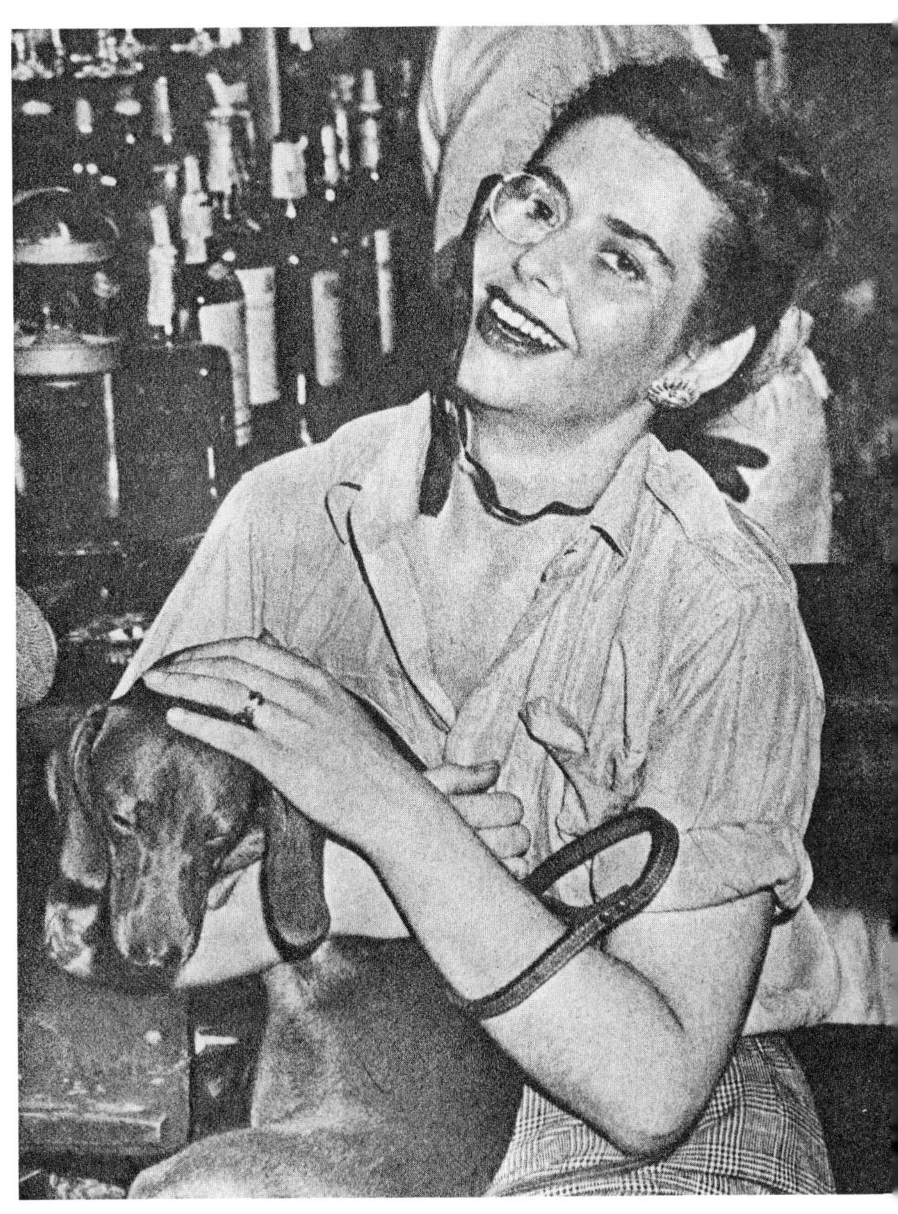

but all that the honeys wanted was Four Roses with a beer chaser. . . .

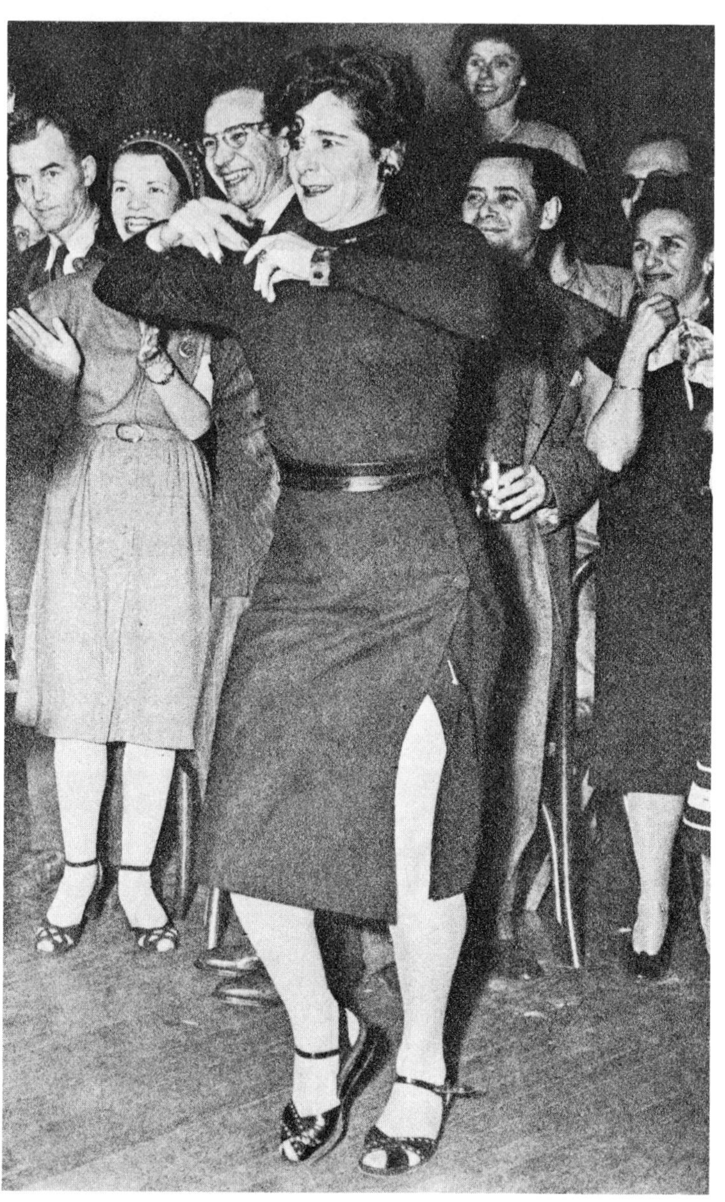

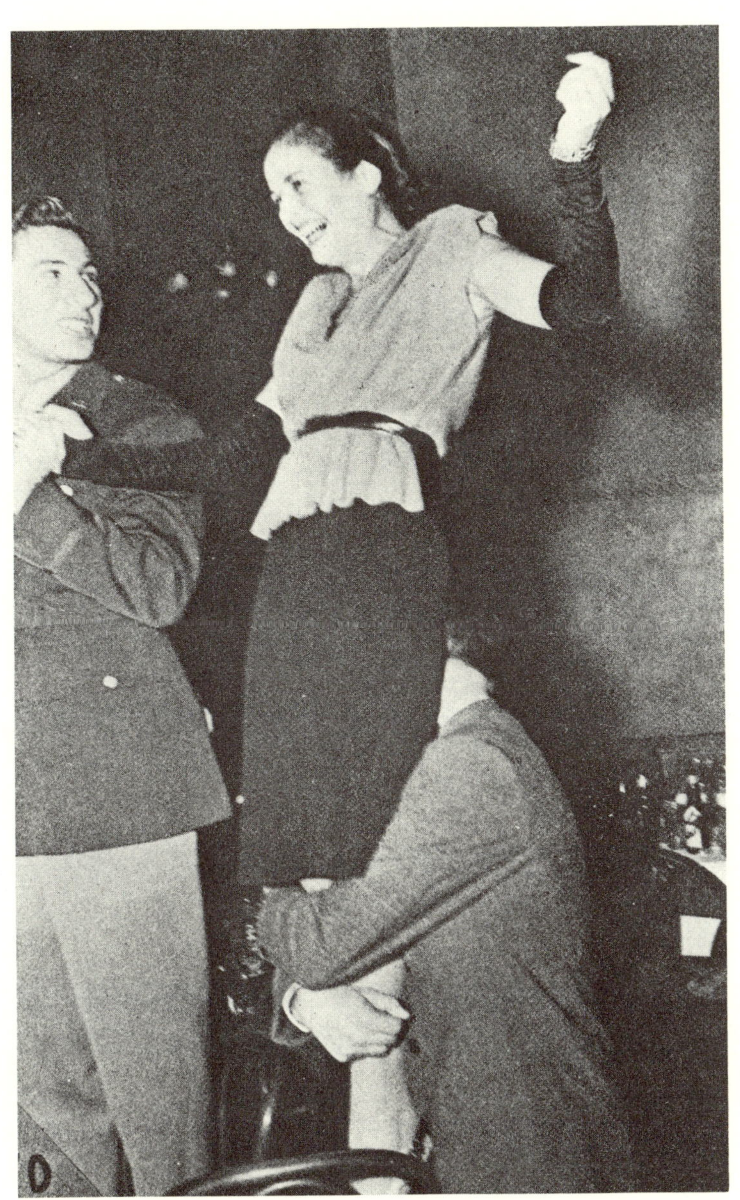

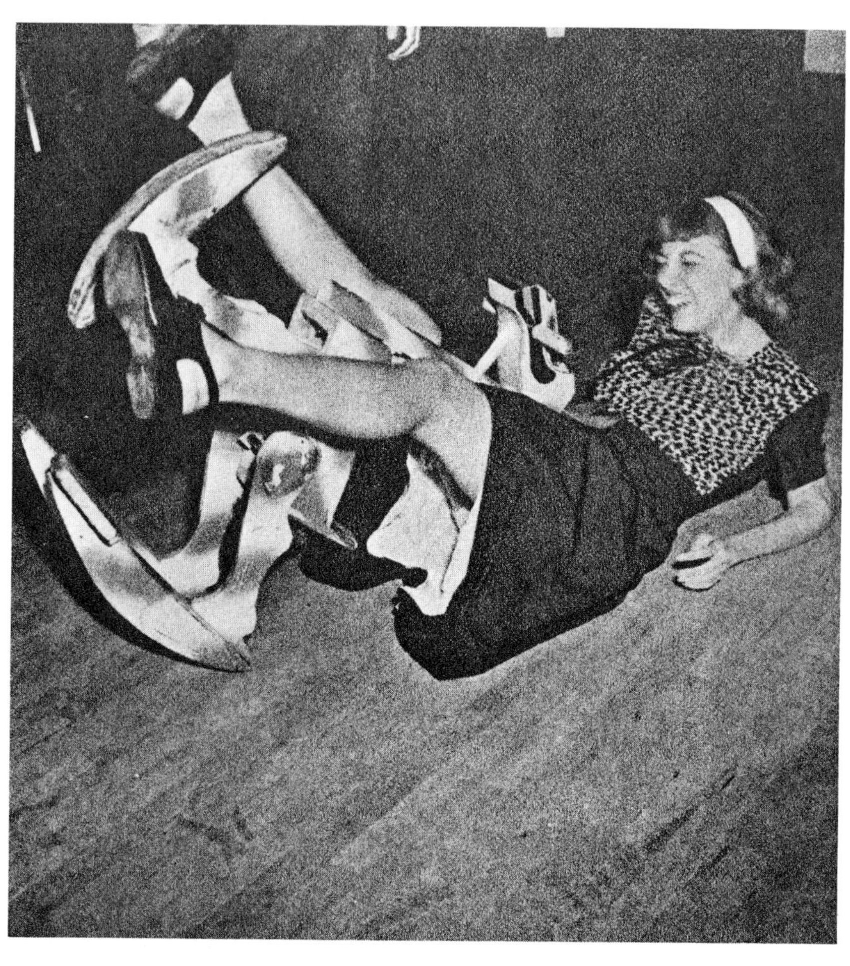

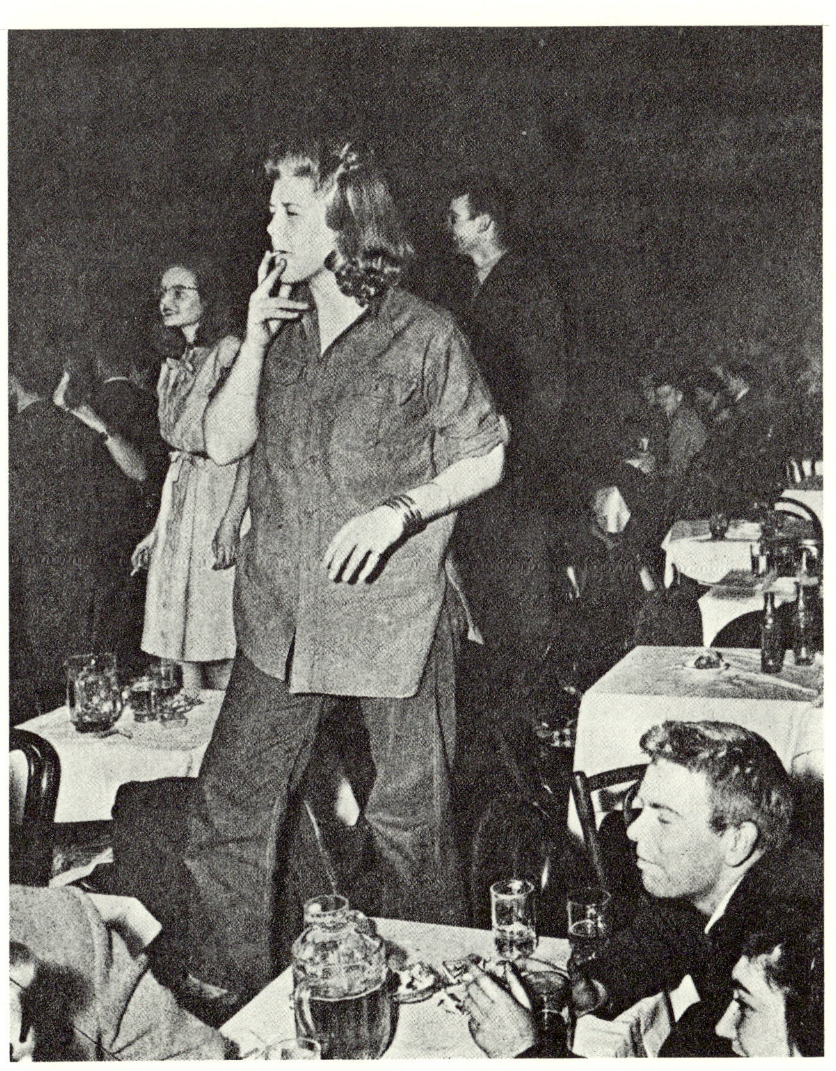

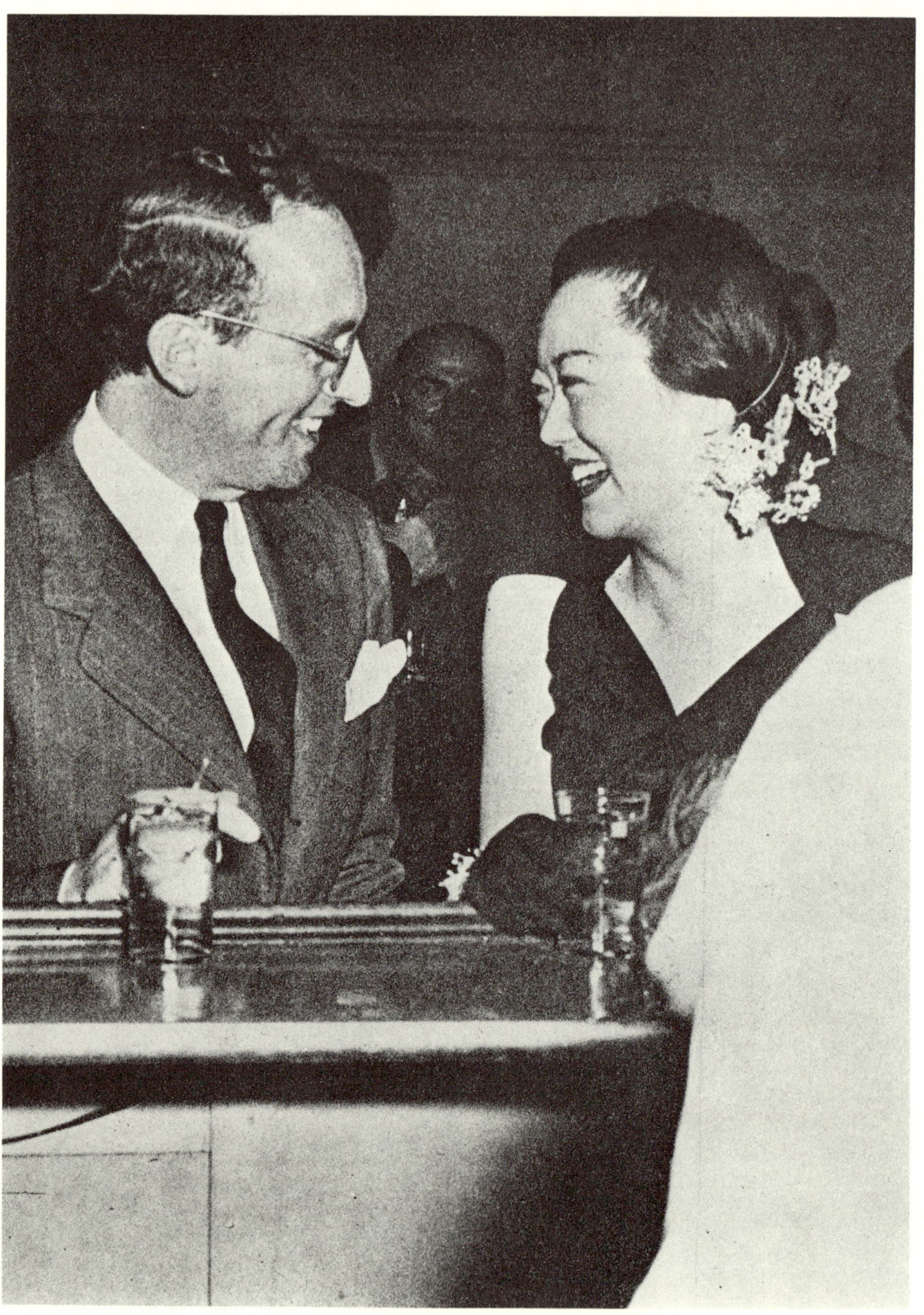

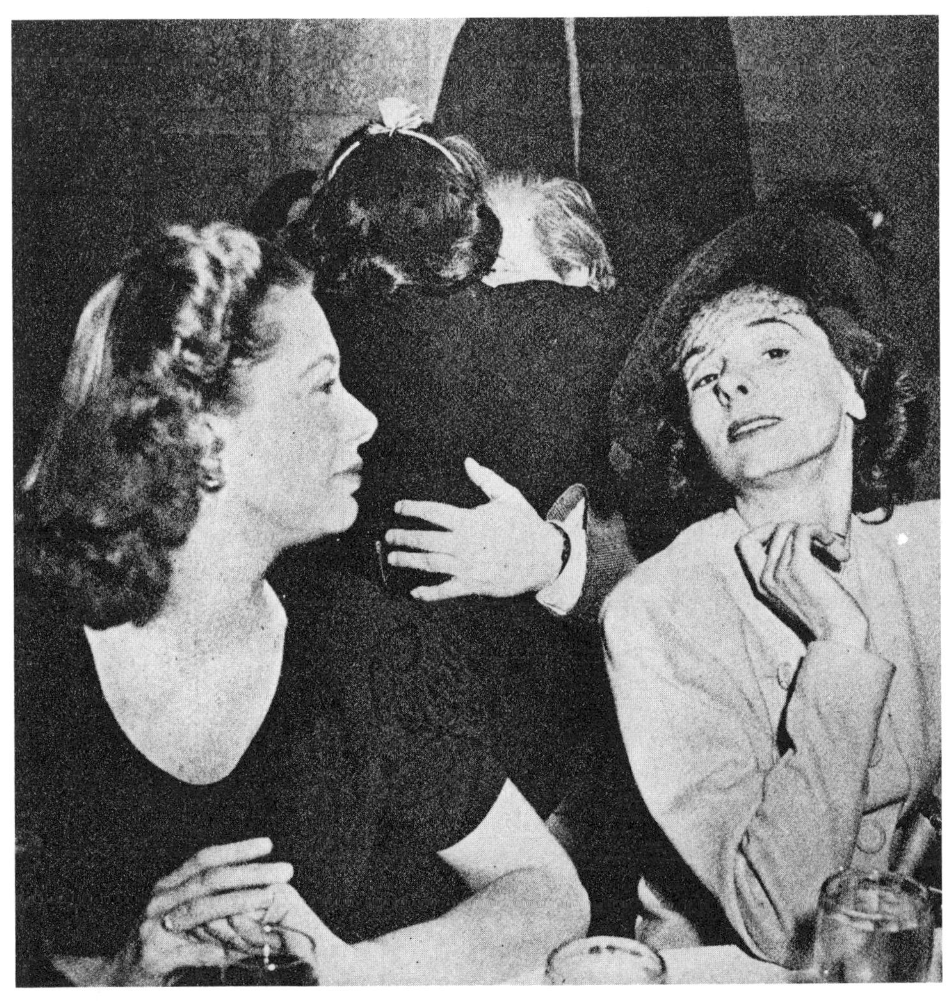

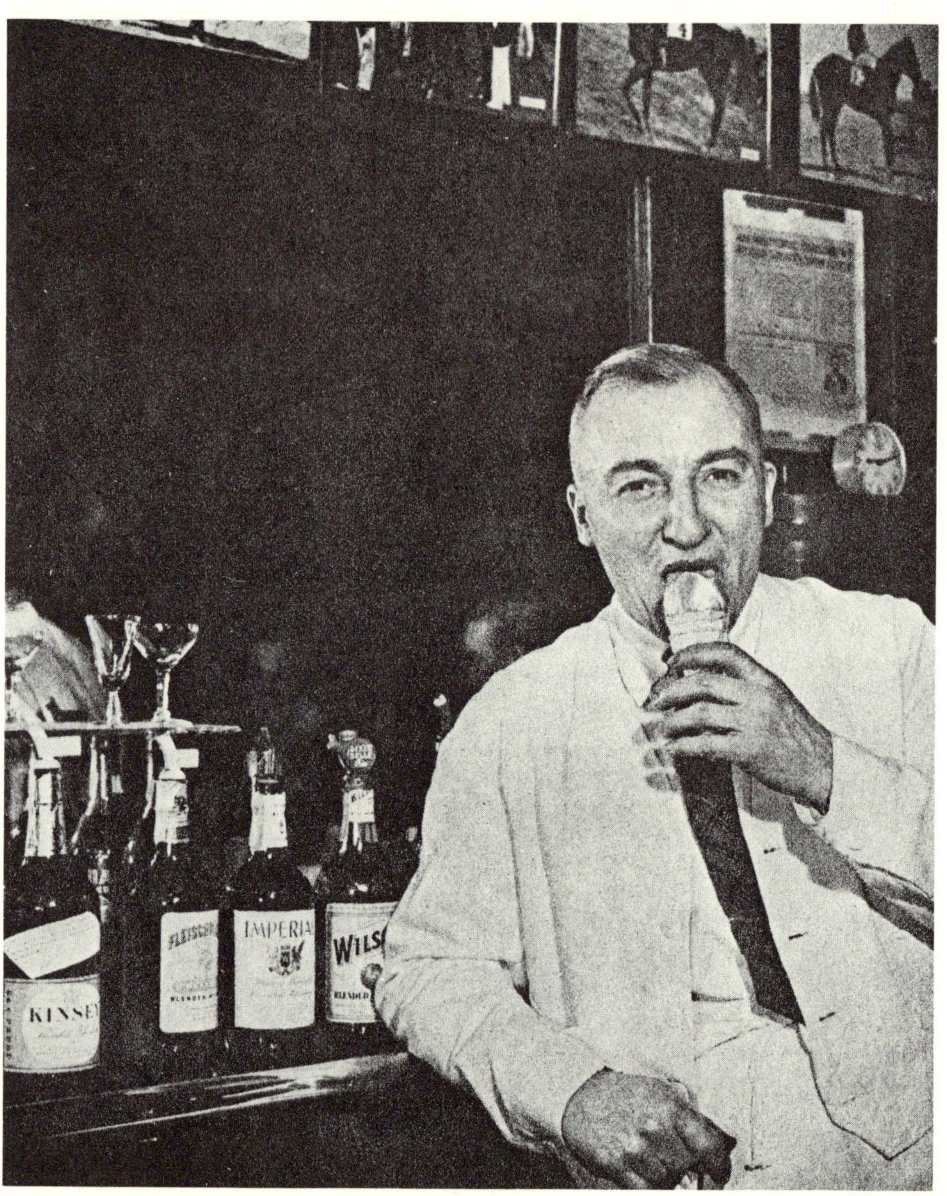

Julius', the oldest bar in the Village at Tenth Street and Waverly Place, rendezvous of artists and writers. . . . Even the musicians from Nick's across the way drop in here for a fast one. . . . Joe, the bartender, answers your phone calls, solves life's complicated problems, and even cashes your checks . . . provided they are OK'd by Packy, the manager.

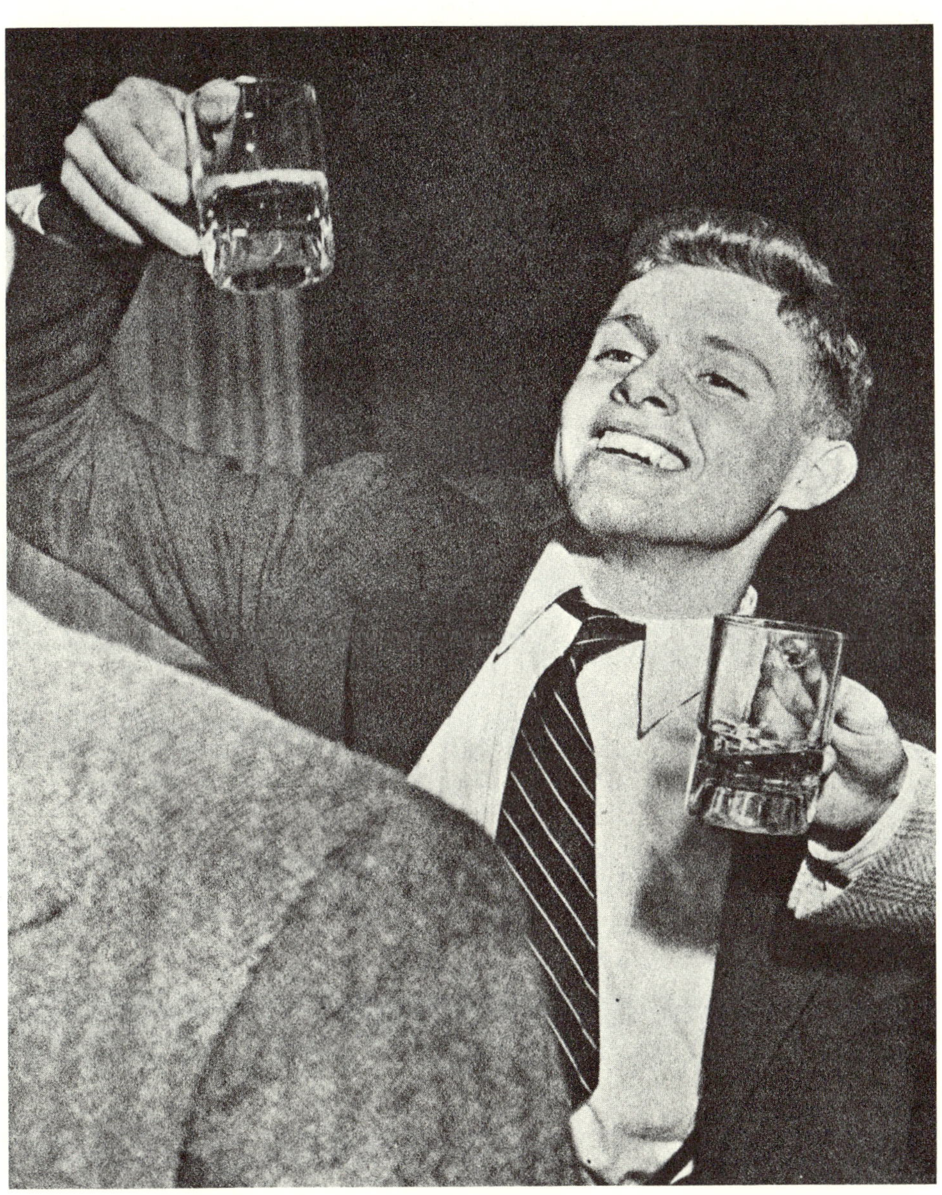

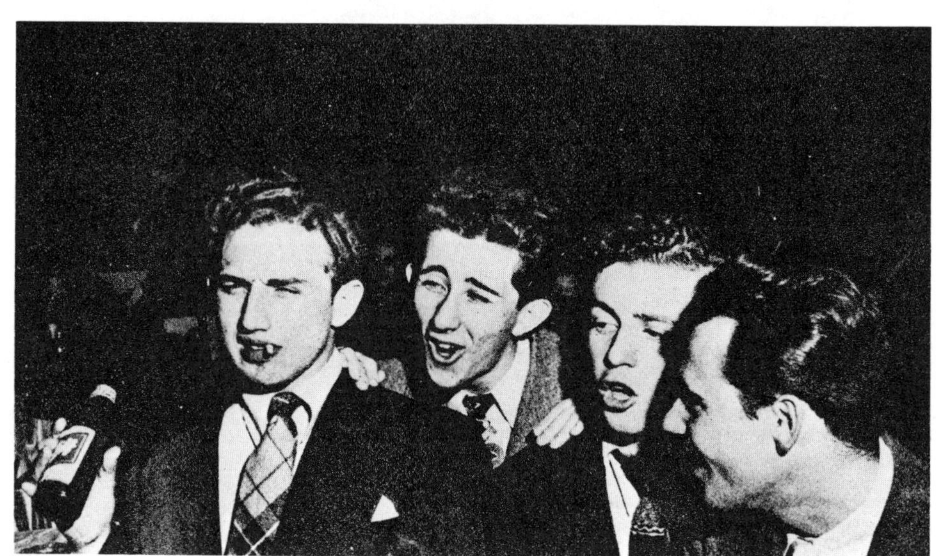

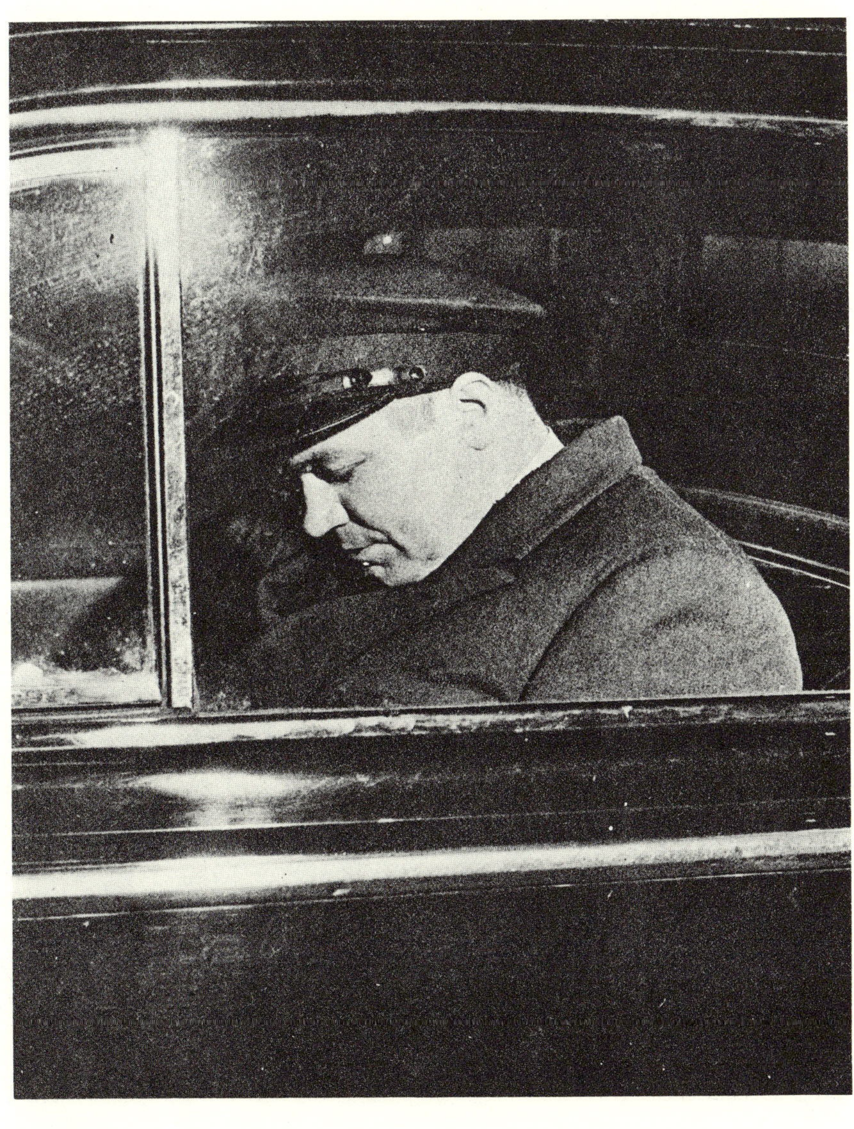

Here's Bunk Johnson again . . . after a busy Saturday night. . . .

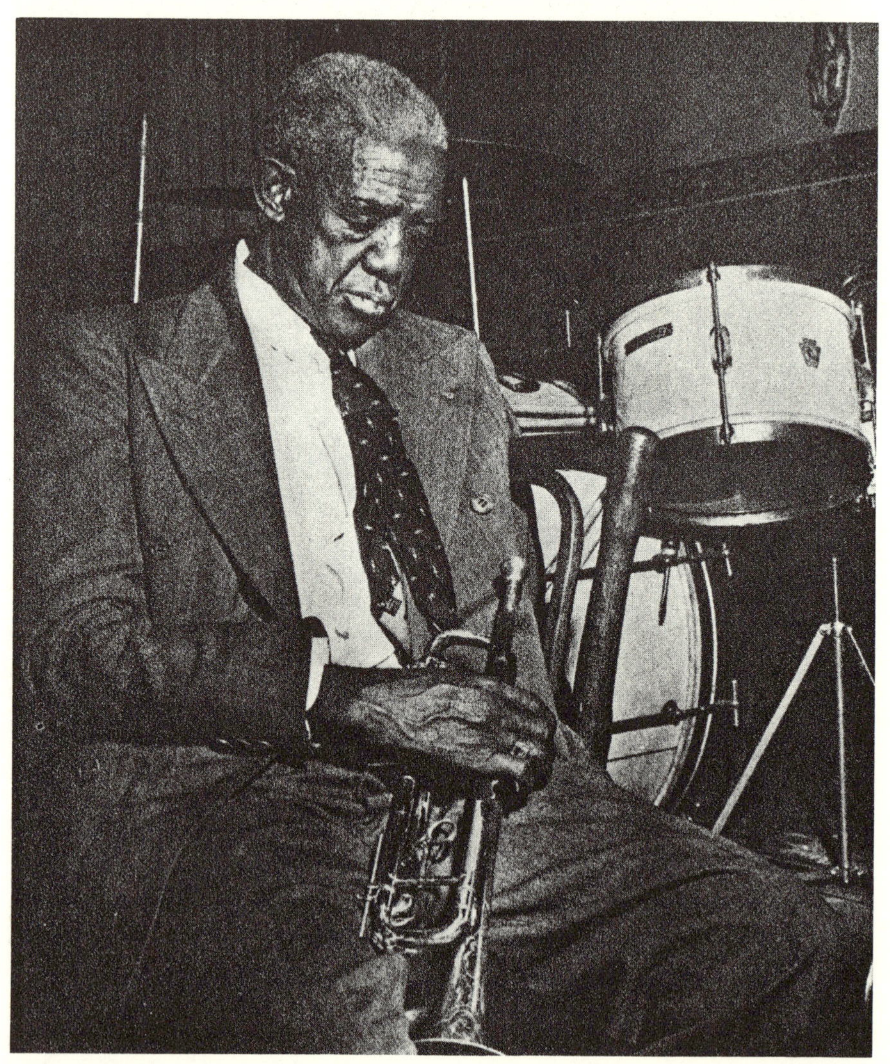

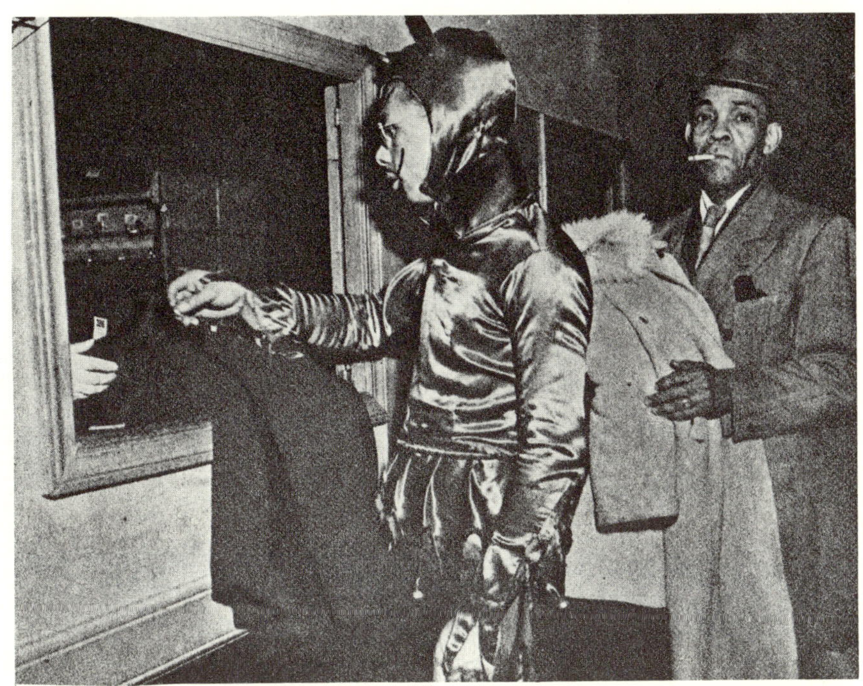

Masquerade

Competition was keen for the first prize winner

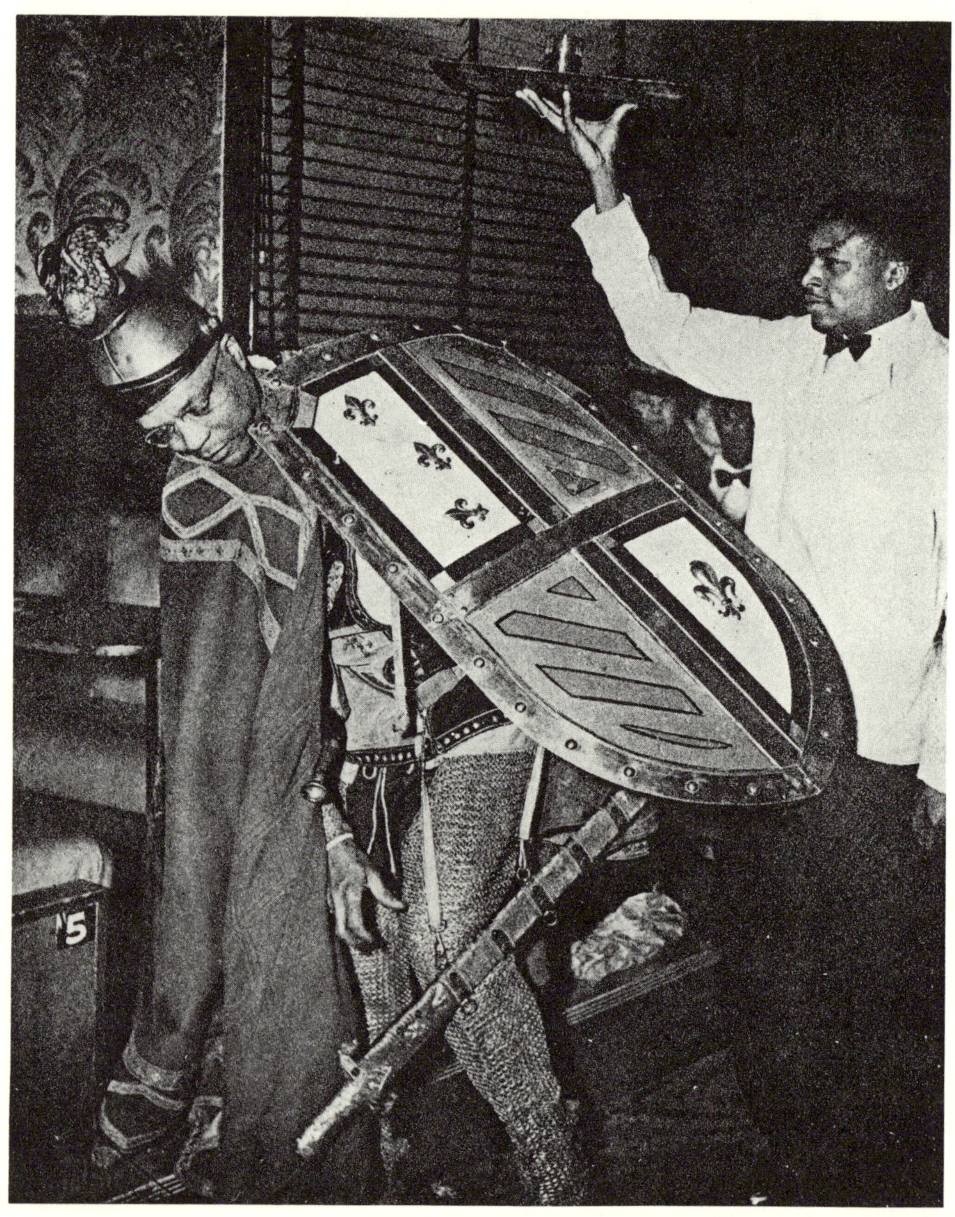

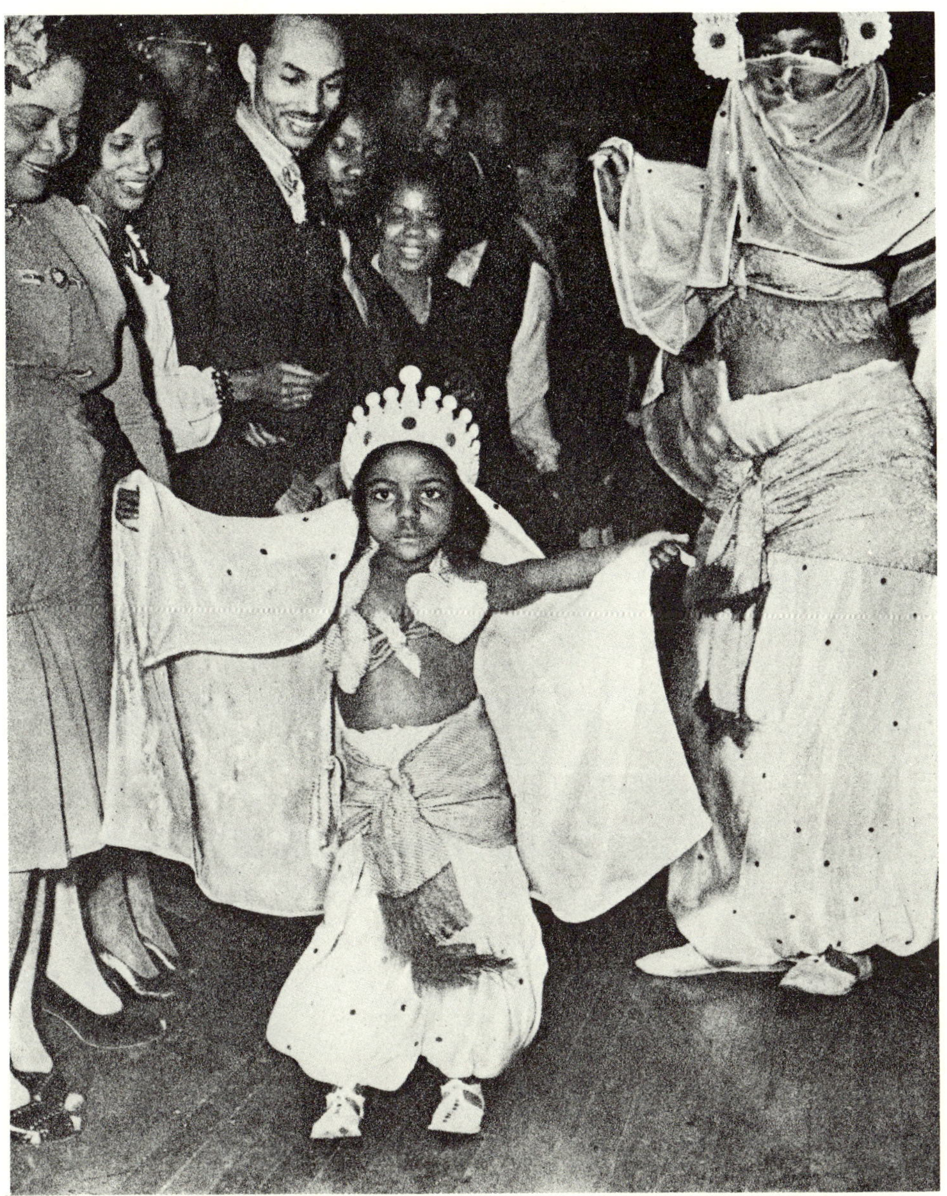

Prize

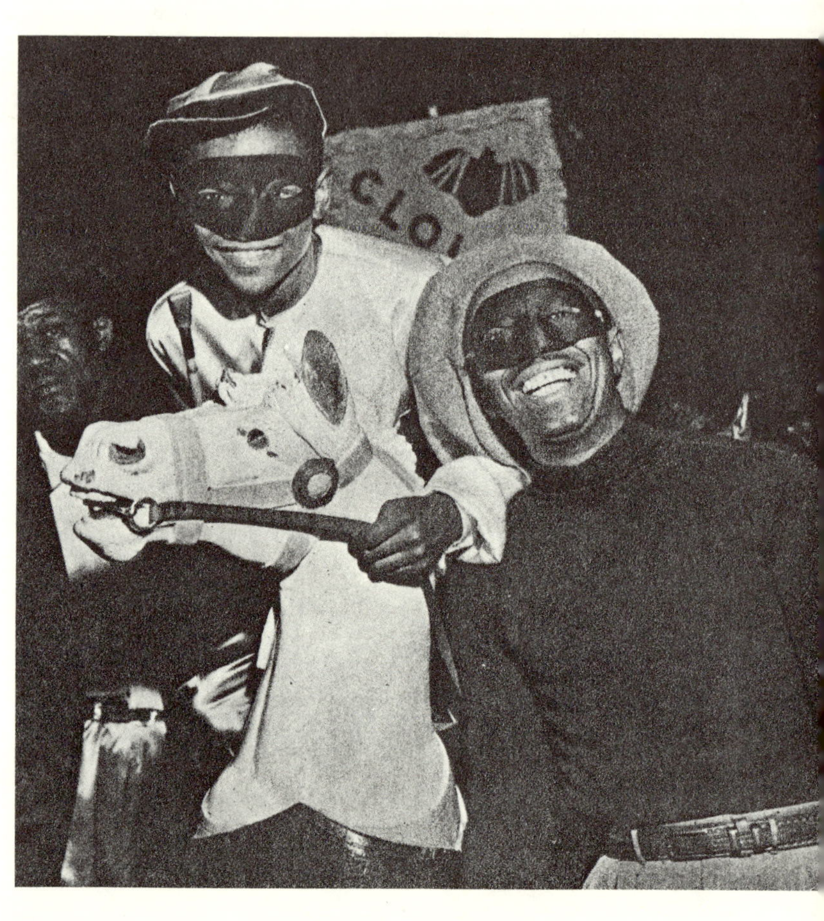

CLO

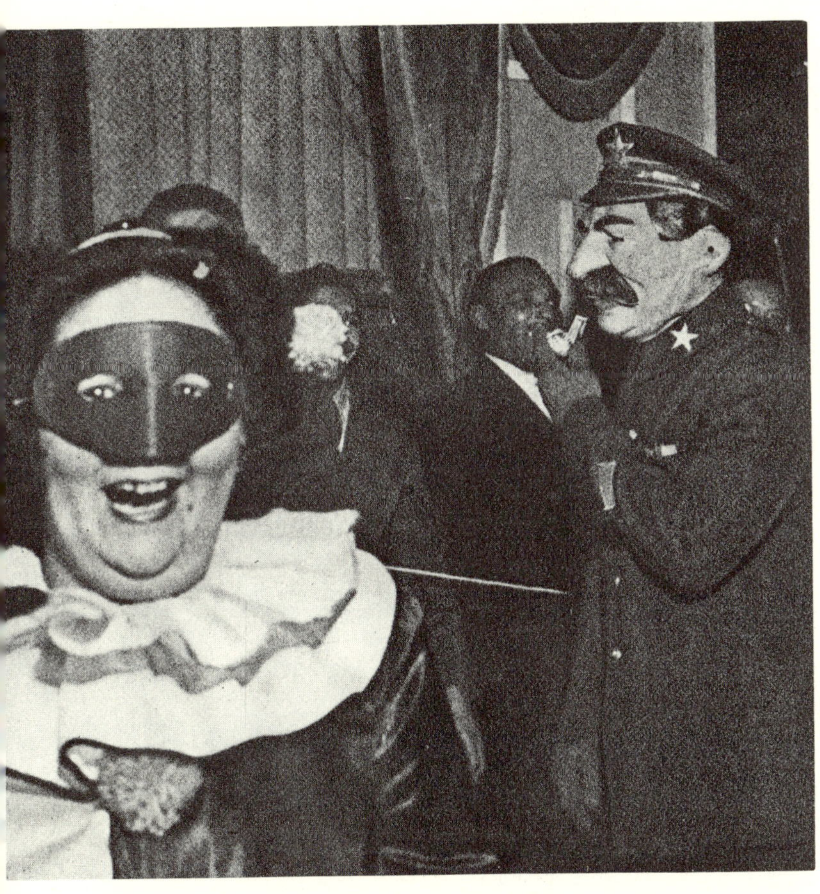

Uncle Joe

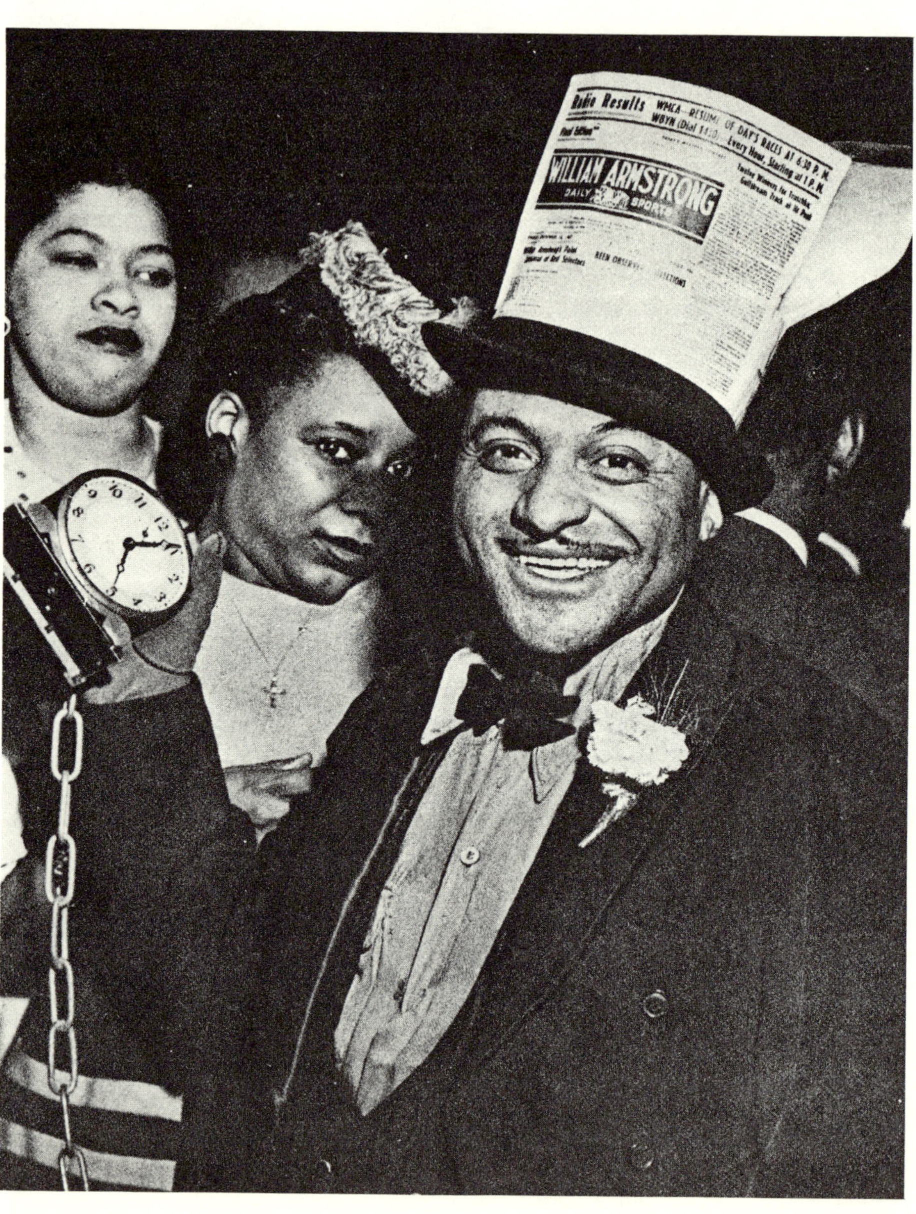

Radio Results   WMCA—RESUME OF DAY'S RACES AT 6:30 P. M.
WBYN (Dial 1430)   Every Hour, Starting at 1 P. M.
WILLIAM ARMSTRONG
DAILY SPORTS

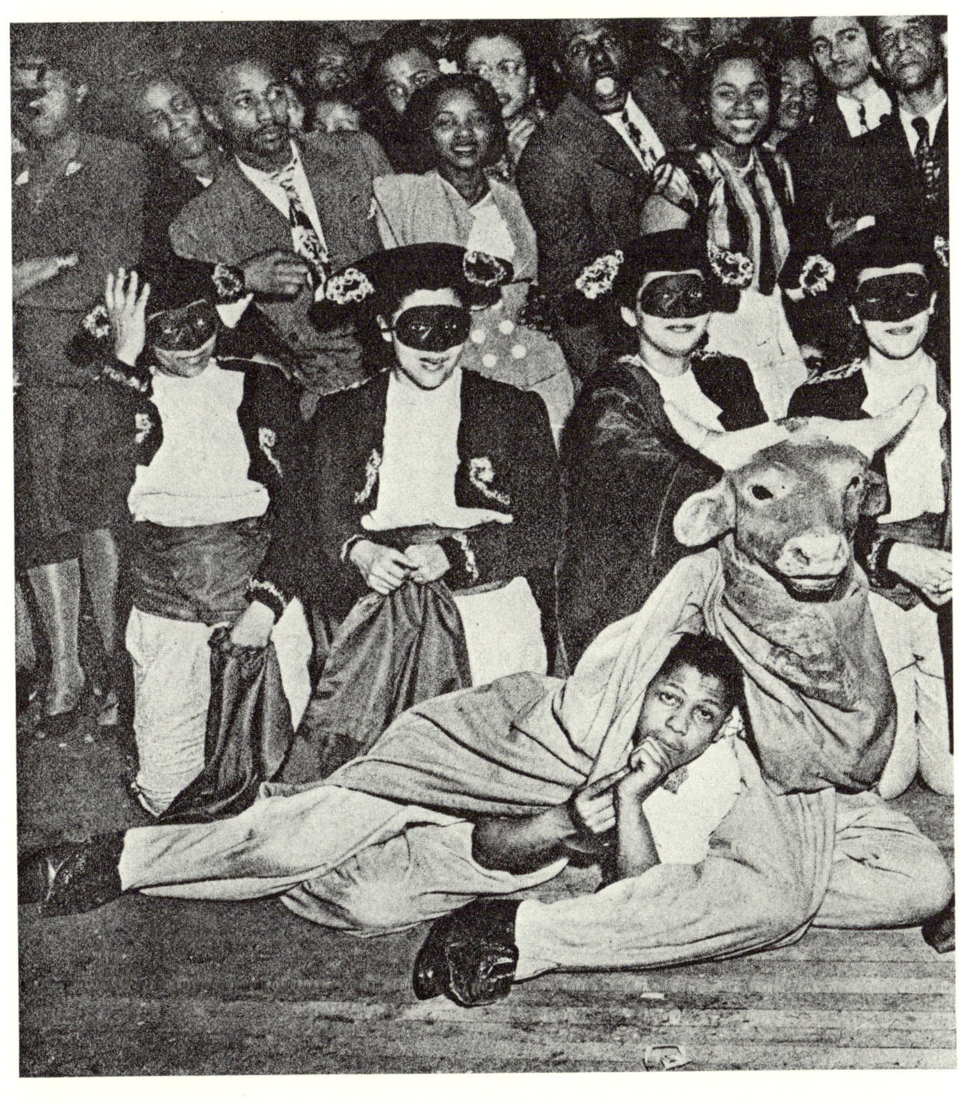

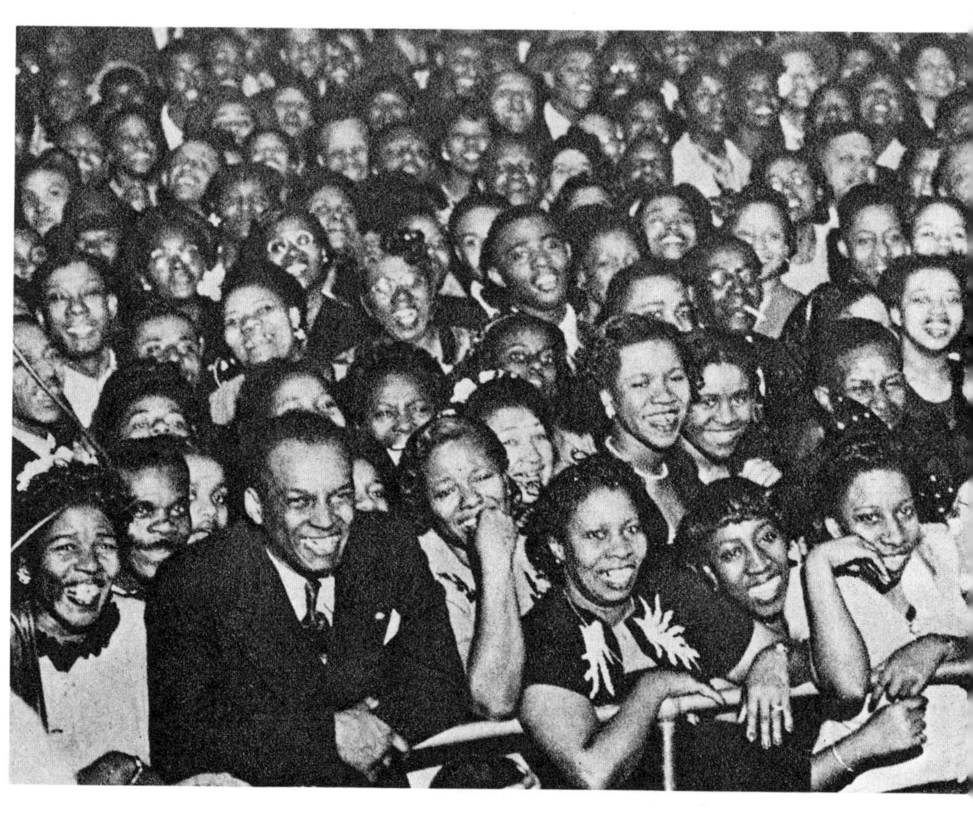

Calypso

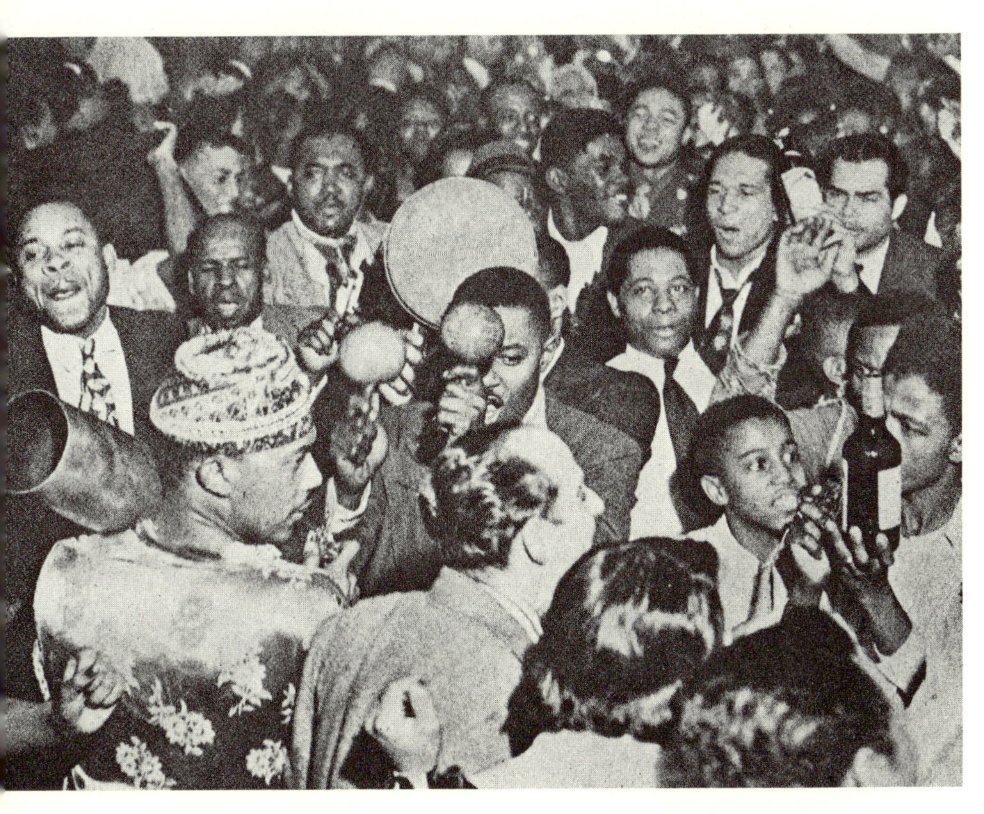

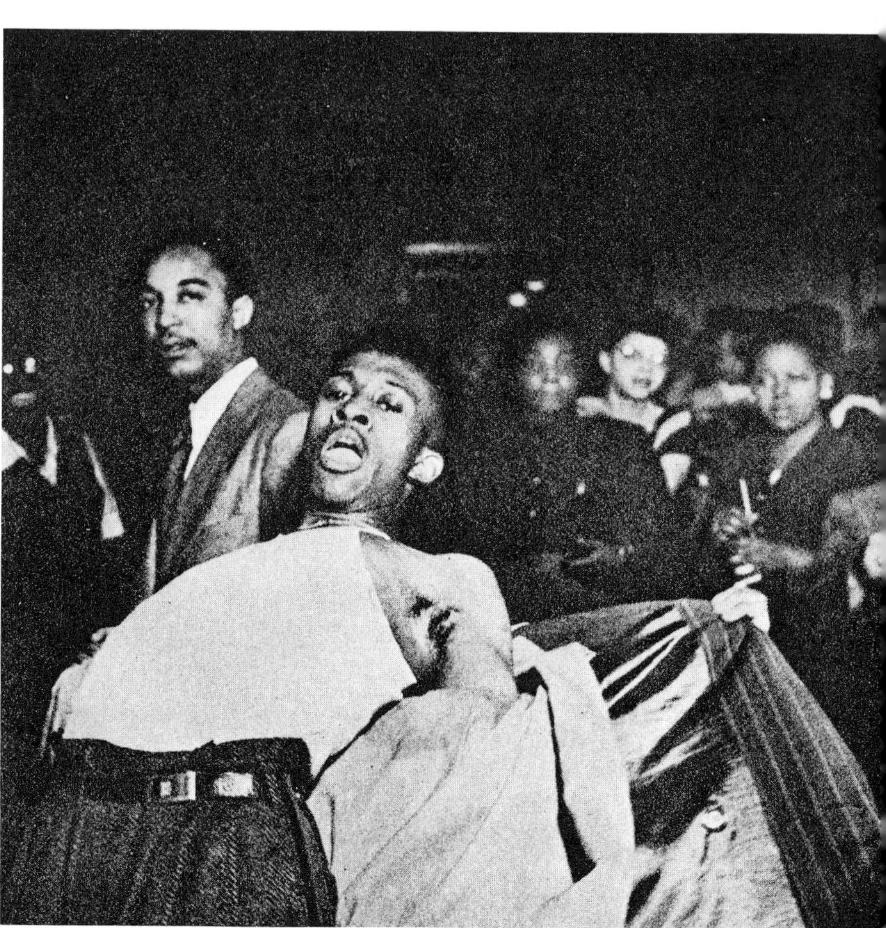

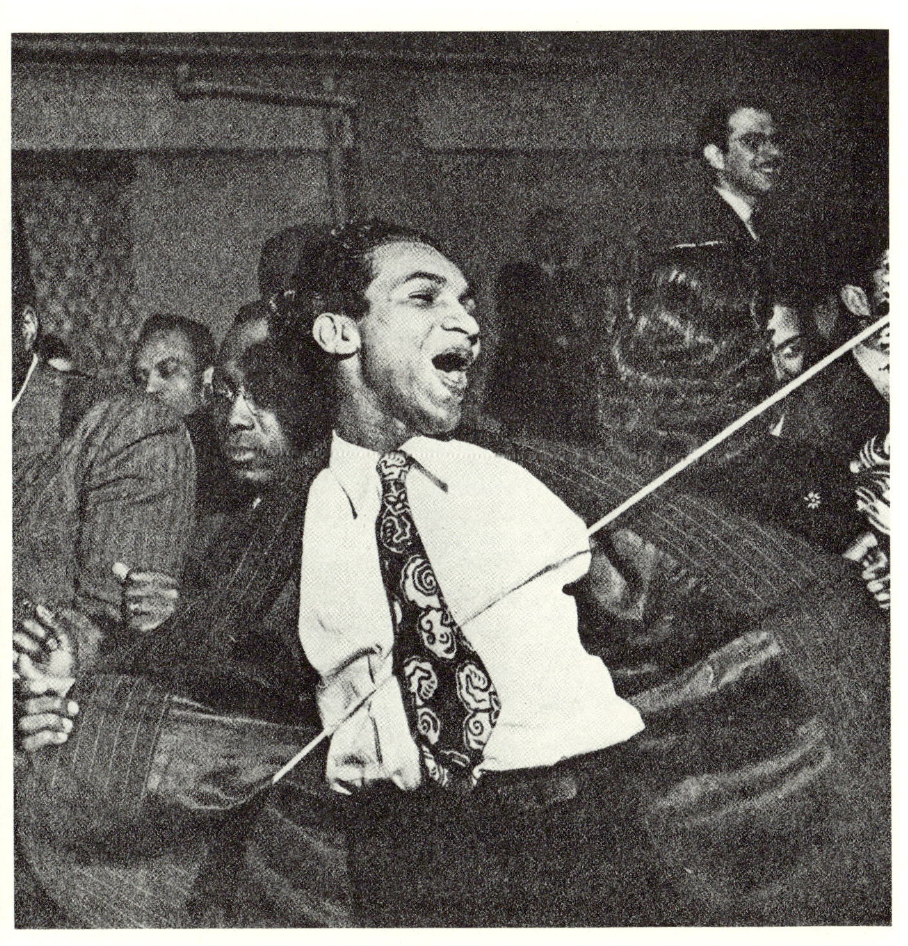

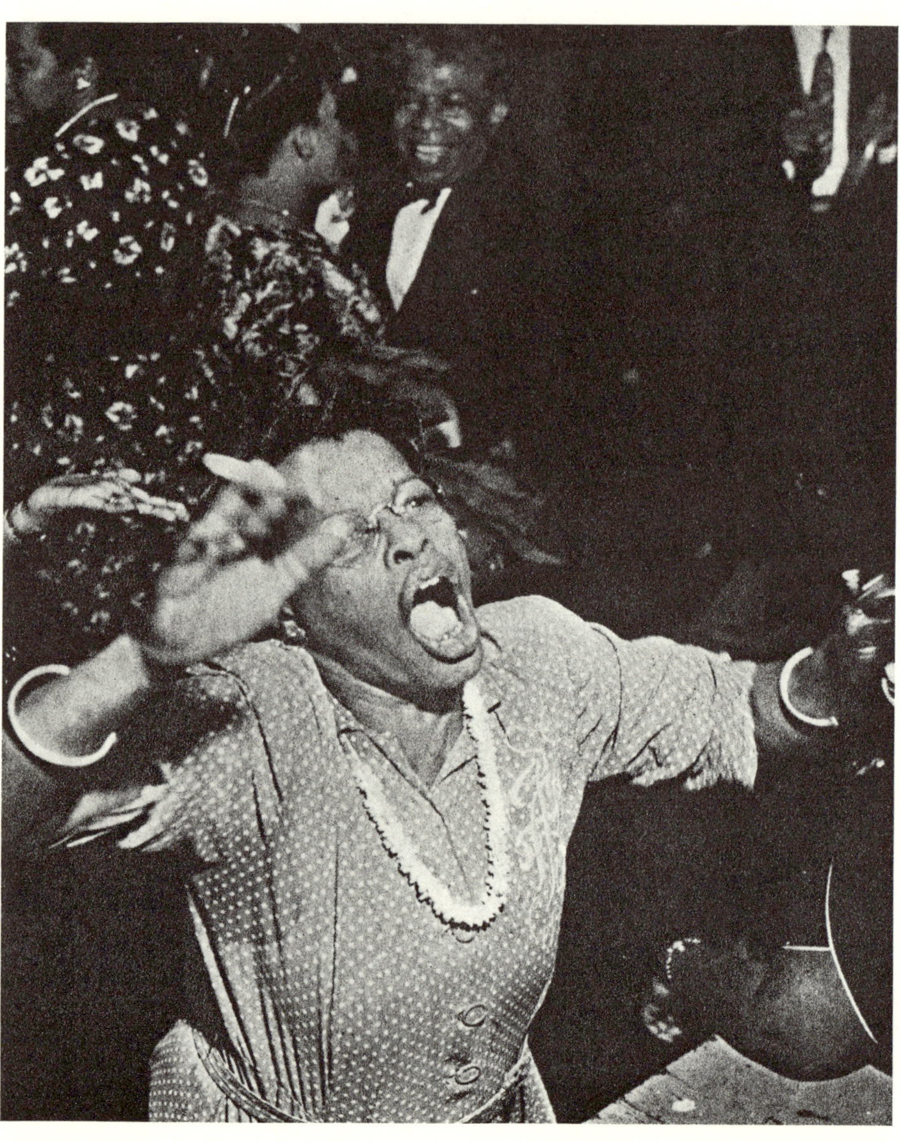

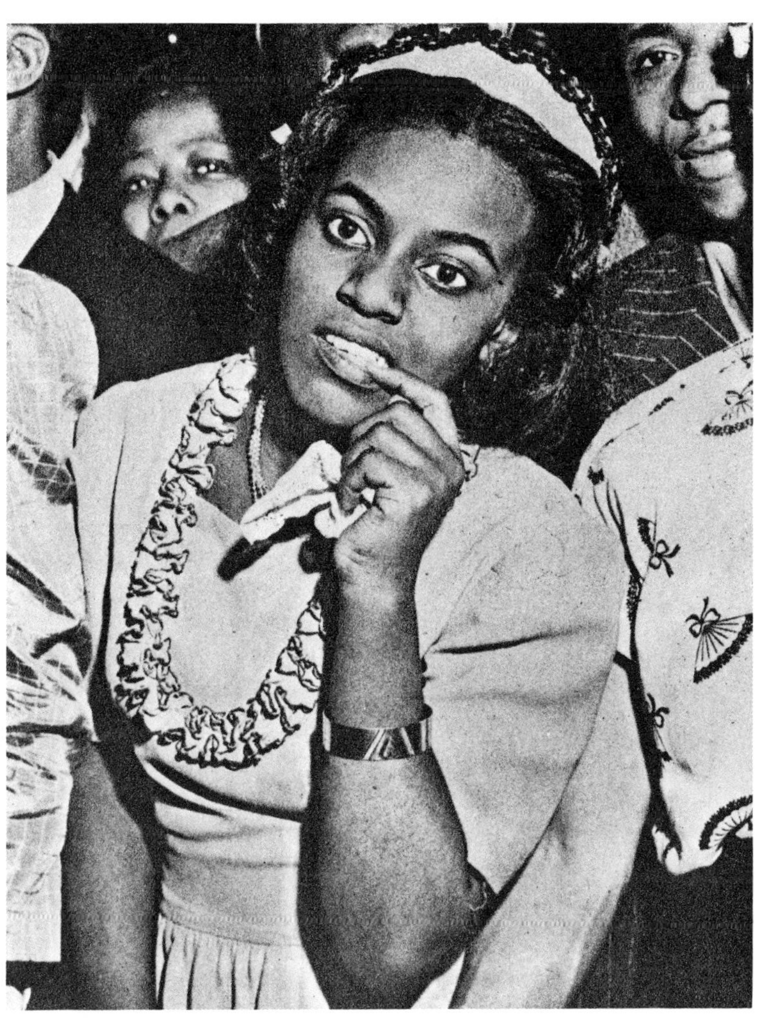

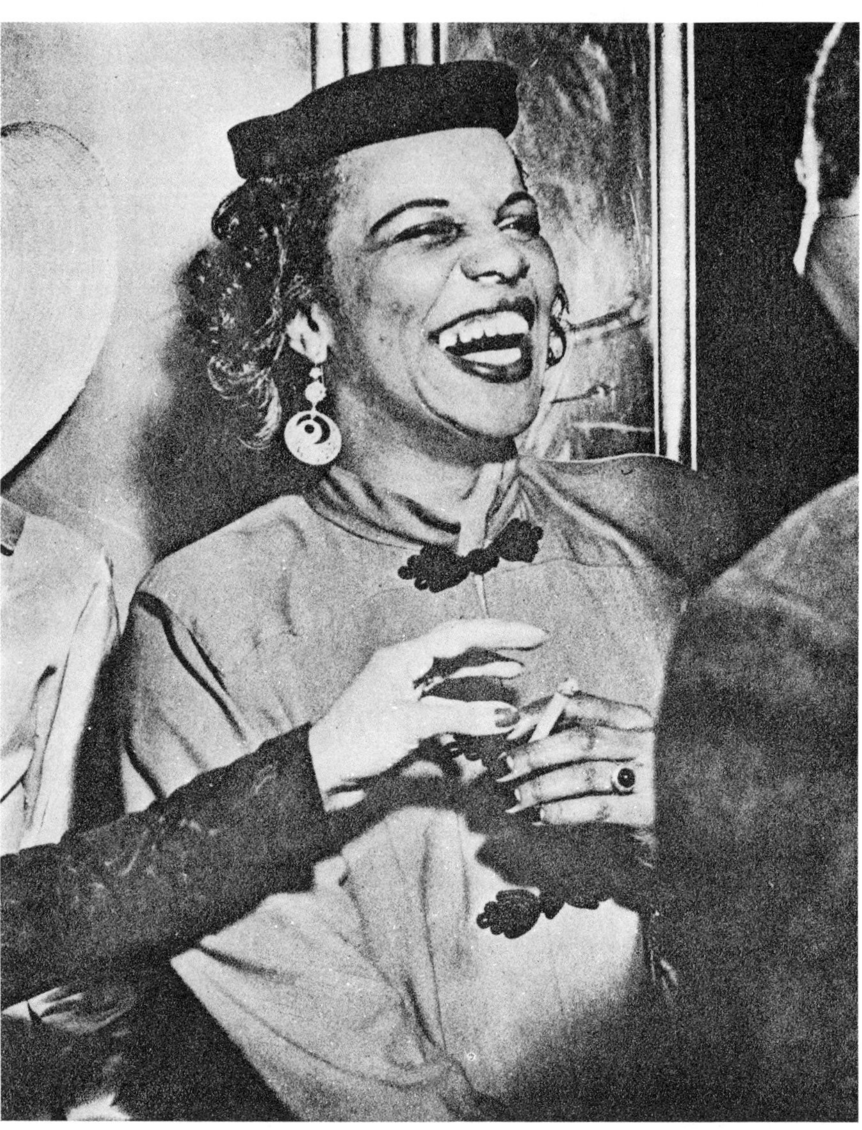

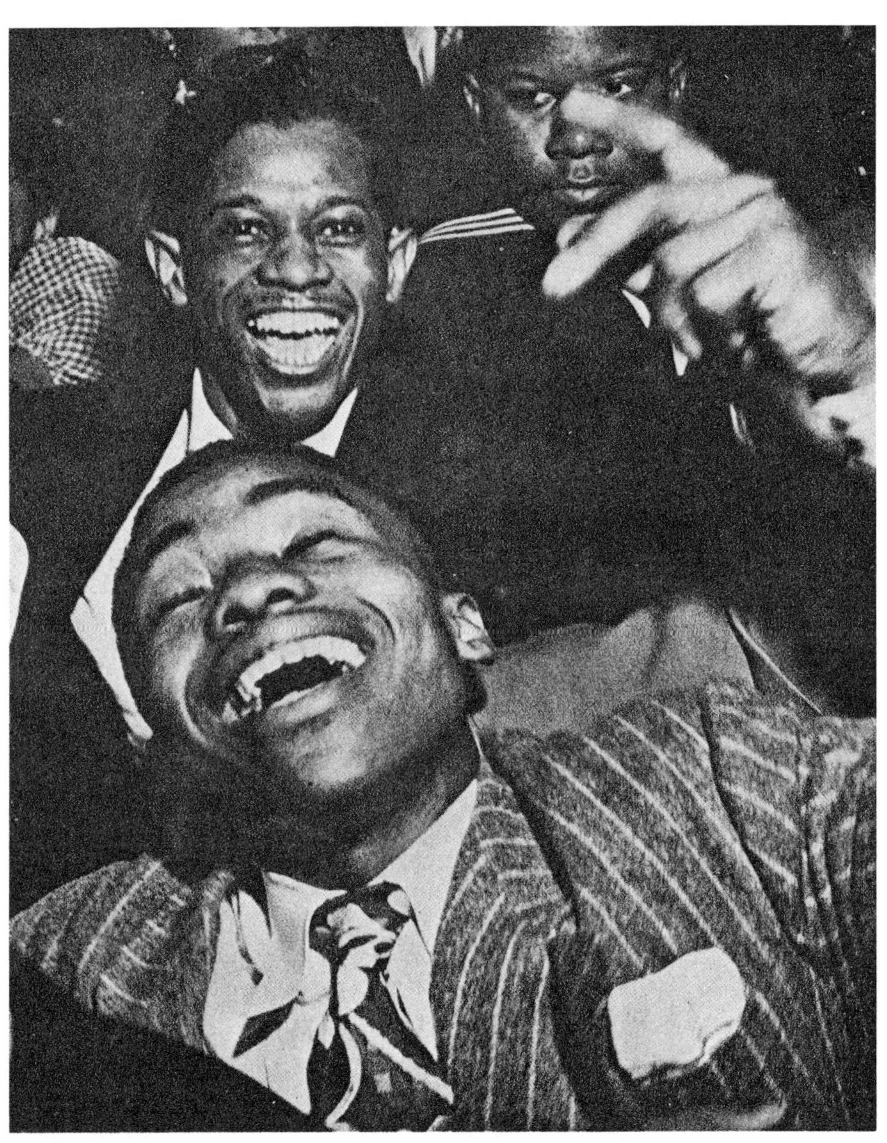

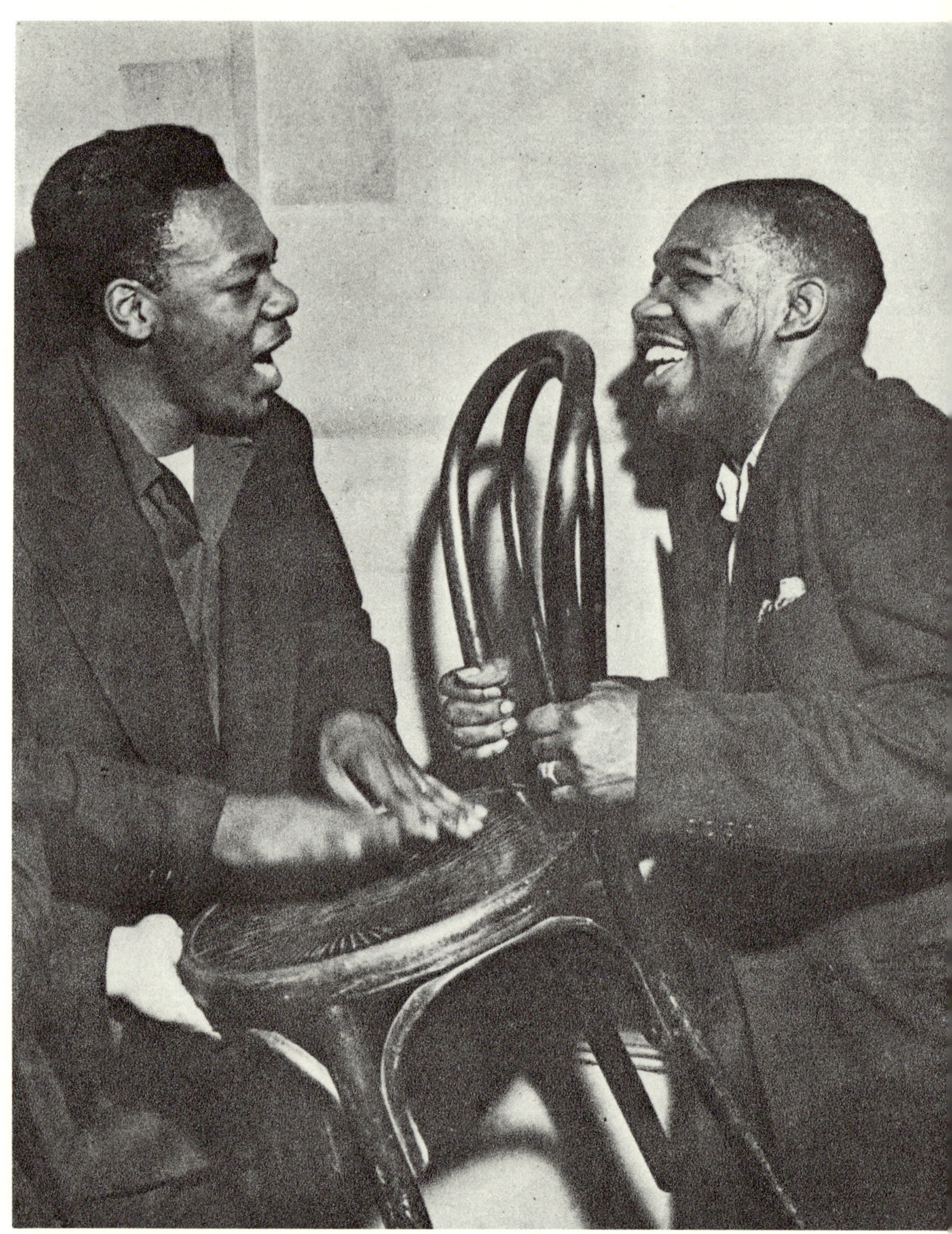

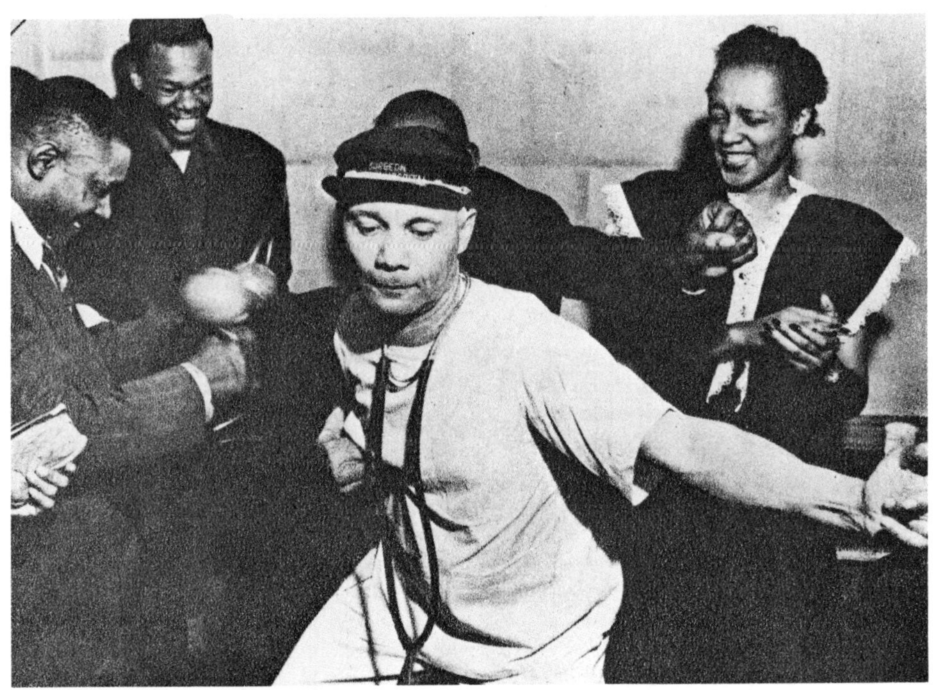

Surgeon "cutting up" on the dance floor

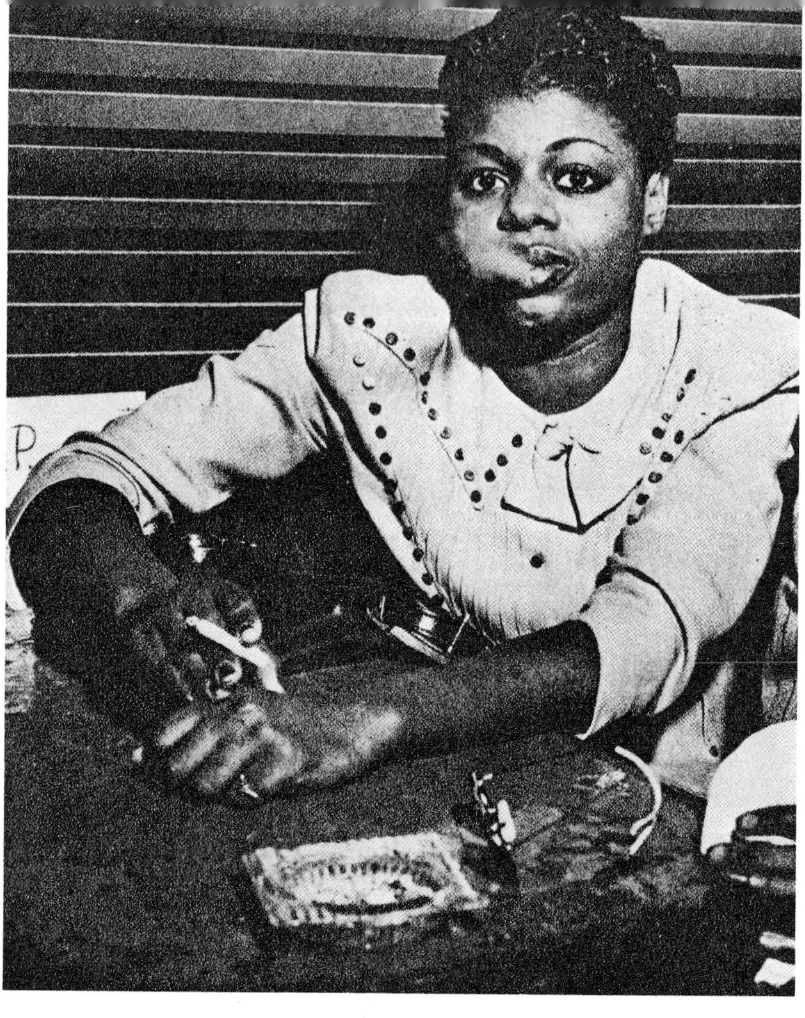

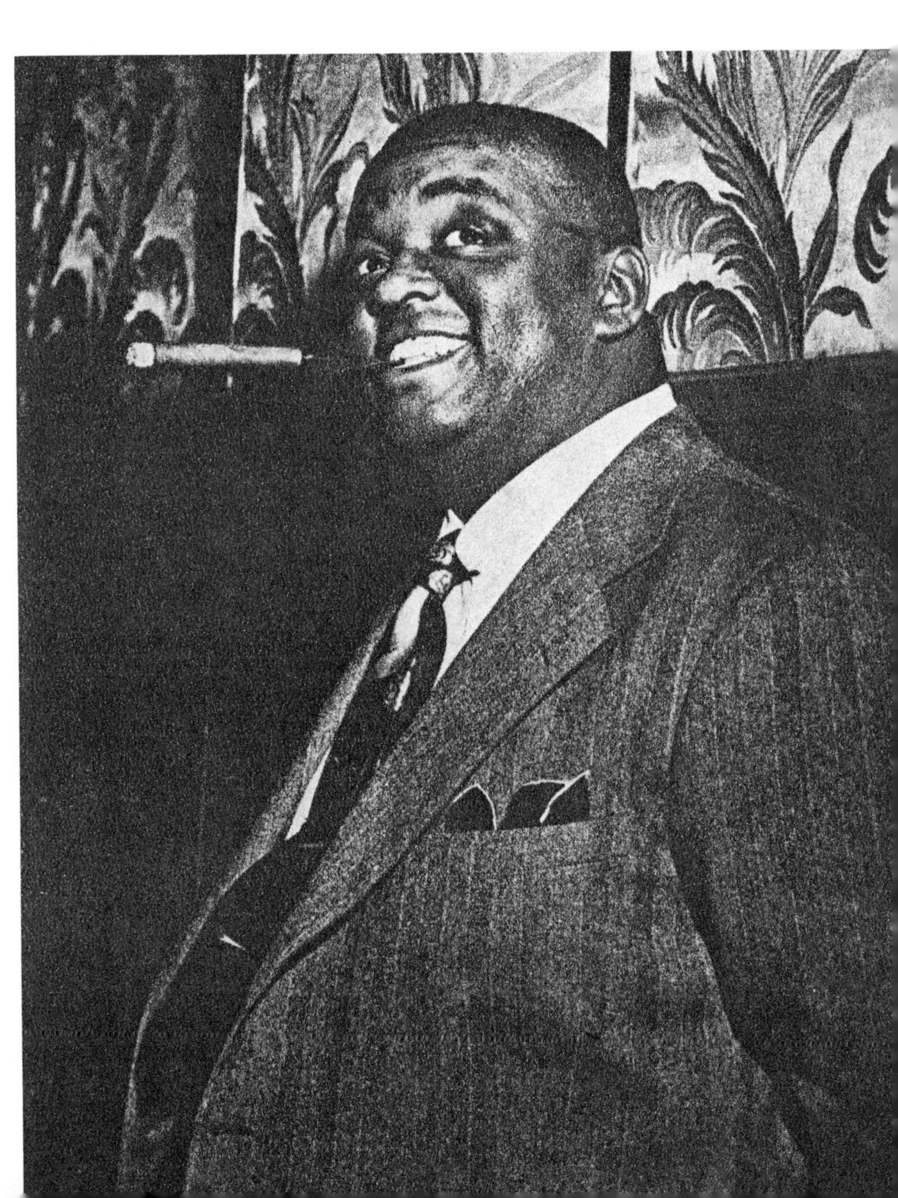

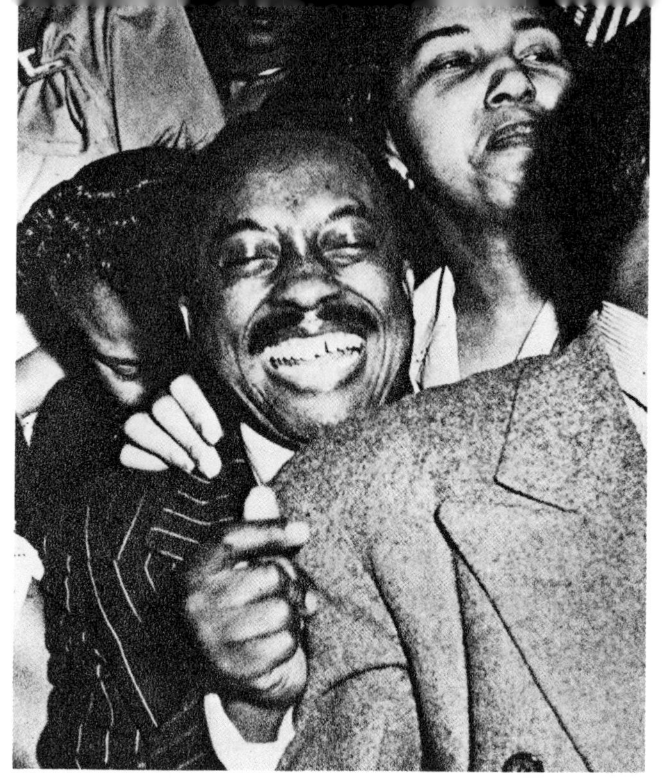

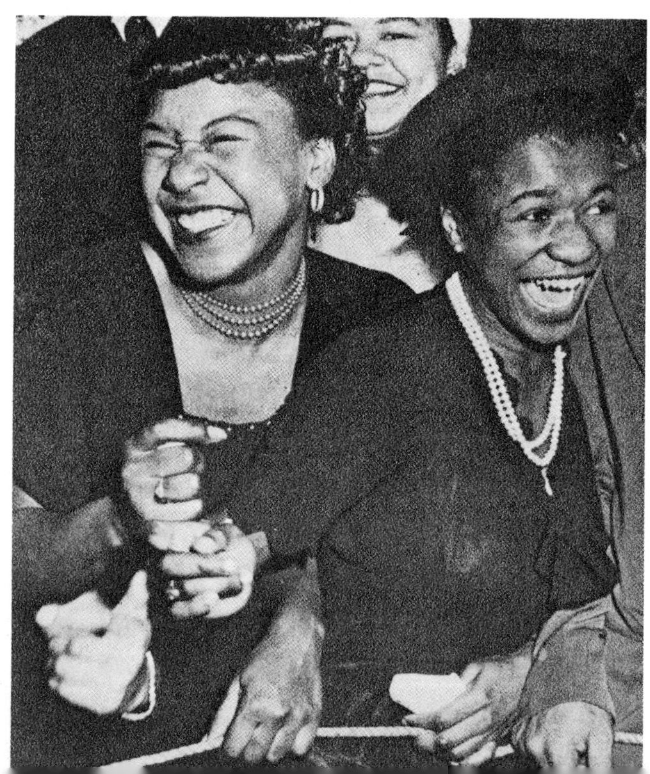

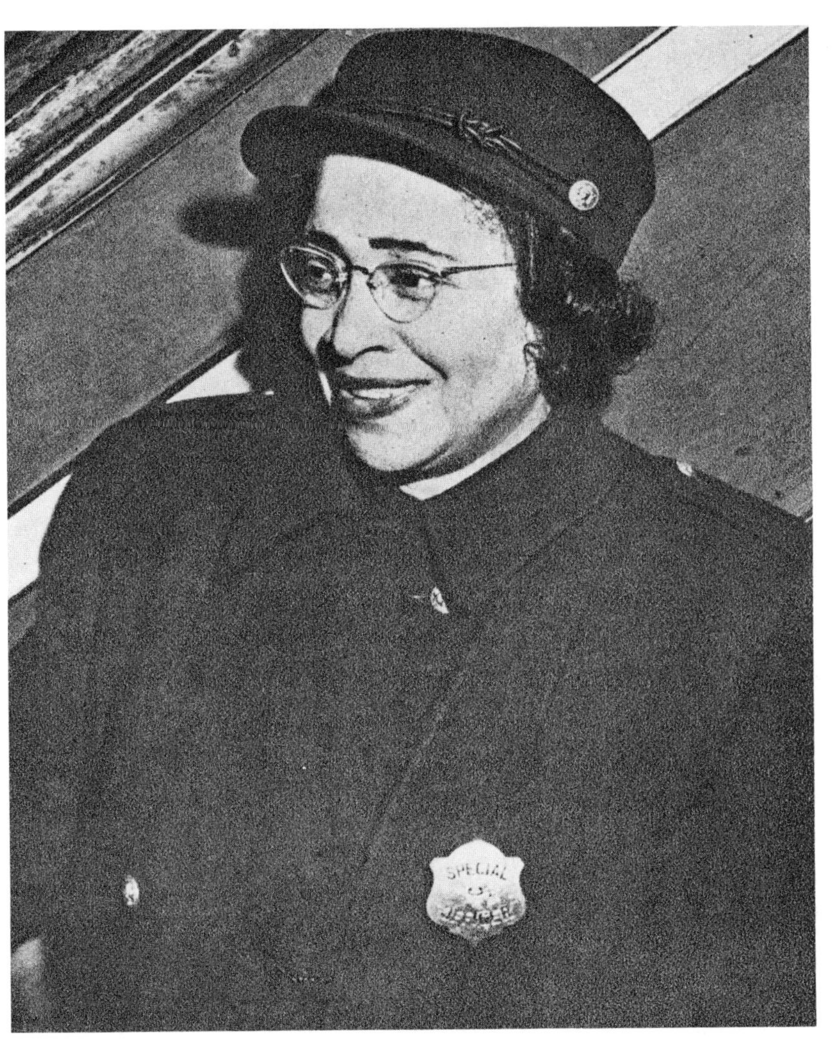

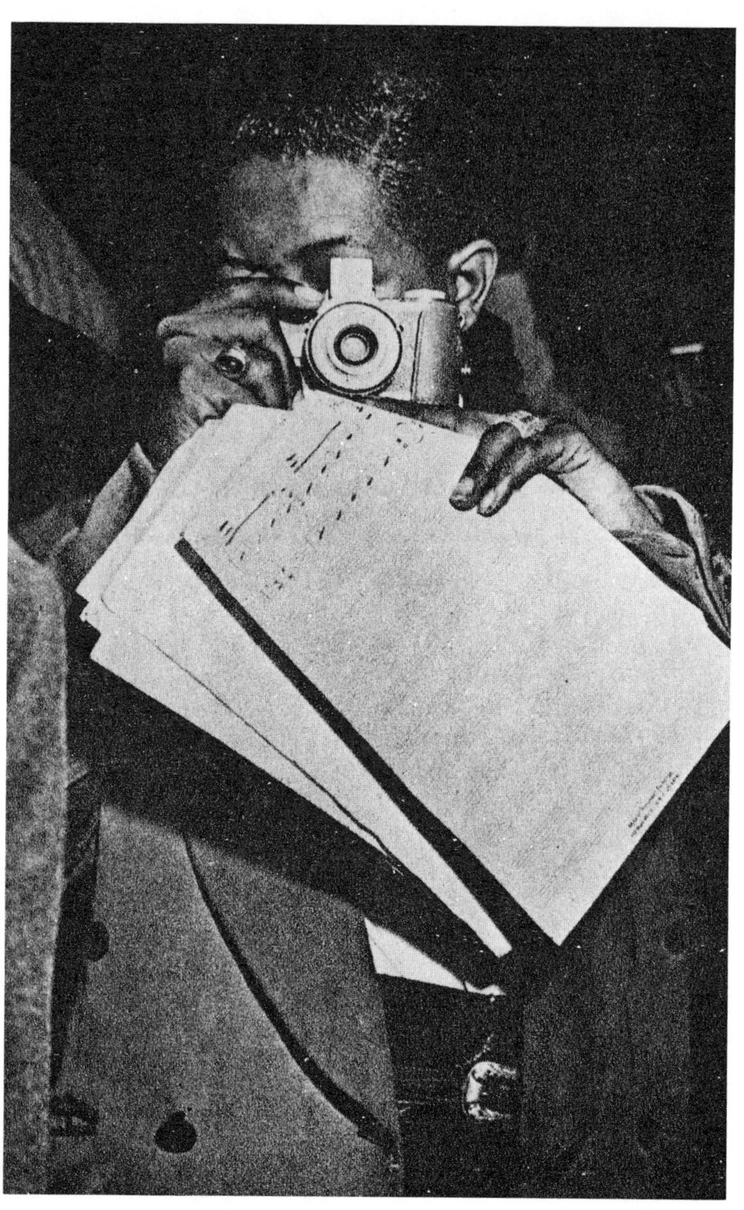

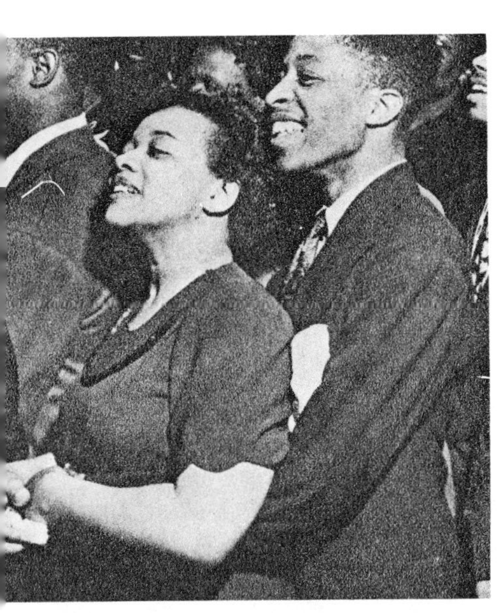
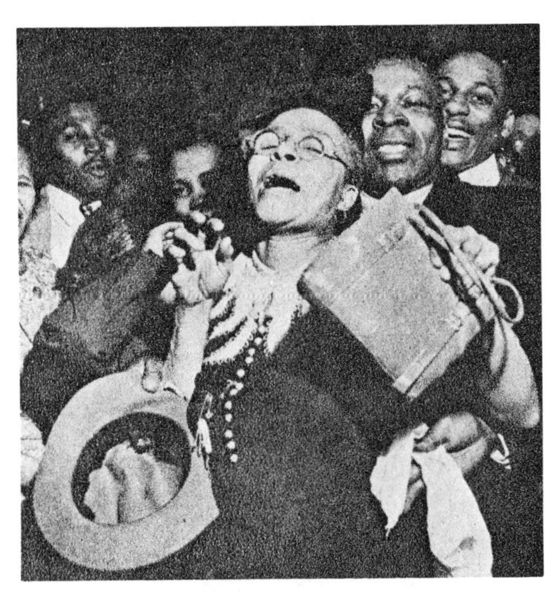
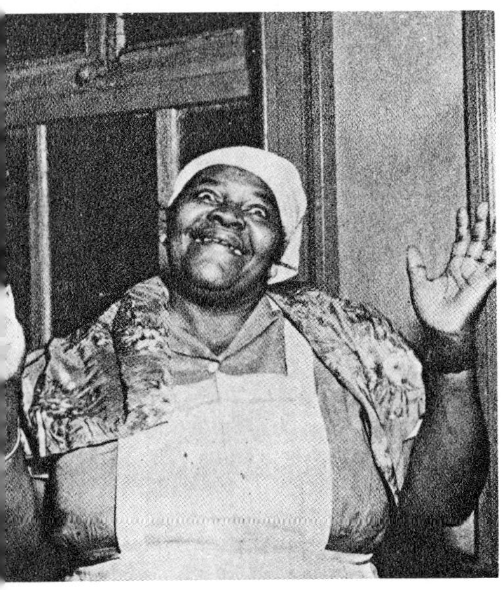
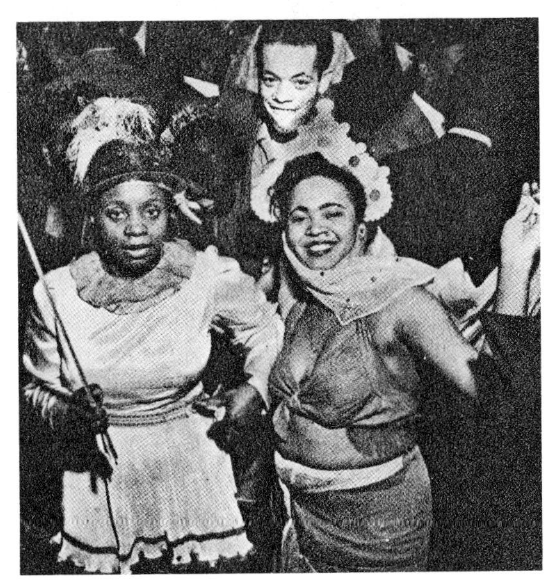

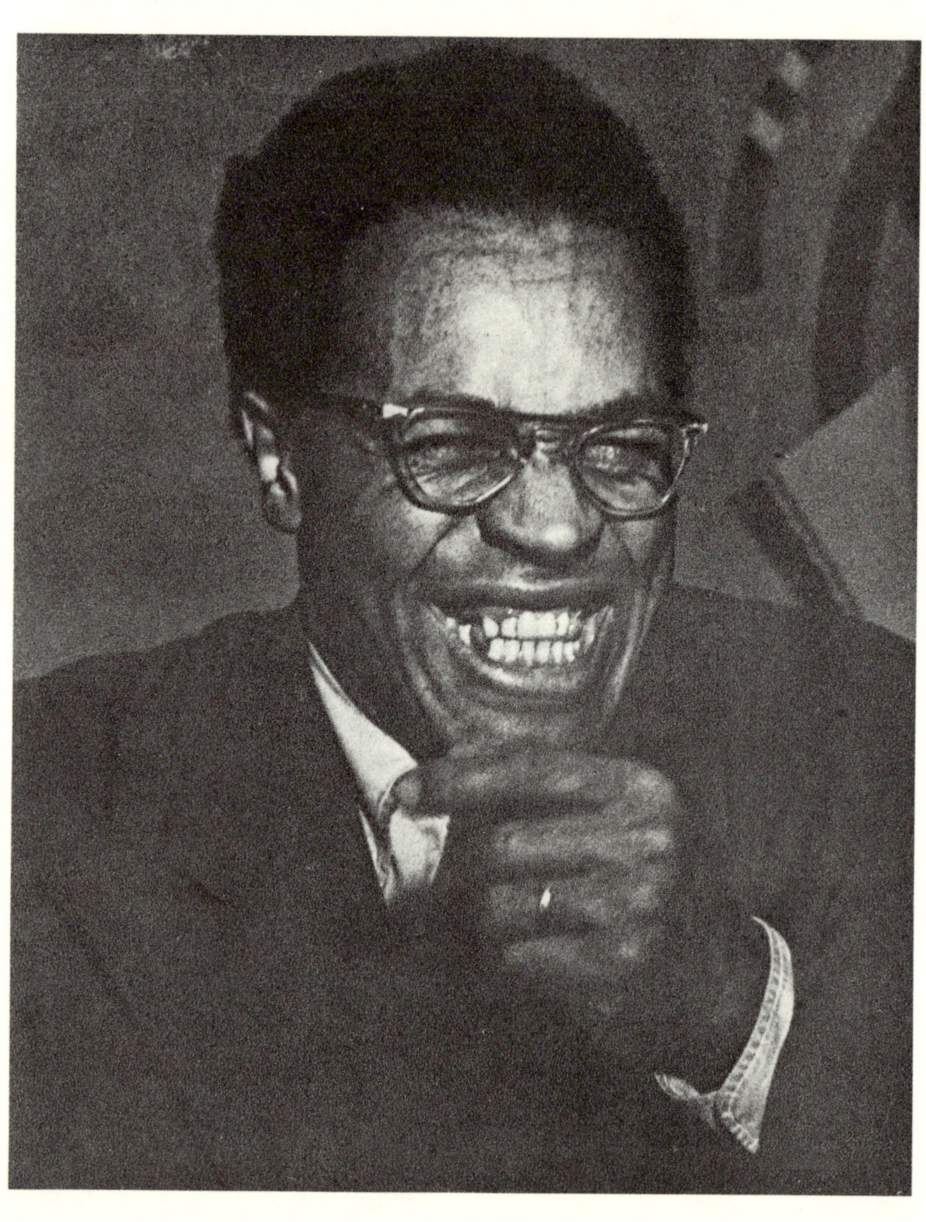

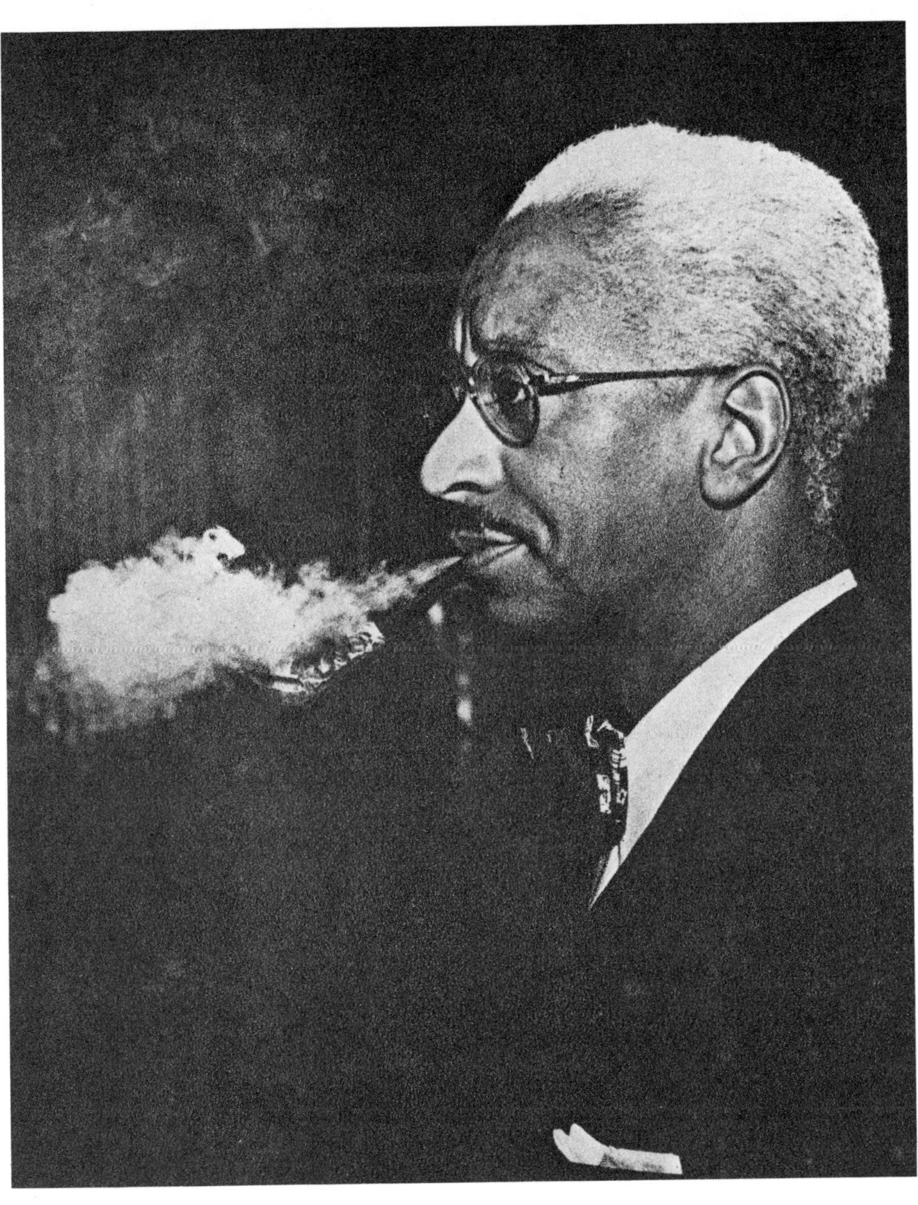

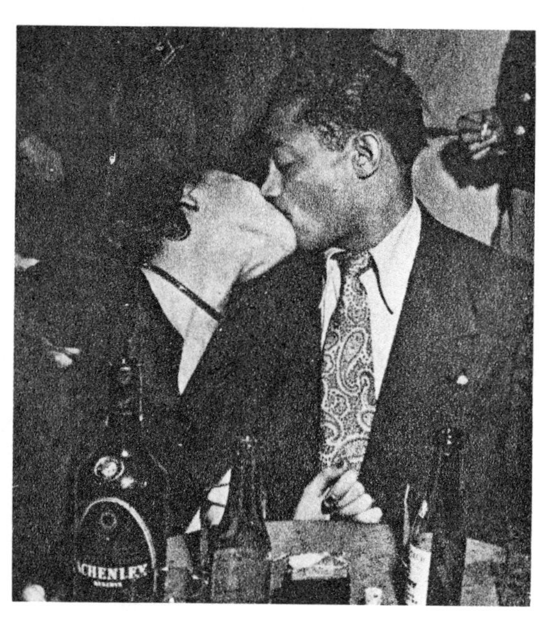

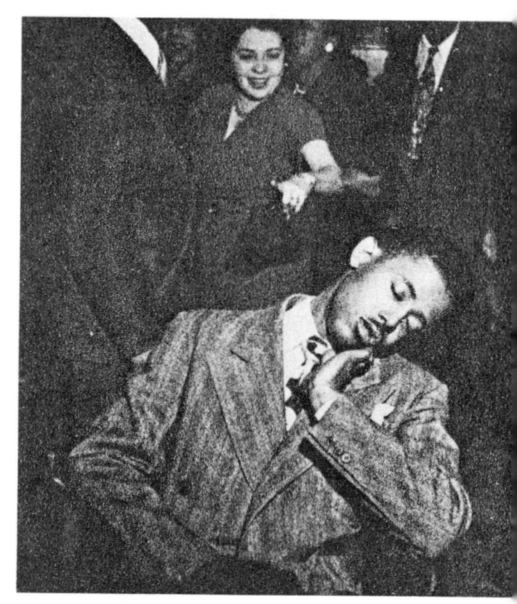

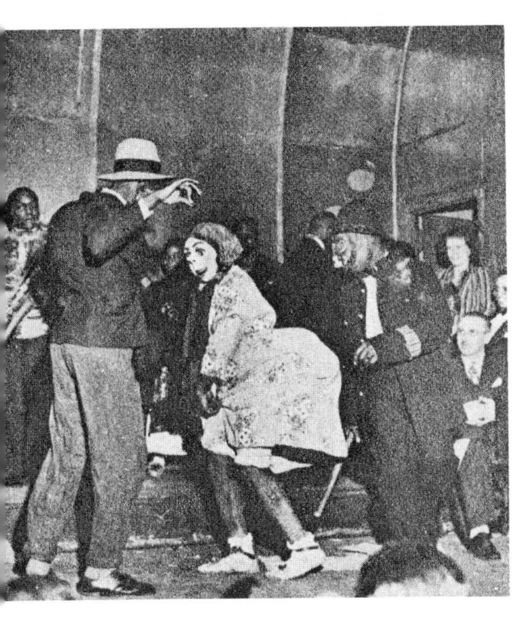 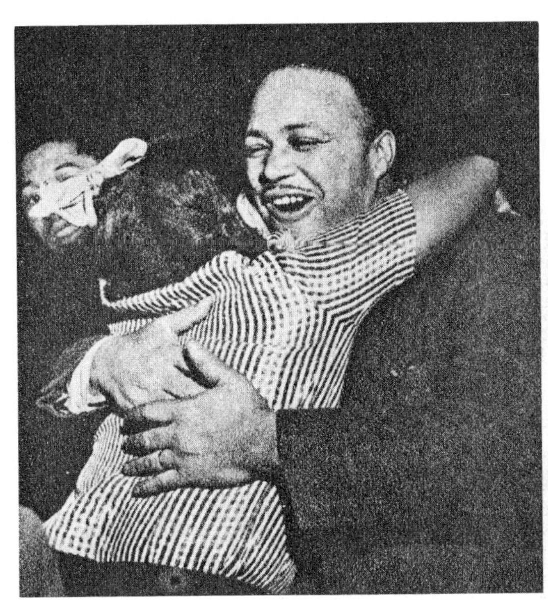

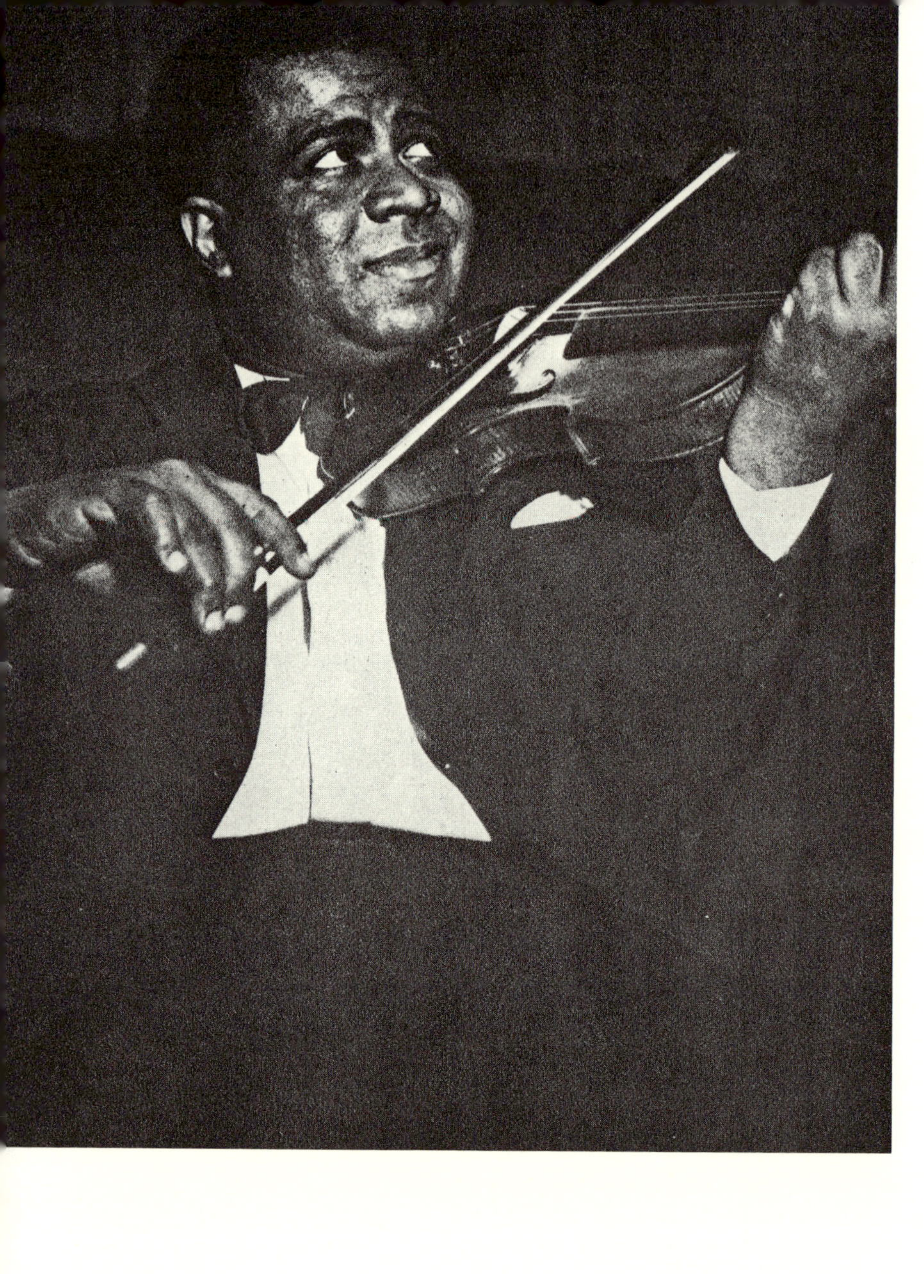

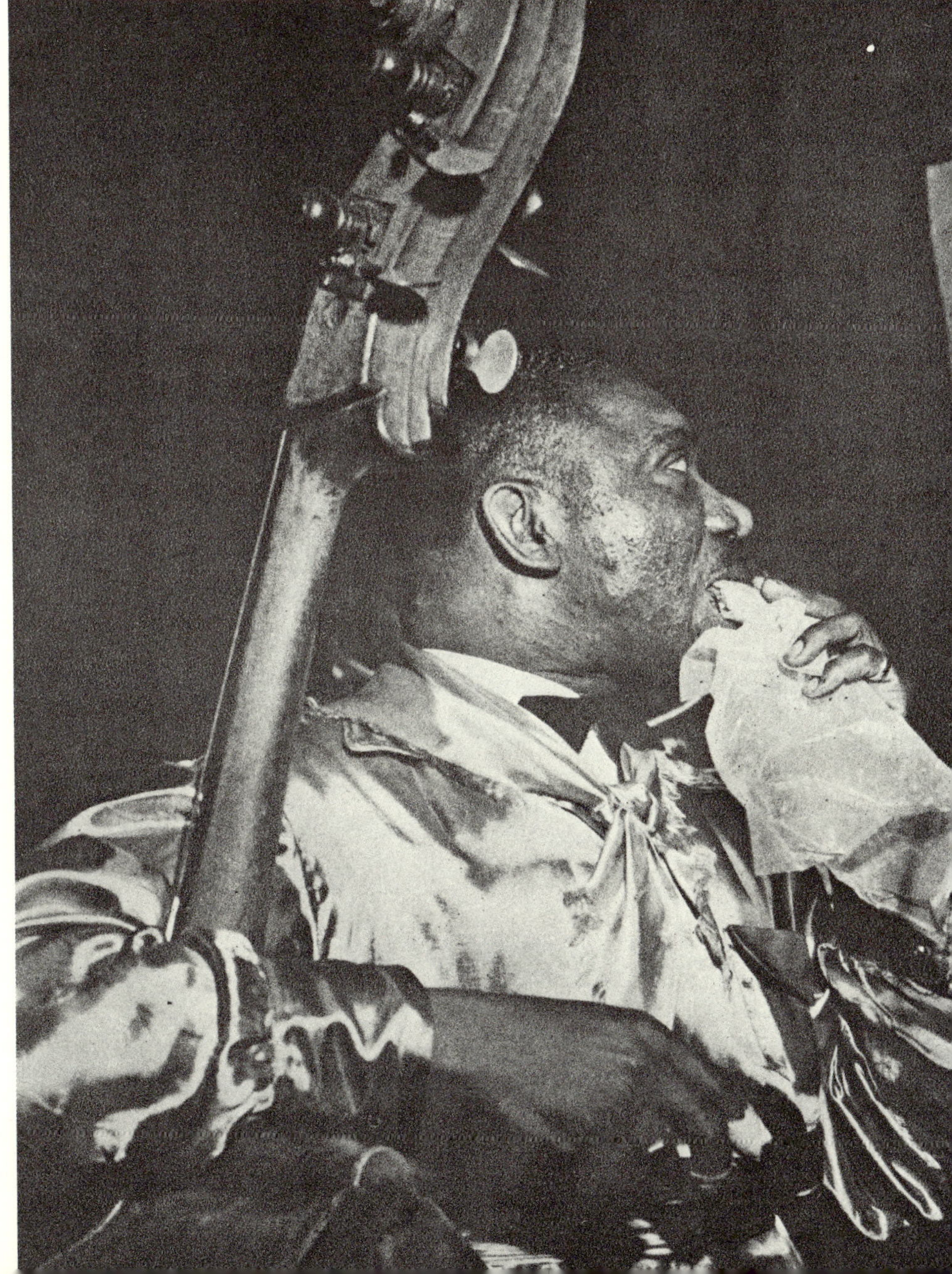

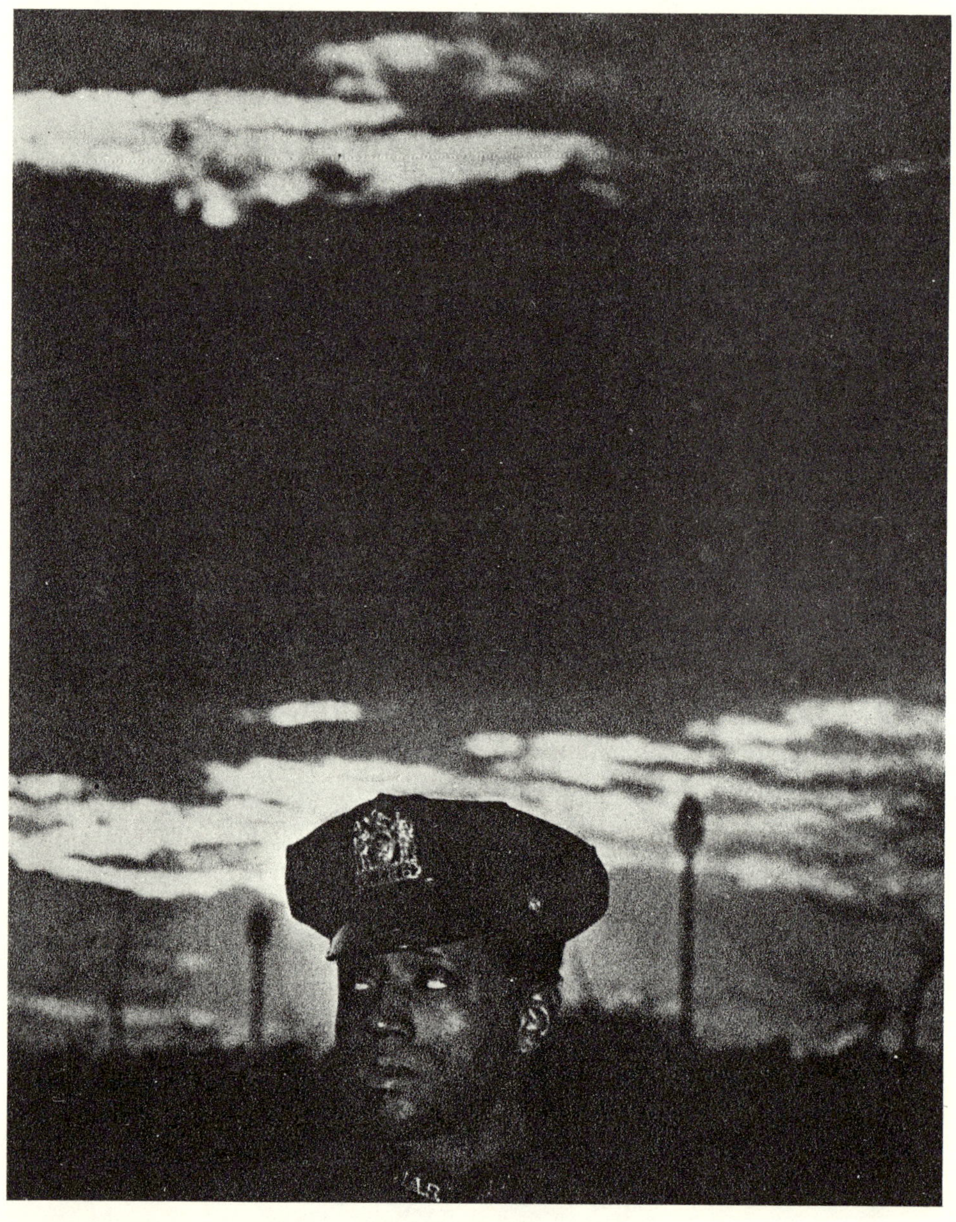

THE BUILDING

The sun pushes its way through the dark
canyons of Wall Street to alight on this
magnificent mountain of stone and steel.
. . . This is the Sixty Wall Street Tower,
third largest skyscraper in the world . . .
owned by the Cities Service Company. . . .

10

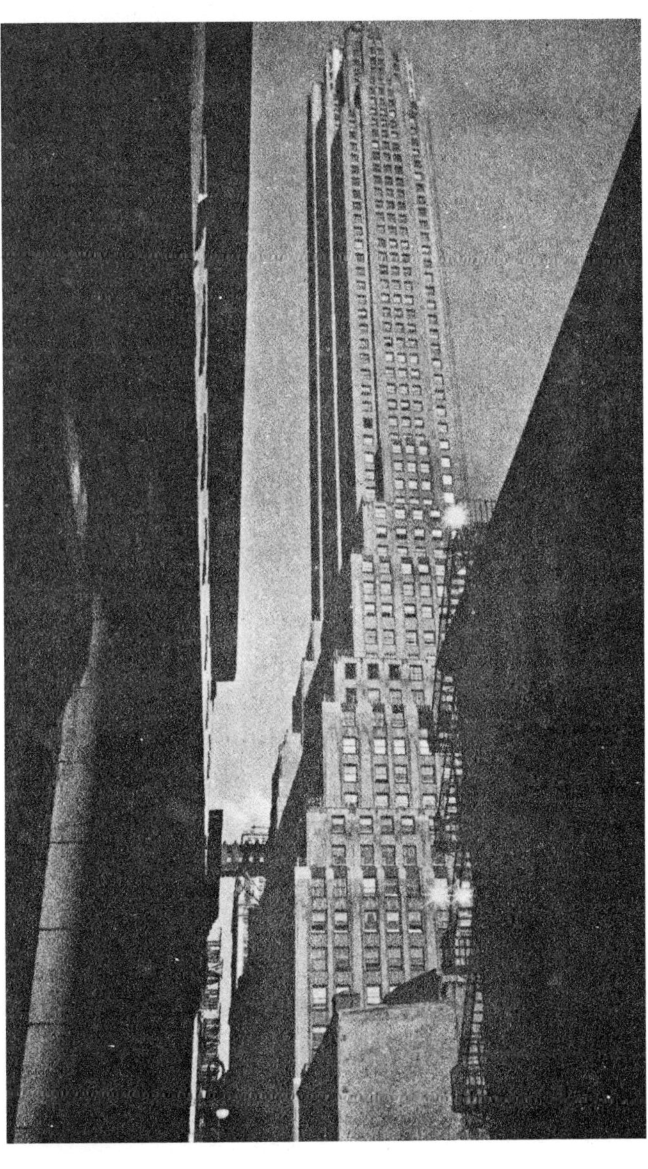

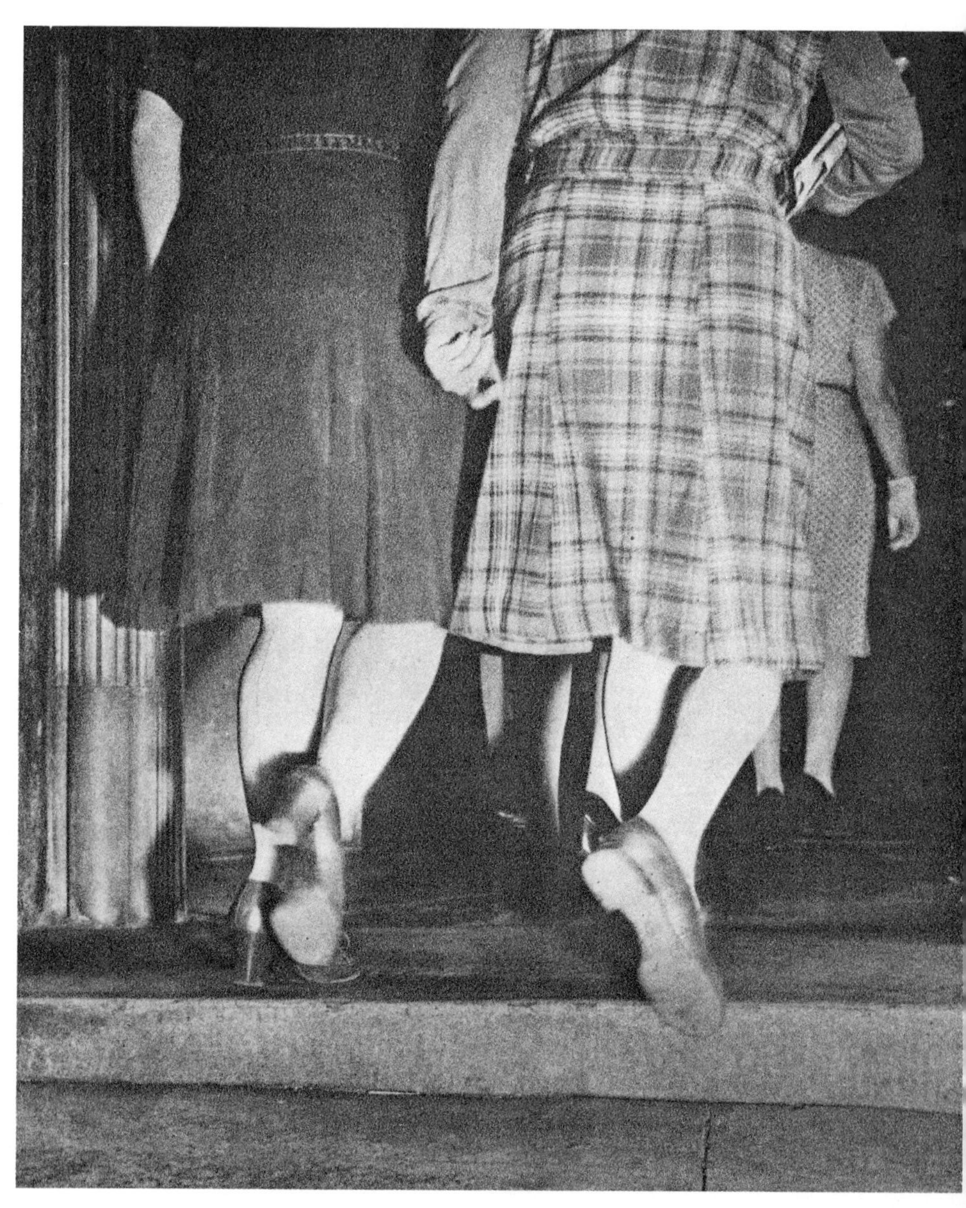

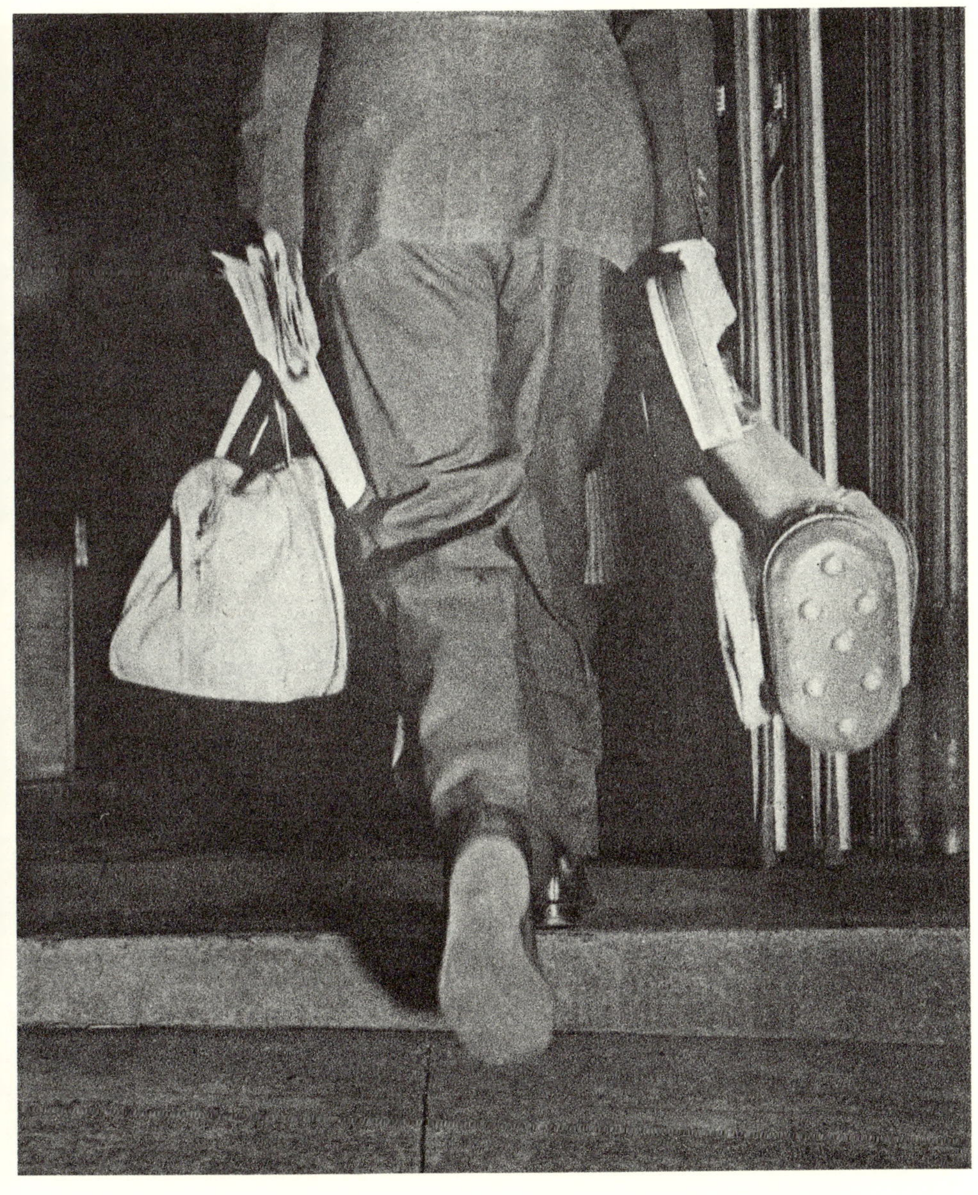

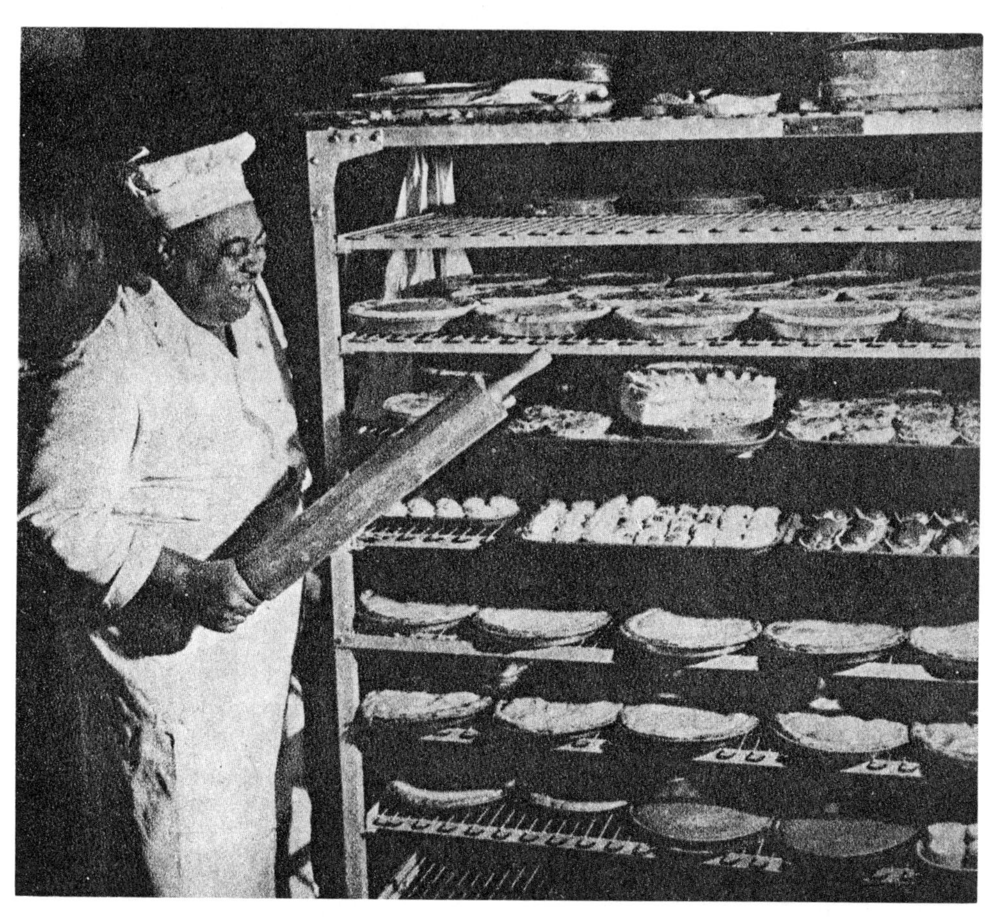

The building has its own restaurant . . .

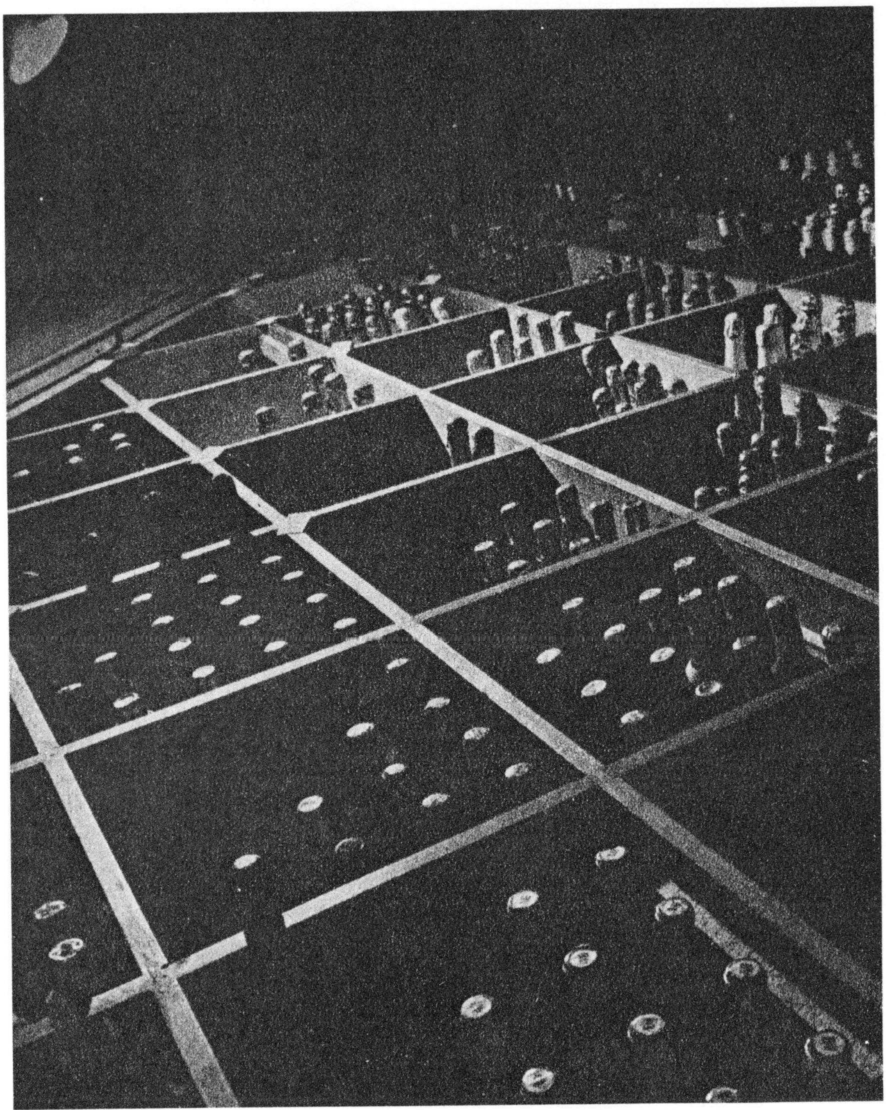

And wine cellars . . .

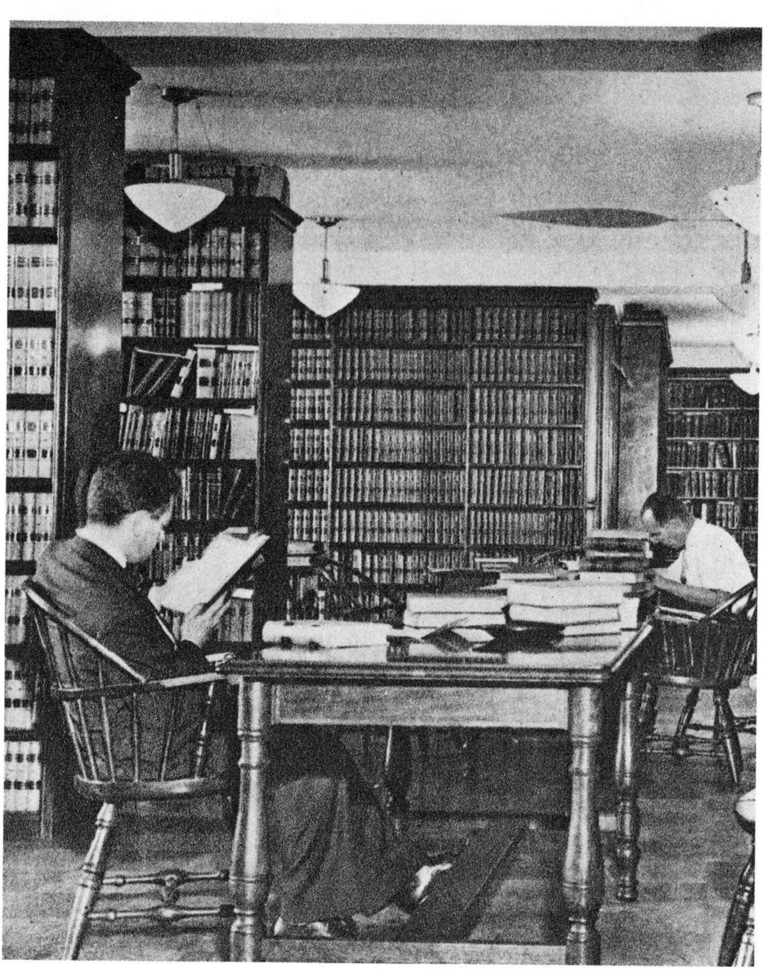

Its own library . . .

And gym

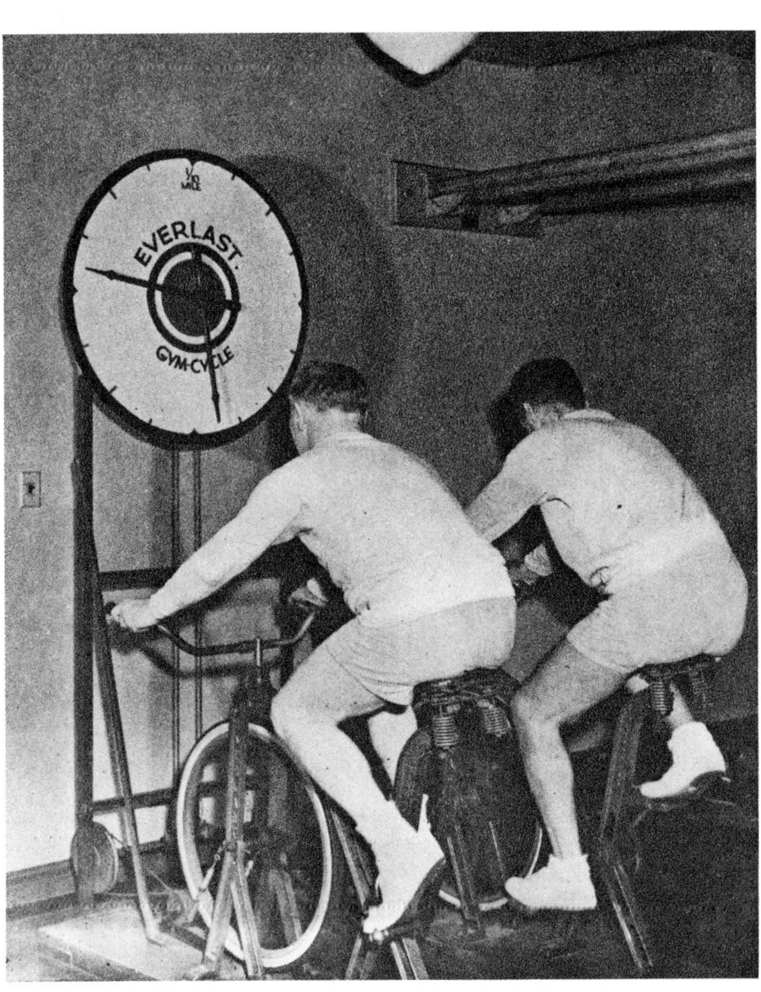

Midnight. . . . The thousands have left . . . except for the lone scrubwoman. . . .

Portrait of a City

11

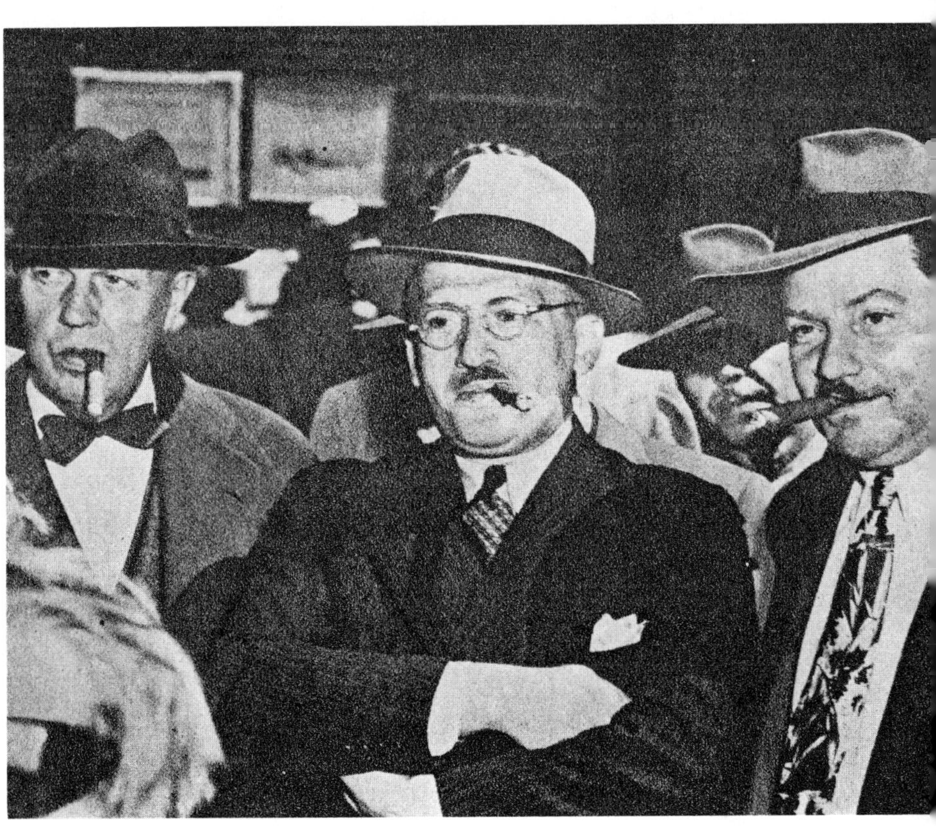

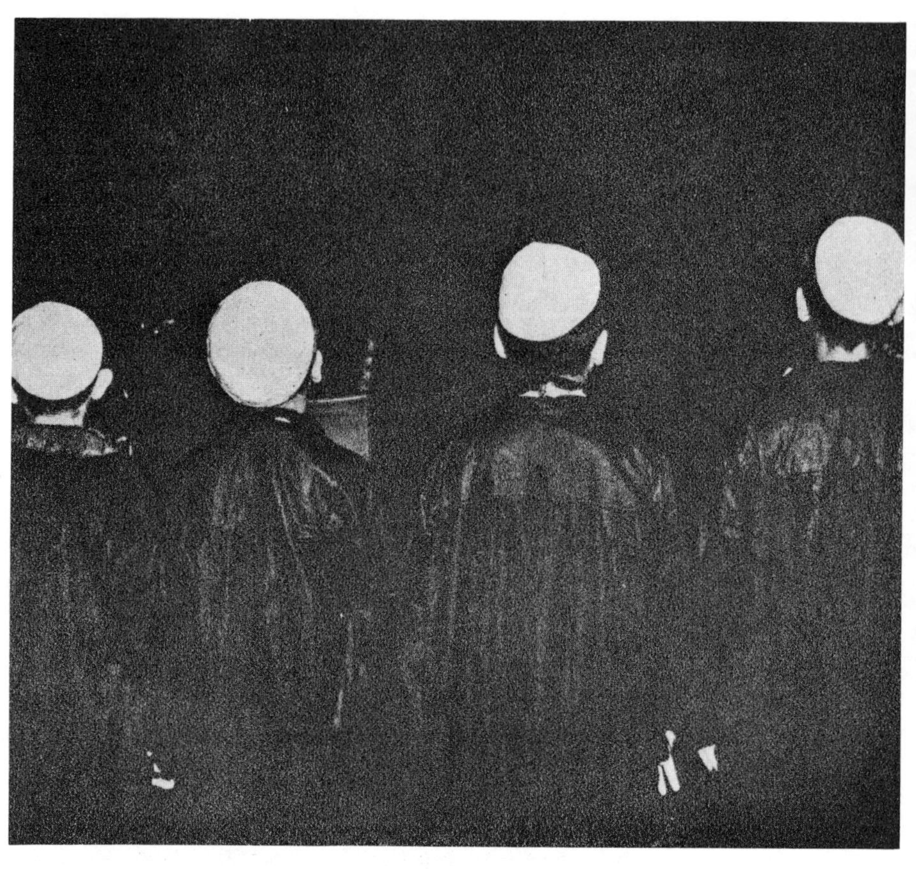

Study in white and black

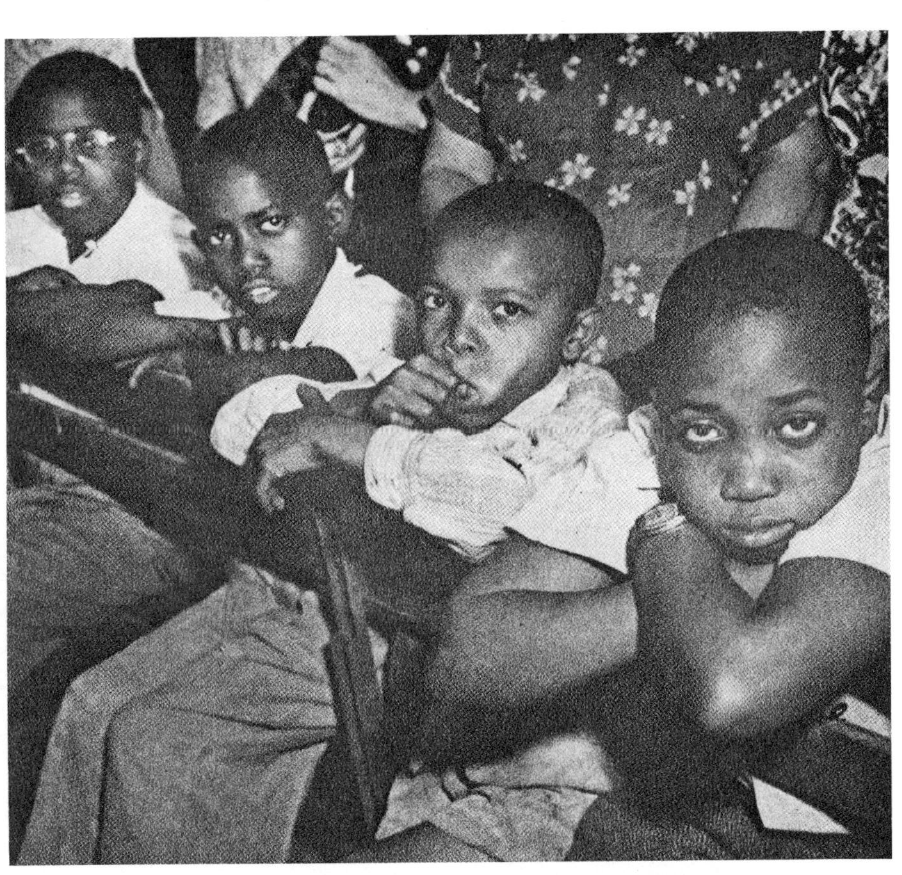

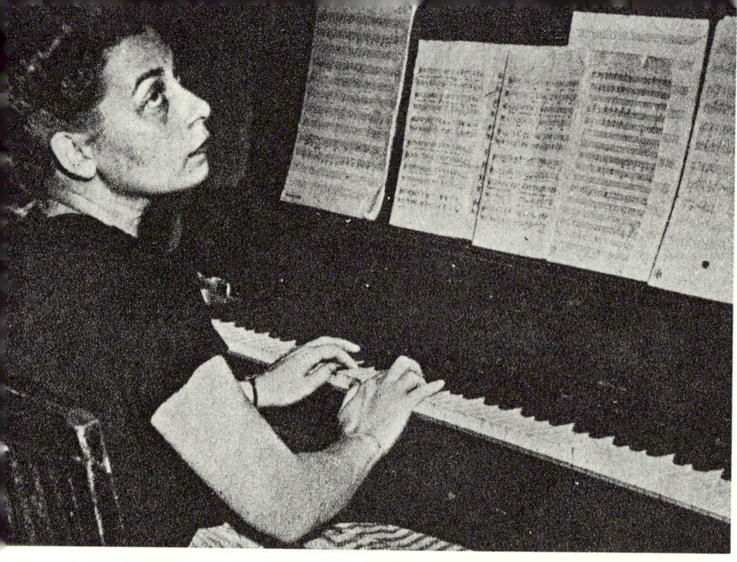

With a song in their hea

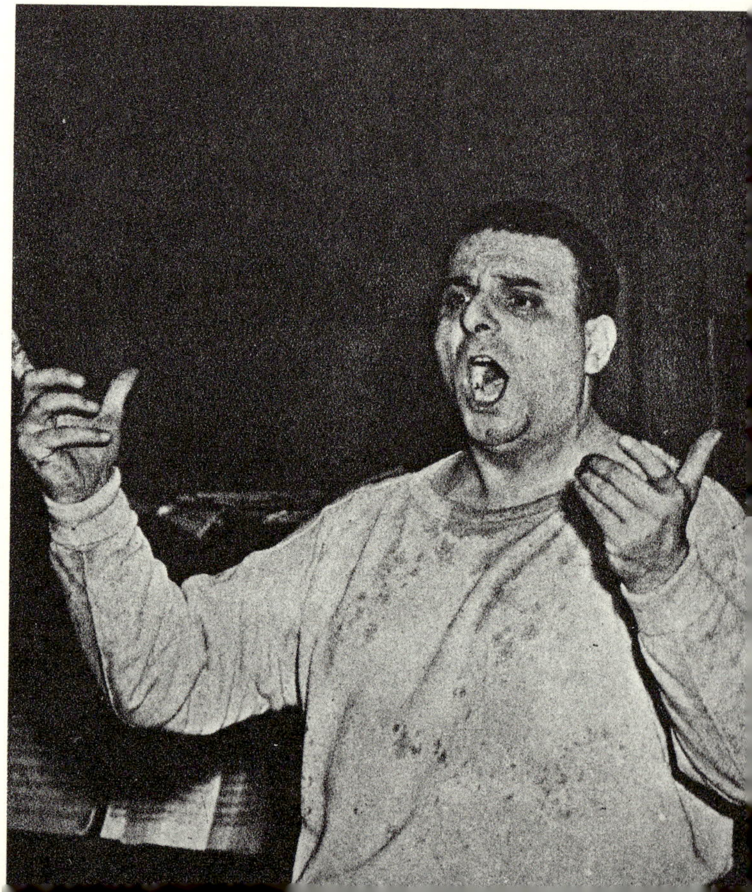

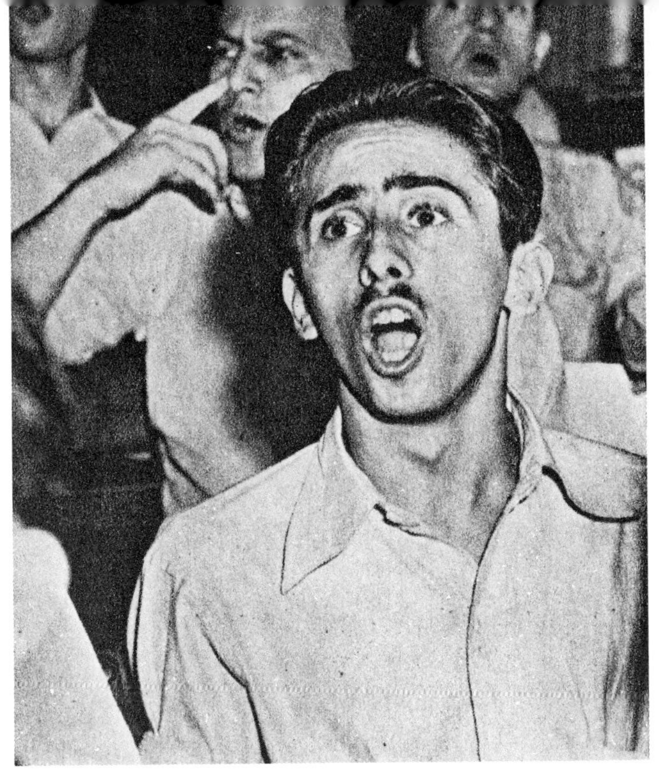

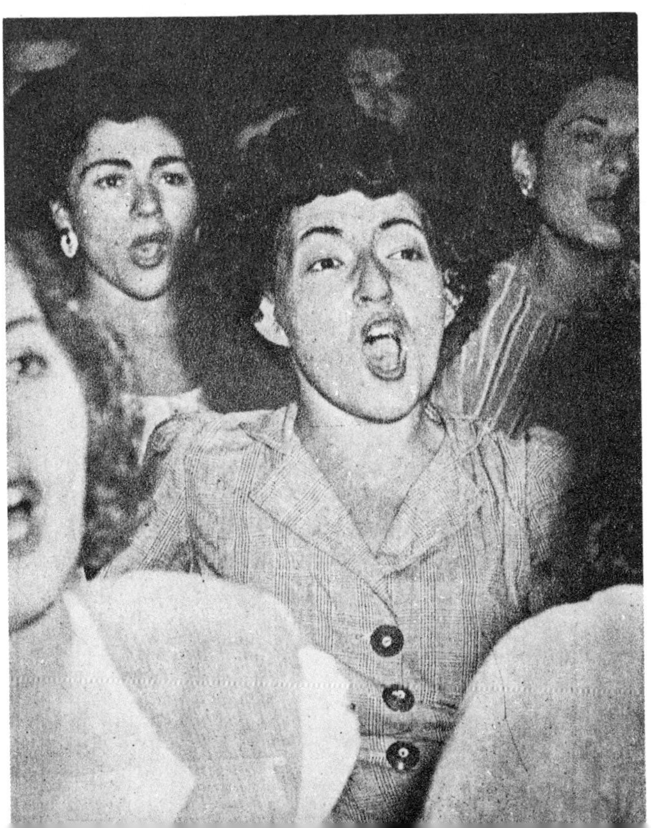

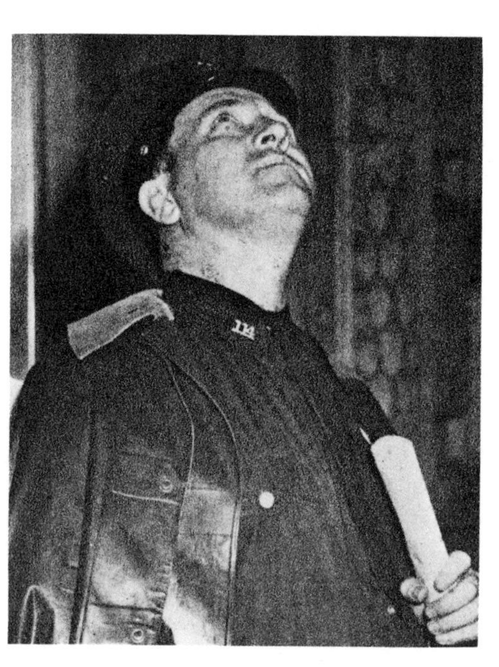

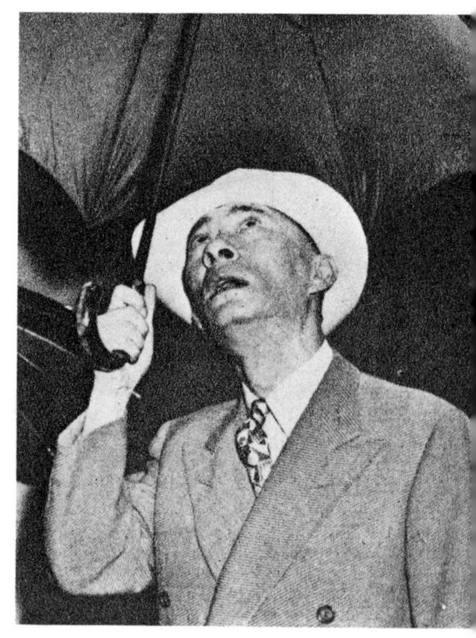

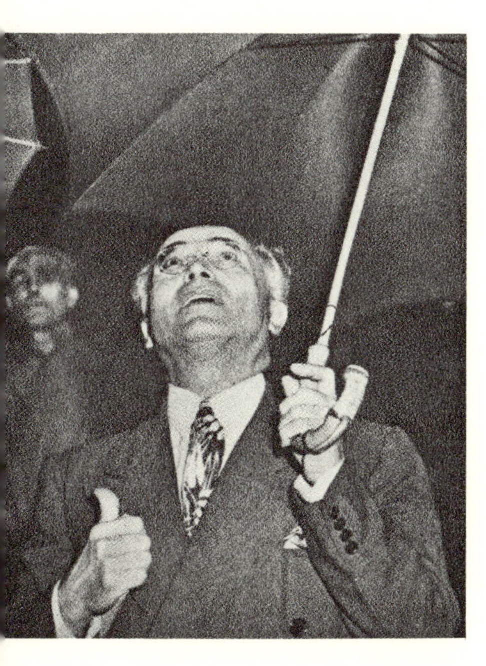

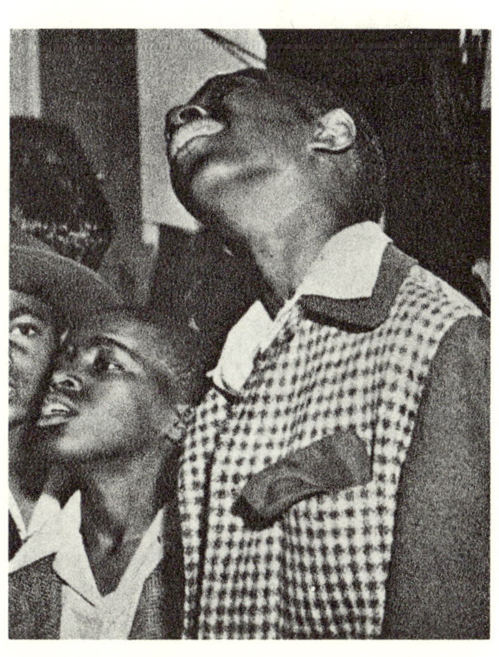

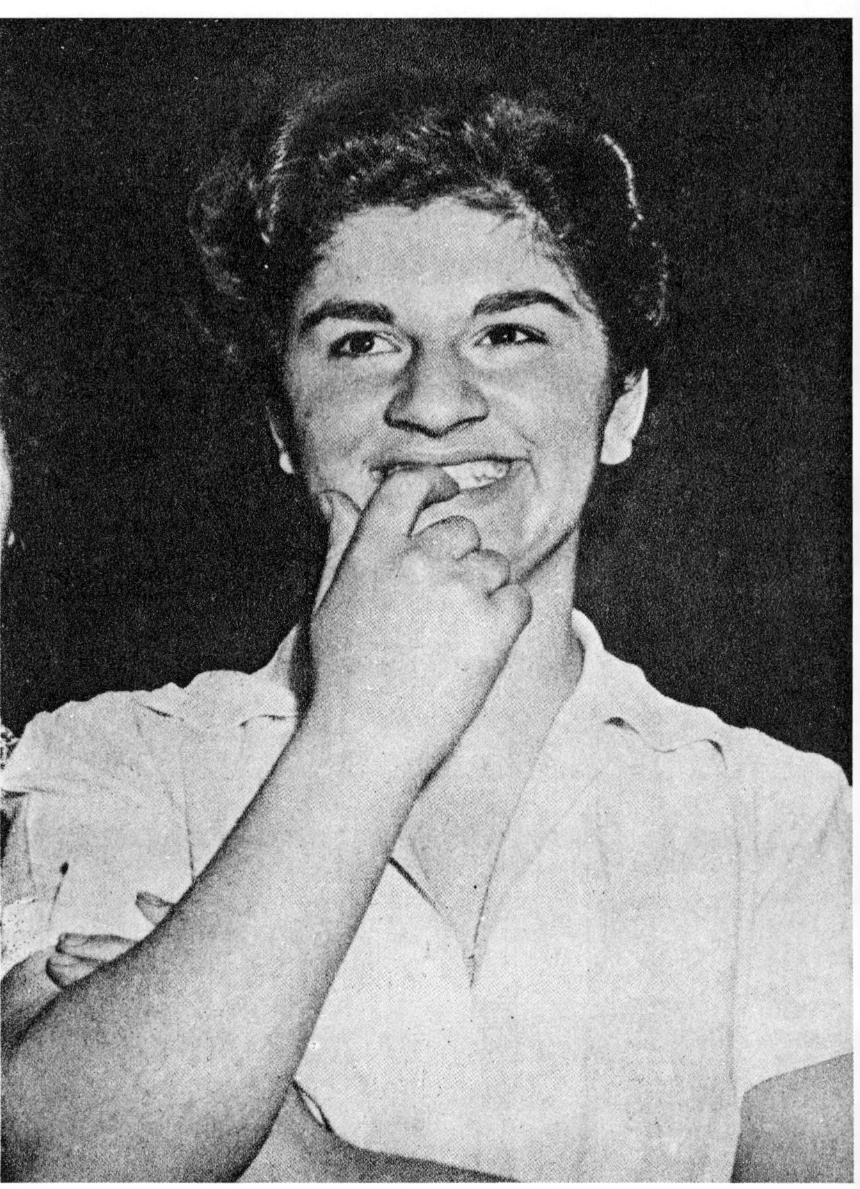

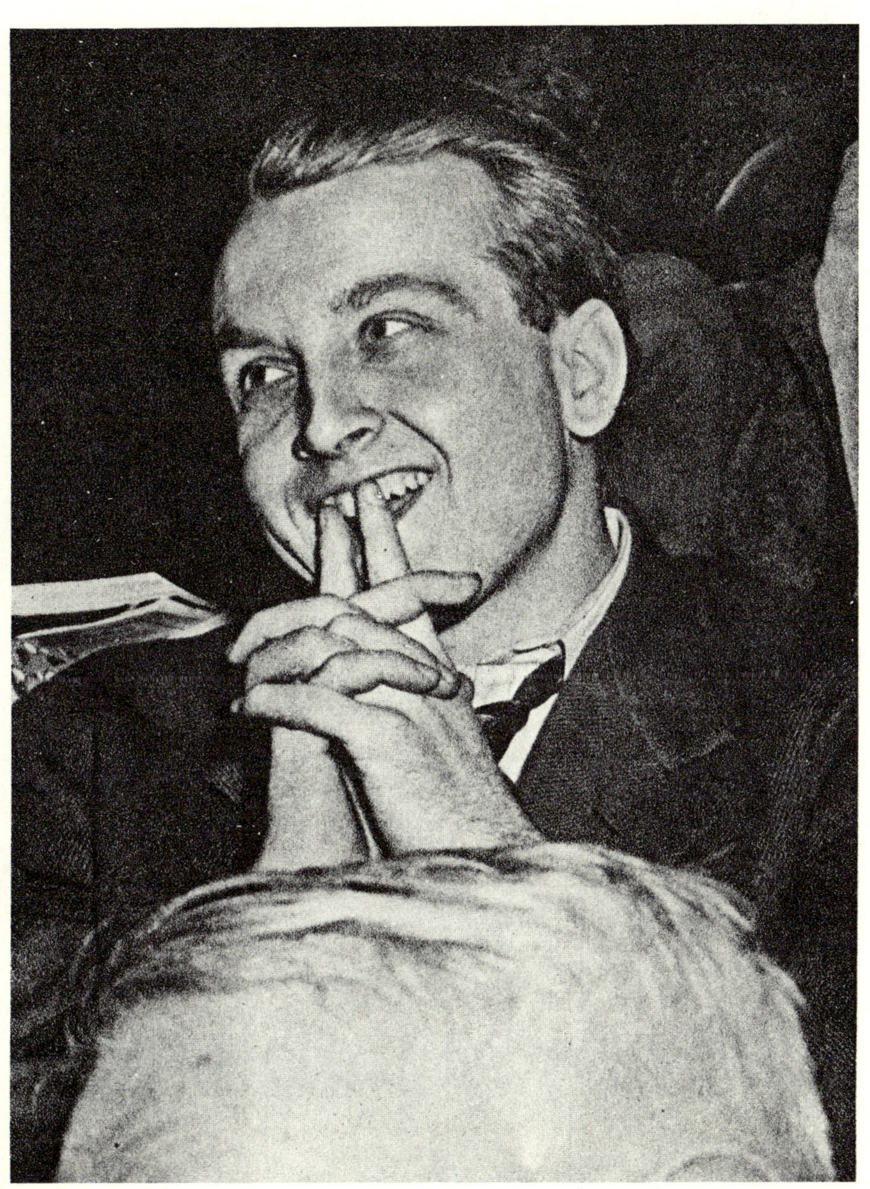

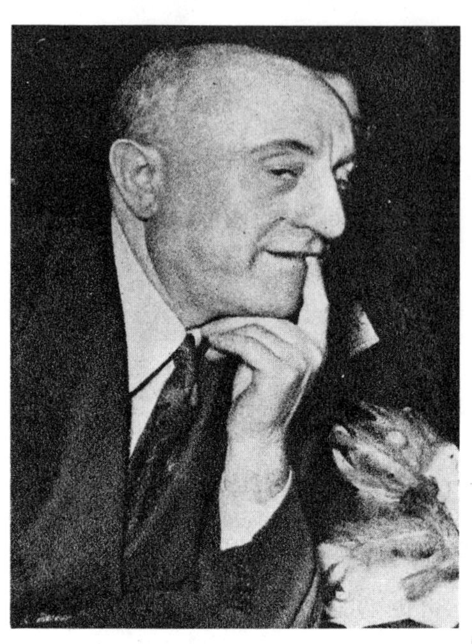

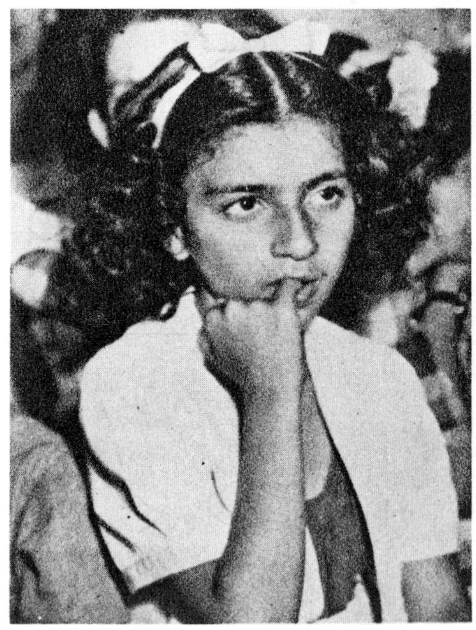

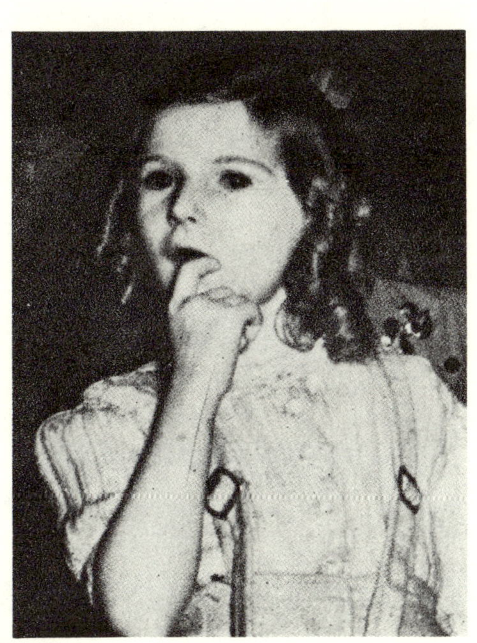

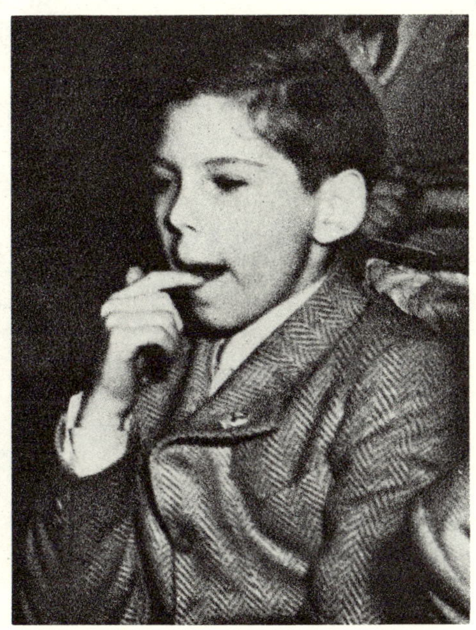

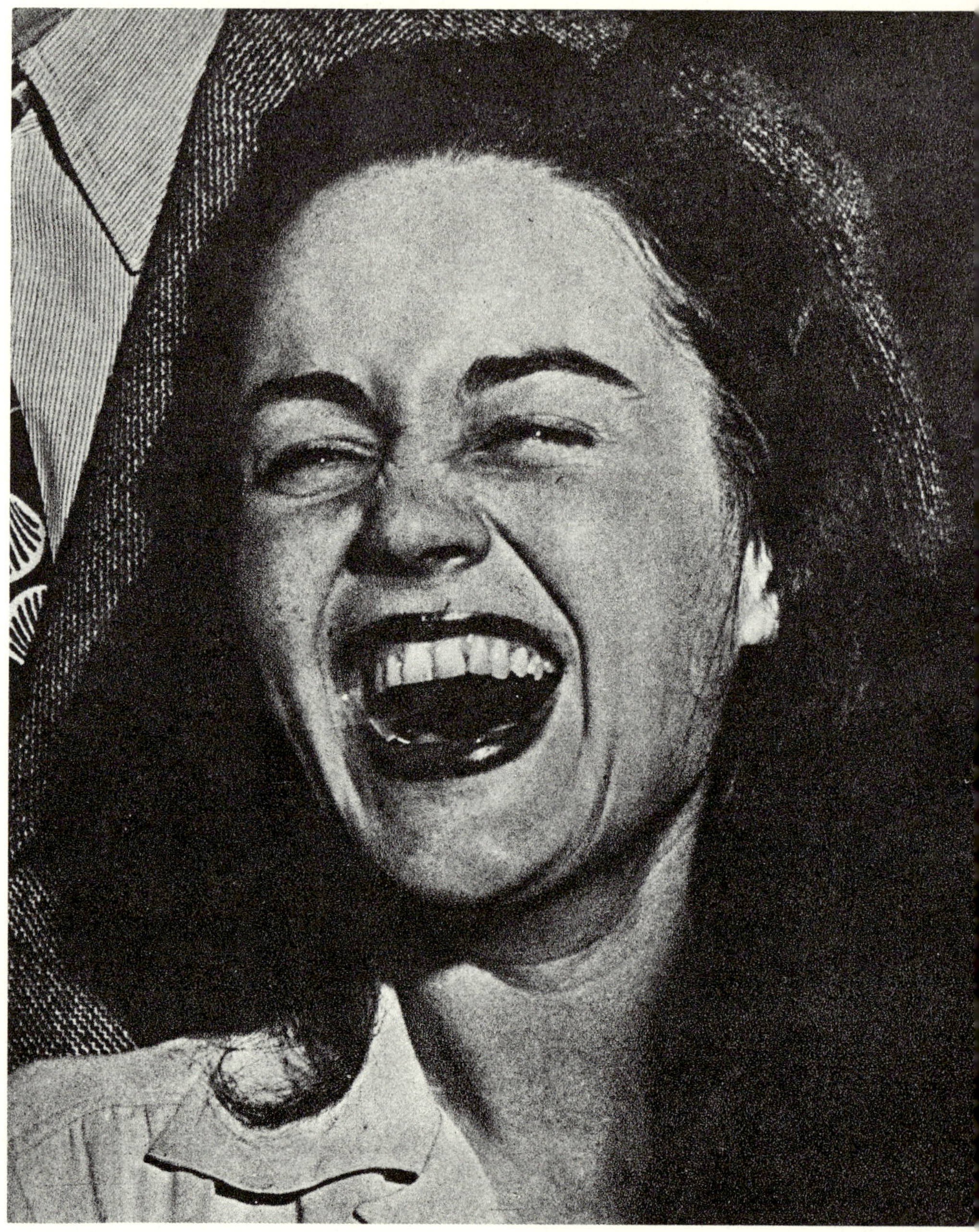

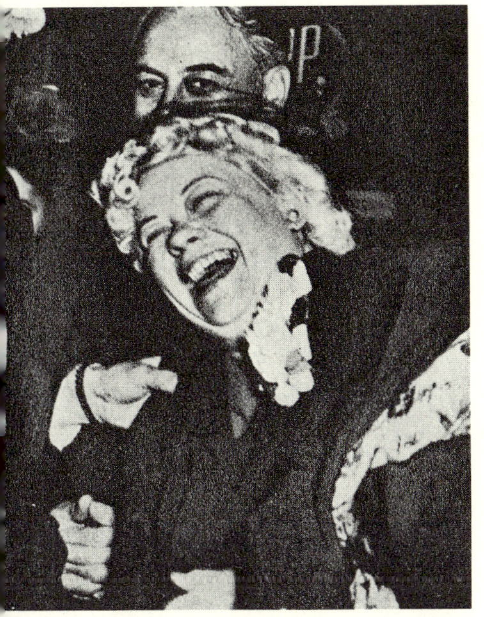
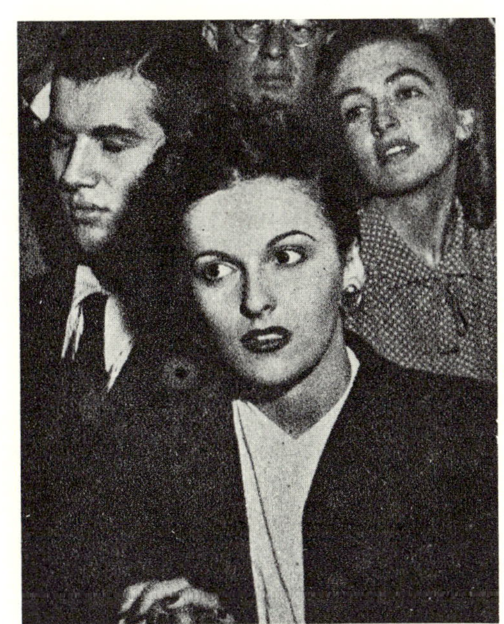
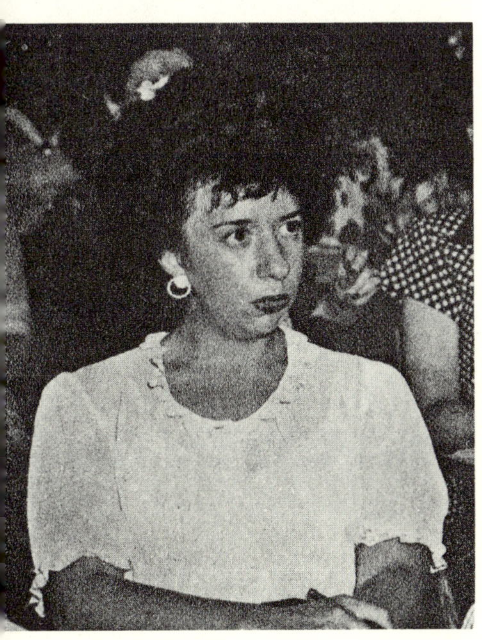
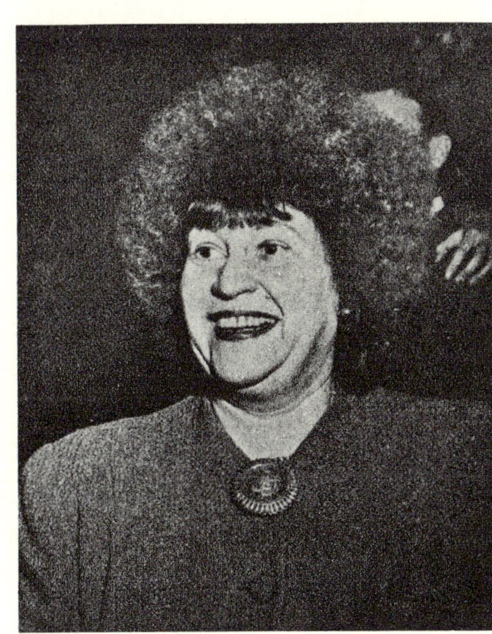

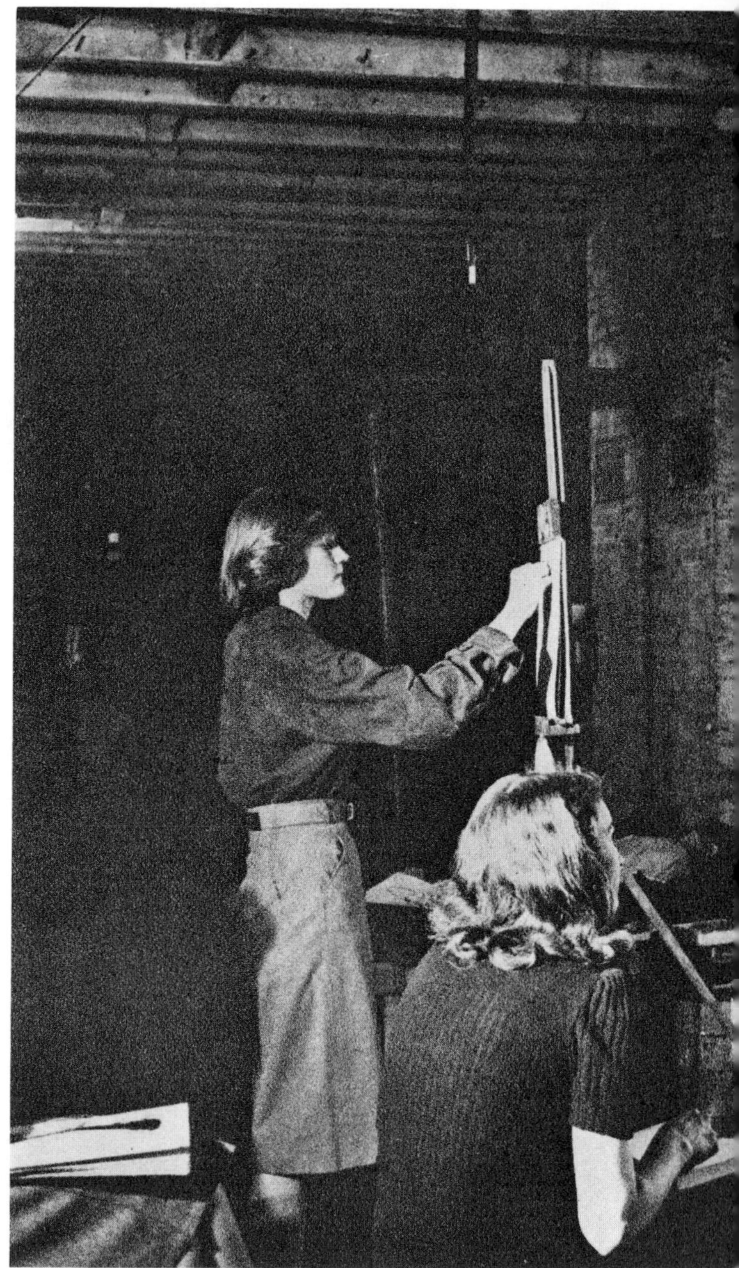

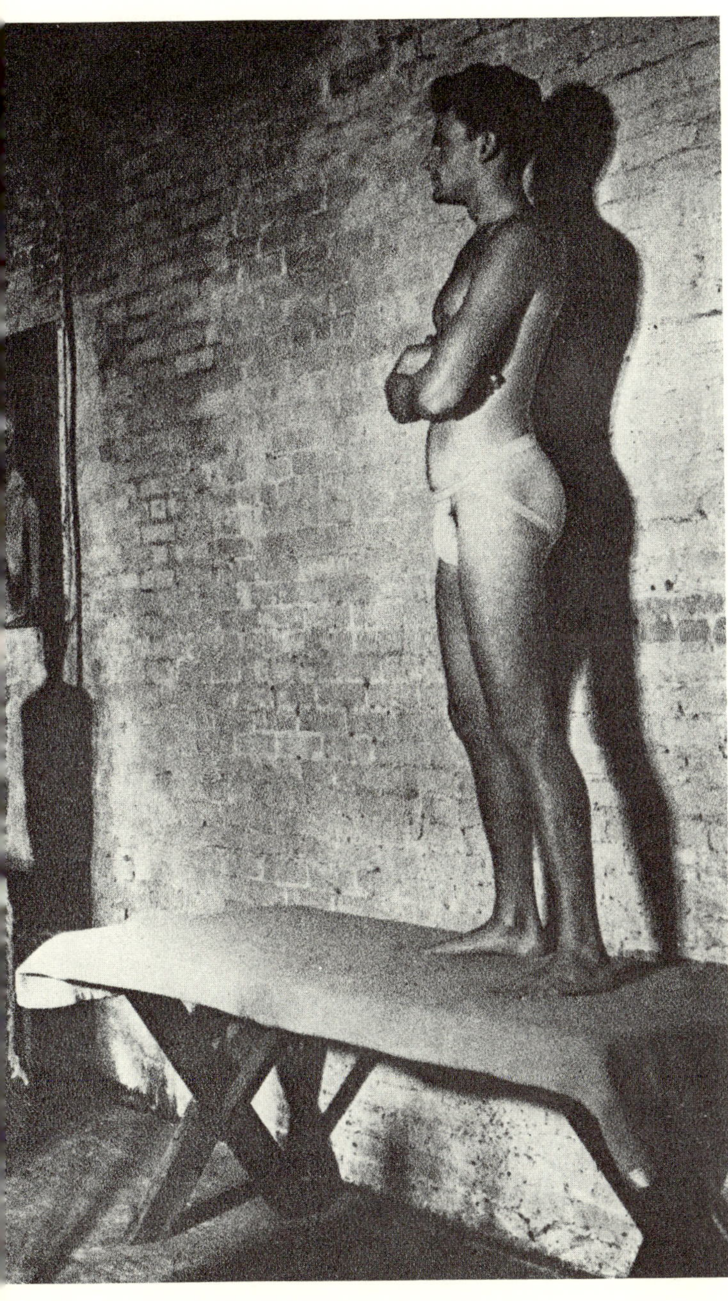

Life class

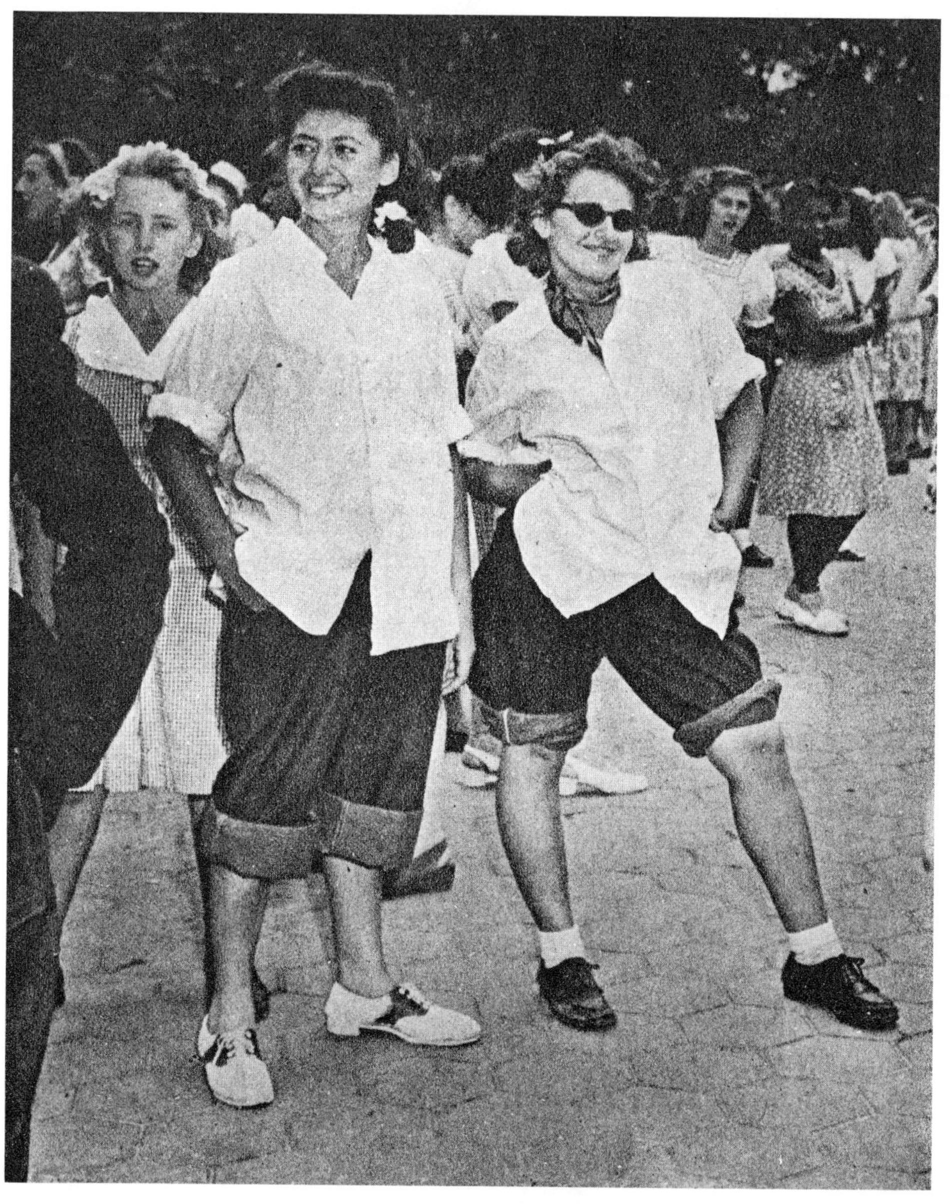

Youth *is* always beautiful

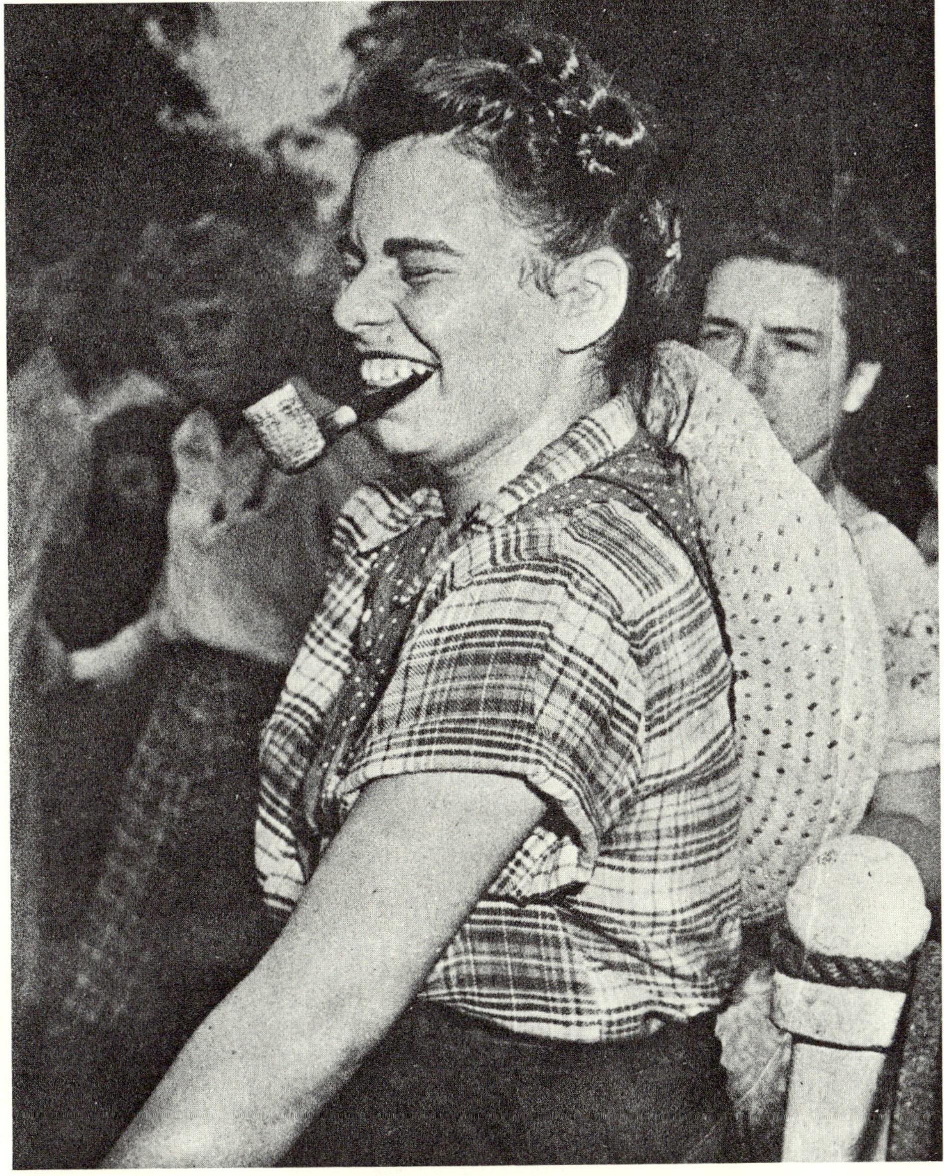

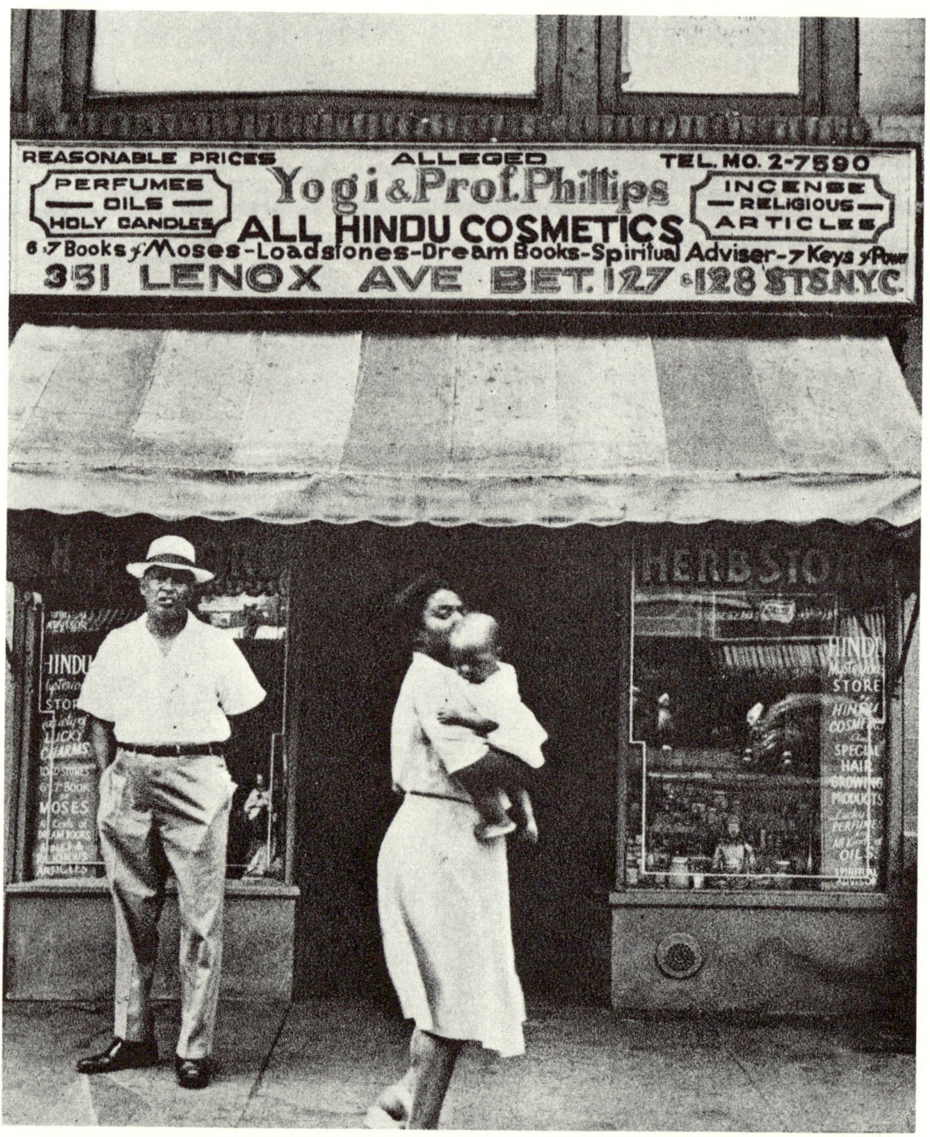

Black magic. . . . This is just one of a dozen stores of the same kind in Harlem. . . . A strange, fantastic mixture of religious articles and superstition, but the customers are not interested in the religious articles. . . . They want the different red, yellow, and blue powders that will make them lucky in love and the numbers game . . . and chase away enemies. . . . I asked the professor why he was called an "alleged" Yoga . . . he told me that the reason was in order to keep him out of trouble with the cops. . . .

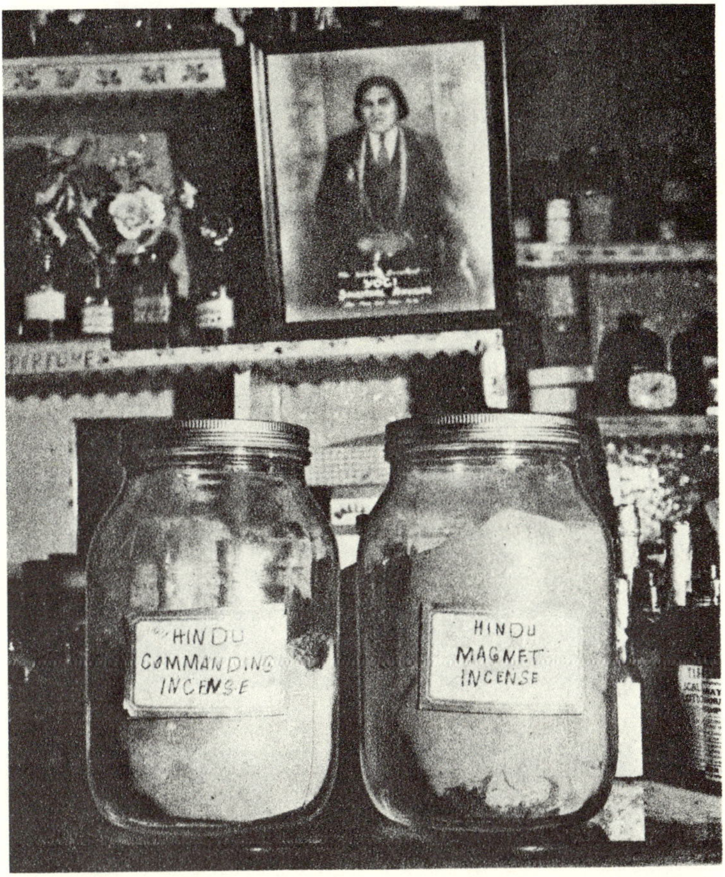

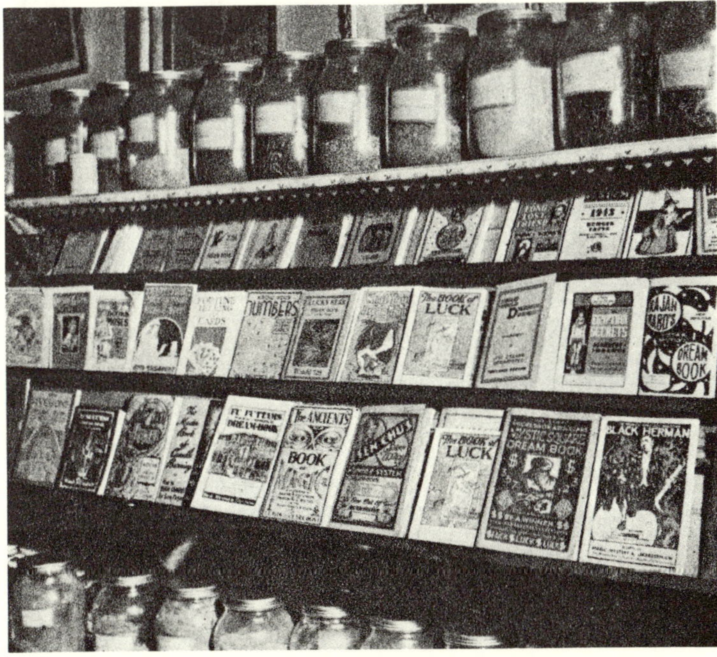

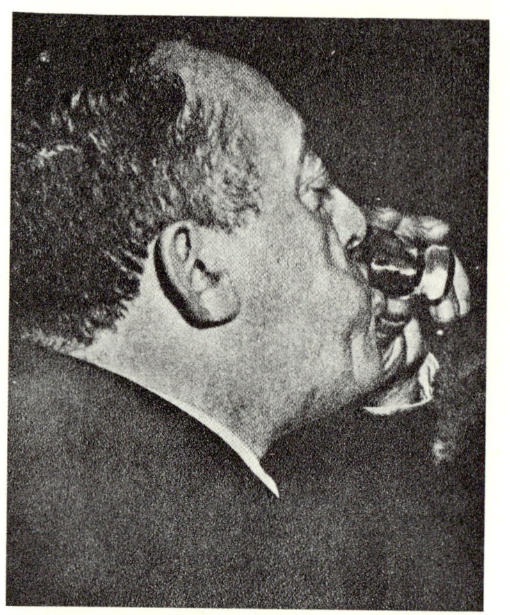
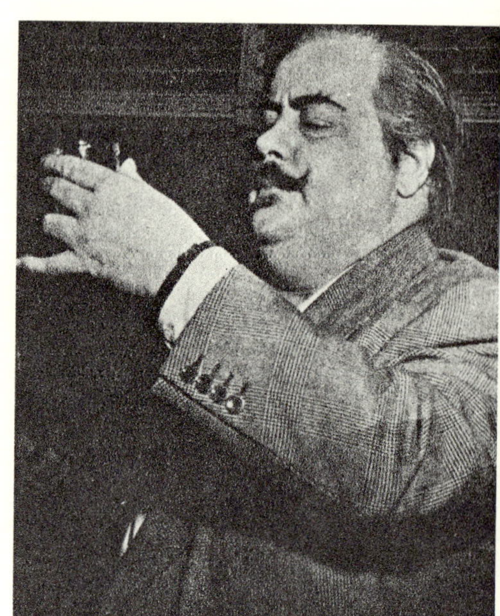
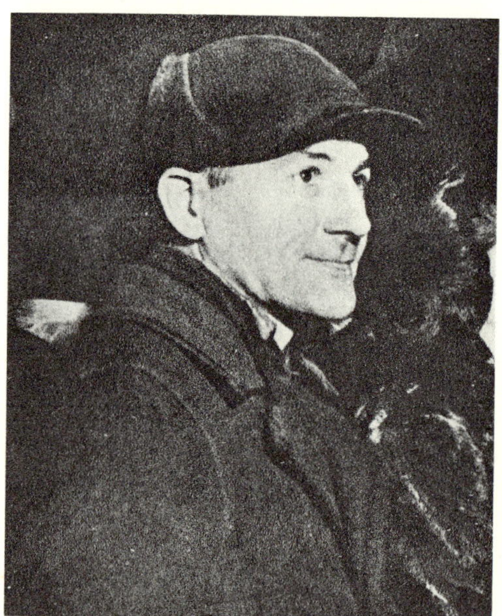
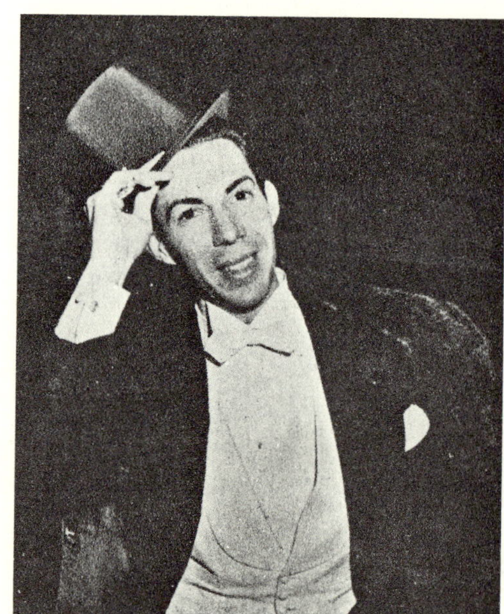

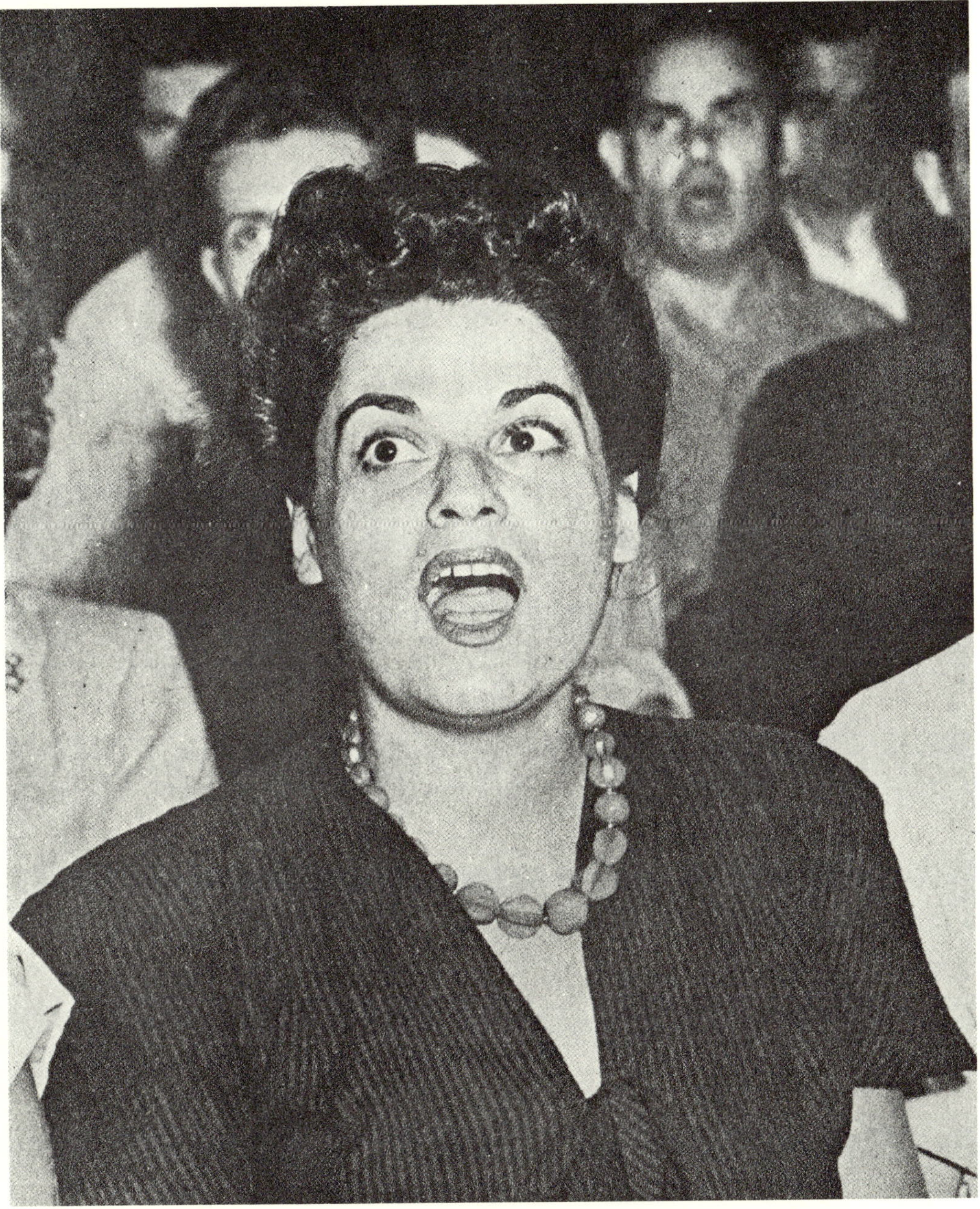

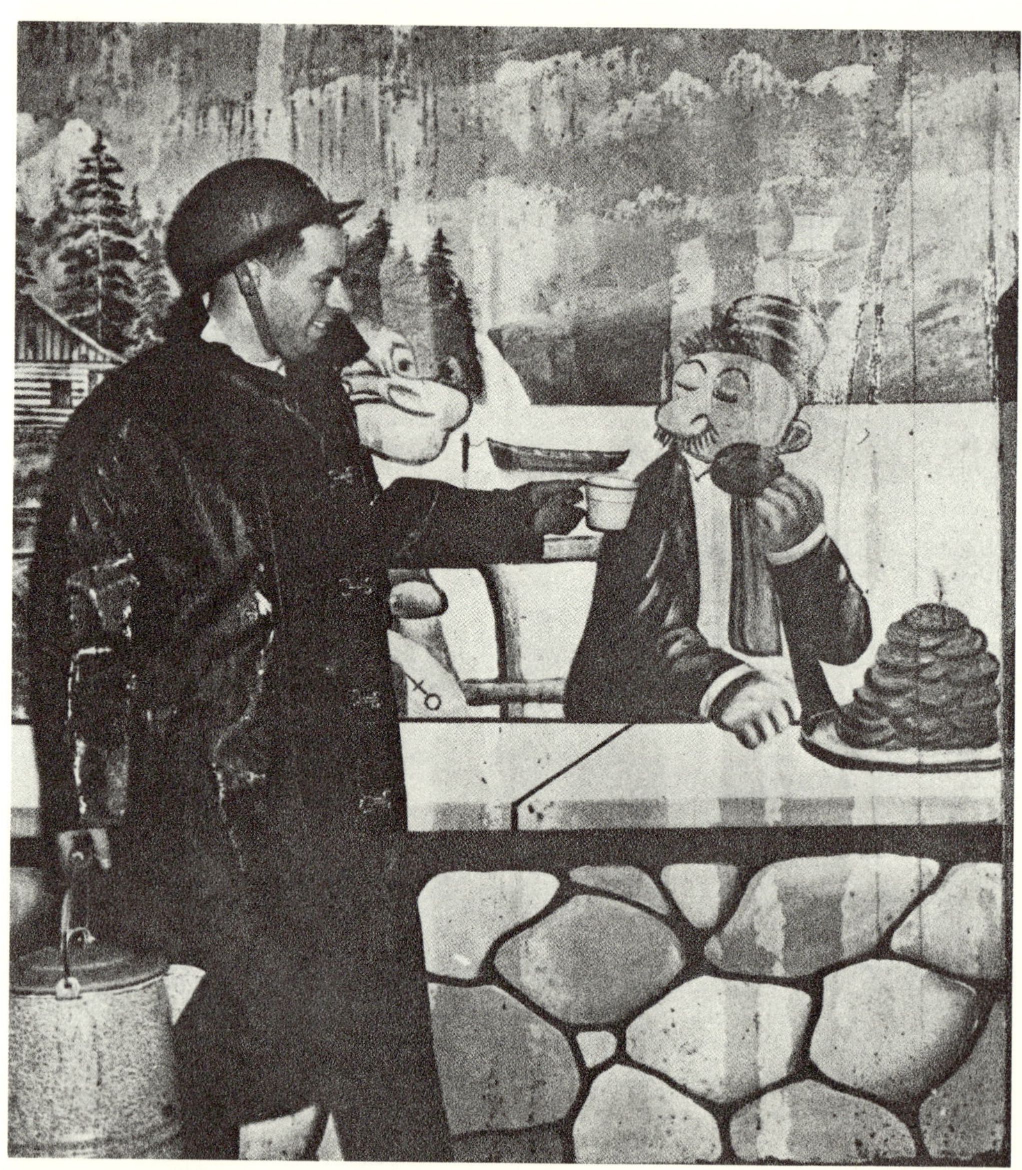

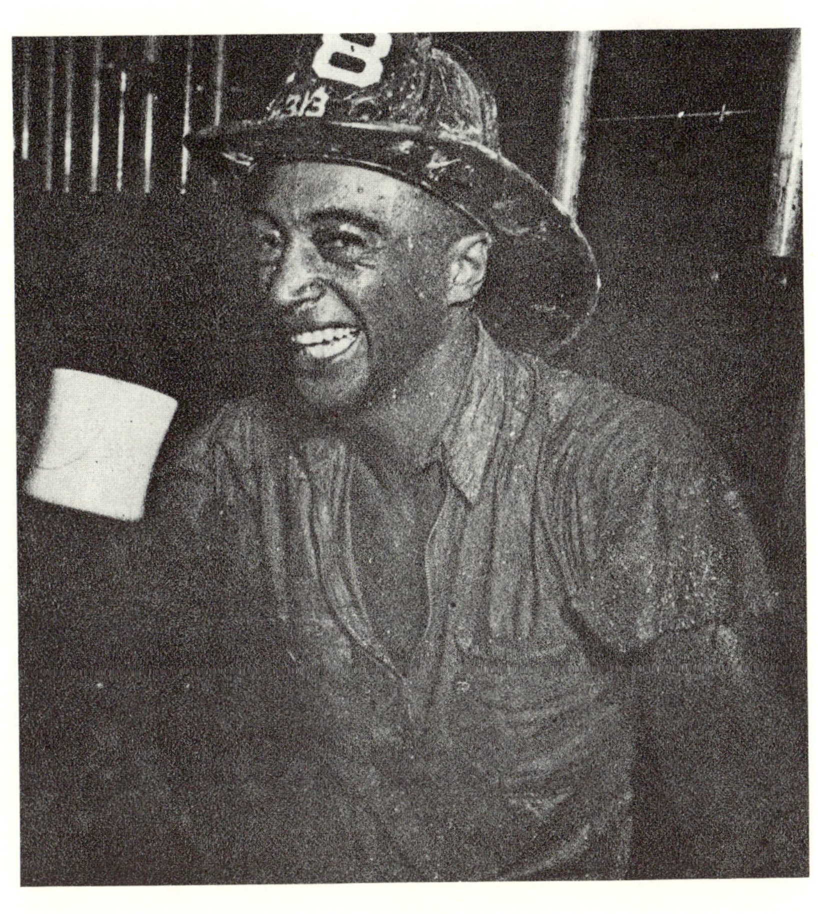

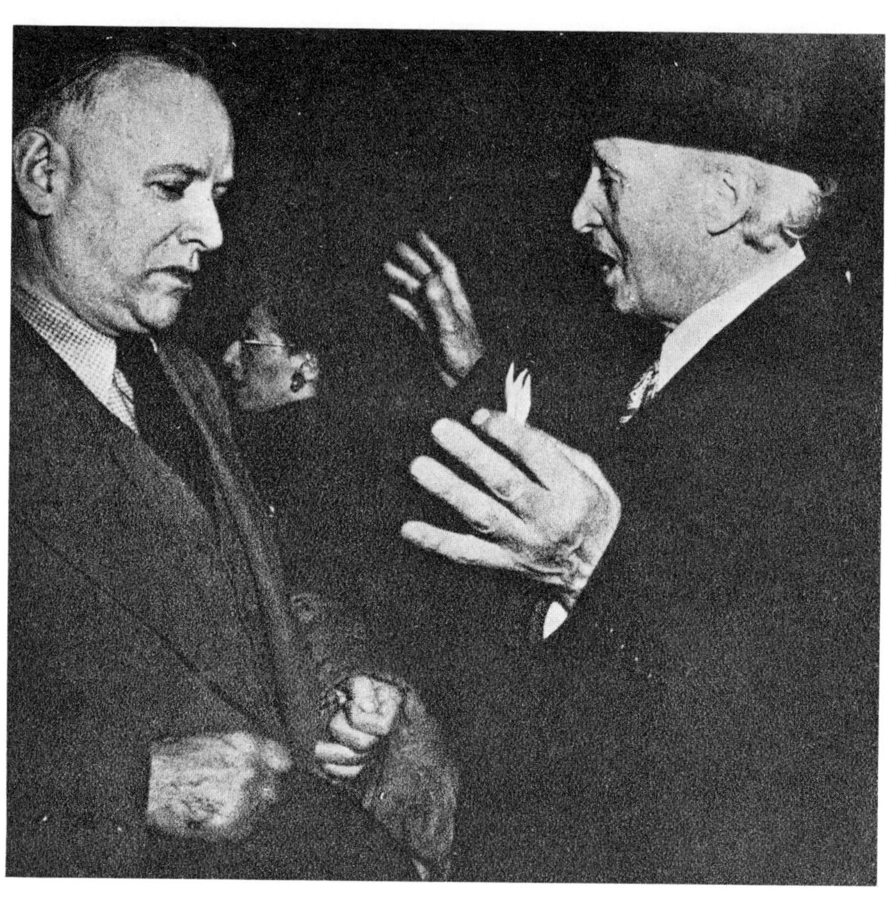

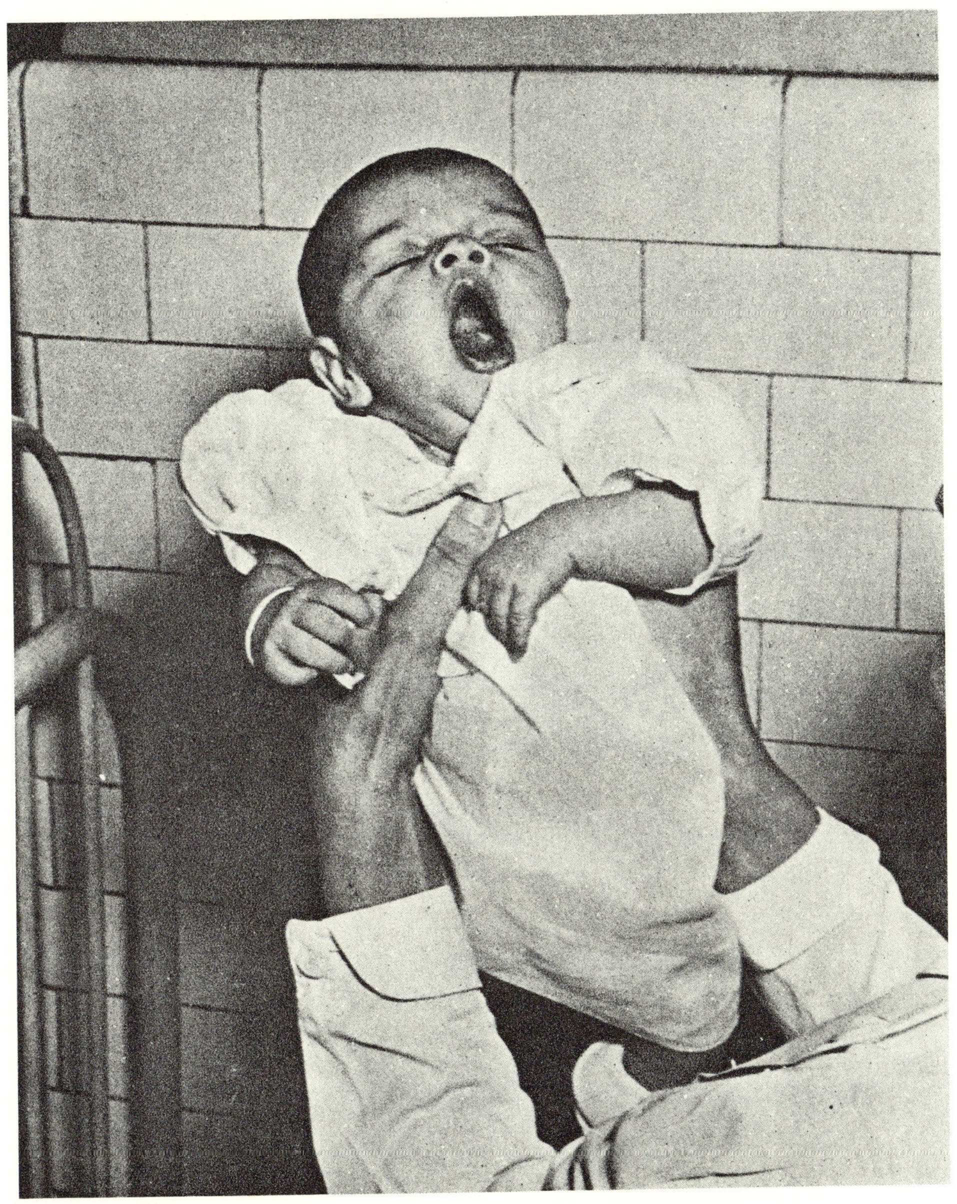

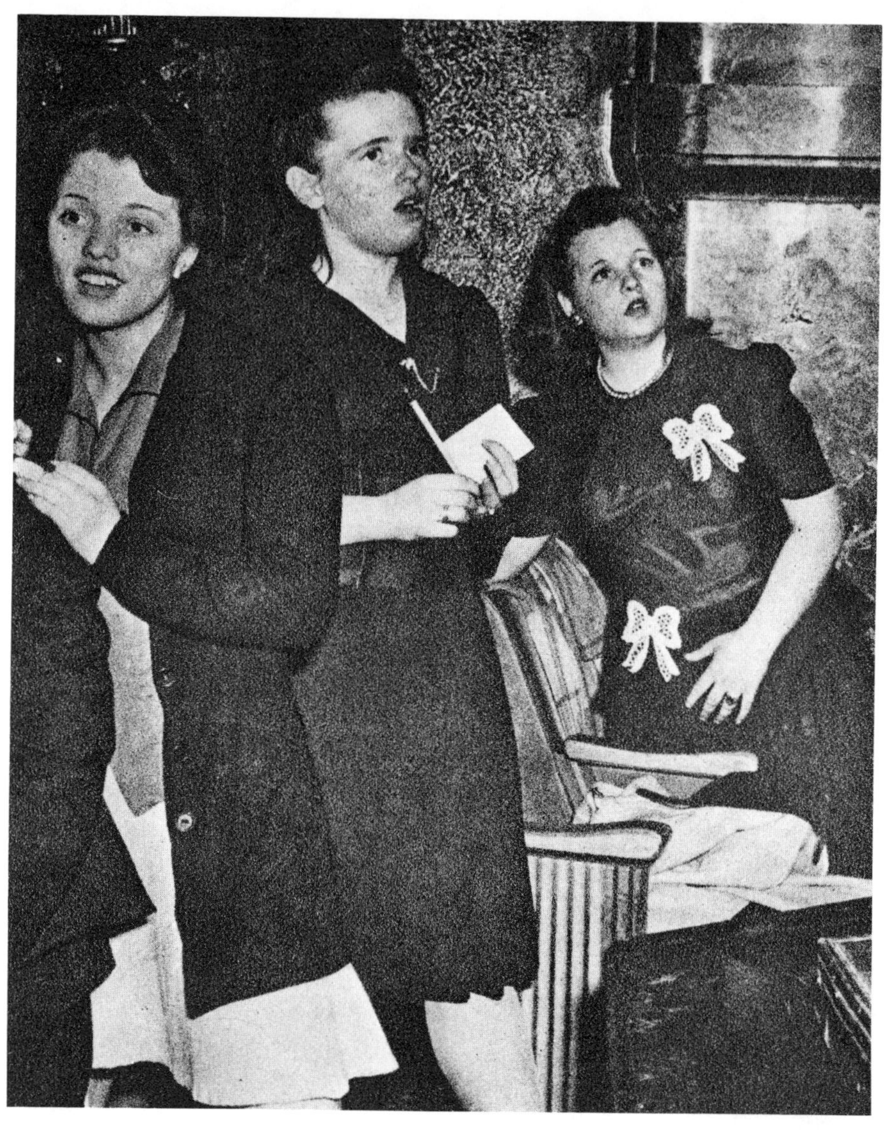

Dream world at the Paramount

Pandemonium at the Roxy

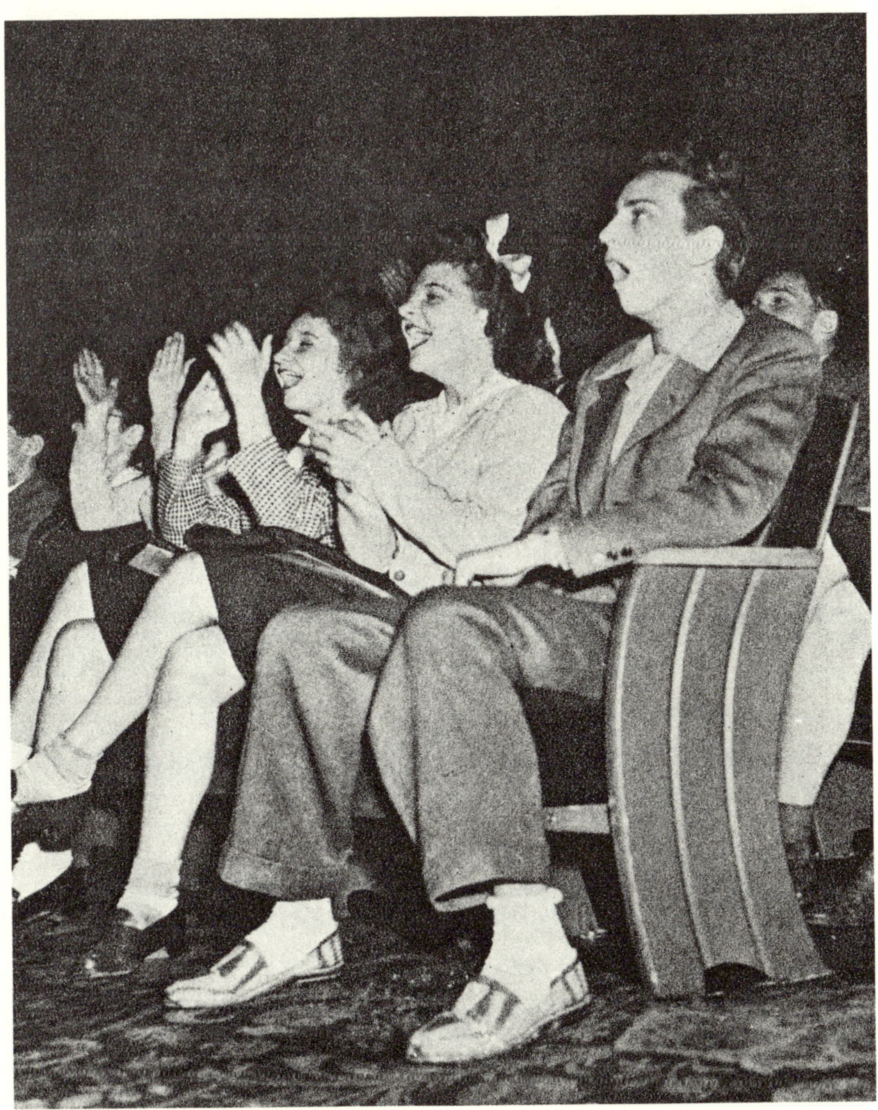

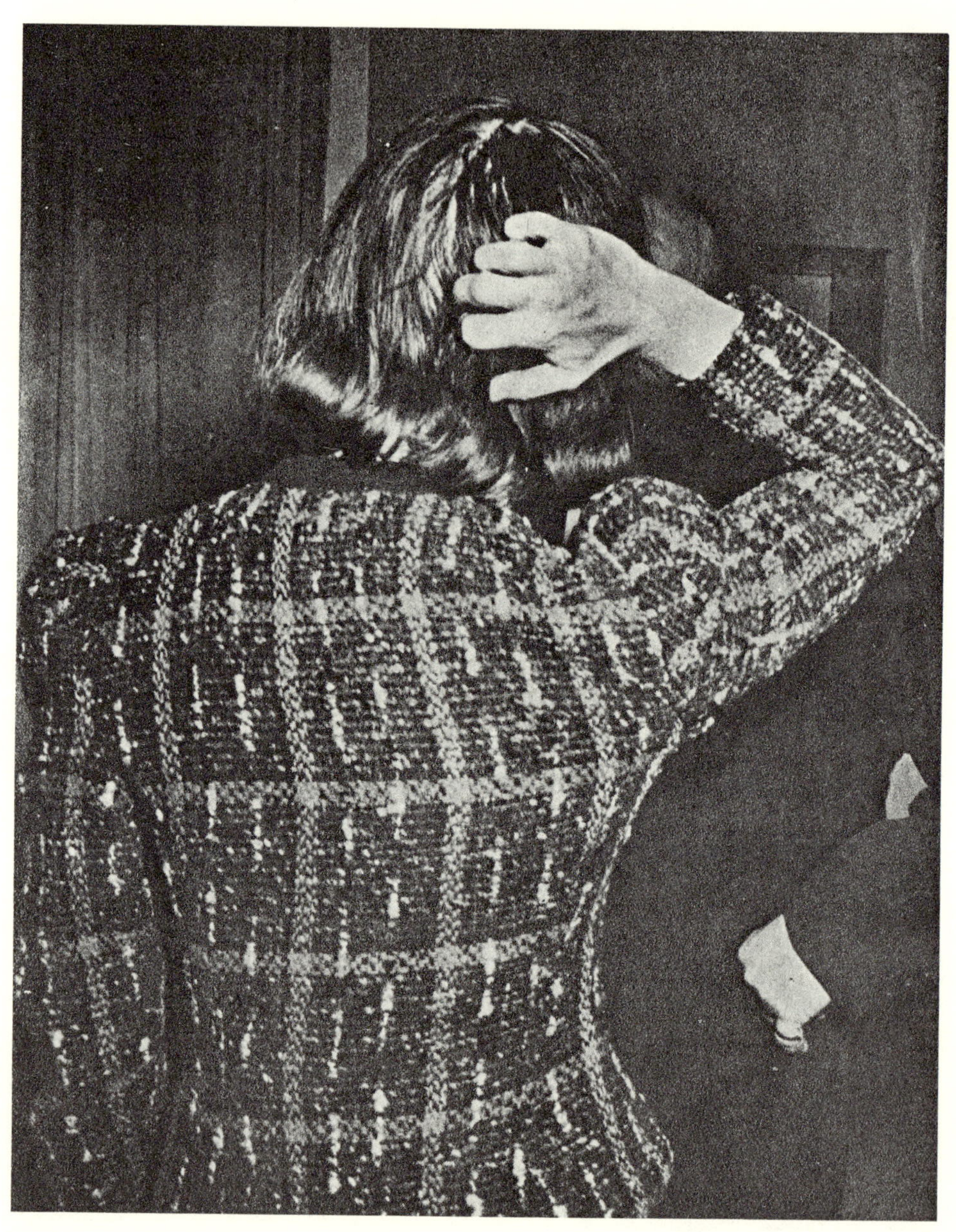

Museum of Modern Art

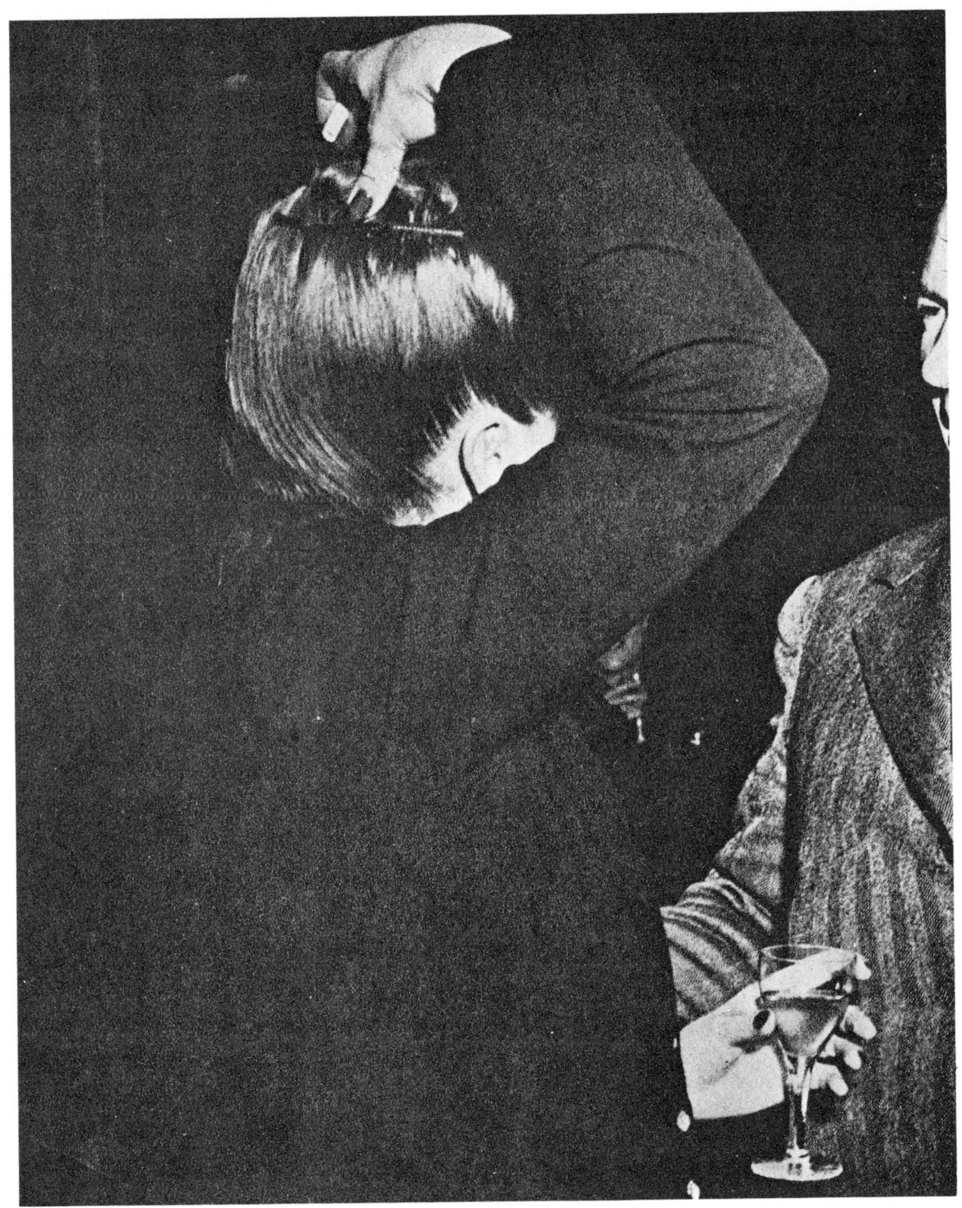

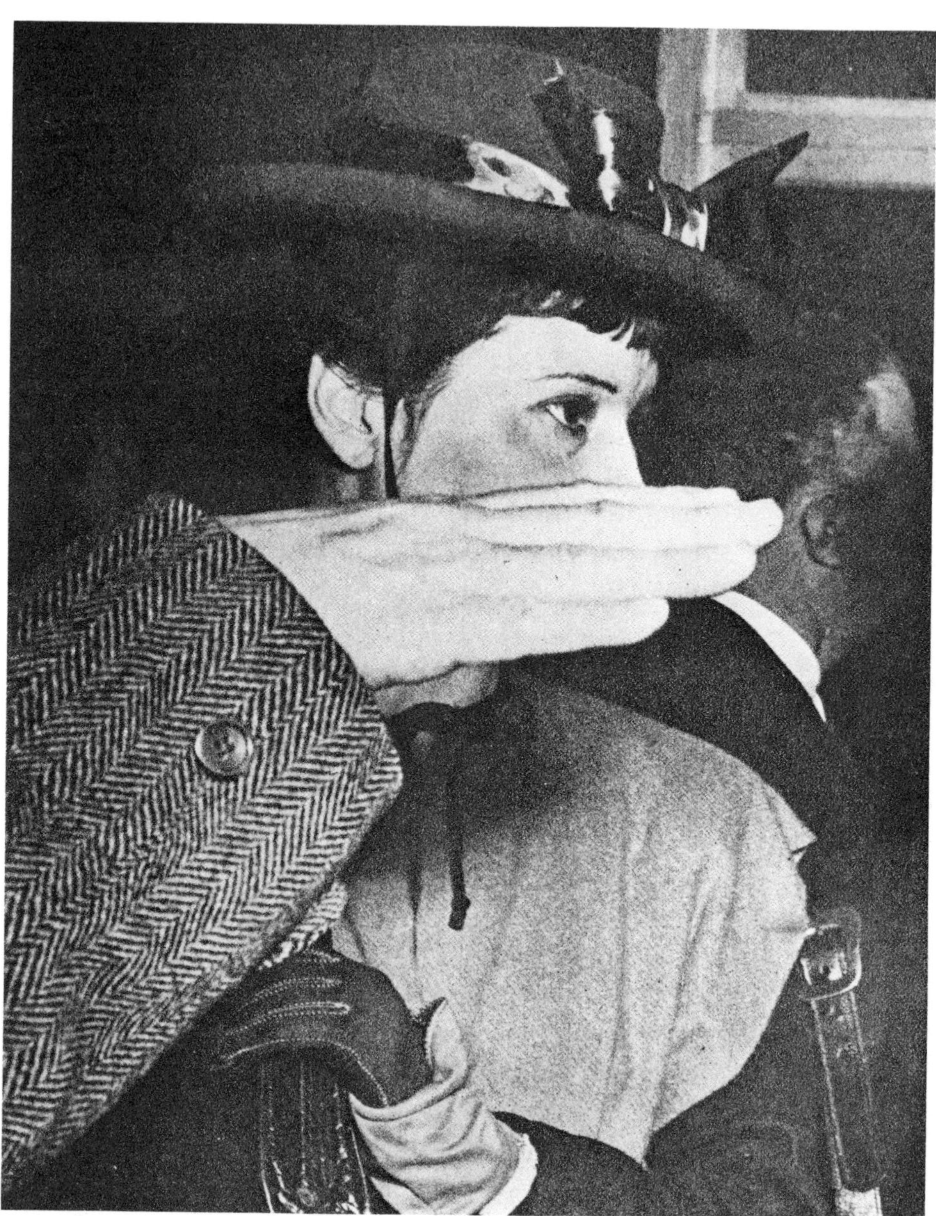

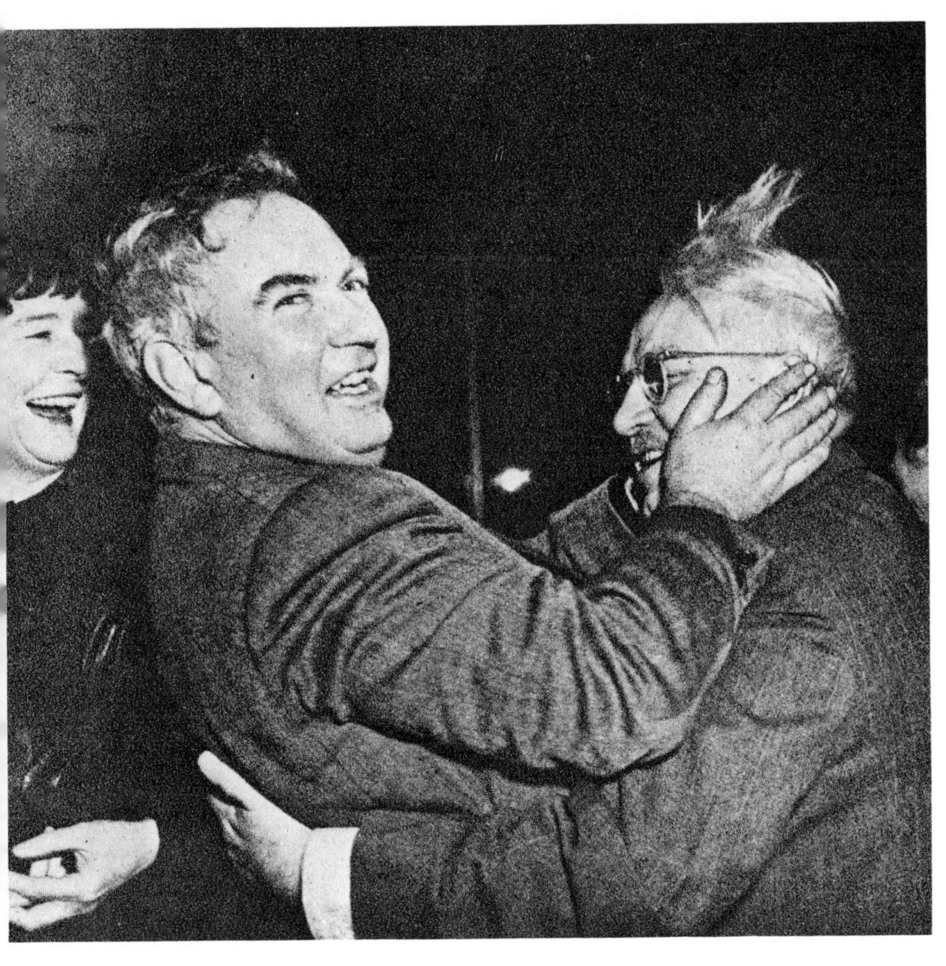

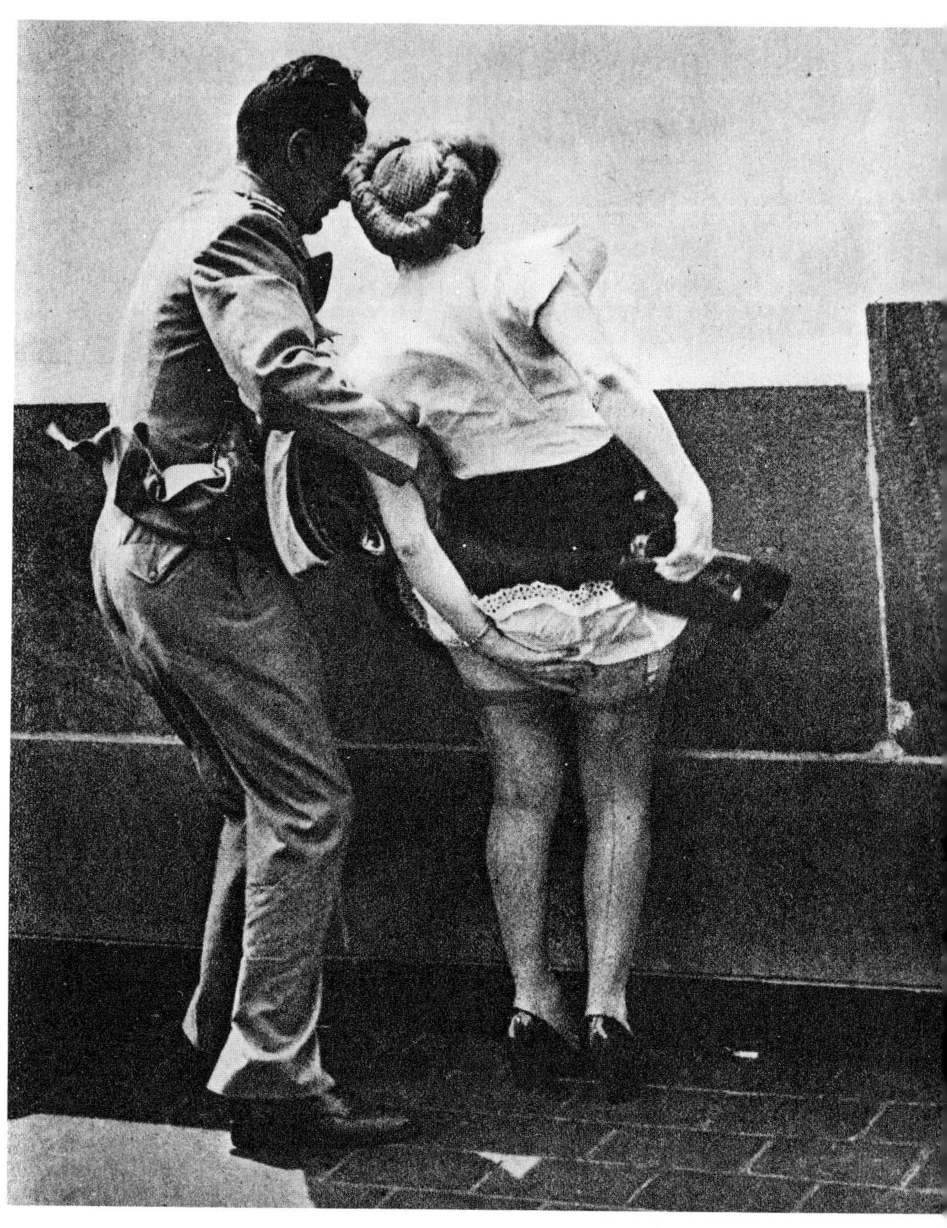

En